Perspectives on Thinking and Reasoning

Essays in Honour of Peter Wason

Edited by

Stephen E. Newstead

and

Jonathan St.B.T. Evans

*Department of Psychology,
University of Plymouth*

LAWRENCE ERLBAUM ASSOCIATES, PUBLISHERS
Hove (UK)
Hillsdale (USA)

Lawrence Erlbaum Associates Ltd., Publishers
27 Church Road
Hove
East Sussex, BN3 2FA
UK

British Library Cataloguing in Publication Data

A catalogue record for this book is available from the British Library

ISBN 0-86377-358-3

Printed and bound by BPC Wheatons Ltd., Exeter

Contents

3. **Content Effects in Wason's Selection Task   41**

4. **Pragmatic Reasoning about Human Voluntary Action:
    Evidence from Wason's Selection Task   67**

5. **Deontic Reasoning   91**

List of Contributors

Patricia Cheng, Department of Psychology, University of California at Los Angeles, Los Angeles, CA 90024-1563, California, USA

Susan Chitwood, Department of Psychology, Bowling Green State University, Bowling Green, OH 43403, USA

Roger Dominowski, Department of Psychology, M/C 285, University of Illinois at Chicago, 1007 W. Harrison Street, Chicago, Illinois 60607, USA

Jonathan Evans, Department of Psychology, University of Plymouth, Drake Circus, Plymouth, PL4 8AA, UK

Vittorio Girotto, Department of Psychology, University of Trieste, Via Dell' Università 7, 34123, Trieste, Italy

Michael Gorman, Technology, Culture and Communications, School of Engineering & Applied Science, University of Virginia, Charlottesville, VA 22903, USA

David Green, Department of Psychology, Centre for Cognitive Science, University College London, Gower Street, London WC1E 6BT, UK

Richard Griggs, Department of Psychology, University of Florida, Gainesville, FL 32611, USA

Keith Holyoak, Department of Psychology, University of California at Los Angeles, Los Angeles, CA 90024-1563, California, USA

Philip Johnson-Laird, Department of Psychology, Princeton University, Green Hall, Princeton, NJ 08544, USA

Paolo Legrenzi, Institute of Psychology, State University of Milan, Via Larga 19, 20122, Milan, Italy

Ken Manktelow,   Division of Psychology, University of Wolverhampton, 62–68 Lichfield Street, Wolverhampton, WVI IDJ, UK

Stephen Newstead,   Department of Psychology, University of Plymouth, Drake Circus, Plymouth, PL4 8AA, UK

David O'Brien,   Department of Psychology, Box G1126, Baruch College, City University of New York, 17 Lexington Avenue, New York, NY 10010, USA

David Over,   School of Social and International Studies, University of Sunderland, Langham Tower, Ryhope, Sunderland, SR2 7EE, UK

Ryan Tweney,   Department of Psychology, Bowling Green State University, Bowling Green, OH 43403, USA

Peter Wason,   Greycourt, Manor Road, Goring-on-Thames, Oxon., RG8 9ED, UK

CHAPTER ONE

Creating a Psychology of Reasoning: The Contribution of Peter Wason

Jonathan St.B.T. Evans and Stephen E. Newstead

Department of Psychology, University of Plymouth, UK

This book presents a series of essays on the contemporary psychology of reasoning, provided by a representative group of the leading researchers in the area. It is also a tribute to the work of Peter C. Wason, formerly of University College London, and now honourably retired. The fact that it has been easy to combine these two objectives in a single work is in itself a testament to the enormous influence of Wason in creating the field of research that we know today as the psychology of reasoning. In this opening chapter we intend to provide a brief account both of the development of the field and the role that Wason has played in it. First, we give some background to the origins of this book.

In July 1992, the Cognitive Psychology Section of the British Psychological Society organised its Second International Conference on Thinking, held at the University of Plymouth in England. With hindsight, we can see that the success of this conference—at which the attendance and quality of contribution exceeded all expectation—was largely inspired by a decision to hold within it a full-day symposium to honour the work of Peter Wason. Invitations were sent to a number of leading researchers known to have been influenced by personal contacts with Wason or to be researching one of his three famous reasoning problems. The response was tremendous. Everyone we asked wanted to come, and most managed to do so, despite—in a number of cases—the need to travel long distances with little or no financial assistance from the conference budget. The result was a remarkable gathering of a large proportion of the major workers in the field, and a special day that few present will be likely to forget.

The idea for this book arose from the "Wason symposium" at the Plymouth conference. Most of the participants in the symposium have contributed a chapter to this volume, and most contributors to this volume participated in the symposium. However, the papers written for this volume are only loosely, if at all, based on the content of the conference papers. It was agreed that each author should write an essay to provide their own theoretical perspective on an issue of importance in the contemporary psychology of reasoning. Links with Peter Wason's own work did not need to be contrived in the process, for, as we shall see, his ideas and his tasks hold a pervasive influence in the field.

Those coming new to the field now may think that Wason's prime contribution was the development of three tasks which between them provide the basis for the majority of all contemporary experimental studies in the psychology of reasoning. The tasks (discussed later) are the four card problem, best known simply as the "selection task"; the 2-4-6 problem; and the THOG problem. Profoundly important though this legacy has been, it would be a grave misjudgement to equate the provision of the paradigms with Wason's contribution. First of all, his research and his ideas revolutionised the study of reasoning and laid the foundations for the current field. Secondly, his direct and indirect influence has inspired many of the researchers who continue to be active in this field. His collaborators and PhD students (including Phil Johnson-Laird and Jonathan Evans) and his students' students, colleagues and collaborators form the nucleus of a large family of researchers—albeit a family with many adopted members.

ORIGINS OF THE PSYCHOLOGY OF REASONING AND THE "BRITISH TRADITION"

Historically, the psychology of reasoning has two major traditions which we might term an American and a British school. These terms refer only to where the schools originate and hence may be misleading. The "British" tradition, founded by Peter Wason, has many American and European followers among contemporary researchers in the field, as inspection of the list of authors in this book will confirm.

The earliest experiments on deductive reasoning were based on reasoning with classical, Aristotelian syllogisms, early examples of which can be found in the papers of Wilkins (1928) and Woodworth and Sells (1935). (Of contemporary research not employing one of Wason's three tasks, syllogistic reasoning remains the most popular paradigm. It is interesting to note that Wason himself never worked with syllogisms.) The distinctive American tradition is perhaps best traced to the paper of Henle (1962), which adopted a rationalist and logicist perspective. Henle argued that formal logic provided not simply a normative but a descriptive model of human reasoning—a view consistent with a large philosophical tradition. She claimed that apparent errors of reasoning observed by psychologists resulted from subjects either adopting personalised representations of the premises of problems or else "refusing to accept the logical task".

Contemporary inheritors of the American tradition continue to stress rationality and logicality in reasoning (for examples, see Revlin, Leirer, Yopp, & Yopp, 1980; Rips, 1983; 1990; Braine, 1978; Braine & O'Brien, 1991; O'Brien, 1993; and also O'Brien, Chapter 9 in this volume). Many in this tradition are associated with a theoretical position known as "mental logic" in which it is proposed that people have a natural logical system comprised of a set of abstract and general purpose inference rules which can be applied across a wide range of problem domains. This idea has its origins also in a major European school: the genetic epistemology of Jean Piaget. This enormously influential theory includes an assumption that adults achieve a level of thinking known as "formal operations" which permits them to reason by formal logical analysis (see Inhelder & Piaget, 1958).

Peter Wason's own work on reasoning grew originally from an interest in language and the emerging field of psycholinguistics in the late 1950s and early 1960s. Wason conducted important early research on the sentence verification task and the effects of negation (see Wason & Johnson-Laird, 1972; Evans, 1982, Chapter 2). His distinctive view of the psychology of reasoning emerged most clearly, however, in his early studies of inductive reasoning (Wason, 1960) and deductive reasoning (Wason, 1966). This work demonstrated two important facets of his creativity. First, he invented entirely new problems for studying reasoning. Hence, the worthy but dull traditional concept-learning paradigm employed by Bruner, Goodnow, and Austin (1956)—and many followers—was ignored as a means of studying inductive inference, and the 2-4-6 task was born. When he later turned to deduction, Wason once again dispensed with the contemporary paradigm (syllogistic inference) and invented what has since become the single most studied reasoning problem—the selection task.

The second facet of Wason's creativity lay in his theoretical thinking, which challenged the rationalistic orthodoxy of the time. The dominant schools of Henle and Piaget maintained, as we have seen, that humans reasoned by logical analysis. Wason's elegant and deceptively simple tasks trapped the majority of his subjects into clear logical errors. In the discussions of his papers, Wason argued that subjects were prey to confirmation biases, that they were poor Popperians, and that their thinking was self-contradictory. He showed that reasoning was content dependent (e.g. Wason & Shapiro, 1971) and used this—and the prevalence of error—to argue against logicism, especially that of Piaget, throughout his career (e.g. Wason, 1983). He also argued that people were driven by unconscious biases and that their introspective reports served to rationalise their behaviour (Wason & Evans, 1975).

In short, Wason was the original bias psychologist in the psychology of reasoning. In many ways his influence stands in parallel to the work of Amos Tversky and Daniel Kahneman, whose famous series of papers on heuristics and biases in statistical judgement (see Kahneman, Slovic, & Tversky, 1982) similarly challenged the orthodoxy of rational, normative behaviour in the study of decision making (Peterson & Beach, 1967). Along with Tversky and Kahneman, Wason was a prime target for the famous critique of bias research provided by the philosopher L. Jonathan Cohen (1981). Some comments of Wason in response to this are characteristic not only of his view of rationality but of his belief in the real-world relevance of the tasks that he studied:

> It seems to me that Cohen overestimates the pervasiveness of rational thought in everyday life. And it could be argued that irrationality, not rationality, is the norm. People all too readily succumb to logical fallacies, especially when trying to be persuasive ...
>
> What Cohen calls "cognitive illusions" ... far from being the unique prerogative of the academic conjuror, may not be radically different from the circumstances and contingencies which are sometimes met in everyday life and which are quite irrational, e.g. incorrigible convictions about quite ordinary things, delusions of reference, and other transient symptoms such as falling in love (Wason, 1983, pp. 59–60).

The University College London school of work was strong through the 1960s and early 1970s and culminated in the widely read and influential book, *Psychology of Reasoning: Structure and Content*, by Wason and Johnson-Laird (1972). During this period a number of visitors to UCL were inspired by Wason's work. Among these were such as Ryan Tweney and Paolo Legrenzi who have remained active in reasoning research ever since and who have shared their interests with a number of collaborators. During the 1970s, however, the London based "school" started to break up. Phil Johnson-Laird went first to Sussex University and later to Cambridge and Princeton, and Jonathan Evans moved to Plymouth. Evans, together with Stephen Newstead, founded a second generation school of bias research at Plymouth—see, for example, Evans (1989) and chapters by Evans and by Newstead et al. in this volume (Chapters 7 and 12 respectively). Students of the Plymouth group included Ken Manktelow and Paul Pollard. Johnson-Laird, working with Ruth Byrne, Jane Oakhill, and many other collaborators, developed the major school of work based upon the mental model theory of reasoning (see Johnson-Laird, 1983; Johnson-Laird & Byrne, 1991).

In parallel with these developments, the late 1970s and the 1980s saw a major period of expansion in the reasoning field in which a number of other psychologists, based outside the UK, began to work on the tasks invented by Peter Wason. Ryan Tweney, together with colleagues such as Mike Doherty and Jack Mynatt, launched a programme of studies on inductive and scientific reasoning at Bowling Green, Ohio, which originally focused on the 2-4-6 problem (see Tweney and Chitwood, this volume, Chapter 11). Richard Griggs at the University of Florida began what has become a massive programme of experimental research using the Wason selection task and THOG problems (see, for example, Griggs, this volume, Chapter 2). Other US based researchers developed major new reasoning theories based upon the notion of content-dependent rules and schemas (Cheng & Holyoak, 1985; Holyoak & Cheng, this volume, Chapter 4; Cosmides, 1989) which utilised the selection task as the principal paradigm for their research. A new generation of Italian reasoning researchers (such as Vittorio Girotto, Bruno Bara and Pat Tabossi) emerged from the Legrenzi connection.

The field is now so large that we must apologise to all those contributors that we have omitted to name in this attempt to trace the history of Wason's influence. What we hope to have illustrated is the way in which Wason's work inspired first a London, then British, and now an international tradition of work. More than any other one individual, Wason served to create the field now described as the psychology of reasoning. We now turn to a brief consideration of the three tasks which Wason gave to the field and the contribution that their investigation has made.

THE WASON 2-4-6 PROBLEM

Wason (1960) presented the 2-4-6 problem as a test of inductive reasoning and as a model of scientific thinking. At that time, inductive reasoning was conventionally studied using the concept-learning paradigm of Bruner, Goodnow, and Austin (1956). A typical method would involve presenting subjects with a sequence of instances which varied on a number of dimensions: for example, coloured shapes. Subjects initially would guess whether or not the instance conformed to the experimenter's rule and then receive feedback. Eventually they learned correctly to classify the cases and to transfer this ability to some new set of instances. Some authors offered cognitive accounts of rule learning in terms of hypothesis testing whilst others offered learning theory explanations. Following Bruner et al.'s (1956) imaginative investigation of complex logical rules involving several attributes in conjunction or disjunction, researchers started to concentrate on simple concepts involving one dimension only, and to build mathematical models of the learning process (e.g. Bower & Trabasso, 1964).

We mention this tradition in order to provide a context for Wason's innovation. The 2-4-6 problem also involved an experimenter's rule, positive and negative instances, and hypothesis testing. However, by liberating himself from the orthodox paradigm, and producing a task intended as a more accurate model of scientific thinking, Wason discovered a new phenomenon—described at the time as a verification of confirmation bias—that had eluded the concept-learning tradition. The critical change, with hindsight, lay in the freedom given to subjects (as to scientists) to choose their own experiments from an open and infinite number of possibilities.

In the original form of the task, subjects are told that the experimenter has in mind a rule which applies to groups of three whole numbers (often referred to in the literature as "triples"). The subject is to attempt to discover the rule by offering triples of his/her own which the experimenter will then classify. The subject is then given a single example of a triple which conforms to the 2-4-6 rule. Subjects are provided with a sheet on which they write down the triple tested, the reason for testing it, and the feedback they are given. They are told to announce the rule only when they are sure it is correct. If a wrong rule is announced, however, subjects are permitted to continue. The correct rule is "any ascending sequence". Table 1.1 shows a typical protocol from Wason (1960).

TABLE 1.1
Sample Protocol from Wason (1960)

8-10-12: two added each time; 14-16-18: even numbers in order of magnitude; 20-22-24: same reason; 1-3-5: two added to preceding number.
The rule is that by starting with any number, two is added each time to form the next number.

2-6-10: middle number is arithmetic mean of outer two; 1-50-99: same reason.
The rule is that the middle number is the arithmetic mean of the other two.

3-10-17: same number, seven added each time; 0-3-6: three added each time.
The rule is that the difference between two numbers next to each other is the same.

12-8-4: the same number subtracted each time to form the next number.
The rule is adding a number, always the same one, to form the next number.

1-4-9: any three numbers in order of magnitude.
The rule is any three numbers in order of magnitude.

The basic finding is that subjects form an hypothesis that is more specific than the real rule and test only positive examples of it. Because these positive examples form a subset of the correct ones, they can never receive disconfirmation except by announcing the rule. What subjects fail to do is to test instances that are inconsistent with their hypothesis. Wason interpreted this as strong evidence for a confirmation bias. He and a number of later researchers raised doubts about the adherence to falsification in science as recommended by the philosopher Karl Popper (e.g. 1959).

It is not our purpose to review research on the 2-4-6 problem here. What we must note, however, is the large number of studies that have subsequently been run using the task. Many of the authors, like Wason, see it as a test of scientific reasoning and as evidence of confirmation bias; many subsequent studies have thus focused on means by which the bias might be reduced. Other authors—equally impressed by the importance of the findings—have argued for other interpretations. For example, Klayman and Ha (1987) suggested that people have a "positive test heuristic" which is often successful but fails on the selection task. Evans (1989) argued that the bias was due to a cognitive constraint which he terms "positivity bias" rather than to any lack of motivation to falsify hypotheses. The degree of continuing current interest in the task is evidenced by the inclusion in a recent journal special issue (edited by Evans, 1993) of no fewer than 3 papers reporting 2-4-6 experiments.

As with the selection task, we feel that researchers coming new to the field will miss valuable insights if they fail to read the original papers of Peter Wason. We strongly recommend, for example, that Wason's (1967) review of early research on the 2-4-6 problem be required reading for all students of reasoning research. Wason was fascinated by irrationality and probed the significance of his protocols in a manner rarely imitated by later researchers. In particular, he was interested in an effect illustrated in the protocol quoted in Table 1.1, and generally neglected in the subsequent literature. Notice that the three middle rules announced by this subject were all verbal reformulations of the same rule. This was by no means an isolated case. Wason's interest in this apparent rationalisation of an unconsciously driven bias was an early forerunner of the dual process theory of reasoning published some years later (Wason & Evans, 1975).

THE WASON SELECTION TASK

Wason (1966) described a simple reasoning problem that he had invented. Subjects were told that a pack of cards each had a letter written on one side and a number written on the other side. The experimenter claimed that the following rule held true: "If a card has a vowel on one side then it has an even number on the other side". Subjects were shown four cards from the pack which had on their exposed sides, a vowel, a consonant, an even number, and an odd number. For example:

E   T   4   7

The task was to decide which cards to turn over in order to decide whether the rule was true or false. The correct choice, Wason argued, was the vowel and the odd number, since only this combination on a card could falsify the rule. Most subjects, however, chose either the vowel and the even number, or just the vowel. In general terms, for a rule of the form "if p then q", the correct choice is p and not-q, but most subjects fail to choose the latter card. Wason concluded, that the subjects—like those on the 2-4-6 task—were again susceptible to a confirmation bias and again lacking in insight into the need for falsification.

This problem, known most commonly and simply as the "selection task", has since become the single most investigated problem in the history of the psychology of reasoning and there is no sign as yet that interest in it is abating. Indeed, in the current volume, a majority of chapters take the selection task as a major—and in some cases exclusive—focus of discussion. The most recent review of the many studies of the selection task is that of Evans, Newstead and Byrne (1993, Chapter 4). Such was the volume of papers to consider, that this review was of necessity biased towards work reported within the past decade. For a full history of the development of the problem the reader would be advised first to read Wason and Johnson-Laird's (1972) own discussion of their early studies of the task, and then perhaps the intermediate review of Evans (1982, Chapter 9).

Again, it is not our purpose to attempt a review of the selection task here, but we will attempt briefly to plot the major stages of development of work with the problem and to highlight Wason's personal contribution. Most of the early studies of Wason and Johnson-Laird (1972) were concerned with the prevalence of error and the difficulty of persuading subjects to select the not-q card. They found that 10% or fewer subjects could solve the problem despite various changes to the task, such as the use of a quantified rule (Every card which has an A on one side has a 4 on the other), binary materials (cards which could only have one of two values on either side), use of cards with both values on the same side (one masked), and so on. Most interesting in these early studies were the "therapy" experiments in which Wason tried to persuade subjects of the error of their thinking. He found extraordinary resistance in his subjects. Some would even turn over the not-q card, discover the falsifying p on the back, and still say it was not necessary to select it. They effectively claimed that a card with a vowel on the front and an odd number on the back falsified the rule, but the same card lying the other way up did not!

Wason was fascinated by the apparent irrationality of his subjects: their inconsistency, rationalisation and lack of Piagetian "reversibility" (for good examples, see Wason, 1969; Wason & Golding, 1974). Although much recent research has been reported using the selection task, no current papers provide either experimental manipulations or psychological discussion comparable to these early Wason papers. They should be read not just for their historical significance but for the psychological insights they still provide.

Around about 1970, two factors were discovered at UCL which finally broke the pattern of invariable error on the selection task. One of these was the so-called "thematic facilitation effect". The early experiments (published by Wason & Shapiro, 1971; Johnson-Laird, Legrenzi, & Legrenzi, 1972) appeared to show that people could solve the problems as long as they were couched in familiar terms—for example, "Every time I go to Manchester I travel by car". (We now know that the conditions for facilitation are rather more complex and depend upon the precise nature of the prior knowledge the subject brings to bear—see Evans, Newstead, & Byrne, 1993, Chapter 4.) Wason quickly adapted to this turn of events, using the finding of content-dependent reasoning, for example, to argue against the Piagetian theory that people attain the stage of formal operational thinking.

The other development was more problematic as it appeared to undermine the notion of confirmation bias which was dominant in Wason's early thinking about the selection task as well as the 2-4-6 problem. Jonathan Evans, as part of his PhD work, discovered by rotating the presence of negative components in conditional rules that subjects showed a "matching bias" on a related task known as the truth table task (Evans, 1972). That is, they tended to choose the values named in the rules, regardless of negations (see Evans, this volume, Chapter 7, for details). The first experiment that Evans ran on completion of his doctorate was designed to distinguish between verification and matching bias on the selection task (Evans & Lynch, 1973) and did so decisively in favour of matching.

Wason immediately and graciously accepted the matching bias finding, despite the theoretical difficulties that it caused him at the time. He was, however, puzzled by the fact that verbal protocols appeared to provide evidence for confirmation bias (Goodwin & Wason, 1972). This led to a collaboration in which the "dual process" theory of reasoning was developed (Wason & Evans, 1975). In this paper it was argued that subjects' verbalisations (type 2 processes) served only to rationalise choices stemming from unconscious (type 1) processes—in this case causing subjects to match. Wason was very pleased with this theory which he could relate to much of his earlier discussions of irrationality and inconsistent verbalisations on the selection task and 2-4-6 problem. The dual process theory in turn laid the foundation for the later heuristic-analytic theory of Evans (1984; 1989) and its contemporary emphasis on relevance effects in reasoning (see Evans, this volume, Chapter 7).

From the late 1970s, work on the selection task started to take off and become an international enterprise. Following discovery that thematic material did not always facilitate (Manktelow & Evans, 1979), the first of many excellent papers by Richard Griggs and collaborators at the University of Florida was directed to understanding why (Griggs & Cox, 1982). These findings created a new interest in the field and led eventually to major theoretical contributions from other researchers based in the USA (e.g. Cheng & Holyoak, 1985; Cosmides, 1989). Interest in the thematic selection task continues unabated, with some researchers emphasising the importance of deontic terms such as must and may and the effect of pay-offs on choices (see Manktelow & Over, 1991; and this volume, Chapter 5). In recent times, interest in the abstract selection task—which had waned in the 1980s—has revived considerably (see, for example, Platt & Griggs, 1993; Griggs, this volume, Chapter 2; Evans, this volume, Chapter 7).

There are a variety of contemporary views of the selection task, some of which presume that it tells more about decision making than it does about reasoning *per se* (see, for example, Evans, Over, & Manktelow, 1993; Oaksford & Chater, 1993). What everyone seems to agree on, however, is that the task provides a remarkable vehicle for the study of human thinking.

THE THOG PROBLEM

The THOG problem is in many ways the poor relation to the other two tasks that Peter Wason has devised. The special issue of the *Quarterly Journal of Experimental Psychology* on the psychology of reasoning (Evans, 1993), to which we have already referred, contained just one article covering research on this problem. Similarly, the present book contains only a single chapter on the problem. Wason himself, after initial enthusiasm for the task, actually published just one empirical paper on it—that by Wason and Brooks (1979).

This is not just because the problem was devised rather later than the others (in the late 1970s rather than the 1960s). There is also something a little less elegant about this task than either the selection task or the 2-4-6 problem. These latter two are both simple, easy to understand problems on which the great majority of people make mistakes. The THOG problem, on the other hand, is not quite as simple to understand: the instructions are longer and more complex than with the other tasks. Paradoxically, it is also less difficult to solve than the others, and around a third of subjects get the problem right first time round. Hence the problem does not have quite the same dramatic impact as the others. It may not, in addition, have the same implications for scientific reasoning in general as the other problems are claimed to have.

Nevertheless, in other respects the task has had a similar history to the others. After initial research by Wason and his collaborators in the United Kingdom, the task was taken up by international researchers. Richard Griggs at the University of Florida and David O'Brien at the City University of New York have both carried out studies of the problem, and in Italy Vittorio Girotto and Paolo Legrenzi have been regular publishers of research on it. Some of the issues that have been researched carry parallels with research on the other tasks; for example, the effects of realistic material have been widely investigated, and matching bias is frequently evoked as an explanation of reasoning errors. Furthermore, although research on the problem is nothing like as prolific as that on the selection task, it is still one of the more widely researched reasoning tasks.

This is what has been termed the standard version of the task:

"In front of you are four designs:
  black diamond;
  white diamond;
  black circle; and
  white circle.

"You are to assume that I have written down one of the colours (black or white) and one of the shapes (diamond or circle). Now read the following rule carefully: *If, and only if, any of the designs includes either the colour I have written down, or the shape I have written down, but not both, then it is called a THOG.*

"I will tell you that the black diamond is a THOG".

Subjects are then asked to indicate which of the other designs, if any, is a THOG.

In order to solve this problem, subjects need to carry out a combinatorial analysis—something which should be well within the capabilities of adult subjects according to theorists such as Piaget. The fact that well over half the subjects get it wrong provided further ammunition for Wason's armoury in his attack on the orthodoxies of the time. Using more realistic material does not seem to help (see, for example, Smyth & Clark, 1986), unless this material cues in the correct answer (Newstead, Griggs, & Warner, 1982) or in some way makes the problem structure very clear (Girotto & Legrenzi, 1989). The reason why some of these realistic versions produce facilitation—as with the selection task—is still a matter for debate, though this debate has proved somewhat less theoretically productive in the case of the THOG problem.

The research on the THOG problem is summarised in Newstead, Girotto, & Legrenzi (this volume, Chapter 12) and will not be repeated here. Perhaps the most revealing aspect of this research is that there is still no completely accepted account of the difficulty of the problem, nor of the common errors that are made. Many of the suggestions put forward by Wason when he first devised the problem some 15 years ago are still strong contenders, though newer theories have also been proposed (e.g. confusion theory, Girotto & Legrenzi, 1989; Newstead & Griggs, 1992), and attempts have been made to explain performance in terms of mental models theory. However, it seems clear that the THOG problem, like the others devised by Wason, is likely to fascinate researchers for many years to come.

OVERVIEW OF THIS BOOK

The chapters in this book reflect quite closely the relative interest that has been shown in the three tasks described. There are eight chapters on the extensively researched selection task, two on the 2-4-6 task and just one on the THOG problem.

The authors of the chapters on the selection task include almost all the major researchers in this field, and all the major theoretical perspectives are well covered. Chapter 2 by Richard Griggs examines recent research on the original version of the task using an affirmative rule with abstract materials. He reports evidence to support the claim that, in appropriately favourable circumstances, the abstract version can be solved by the majority of naive subjects. When the rule is suitably clarified, when subjects are asked to justify their choices, and when violation instructions are given, the problem becomes almost easy.

Most of the remaining chapters are concerned, directly or indirectly, with the effects of content on performance. Roger Dominowski presents (in Chapter 3) an attempt to characterise the various different types of realistic content that have been used. Realism can vary along a number of dimensions, including the abstractness/concreteness of the terms, the plausibility/implausibility of the relations, and the familiarity/non-familiarity of the scenarios. Evidence suggests that all of these aspects can play a role in determining problem difficulty.

The chapters by Holyoak and Cheng and by Manktelow and Over (Chapters 4 and 5, respectively) both focus on the contextual dependency of reasoning. Holyoak and Cheng provide a vigorous defence of their theory of pragmatic reasoning schemas which has recently come under fire as being possibly based on an experimental artefact. Manktelow and Over summarise the theoretical position that they have espoused in recent years involving deontic reasoning. This puts reasoning into the social context of duties and obligations, and these authors claim that many of the contents which produce facilitation can be explained in terms of such deontic factors.

The principal proponent of the mental models theory of reasoning has been Phil Johnson-Laird, and in Chapter 6 he explains how this theory can account for performance on the selection task—something that has been done in outline before but not previously in the kind of detail presented here. Jonathan Evans has been the champion of the heuristic-analytic theory, which is usually seen as an alternative to the mental models position. In Chapter 7, he summarises his recent work on relevance in reasoning, and suggests how there might be a *rapprochement*, even an integration, between this approach and that of the mental models theory. David Green (Chapter 8) also supports a mental models approach but of a rather different kind. He attempts to explain why people can be both illogical and logical in the selection task, in the sense that they tend to choose non-logical matching cases but can then justify these choices in seemingly logical terms. He suggests that this paradox results from "internal argumentation", and that the rules involved in this can be regarded as types of mental models.

The final chapter on the selection task (Chapter 9) is by David O'Brien. He is one of the main supporters of the mental-logic approach which supposes that people reason using general purpose rules. It has often been claimed that this approach cannot explain various aspects of performance on the selection task—for example, the fact that so many errors are made or that realistic content can improve performance. He provides a thought-provoking analysis of research in this area, arguing that the underlying logic of the problem is so complex that the failure of subjects to solve it is perfectly understandable, even predictable, within the mental logic approach.

The chapters by Gorman and by Tweney and Chitwood (Chapters 10 and 11, respectively) summarise research on the 2-4-6 task but also go much further than this. Gorman argues that research on this task can reveal much about hypothesis testing and scientific reasoning in general. Tweney and Chitwood discuss the role of confirmation bias in scientific thinking, and illustrate this with reference to studies of eminent scientific thinkers and to their own laboratory studies. They also place this research in context by discussing how it relates to other approaches to the study of scientific thinking. Next is Chapter 12 on the THOG problem by Newstead, Girotto, and Legrenzi, which both summarises research on the task and also attempts to place it in the context of recent developments in reasoning theory and research.

A common theme running through all these chapters—one which is almost too obvious to need stating—is the debt that is owed to Peter Wason.

Many of the present authors explicitly acknowledge this, while others do so implicitly by the frequency with which they quote his research and theoretical ideas. The final chapter in this book is thus, appropriately, written by Wason himself. In it, he summarises his life and career and discusses creativity in science, with special reference to his own contributions in generating new ideas and new ways of approaching problems.

ACKNOWLEDGEMENTS

We wish to acknowledge a number of people who have helped make this book possible. Without the help of Sue Smith, the conference which provided the impetus for this book might never have occurred. We thank the contributors themselves who have not only written their own chapters but in most cases have served also as commentators on the contributions of others. Our long-suffering wives and families also deserve our thanks and grateful acknowledgement for their support throughout this project.

Most of all, however, we wish to acknowledge the debt that we and all the other contributors owe to Peter Wason. Without him, not only would this book obviously never have been conceived, but the study of human reasoning itself would not exist in the form that we know it. The entire book is in essence a tribute to him and his work, and it is with great pleasure and gratitude that we dedicate it to him.

REFERENCES

Bower, G.H., & Trabasso, T.R. (1964). Concept identification. In R.C. Atkinson (Ed.), *Studies in mathematical psychology*. Stanford: Stanford University Press.

Braine, M.D.S. (1978). On the relation between the natural logic of reasoning and standard logic. *Psychological Review, 85*, 1–21.

Braine, M.D.S., & O'Brien, D.P. (1991). A theory of If: A lexical entry, reasoning program, and pragmatic principles. *Psychological Review, 98*, 182–203.

Bruner, J.S., Goodnow, J.J., & Austin, G.A. (1956). *A study of thinking*. New York: Wiley.

Cheng, P.W., & Holyoak, K.J. (1985). Pragmatic reasoning schemas. *Cognitive Psychology, 17*, 391–416.

Cohen, L.J. (1981). Can human irrationality be experimentally demonstrated? *The Behavioral and Brain Sciences, 4*, 317–370.

Cosmides, L. (1989). The logic of social exchange: Has natural selection shaped how humans reason? Studies with the Wason selection task. *Cognition, 31*, 187–276.

Evans, J.St.B.T. (1972). Interpretation and matching bias in a reasoning task. *British Journal of Psychology, 24*, 193–199.

Evans, J.St.B.T. (1982). *The psychology of deductive reasoning.* London: Routledge and Kegan Paul.

Evans, J.St.B.T. (1984). Heuristic and analytic problems in reasoning. *British Journal of Psychology, 75,* 451–468.

Evans, J.St.B.T. (1989). *Bias in human reasoning: Causes and consequences.* Hove, UK: Lawrence Erlbaum Associates Ltd.

Evans, J.St.B.T. (1993, Ed.). The cognitive psychology of reasoning. *Special Issue of The Quarterly Journal of Experimental Psychology.* Hove, UK: Lawrence Erlbaum Associates Ltd.

Evans, J.St.B.T., & Lynch, J.S. (1973). Matching bias in the selection task. *British Journal of Psychology, 64,* 391–397.

Evans, J.St.B.T., Newstead, S.E., & Byrne, R.M.J. (1993). *Human reasoning: The psychology of deduction.* Hove, UK: Lawrence Erlbaum Associates Ltd.

Evans, J.St.B.T., Over, D.E., & Manktelow, K.I. (1993). Reasoning, decision making, and rationality. *Cognition, 49,* 165–187.

Girotto, V., & Legrenzi, P. (1989). Mental representation and hypothetico-deductive reasoning: The case of the THOG problem. *Psychological Research, 51,* 129–135.

Goodwin, R.Q., & Wason, P.C. (1972). Degrees of insight. *British Journal of Psychology, 63,* 205–212.

Griggs, R.A., & Cox, J.A. (1982). The elusive thematic materials effect in the Wason selection task. *British Journal of Psychology, 73,* 407–420.

Henle, M. (1962). On the relation between logic and thinking. *Psychological Review, 69,* 366–378.

Inhelder, B., & Piaget, J. (1958). *The growth of logical thinking.* New York: Basic Books.

Johnson-Laird, P.N. (1983). *Mental models.* Cambridge: Cambridge University Press.

Johnson-Laird, P.N., & Byrne, R. (1991). *Deduction.* Hove, UK: Lawrence Erlbaum Associates Ltd.

Johnson-Laird, P.N., Legrenzi, P., & Legrenzi, M.S. (1972). Reasoning and a sense of reality. *British Journal of Psychology, 63,* 395–400.

Kahneman, D., Slovic, P., & Tversky, A. (1982). *Judgement under uncertainty: Heuristics and biases.* Cambridge: Cambridge University Press.

Klayman, J., & Ha, Y-W. (1987). Confirmation, disconfirmation and information in hypothesis testing. *Psychological Review, 94,* 211–228.

Manktelow, K.I., & Evans, J.St.B.T. (1979). Facilitation of reasoning by realism: Effect or non-effect? *British Journal of Psychology, 70,* 477–488.

Manktelow, K.I., & Over, D. (1991). Social roles and utilities in reasoning with deontic conditionals. *Cognition, 39,* 85–105.

Newstead, S.E., & Griggs, R.A. (1992). Thinking about THOG: Sources of error in a deductive reasoning task. *Psychological Research, 54,* 299–305.

Newstead, S.E., Griggs, R.A., & Warner, S.A. (1982). The effects of realism on Wason's THOG problem. *Psychological Research, 54,* 299–305.

Oaksford, M., & Chater, N. (1993). *A rational analysis of the selection task as optimal data selection.* Technical Report UWB-CNU-TR-93-2, Department of Psychology, University of Wales, Bangor.

O'Brien, D.P. (1993). Mental logic and irrationality: We can put a man on the moon, so why can't we solve those logical reasoning problems. In K.I. Manktelow & D.E. Over (Eds.), *Rationality.* London: Routledge & Kegan Paul.

Peterson, C.R., & Beach, L.R. (1967). Man as an intuitive statistician. *Psychological Bulletin, 68*, 29–46.

Platt, R.D., & Griggs, R.A. (1993). Facilitation in the abstract selection task: The effects of attentional and instructional factors. *Quarterly Journal of Experimental Psychology, 46A*, 591–613.

Popper, K.R. (1959). *The logic of scientific discovery*. London: Hutchinson.

Revlin, R., Leirer, V., Yopp, H., & Yopp, R. (1980). The belief bias effect in formal reasoning: The influence of knowledge on logic. *Memory and Cognition, 8*, 584–592.

Rips, L.J. (1983). Cognitive processes in propositional reasoning. *Psychological Review, 90*, 38–71.

Rips, L.J. (1990). Reasoning. *Annual Review of Psychology, 41*, 85–116.

Smyth, M.M., & Clark, S.E. (1986). My half-sister is THOG: Strategic processes in a reasoning task. *British Journal of Psychology, 77*, 275–287.

Wason, P.C. (1960). On the failure to eliminate hypotheses in a conceptual task. *Quarterly Journal of Experimental Psychology, 12*, 129–140.

Wason, P.C. (1966). Reasoning. In B.M. Foss (Ed.), *New horizons in psychology, I*. Harmondsworth: Penguin.

Wason, P.C. (1967). On the failure to eliminate hypotheses: A second look. In P.C. Wason & P.N. Johnson-Laird (Eds.), *Thinking and reasoning*. Harmondsworth: Penguin.

Wason, P.C. (1969). Regression in reasoning? *British Journal of Psychology, 60*, 471–480.

Wason, P.C. (1983). Realism and rationality in the selection task. In J.St.B.T. Evans (Ed.), *Thinking and reasoning: Psychological approaches*. London: Routledge & Kegan Paul.

Wason, P.C., & Brooks, P.G. (1979). THOG: The anatomy of a problem. *Psychological Research, 41*, 79–90.

Wason, P.C., & Evans, J.St.B.T. (1975). Dual processes in reasoning? *Cognition, 3*, 141–154.

Wason, P.C., & Golding, E. (1974). The language of inconsistency. *British Journal of Psychology, 65*, 537–546.

Wason, P.C., & Johnson-Laird, P.N. (1972). *Psychology of reasoning: Structure and content*. London: Batsford.

Wason, P.C., & Shapiro, D. (1971). Natural and contrived experience in a reasoning problem. *Quarterly Journal of Experimental Psychology, 23*, 63–71.

Wilkins, M.C. (1928). *The effect of changed material on the ability to do formal syllogistic reasoning*. Archives of Psychology, New York, No.102.

Woodworth, R.S., & Sells, S.B. (1935). An atmosphere effect in syllogistic reasoning. *Journal of Experimental Psychology, 18*, 451–460.

CHAPTER TWO

The Effects of Rule Clarification, Decision Justification, and Selection Instruction on Wason's Abstract Selection Task

Richard A. Griggs

Department of Psychology, University of Florida, USA

INTRODUCTION

The four card selection task was first described by Wason (1966) who can hardly have suspected that in the next quarter of a century it would become the most intensively researched single problem in the history of the psychology of reasoning. At the time of writing, there is no sign that interest in this task is abating, and submissions of papers on the problem to learned journals continue with great regularity (Evans, Newstead, & Byrne, 1993, p. 99).

This chapter is concerned with Peter Wason's selection task—specifically with the original version that has become known as the *standard abstract* form of the task. It is, in Wason's words, "deceptively simple (not *'deceptively difficult'* as some people write for reasons which escape me), with the corollary that it is really very difficult" (Wason, 1983, p. 48). Wason goes on to point out that this task has been called "really very complicated" (Finocchiaro, 1980), a "laboratory game" (Wetherick, 1970), a "cognitive illusion" (Cohen, 1981), or quite simply "irritating" (Vuyk, 1981). What then is this sometimes maligned but so intensively studied task?

In its standard form (Evans et al., 1993), the task presents the subject with four cards and an "If p then q" rule that refers to these cards. It is made clear to the subject that the cards each have a letter on one side and a number on the other side. The subject can see only one side of each card and is asked to select only the card or cards that must be turned over so as to determine whether the rule is true or false. The visible sides of the four cards represent cases of p, not-p, q, and not-q. For example, the rule might be "If a card has a vowel on one side, then it has an even number on the other side", and the four cards would show a vowel (p), a consonant (not-p), an even number (q), and an odd number (not-q). Often the rule relates specific instances (e.g. "If a card has an A on one side, then it has a 3 on the other side"). The correct answer is to select the p and the not-q cards (the cards with the vowel and the odd number showing in the first example) because only cases of p and not-q can falsify the "If p then q" implication rule. The rule is true regardless of what is on the other side of the not-p and the q cards.

Why the fascination with this particular task? The answer is simple. For the past 27 years, no one has figured out how to reliably facilitate performance on the standard abstract version. The correct selection rate is usually less than 10% (Evans et al., 1993). Reliably good performance on some thematic versions of the task (e.g. Griggs & Cox's drinking-age version, 1982) and on some abstract schema versions (e.g. Cheng & Holyoak's abstract permission schema version, 1985) has been observed, but such facilitation on the standard abstract task has remained an elusive result. Recently, however, Richard Platt and I managed to produce such facilitation (Platt & Griggs, 1993b). We replicated our findings, but given the history of non-replication in the selection task literature, independent replication is clearly necessary.

Three factors were important in obtaining our results. The factors are given in the title of this chapter—rule clarification, decision justification, and selection instruction. In order to provide a frame for the Platt and Griggs findings, I will review the previous research on each factor, highlighting the studies most relevant to our experiments. However, because I want these reviews to be valuable to researchers planning to do empirical work involving these factors, the reviews will be relatively complete. Thus, some studies (e.g. my 1989 work on Howard Margolis's ambiguity theory) will not bear quite as directly on the Platt and Griggs experiments. Following these reviews, I will describe the Platt and Griggs findings and then conclude by positioning these findings within the previous literature and the current major theories of performance on the standard abstract selection task, specifically Evans's two-stage theory (see Evans, this volume, Chapter 7) and Johnson-Laird and Byrne's mental models theory (see Johnson-Laird, this volume, Chapter 6).

RULE CLARIFICATION

By rule clarification I mean any change in the wording of the rule or the addition of any text material to clarify the implication meaning of the "if ... then" rule statement. Given the rather large literature on difficulties in comprehending "if ... then" statements (e.g. see Fillenbaum, 1975; Taplin & Staudenmayer, 1973) and the popularity of Henle's rationalist argument in reasoning research (e.g. Falmagne, 1975; Revlin & Mayer, 1978), it is surprising that few researchers have examined the role of rule clarification in the selection task.

It appears that the first researcher to investigate rule clarification was Bracewell (1974). He presented a paper at the "The Selection Task Conference" in Trento, Italy, in 1974 that described attempts to facilitate performance on the abstract task by clarifying the conditional meaning of the rule. To the best of my knowledge, this paper was never published and it has seldom been cited. I only know about it because Peter Wason graciously sent me a copy years ago. Since it is unpublished and not widely cited, I will provide a little more detail about it than one might expect. Because it is a conference paper, however, the detail available is already limited.

Bracewell described two experiments that were rather complex, but I will isolate the details relevant to this discussion. In the first experiment, the rule used was, "If J is on one side of the card then 2 is on the other side", and the selection instructions made it clear that the task was to select the card or cards that could possibly falsify the rule. To explicate the meaning of the rule, an equivalence interpretation sheet on which three equivalence interpretations of the rule were typed was used. (Please note that Bracewell referred to the rule as the "hypothesis".)

The three equivalence statements were the following:

1. Please do not make the interpretation that the hypothesis means in addition that "If 2 is on one side of the card then J is on the other side".
2. In other words we do not want you to take the hypothesis to mean "If and only if J is on one side is 2 on the other side".
3. To put it another way, the hypothesis should not be interpreted to mean that 2 occurs only with J.

With respect to procedure, after the hypothesis (rule) was presented, the subject was then presented with the first equivalence interpretation and asked if it and the hypothesis differed in meaning. If the difference was not clear, then the second equivalence statement was presented and the subject was asked if the difference was clear. If still not clear, the third statement was presented and the question about the difference repeated. Then the subject was asked to select the possible falsifying cards. After selection, the subject was asked to justify the choice of each card. If mistakes were made, the experimenter went back to the original task instructions and the equivalence interpretation sheet and then asked the subject to do the task again.

Because we are not interested in training, only the first-trial data are of interest in this discussion. Only 1 of 12 subjects (university graduates enrolled in the Faculty of Education at the University of Toronto) made the correct selection. Although no facilitation was observed in this experiment, Bracewell did find facilitation in a second experiment with subjects from the same population but with two important methodological differences. First, explicit reference was made to the sides of the selection cards in the statement of the rule (i.e. "If either the showing face or the underside face of the card has J on it, then 2 is on the remaining side"). Secondly, and probably most important, the three statements on the equivalence interpretation sheet were changed to the following:

1. The hypothesis should not be interpreted to mean in addition that 2 occurs only with J.
2. In other words, we do not want you to take the hypothesis to mean in addition that "If either the showing face or the underside face of the card has a 2 on it then J is on the remaining side".
3. To put it another way, the hypothesis should not be interpreted to mean "If and only if either the showing face or the underside face of the card has J on it will 2 be on the remaining side".

This time 7/12 (58%) made the correct selection on the first trial. Bracewell points out that the source of this improvement is not clear given that both rule wording and the equivalence statements were changed. He does, however, present some evidence that more subjects in Experiment 1 made equivalence interpretations than in Experiment 2, and entertains the possibility that the first equivalence interpretation statement used in Experiment 2 may be a better cue for restricting the interpretation of the rule to the conditional.

Although there are obviously many constraints upon drawing very strong conclusions from Bracewell's results (e.g. no data relating equivalence interpretation performance to selection task performance are provided), these findings do at least indicate that rule explication *may* lead to task facilitation. These data also suggest, however, that not every type of explication will do so. Two other aspects of Bracewell's procedure should be noted because of their relevance to the other two factors to be reviewed: (1) selection instructions that clearly asked the subject to choose the card or cards that could possibly falsify the rule were used; and (2) subjects were asked to justify their selections (but this justification stage was used as part of a training procedure and could not affect first-trial data).

Interestingly, a second presentation at the Trento conference described another attempt to facilitate performance by reducing the ambiguity in interpretation. Mosconi and D'Urso (1974) proposed that a formulation of the rule that will make the not-q value more salient will help in the consideration of the not-q card and the recognition of its relevance to the selection task. In their Experiment 2, the instructions were as follows:

> These cards are divided into two parts. To the left there will always be either the letter A or some other letter different from A. To the right there will always be either the number 2 or some other number different from 2. Only one of the two halves of each card is visible. With respect to these cards this hypothesis has been proposed: "If to the left there is the letter A, then to the right there is the number 2, and never a number different from 2." I would like to know which of these four cards, if uncovered, could demonstrate that this hypothesis is false. Thus, you should show me which card or cards you would uncover in order to find an instance that could be contrary to the hypothesis.

The result was that 6 of 12 students at the University of Padova got this version of the task correct compared to only 1/12 students on a comparable standard version of the task. Mosconi and D'Urso argued that this version of the task facilitated performance because it made the subjects aware of the logical value of the card that represents not-q. In the standard version, the card that represents not-q is not clearly indicated as such. Like Bracewell's paper, this paper also seems not to have been published, but it has recently been cited by other Italian reasoning researchers (e.g. Girotto, Mazzocco, & Cherubini, 1992).

After the Trento conference, nobody seems to have pursued this line of research until Hoch and Tschirgi did so in the early 1980s; but their studies arose from a very different motivation and focus. Using a Brunswikian cue-redundancy framework (Brunswik, 1952), Hoch and Tschirgi (1983; 1985) provide some cleaner experimental evidence that rule explication may facilitate performance on the standard abstract selection task. Hoch and Tschirgi (1983) argued that the difficulty subjects have on the abstract task stems from their inability to generate all possible pairwise card combinations (p, q; p, not-q; not-p, q; etc.) and then identify the truth value of each pair. The rule most often cues the p, q pair and its *true* value. Hoch and Tschirgi hypothesised that thematic contents which improve performance on the task do so because they provide the subject with alternate cues for the generation of the other relevant pairs and the identification of their truth values (especially the p, not-q pair). Thus, thematic content provides redundant cues to the logical structure of the problem (i.e. the material implication relation), and the subject no longer has to depend solely upon the implication rule to solve the problem.

Hoch and Tschirgi's 1983 experiment was rather complex. Their "abstract-explicit" condition is most relevant to the present discussion. In this condition, the rule was "If there is an A on one side of the card, then there must be a 2 on the other side", and the cards could have the letters A or B on one side and the numbers 1 or 2 on the other side. The statement "Cards with the letter A on the front may only have the number 2 on the back, but cards with the letter B on the front may have either 1 or 2 on the back" was presented immediately after the rule statement. The correct selection was made by 56% of the subjects (students in the Northwestern Graduate School of Management). Performance on the standard abstract task was 28% correct.

In addition to rule explication, Hoch and Tschirgi's study contained other procedural differences that may have contributed to the improved performance in the explicit-relation condition as well as the higher-than-normal baseline performance. Instead of true-false instructions, subjects were asked to make sure the rule was followed. Subjects were also asked to explain their selection decisions in writing, and they were not prevented from changing their answers while generating their explanations. The subject population also differed from the more typical undergraduate students of previous studies.

To examine the possible effects of these differences, Hoch and Tschirgi (1985) conducted a follow-up study in which the original true-false selection instruction was used and subjects were not allowed to change their first answer but were given an opportunity to do so later so that first responses and changes arising from the justification task could be monitored. In addition, they sampled subjects from three different education levels based on highest level of schooling completed (high school, bachelor's degree, and master's degree). The rule was taken from Wason (1966): "If a card has a vowel on its letter side, then it has an even number on the other side." The rule explication statements—"However, a card with a vowel showing may only have an even number on the back side. A card with a consonant showing may have either an odd or an even number on the back side"— immediately followed the statement of the rule.

Performance for the group most comparable to the typical subjects used in selection task studies (i.e. high school graduates) was 8% correct for the standard abstract task and 24% correct for the explicit-cue version. In addition, the correct selection rate remained the same for both versions when first-choice and second-choice data were compared. Hoch and Tschirgi also found what they interpreted to be a level-of-education effect, but what later research by Jackson and Griggs (1988) found to be *probably* an area of expertise effect. Nevertheless, rule clarification had a significant facilitating effect on performance.

More recently, however, as part of a series of experiments examining differences in performance on the standard abstract task and abstract permission schema versions of the task, Kroger, Cheng, and Holyoak (1993) did not observe any facilitation for university undergraduates on the standard task when a rule clarification statement was employed. In Experiment 1b, the rule "If a card says 'A' on one side, then the other side must say 'X' " was followed by the clarification, "The rule does not imply that if a card does not say 'A' on one side, then the other side must not say 'X'." This latter statement was intended to block a biconditional interpretation of the conditional rule. A violation-checking context (described below in the Selection Instruction section) was employed, but no significant facilitation was observed. This result was replicated in their Experiment 2, and Kroger et al. concluded that their rule clarification statement was not sufficient to produce facilitation in the standard task. This should not be surprising given the difficulty humans have in processing negatives (Wason & Johnson-Laird, 1972) and the presence of three negatives in the Kroger et al. rule clarification statement.

I have recently attempted to reduce ambiguity in the task in a more general way that included some rule clarification (Griggs, 1989). I tested Margolis's (1987) hypothesis concerning scenario and linguistic ambiguities in the selection task. Margolis argues that we misinterpret the selection task as an open scenario task, but that it is really a closed scenario task. According to Margolis, an open scenario is a situation in which a person is choosing how to search, whereas a closed scenario is a situation in which the choice of how to search is already foreclosed and the choice remaining is limited to a selection within a constrained set of possibilities.

Margolis argues further that the open scenario is more typical of real life and that people ordinarily encounter a closed scenario after they have gone through the open phase. Because of this and because the context is so impoverished in the selection task, subjects are prompted to give an open scenario interpretation to the selection task. In addition to this main source of difficulty (scenario ambiguity), Margolis proposes a linguistic ambiguity stemming from the multiple possible readings (primarily as being reversible) that may be given to "if ... then" statements.

With an open scenario interpretation, you choose categories that must be checked to find out whether the rule has been violated or not. When you choose a category, you get to check all of the cards with that category on them. Thus, the correct answer would be to check either p or not-q but not both categories; and p-only (one of the frequent errors on the standard task) would be a correct response. Given a reversible interpretation of the rule and an open scenario interpretation of the problem, then a p and q selection (the other frequent error on the standard task) would be a correct answer; and so would not-p and not-q, p and not-p, and q and not-q.

For more details on the open/closed scenario distinction and Margolis's hypothesis, see Margolis (1987, Chapter 8). In summary, Margolis hypothesises that most subjects should make the correct selection if the two ambiguities that he proposes are removed.

I tested this hypothesis and found reliable facilitation (an average of 74% correct in 3 experiments) for an abstract version of the task that, according to Margolis, removed the ambiguities. This remedial version of the abstract task was:

> Four cards have been picked from a mixed pack (some red backs, some blue). The person who chose the cards was told to obey the following rule: "Pick any four cards except that if a card has a red back, it must be at least a 6." You see the cards lying on the table, with two face down and two face up. Circle each card that must be turned over in order to be sure whether it violates the rule. (The four cards were red back, blue back, 7 of hearts, and 5 of clubs.)

Margolis argues that this version is more likely to be interpreted as a closed scenario because people are familiar with handling playing cards in a closed scenario situation and that the new statement of the rule also reduces the likelihood of a reversible interpretation of the "if ... then" language.

I found this facilitation to be reliable; but in order to observe the facilitation, the consequent part of the rule had to be phrased to prevent matching. Matching means that subjects simply select those cards with values that match those mentioned in the rule (see Evans, this volume, Chapter 7). When matching was possible (i.e. the rule was "If a card has a red back, then it must be a 7", and the cards were red back, blue back, 7, and 5), then the facilitation disappeared. It should also be noted that Dominowski (1990a) failed to replicate the high level of facilitation that I observed when matching was not possible (see Chapter 3, this volume). David O'Brien and Maria Dias, however, have found that the first sentence of the problem may be confusing and subjects may not appreciate what the universe of discourse for the problem is (David O'Brien, personal communication, 20th December, 1993). When the universe of discourse was made clear, they observed substantial facilitation (over 50% correct) for non-matching versions of Margolis's remedial task with violation selection instructions. Thus, such confusion may play an important role in Dominowski's failure to replicate my earlier findings.

Conclusions

Given a rather limited set of studies with varying objectives, types of subjects, and factors, firm conclusions about the effects of rule clarification are difficult if even possible. However, one conclusion does seem clear. Facilitation, if it is reliable, does not occur for just any type of rule clarification or explication. Bracewell's results hinted at this, and Kroger et al.'s results confirm it. In addition, the degree of facilitation may vary not only with the type of explication but also with the presence or absence of other factors—possibly the decision justification format and the type of selection instruction employed. We turn next to a discussion of the research literature on the first of these factors.

DECISION JUSTIFICATION

The decision justification factor refers to any procedure that requires subjects to provide reasons (justification) for their decisions to select or not to select each card. It has a very limited history as an experimental variable in selection task studies, probably because of the prominence of Wason and Evans's dual process theory in the 1970s, which questioned the validity of such justifications. Wason and Evans contended that such reports were *post hoc* rationalisations and therefore not reliable evidence of any internal process (for more detail see Wason & Evans, 1975, and Evans & Wason, 1976).

Ironically, however, decision justification seems to have been studied first by Wason (Goodwin & Wason, 1972). The rule "Every card which has a triangle on one half has red on the other half " and a true-false selection instruction were employed. When subjects had made their selections, they were given paper and pencil and asked to write down their reasons for selecting or not selecting each card. Subjects were allowed to change their selections. Summing across their experimental manipulation (i.e. the availability of the four cards during selection), which had no effect, 6/32 (19%) made the correct selection before being asked to give reasons for their decisions. The authors credit this slightly higher than normal baseline performance to their presentation of the problem in terms of halves of the card, as opposed to the sides of the card. This is similar to Mosconi and D'Urso's (1974) finding when they clarified the meaning of "sides" of the cards. Both seem to be facilitative effects of clarifying problem presentation.

Of the remaining 26 subjects in the Goodwin and Wason study, 5 attained the correct selection after trying to give reasons for their initial incorrect selections, and one subject changed from the correct selection to an incorrect one. Given this small increase in the correct selection rate (from 19% to 31%), Goodwin and Wason conclude that the "elicitation of written justifications for the selections had only a limited effectiveness in inducing greater insight" (pp. 211–212).

Wason examined selection justification further in a later study with Jonathan Evans (Wason & Evans, 1975). The standard abstract form of the task with letters and numbers and the "if ... then" rule construction was employed, and subjects were informed about the decision justification task before making their selections. For the condition of interest to us, none of the subjects made the correct selection.

During the 1970s there were a few other studies involving the decision justification format, but not directly as a treatment factor. For example, as mentioned earlier, Bracewell incorporated justification within a training procedure. Similarly, Roth (1979) also used a justification procedure in her transfer study on a reduced-array version of the selection task.

Berry (1983) reported a very complex transfer study involving two types of verbalisation—concurrent verbalisation ("thinking aloud") and post verbalisation (providing a retrospective account). Verbalisation, however, was not varied independent of other variables so it is impossible to sort out any possible effects that it may have had in this transfer study.

Jay Chrostowski and I carried out a study using Berry's verbalisation procedures, but with a single-problem format (Chrostowski & Griggs, 1985). A second post-verbalisation procedure in which subjects did not know ahead of time that they would be asked to justify their selections was also employed. We failed to find any effects of these verbalisation instructions; but this may have been due to our subjects' failure to comply completely with the verbalisation instructions. Many subjects gave justifications only after prompts from the experimenter. Thus, subjects responded to all three verbalisation instructions in a highly similar fashion with little actual verbalisation, eliminating any potential effects. In another attempt to clarify Berry's findings, Klaczynski, Gelfand, and Reese (1989, Experiment 1) found no effect of "thinking aloud" verbalisation, but they had compliance problems similar to those that we had observed.

As already mentioned above, Hoch and Tschirgi (1983; 1985) asked their subjects to explain in one or two sentences why they decided to turn over or not turn over each of the cards. In the 1983 study, subjects were not prevented from changing their selections while generating their explanations. Thus, it is possible that explanations had a positive effect on performance; but we have no way of knowing because justification was not a factor in the experiment. In the 1985 study, however, subjects were not allowed to change their initial answers but could do so during the explanation phase. Thus, though justification was still not an experimental factor, Hoch and Tschirgi could assess its impact by comparing the correct selection rate for the initial answers to the rate including any changed answers. As already mentioned, for the subjects of interest (i.e. the high school graduates) there was no effect. There was, however, a level-of-education effect—subjects with master's degrees were more likely to solve the problem after explaining their initial selections than subjects with bachelor's degrees, and subjects with bachelor's degrees were more likely than the high school graduates. Sherri Jackson and I found a similar effect but for area of expertise rather than level of education (Jackson & Griggs, 1988).

Beattie and Baron (1988) used thinking-aloud protocols in their Experiments 2 and 3, but this verbalisation procedure was not an experimental factor. Relevant to this discussion, however, they did find much evidence to indicate misinterpretation of the rule as a biconditional and a large number of task misunderstandings suggesting that "alleged failures of reasoning may often be failures of comprehension" (p. 294).

Given these earlier suggestions in the literature that decision justification might impact performance on the selection task, Dominowski (1990b) reported an experiment on eight versions of the task, including the standard abstract form, in which he directly examined the effects of reason-giving *per se*. In the justification conditions, there was an additional instruction to write briefly the reason for each decision made in the space provided next to each card. Each subject worked through a booklet containing five problems, some thematic and some arbitrary.

Reason-giving generally improved performance (24.9% vs. 12.8% for the no-reason-giving control condition) but not very much on the standard abstract task (10% vs. 4%). To explain the lack of a strong effect on the more difficult abstract problems, Dominowski hypothesised that these problems "seem to present obstacles to comprehending the scenario or the rule that are not removed by the sorts of processing that reason-giving might promote" (pp. 317–318).

Conclusions

One conclusion is obvious—decision justification of any sort has seldom been manipulated as an experimental factor. Dominowski (1990b) provides the cleanest study of this factor. Whereas the other, more muddled studies involving decision justification indicate that this factor may be important, Dominowski's results clearly show that it is, but that its impact may vary across problem content, with the least effect on the standard abstract problem. Thus, it may need to be paired with other factors such as rule clarification to have a more significant impact on the standard task.

SELECTION INSTRUCTION

Although the instruction to select the card(s) that must be turned over to determine whether the rule is true or false has evolved to be the standard selection instruction, many others have been used, but not always as experimental factors. Even in the early studies of the task, different types of selection instruction were used—e.g. to discover whether the experimenter is lying (Wason, 1966); to prove the rule true (Wason, 1968); to pick out values which could break the rule (Wason, 1968); and in order to find whether the sentence is untrue (Wason & Golding, 1974). The effects of such instructions had only slight if any effects on performance (Evans, 1982). The more systematic study of selection instruction as a factor occurred during the early 1980s when researchers became concerned with the elusive thematic content effect (Griggs, 1983).

These studies arose from arguments about the causes of facilitation observed for certain thematic contents (e.g. the drinking-age problem from Griggs & Cox, 1982). Yachanin (1983; Yachanin & Tweney, 1982) argued that the facilitation was mainly the result of violation selection instructions that changed the nature of the task. In the standard abstract true-false version, the truth status of the rule is assessed; but, in a violation version, the rule is given as true, and the task is to select the card or cards that definitely need to be turned over to determine whether or not the rule has been violated. Thus, the standard selection task requires subjects to assess the truth status of an hypothesis (reason about a rule), and the violation selection task asks the subject to check to see whether four instances obey some given rule (reason from a rule).

Yachanin attributed previous failures to observe facilitation for problems with violation instructions and abstract content (e.g. Johnson-Laird, Legrenzi, & Legrenzi, 1972; Griggs & Cox, 1982) to a failure to control role playing in the problems used. A series of studies (Chrostowski & Griggs, 1985; Griggs, 1984; Yachanin, 1986) examined this hypothesis. The results were clear. The type of selection instruction had no effect on the standard abstract task regardless of the role-playing factor. It did, however, have an effect on the thematic versions for which facilitation was observed. More facilitation was observed for violation instructions than for true-false instructions. Valentine (1985) also found no effect of selection instruction on the correct selection rate for the standard abstract task.

Gigerenzer and Hug (1992) have recently proposed an interesting explanation for the instructional effect for the thematic problems and the lack of such an effect for the abstract task (cf. Platt & Griggs, 1993a). It follows from their revised version of Cosmides's (1989) social contract theory. In brief, facilitation would be expected if (1) the rule is perceived as a social contract, and (2) the subject is cued into the perspective of a party that can be cheated. Gigerenzer and Hug argue that both of these conditions were met in the thematic problems examined by Griggs (1984) and Yachanin (1986) but that neither condition is met in the abstract problems examined by Griggs (1984), Yachanin (1986), and Valentine (1985).

Two more recent studies have examined stronger violation-checking treatments (Dominowski, 1989; Kroger et al., 1993). In Dominowski (1989), the violation selection instruction, "to make sure the rule is not being violated", was contrasted with the control selection instruction, "to make sure the rule is being followed". It should be noted that subjects were also required to provide a reason for their decision to select or not select each card.

In addition, before subjects in the violation condition did the selection task, they were asked to indicate outcomes that they thought would violate the rule. They were given five descriptions corresponding to p and q, p and not-q, not-p and q, not-p and not-q, and not-q and p. For example, for the rule, "If a card has a vowel, then it must have an even number", the p and not-q description was "A card with a vowel and odd number." This is very similar to the "project falsity" therapy task used in Experiment 1, Wason (1968), except for the additional fifth description (not-q and p), which reversed the normal order of presentation of the logical cases. Dominowski examined three arbitrary versions, including the standard abstract form, and six thematic versions of the selection task. Each subject was given five problems to solve—some thematic and some arbitrary.

The data that I will describe are given in Dominowski (1992). Dominowski collected some additional data after the 1989 study and reported the complete data set in Dominowski (1992). Across problems, violation checking improved performance (the average increase was 17%). There was improvement for all three arbitrary versions, including the standard abstract problem. Performance on the standard abstract task, however, was the worst (14% correct in the control condition vs. 28% correct in the violation-checking condition). Performance improved more for an arbitrary letters-numbers label problem (up to about 37% correct).

Given that subjects also provided reasons for their card selection decisions, more facilitation might have been expected. Remember, however, that Dominowski (1990b) reported only a very small effect of reason-giving for selections on performance on the standard form of the task. In addition, given Wason's (1968) observation of only a slight effect of his "projecting falsity" procedure, the small effect on performance observed by Dominowski (1989) seems more reasonable. The rule interpretation difficulty still remains.

Even more recently, as pointed out above, Kroger et al. (1993) failed to observe any facilitation for a violation version of the standard task paired with a rule clarification to prevent a biconditional interpretation. Kroger et al. examined what they term "a violation-checking context" for an abstract permission schema version of the task and an arbitrary abstract form of the task very similar to the standard abstract task. The rule in the arbitrary version related letters on the two sides of the cards rather than letters and numbers. The selection instructions used to create the violation-checking context were as follows:

> You want to see if any of the cards violate the rule. Which of the cards below would you have to turn over to check? Turn over as many cards as you think appropriate, but do not turn over a card unless what is on the other side can potentially tell you that the card violates the rule.

In addition, as described above in the Rule Clarification section, a sentence intended to prevent subjects from interpreting the rule as an "if and only if" biconditional followed the statement of the rule. Subjects were not asked to provide justifications for their selection decisions about the cards.

For the arbitrary abstract version of the task, no facilitation was observed. In contrast, a small but reliable degree of facilitation (22% correct) was observed for an abstract permission rule with this violation-checking context. This lack of facilitation for the arbitrary abstract version was observed in Experiment 1A when no rule clarification statement was included, twice in Experiment 1B (for both explicit and implicit negatives on the not-p and not-q cards) with a rule clarification statement, and twice in Experiment 2 (with a rule clarification statement and without one).

Sherri Jackson and I recently observed some other types of instructional effects (Griggs & Jackson, 1990). They stem from some further predictions by Margolis (1987). Margolis argues that the instructional statement for selecting the cards can bias subjects' selections. If in the standard abstract task we constrain the choice to selecting exactly two cards, various changes in selections should be observed. First, if we change the instruction to "Circle two cards to turn over in order to check whether the rule has been violated", then the number of p and q choices should be increased. Because p and q and p-only selections are the most frequent errors on this form of the task, adding the constraint to choose two cards should lead those subjects who might choose only p with the usual selection instruction to select both p and q. I will refer to this selection instruction as the p and q violation instruction.

Margolis, however, further proposes that if the instruction is changed to be "Figure out which two cards could violate the rule, and circle them", then the frequency of the not-p and not-q response (a very infrequent response) should be significantly increased. Margolis argues that this latter change in wording shifts attention to cards not mentioned in the rule. It should also be noted that, according to Margolis, if subjects are interpreting the problem as an open scenario and making an incorrect reversible interpretation of the rule, not-p and not-q would be a correct response (see Margolis, 1987, Chapter 8, and Griggs, 1989, for why this would be the case). I will refer to this selection instruction as the not-p and not-q violation instruction.

We tested both of Margolis's hypotheses by comparing the standard abstract task including a typical violation selection instruction ("Circle the card or cards that must be turned over to determine whether the rule has been violated") with versions using Margolis's two proposed selection instructions (Griggs & Jackson, 1990). The results were just as Margolis predicted. There were significantly more p and q selections for the p and q violation instruction and significantly more not-p and not-q selections for the not-p and not-q violation instruction versus the typical violation instruction. Because the not-p and not-q response is so unusual for this task, this latter result was replicated.

A second experiment using the not-p and not-q instruction was then conducted, but this time with the abstract permission schema problem (Cheng & Holyoak, 1985). In the abstract permission schema task, the subject is instructed to pretend to be an authority checking whether or not people are obeying certain regulations. The regulations all have the general form, "If one is to take action A, then one must first have fulfilled prerequisite P." The four cards, which contain information about four people, are "Has taken action A", "Has not taken action A", "Has fulfilled prerequisite P", and "Has not fulfilled prerequisite P".

The facilitation observed for the abstract permission schema problem can be explained by Margolis's theory. For example, a reversible interpretation would be less likely because a person could certainly fulfil a prerequisite but not take a particular action. Similarly, checking people for following regulations is more likely to be interpreted as a closed scenario.

An interesting aspect of the error frequency data for the abstract permission schema task is that there are far more p-only selections than p and q selections (Jackson & Griggs, 1990; Girotto et al., 1992). The reverse is true for the standard abstract task (Griggs & Cox, 1993). Given this and the probable closed scenario/non-reversible interpretation of this version of the task, Margolis's not-p and not-q violation instruction should increase the facilitation for the permission task rather than lead to an increase in the number of not-p and not-q selections. The instruction should make the not-q card more salient to those who might normally have chosen p-only and, because two cards have to be chosen, a correct p and not-q selection would be likely. This turned out to be the case. For two different groups of subjects, the not-p and not-q violation instruction led to enhanced facilitation—76% and 82% correct. Griggs and Cox (1993) replicated this finding as well as the increase in not-p and not-q selections for the standard abstract task.

Conclusions

Although not extensively studied as an experimental factor, the selection instruction variable has been studied more than the other two reviewed factors. Thus, the conclusions that one can draw are a little more solid. A violation selection instruction leads to better performance than a true-false selection instruction, but this conclusion is definitely qualified by the type of problem. For thematic problems that typically lead to facilitation, more facilitation is observed for the violation instruction version. For the standard abstract problem, little, if any, facilitation has been observed for the violation selection instruction. Dominowski (1989) found some, but it was not substantial.

The effects of Margolis's two violation instructions seem fairly reliable, but still need independent replication. His p and q violation instruction seems to increase the frequency of the incorrect p and q selection on the standard abstract task, and his not-p and not-q violation instruction seems to increase greatly the frequency of the normally atypical not-p and not-q selection on the standard abstract task, but to increase the frequency of the correct selection on the abstract permission schema problem.

THE PLATT AND GRIGGS EXPERIMENTS

Using the Hoch and Tschirgi studies as a base because of their clear finding of facilitation on the standard abstract task, Richard Platt and I conducted a series of three experiments involving the three factors that have been reviewed (Platt & Griggs, 1993b). The subjects in all of the experiments were university undergraduates (the typical subjects in selection task research). The first experiment examined the rule clarification factor.

The effects of the presence versus absence of four different rule clarification statements, including the one employed by Hoch and Tschirgi (1985), as well as the presence versus the absence of the standard rule were examined. When the standard rule was absent, the clarification statement took the place of the rule. We hypothesised that the correct selection rate (only 24%) in the Hoch and Tschirgi 1985 study may have been lessened by the presence of the actual rule statement. Some subjects may have ignored the clarification statement, relying on matching the two cases mentioned in the rule to guide their selections. A pilot study had indicated some support for this hypothesis. (It should be noted that in previous studies in which no effect of rule clarification was observed, subjects may have ignored the clarification and used only the rule statement.)

The standard abstract version of the task with the rule, "If a card has a vowel on its letter side, then it has an even number on its number side", and a true-false selection instruction was used. Because the clarification statement mentioned all four card values, we used four different explication statements in order to check for possible attentional effects due to the position of each card value in the clarification statement. The four clarification statements varied according to the logical value referred to first in the sentence. The four types were referred to as p-explication, not-p explication, q-explication, and not-q explication. Hoch and Tschirgi's clarification comprised the p-explication statement, "A card with a vowel on it can only have an even number, but a card with a consonant on it can have either an even or an odd number." The not-p explication statement was "A card with a consonant on it can have either an even or an odd number, but a card with a vowel on it can only have an even number", and so on. The standard abstract task with no rule clarification was included for comparison purposes.

For the eight problems with explication statements, correct performance was greater when the rule was not present (31% vs. 20%, respectively), but this difference was not significant. With the standard rule absent, correct responding ranged from 25–40%. The correct selection rates for both the standard-rule-absent and the standard-rule-present conditions were significantly greater than that for the standard abstract task (0% correct).

In agreement with the findings of Hoch and Tschirgi, the results of this first experiment provide evidence that explicit clarification of the rule can facilitate performance. Even in the best condition, however, only 40% of the subjects made the logically correct response; but subjects were not required to provide reasons for their selection or non-selection of each card as in the Hoch and Tschirgi studies. Thus, in the second experiment we compared performance on the standard abstract task and the p-explication version with the rule absent; and subjects were either asked or not asked to write down reasons for their decisions about each card. Subjects were allowed to change their answers during the justification, but such changes were not monitored. The correct selection rate increased to 67% in the reason-giving condition.

In an attempt to increase correct performance further, in a third experiment we changed from the true-false selection instruction to a typical violation instruction (i.e. "Your task is to decide which card or cards must be turned over in order to find out whether the rule is being violated"). The correct selection rate increased to 81%. We replicated this result twice (69% correct with 3 of the 5 subjects making errors showing partial insight p, q, and not-q selections for the typical violation instruction, and 87% correct for the Margolis not-p and not-q violation instruction).

The results of this series of experiments seem to clearly indicate facilitation for the standard abstract task with an explicated rule. To observe a correct selection rate greater than 50%, however, 2 other factors (a decision justification procedure and a violation selection instruction) were necessary.

SYNTHESIS

In this final section I want to consider the congruency of the Platt and Griggs findings first, briefly, with previous findings on the effects of the three reviewed factors and, secondly, with current theories of performance on the standard abstract task.

In general, the Platt and Griggs results are consistent with the previous findings for the three factors. There are certainly indications of facilitation for rule clarification in the literature that was reviewed, but it should be noted that not any type of rule clarification leads to facilitation (e.g. Kroger et al., 1993). The Hoch and Tschirgi (1985) findings are most relevant since they employed comparable rule explication. In their study, however, the "if ... then" rule was present, and subjects may have ignored the explication, using the rule to make their selections thereby reducing the amount of facilitation observed. The Platt and Griggs results suggest that this may have been the case.

With respect to decision justification, the Platt and Griggs results are clearly congruent with Dominowski's (1990b) study in which reason-giving was an experimental factor. It should be noted that in addition to reason-giving, Platt and Griggs used an explicated rule that had already been shown to lead to facilitation. Thus, more facilitation should have been observed—and it was.

The effect of violation instructions on the amount of facilitation observed is probably the most congruent with the previous literature. It is clear in previous studies that for versions of the task that lead to facilitation, the violation selection instruction leads to better performance than the true-false instruction (e.g. Griggs, 1984). The additional result that the Margolis not-p and not-q violation instruction leads to further facilitation is also consistent with the Griggs and Jackson (1990) finding for the abstract permission schema task.

Given that the results are congruent with the previous literature, how do they fare with respect to current theories of performance on the standard abstract task. Because Evans's two-stage theory and Johnson-Laird and Byrne's mental models theory comprised the theoretical basis for the Platt and Griggs experiments, it should come as no surprise that the results are congruent with these theories.

First, consider mental models theory. According to Johnson-Laird and Byrne (1991), facilitation should occur when subjects "flesh out" their model to include not-q. P must be exhaustively paired with q, leaving not-q paired only with not-p. It might also be necessary to represent explicitly the impossibility of pairing p with not-q. By explicitly mentioning all four card values in the explicated rule statement, the probability that subjects will flesh out their models and include not-q in them should increase. Thus, the correct selection rate should increase—and it did.

Johnson-Laird and Byrne (1991, p. 81) claim that reason-giving should make subjects "more likely to envisage the alternatives explicitly". Thus, in writing their reasons for their selections, subjects should realise the need to flesh the model out to include not-q. Similarly, a violation selection instruction would make it more likely that the violating case, p and not-q, would be explicitly represented in the model. The subject should be drawn to represent in the model what a violation would entail if the task is to find instances that might violate the rule. With a true-false selection instruction, the subject could more easily opt to represent only verifying instances. Thus, in both cases, as with the rule explication, subjects' models should be fleshed out in a correct manner; and performance should improve, as it did.

Evans's two-stage bias model (1984; 1989) could explain the findings in a similar fashion. The explicit rule could block matching bias in the first stage and increase the judgement of relevance for all four card values because they are all mentioned in the explicated rule statement. Thus, the probability that not-q would be considered in the second stage would be increased. The second stage of analytic processing could then account for not only the explication effect but Platt and Griggs's other results as well. This stage, however, has remained so underspecified that the mechanisms to account for such effects have not been defined. Mental models theory, however, could provide the explanation for this second stage (e.g. see Evans, 1991), and the results could be explained as above in terms of fleshing out the model correctly. Nevertheless, the Platt and Griggs findings are not inconsistent with Evans's theory.

In conclusion, the Platt and Griggs findings should stimulate renewed interest in empirical work on the standard abstract selection task. Most of the recent selection task research has revolved around competing theories for schema versions of the task (e.g. Cheng & Holyoak's pragmatic reasoning schemas, 1985; Cosmides's social contract schemas, 1989; Manktelow & Over's deontic schemas, 1990). Certainly the mental logicians (e.g. O'Brien, 1993; this volume, Chapter 9) will be interested. If the Platt and Griggs findings prove to be reliable, one must wonder why 27 years elapsed before their discovery. Two possibilities seem especially intriguing to me. First, is it possible that confirmation bias has played a major role? Hasn't there been far more research attempting to explain why we cannot solve the task rather than to explain how we can do so? Secondly, could it be that researchers have approached the empirical study of the task much like most subjects appear to approach the task itself—with a biased misinterpretation followed by an incomplete analysis of the problem. If so, 27 years would not seem so long.

ACKNOWLEDGEMENTS

I would like to thank James Cox, Sherri Jackson, and Richard Platt for their invaluable contributions to my thinking about the selection task. All of our projects were true collaborations and extremely rewarding experiences. My debt to Peter Wason is obvious. Without him, these experiences would almost certainly never have occurred.

REFERENCES

Beattie, J., & Baron, J. (1988). Confirmation and matching biases in hypothesis testing. *Quarterly Journal of Experimental Psychology, 40A*, 269–297.

Berry, D.C. (1983). Metacognitive experience and transfer of logical reasoning. *Quarterly Journal of Experimental Psychology, 35A*, 39–49.

Bracewell, R. J. (1974, April). *Interpretation factors in the four card selection task.* Paper presented at The Selection Task Conference, Trento, Italy.

Brunswik, E. (1952). The conceptual framework of psychology. In *International encyclopedia of unified science (Vol. 1, No. 10).* Chicago: University of Chicago Press.

Cheng, P.W., & Holyoak, K.J. (1985). Pragmatic reasoning schemas. *Cognitive Psychology, 17*, 391–416.

Chrostowski, J.J., & Griggs, R.A. (1985). The effects of problem content, instructions, and verbalisation procedure on Wason's selection task. *Current Psychological Research and Reviews, 4*, 99–107.

Cohen, L.J. (1981). Can human irrationality be experimentally demonstrated? *The Behavioral and Brain Sciences, 4*, 317–370.

Cosmides, L. (1989). The logic of social exchange: Has natural selection shaped how humans reason? *Cognition, 31*, 187–286.

Dominowski, R.L. (1989, September). *Success and failure on the four card problem.* Paper presented at the Sixth Annual Conference of the Cognitive Psychology Section, British Psychological Society, Cambridge, England.

Dominowski, R.L. (1990a, September). *Arbitrary and thematic versions of the four card problem.* Paper presented at the Seventh Annual Conference of the Cognitive Psychology Section, British Psychological Society, Leicester, England.

Dominowski, R.L. (1990b). Problem solving and metacognition. In K.J. Gilhooly, M.T.G. Keane, R.H. Logie, & G. Erdos (Eds.), *Lines of thinking: Reflections on the psychology of thought: Vol. 2. Skills, emotions, creative processes, individual differences and teaching thinking* (pp. 313–328). Chichester: Wiley.

Dominowski, R.L. (1992, July). *Wason's four card task: The multiple effects of changing content.* Paper presented at the Second International Conference on Thinking, Plymouth, England.

Evans, J.St.B.T. (1982). *The psychology of deductive reasoning.* London: Routledge & Kegan Paul.

Evans, J.St.B.T. (1984). Heuristic and analytic processes in reasoning. *British Journal of Psychology, 75,* 451–468.

Evans, J.St.B.T. (1989). *Bias in human reasoning: Causes and consequences.* Hove, UK: Lawrence Erlbaum Associates Ltd.

Evans, J.St.B.T. (1991). Theories of human reasoning: The fragmented state of the art. *Theory and Psychology, 1,* 83–105.

Evans, J.St.B.T., Newstead, S.E., & Byrne, R.M.J. (1993). *Human reasoning: The psychology of deduction.* Hove, UK: Lawrence Erlbaum Associates Ltd.

Evans, J.St.B.T., & Wason, P.C. (1976). Rationalisation in a reasoning task. *British Journal of Psychology, 67,* 479–486.

Falmagne, R.J. (Ed.) (1975). *Reasoning: Representation and process.* New York: Wiley.

Fillenbaum, S. (1975). If: Some uses. *Psychological Research, 37,* 245–260.

Finocchiaro, M.A. (1980). *Galileo and the art of reasoning.* Dordrecht: Reidel.

Gigerenzer, G., & Hug, K. (1992). Domain-specific reasoning: Social contracts, cheating, and perspective change. *Cognition, 43,* 127–171.

Girotto, V., Mazzocco, A., & Cherubini, P. (1992). Pragmatic judgements of relevance in reasoning: A reply to Jackson and Griggs. *Quarterly Journal of Experimental Psychology, 45A,* 547–574.

Goodwin, R.Q., & Wason, P.C. (1972). Degrees of insight. *British Journal of Psychology, 63,* 205–212.

Griggs, R.A. (1983). The role of problem content in the selection task and THOG problem. In J.St.B.T. Evans (Ed.), *Thinking and reasoning: Psychological approaches* (pp. 16–43). London: Routledge & Kegan Paul.

Griggs, R.A. (1984). Memory cueing and instructional effects on Wason's selection task. *Current Psychological Research and Reviews, 3,* 3–10.

Griggs, R.A. (1989). To "see" or not to "see": That is the selection task. *Quarterly Journal of Experimental Psychology, 41A,* 517–529.

Griggs, R.A., & Cox, J.R. (1982). The elusive thematic-materials effect in Wason's selection task. *British Journal of Psychology, 73,* 407–420.

Griggs, R.A., & Cox, J.R. (1993). Permission schemas and the selection task. *Quarterly Journal of Experimental Psychology, 46A,* 637–651.

Griggs, R.A., & Jackson, S.L. (1990). Instructional effects on responses in Wason's selection task. *British Journal of Psychology, 81,* 197–204.

Hoch, S.J., & Tschirgi, J.E. (1983). Cue redundancy and extra logical inferences in a deductive reasoning task. *Memory and Cognition, 11,* 200–209.

Hoch, S.J., & Tschirgi, J.E. (1985). Logical knowledge and cue redundancy in deductive reasoning. *Memory and Cognition, 13,* 435–462.

Jackson, S.L., & Griggs, R.A. (1988). Education and the selection task. *Bulletin of the Psychonomic Society, 26,* 327–330.

Jackson, S.L., & Griggs, R.A. (1990). The elusive pragmatic reasoning schemas effect. *Quarterly Journal of Experimental Psychology, 42A,* 353–373.

Johnson-Laird, P.N., & Byrne, R.M.J. (1991). *Deduction.* Hove, UK: Lawrence Erlbaum Associates Ltd.

Johnson-Laird, P.N., Legrenzi, P., & Legrenzi, M.S. (1972). Reasoning and a sense of reality. *British Journal of Psychology, 63*, 395–400.

Klaczynski, P.A., Gelfand, H., & Reese, H.W. (1989). Transfer of conditional reasoning: Effects of explanations and initial problem types. *Memory and Cognition, 7*, 208–220.

Kroger, J.K., Cheng, P.W., & Holyoak, K.J. (1993). Evoking the permission schema: The impact of explicit negation and a violation-checking context. *Quarterly Journal of Experimental Psychology, 46A*, 615–635.

Manktelow, K.I., & Over, D.E. (1990). Deontic thought and the selection task. In K.J. Gilhooly, M.T.G. Keane, & G. Erdos (Eds.), *Lines of thinking, Volume 1* (pp. 153–164). London: Wiley.

Margolis, H. (1987). *Patterns, thinking and cognition: A theory of judgment.* Chicago: The University of Chicago Press.

Mosconi, G., & D'Urso, V. (1974, April). *The selection task from the standpoint of the theory of double code.* Paper presented at The Selection Task Conference, Trento, Italy.

O'Brien, D.P. (1993). Mental logic and irrationality: We can put a man on the moon, so why can't we solve these logical problems. In K.I. Manktelow & D.E. Over (Eds.), *Rationality*. London: Routledge & Kegan Paul.

Platt, R.D., & Griggs, R.A. (1993a). Darwinian algorithms and the Wason selection task: A factorial analysis of social contract selection task problems. *Cognition, 48*, 163–192.

Platt, R.D., & Griggs, R.A. (1993b). Facilitation in the abstract selection task: The effects of attentional and instructional factors. *Quarterly Journal of Experimental Psychology, 46A*, 591–613.

Revlin, R., & Mayer, R.E. (Eds.) (1978). *Human reasoning.* New York: Wiley.

Roth, E.M. (1979). Facilitating insight in a reasoning task. *British Journal of Psychology, 70*, 265–271.

Taplin, J.E., & Staudenmayer, H. (1973). Interpretation of abstract conditional sentences in deductive reasoning. *Journal of Verbal Learning and Verbal Behavior, 12*, 530–542.

Valentine, E.R. (1985). The effects of instructions on performance in the Wason selection task. *Current Psychological Research and Reviews, 4*, 214–223.

Vuyk, R. (1981). *Critique of Piaget's genetic epistemology, 1965–1980, II.* London: Academic Press.

Wason, P.C. (1966). Reasoning. In B. Foss (Ed.), *New horizons in psychology* (pp. 135–151). Harmondsworth: Penguin.

Wason, P.C. (1968). Reasoning about a rule. *Quarterly Journal of Experimental Psychology, 20*, 273–281.

Wason, P.C. (1983). Realism and rationality in the selection task. In J.St.B.T. Evans (Ed.), *Thinking and reasoning: Psychological approaches* (pp. 44–75). London: Routledge & Kegan Paul.

Wason, P.C., & Evans, J.St.B.T. (1975). Dual processes in reasoning? *Cognition, 3*, 141–154.

Wason, P.C., & Golding, E. (1974). The language of inconsistency. *British Journal of Psychology, 65*, 537–546.

Wason, P.C., & Johnson-Laird, P.N. (1972). *Psychology of reasoning: Structure and content.* Cambridge, MA: Harvard University Press.

Wason, P.C., & Shapiro, D. (1971). Natural and contrived experience in a reasoning problem. *Quarterly Journal of Experimental Psychology, 23*, 63–71.

Wetherick, N.E. (1970). On the representativeness of some experiments in cognition. *Bulletin of the British Psychological Society, 23*, 213–214.

Yachanin, S.A. (1983). Cognitive short-circuiting strategies: The path of least resistance in inferential reasoning. (PhD dissertation, Bowling Green State University, 1982). *Dissertation Abstracts International, 43*, 2378B.

Yachanin, S.A. (1986). Facilitation in Wason's selection task: Content and instruction. *Current Psychological Research and Reviews, 5*, 20–29.

Yachanin, S.A., & Tweney, R.D. (1982). The effect of thematic content on cognitive strategies in the four card selection task. *Bulletin of the Psychonomic Society, 19*, 87–90.

CHAPTER THREE

Content Effects in Wason's Selection Task

Roger L. Dominowski

University of Illinois at Chicago, USA

Questions about the nature of human reasoning have long been tied to questions about the ways in which problem content influences reasoning. Proposals concerning reasoning abilities range from postulating content-free rules to arguing that reasoning is tied to specific experiences (see, for example, Johnson-Laird & Byrne, 1991). Determining how reasoning changes with task content thus plays an important part in refining theoretical formulations. Although this paper will focus on content effects in Wason's selection task, I will first briefly review a topic with a longer history—namely, content effects in syllogistic reasoning.

CONTENT EFFECTS WITH SYLLOGISMS

A task commonly used to assess reasoning ability is the syllogism, which focuses on deductive inference and stresses the evaluation of the internal validity of an argument. The basic syllogism consists of two premises and a conclusion; the premises are assumed to be true, and the essential task is to determine if a conclusion necessarily follows from the premises. For example, given the premises "All X are Y" and "All Y are Z", does it follow that "All X are Z?"; yes, it does. Early on, there was interest in whether performance on syllogisms would depend on their content. Wilkins (1928) found (1) that performance was slightly better with realistic sentences (e.g. "All good ballet dancers have many years of training") than with abstract sentences (e.g. "All Bs are Cs"), and (2) that realistic content can trigger beliefs that bias performance. Subsequent research has focused on more precise characterisations of these effects.

When people are given syllogisms with abstract content, such as letters, they frequently make errors in evaluating conclusions. One explanation of such errors is that people misinterpret the premises—for example, interpreting "All X are Y" to also mean that "All Y are X". Such misinterpretations have been shown to lead to erroneous acceptance of illogical conclusions (e.g. Ceraso & Provitera, 1971). For example, given the premises "All X are Y" and "Some Y are Z", it does not follow that "Some X are Z". If, however, the first premise is interpreted as also meaning that "All Y are X", then a person will accept the invalid conclusion.

One notion is that misinterpretations occur because of the ambiguity of abstract premises. In contrast, meaningful premises will be unambiguous and thus allow errors to be avoided. Certainly, meaningful premises reduce or eliminate ambiguity; for example, people do not entertain the idea that "All collies are dogs" might also mean that "All dogs are collies". Given the premises "All collies are dogs" and "Some dogs are greyhounds", people will not accept "Some collies are greyhounds" as a valid conclusion. Using meaningful material can eliminate errors stemming from premise ambiguity (e.g. Revlis, 1975), but meaningful material also introduces belief bias.

Conclusions to syllogisms are either valid or invalid, depending on whether they do or do not necessarily follow from the premises. The reasoner's task is to determine the validity of conclusions. But conclusions that are meaningful statements might also either agree or disagree with what the person believes about the world, and the person might judge them on the basis of belief rather than logical validity. Evans, Barston, and Pollard (1983) found that judgements sometimes appeared to be based primarily on the conclusion itself, resulting in very strong belief biases. More often, reasoners faced a conflict between logic and belief which might be resolved in favour of either alternative. Belief biases were strongest with respect to accepting believable but invalid conclusions; belief–logic conflict is weak here because the conclusions, although not necessarily following from the premises, are consistent with the premises. They are possible conclusions rather than necessary ones; logic does not yield a direct contradiction of belief. The conflict is greater for valid but unbelievable conclusions, as logic and belief lead to opposite responses; belief biases were present but weaker in this instance. There is uncertainty regarding where in the course of syllogistic reasoning belief biases exert their influence. Evans (1989) concluded that non-logical processing (i.e. using beliefs) occurs early and prior to any more analytic processing. Markovits and Nantel (1989), using a different set of findings, concluded that belief effects occur in a second, evaluative stage of processing that follows reasoning.

Research on syllogistic reasoning offers a number of ideas of potential relevance to understanding content effects in the selection task: people are inclined to misinterpret abstract statements, and their errors in judgement can often be traced to such misinterpretations. Introducing meaningful material is not expected simply to improve reasoning. Meaningfulness aids comprehension of the premises but can also evoke biases which affect judgements of conclusions. Both non-logical and logical processes influence performance on a reasoning task.

It is interesting to note that researchers have typically concluded that most people are trying to do the requested reasoning, regardless of problem content. In one study employing arbitrary materials (Dominowski, 1977), the attempt was made to classify reasoners on the basis of their patterns of responding to a series of syllogisms. Of the 70 subjects, 10 responded so inconsistently that no response strategy could be identified; another 5 seemed to respond to "atmosphere" (e.g. accepting conclusions with "some" in them if the premises included "some"), which is a shallow, alogical response strategy. Eight subjects responded logically, while the remaining 47 students seemed best described as trying to work out the syllogisms but making errors because of misinterpreting premises or failing to consider all the ways the premises might be combined. Markovitz and Nantel (1989) found that belief bias existed at all levels of reasoning ability, where ability was based on performance with abstract syllogisms. This result is consistent with Evans et al.'s (1983) finding that it was not the case that some subjects responded consistently on the basis of belief, others on the basis of logic. Evans et al. concluded that subjects generally confronted conflict between logic and belief. Thus, whether the syllogism materials are arbitrary or realistic, subjects are considered to attempt to analyse the problem and work out the inferences, even when the outcome is an error. It is not clear that researchers make the comparable assumption with respect to performance on the selection task.

WASON'S SELECTION TASK

For more than two decades, Wason's selection task has served as a primary focus of reasoning research. The basic elements of the task are illustrated in Fig. 3.1 and can be described as follows: four cards are presented, so that one side of each card is visible with the other side hidden. The participant is told what kinds of information might occur on either side of the cards. A statement or rule is given, in the general form of "If p, then q", with p referring to the information on one side of the cards and q referring to the information on the other side of the cards. The visible sides of the four cards represent the values p, q, not-p, and not-q with respect to the terms mentioned in the rule. The participant is asked to indicate which cards

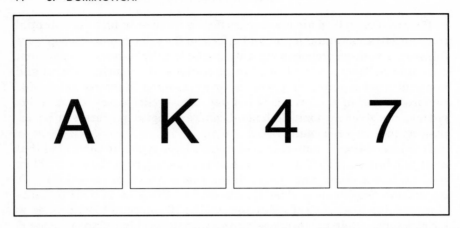

FIG. 3.1. An example of Wason's selection task. Each box represents a card lying on a table. Each card has a letter on one side and a number on the other side. The rule is: "If a card has a vowel, then it has an even number." Which cards do you need to turn over to see if the rule is true or false?

need to be turned over to determine if the statement correctly describes the cards. The designated solution is to select (for turning over) the card showing p and the card showing not-q. The p card should be selected because q on the other side would confirm the rule whereas not-q on the other side would falsify the rule. The card showing not-q should be chosen because it would falsify the rule if p were on the other side.

The original version of the task concerned cards with letters on one side and numbers on the other side (Wason, 1968). A sentence such as "If there is a D on one side of any card, then there is a 3 on its other side" was offered for testing. The four cards showed D, 3, B, and 7 respectively, representing the logical cases p, q, not-p, and not-q. The experimenter pointed to each card in turn, asking the subject if knowing what was on the other side would enable one to find out if the rule were true or false. The correct selections are D (= p) and 7 (= not-q). The basic finding was that only 10% of subjects made the correct selections—a result that has been replicated many times. In addition, subsequent research produced results indicating that, sometimes, one could observe improved performance on the task by changing its content. The greatest attention has been given to improvement associated with introducing meaningful, thematic content.

Two findings have been the cornerstones of research on content effects to the present day: (1) that performance on the abstract, arbitrary version of the selection task is very poor; and (2) that introducing thematic content can result in better performance. I will first consider the multiple differences which exist between abstract and thematic selection tasks.

Differences among thematic versions will be discussed, as well as differences among arbitrary versions. Lastly, attention will be given to the kinds of processes that might lead to differential performance.

Abstract Versus Thematic Content

Research on thematic facilitation has regularly compared performance on a thematic selection task with the letter-number version (Fig. 3.1). A variety of thematic versions has been employed, some of which are described in Table 3.1. These examples have been chosen to illustrate not only variation in topic but also variation in the description of the task. It must be noted that researchers using the same version of the task (e.g. the drinking-age problem) have not necessarily employed the same specific description of the task. The thematic problems in Table 3.1 have been found to yield rates of correct selections as high as 70–90%, far superior to the 10% solution rate often associated with the letter-number version.

Compared to the letter-number selection task (shown in Fig. 3.1), thematic versions differ in many ways. Here is a list of such differences drawn from a collection of thematic versions:

1. The terms in the rule and describing the cards are concrete and meaningful.
2. The subject's task is to determine which cards might be violating the stated rule; with the standard letter-number version, the subject's task is to determine if the rule is true or false.
3. A scenario is provided, and the subject is given a role to play in attempting the task.
4. A rationale or justification is provided for the rule (see the postage rule problem in Table 3.1).
5. The two rule components (if___, then___) have a plausible, meaningful relation. (For a contrasting example, consider, "If a person is drinking beer, then the letter must carry a 20-cent stamp.")

Which of these differences are relevant to success on the selection task? It appears that all of them influence performance. Let's consider some of the research evidence.

Concrete Versus Abstract Terms

Gilhooly and Falconer (1974) created a non-thematic, concrete problem by substituting names of cities and methods of transportation for letters and numbers. The resulting rule was, "Every card which has Manchester on one side has a car on the other side." The use of concrete terms produced

TABLE 3.1
Selection Problems with Thematic Content

A. Drinking-age problem

"Imagine that you are a police officer on duty. It is your job to ensure that people conform to certain rules. The cards below have information about four people sitting at a table. One side of a card has a person's age and the other side has what the person is drinking. Here is a rule: *If a person is drinking beer, then the person must be over 19.* Select those cards that you definitely need to turn over to determine whether or not the people are violating the rule." Cards show:

> *Drinking a beer*
> *Drinking a coke*
> *22 years old*
> *18 years old*

B. Sales receipts problem

"Suppose that you are an assistant manager at Sears, and it is your job to check sales receipts to make sure that *any sale over $30 has been approved by the section manager, Mr. Jones.* (This is a rule of the store.) The amount of the sale is on one side of each receipt, and the space for approval signature is on the other side. Which of the forms shown below would you have to turn over to make sure the sales clerks had followed the regulation?" Cards show:

> *$70*
> *$22*
> *Approval Paul Jones_____*
> *Approval_____*

C. Postage rule problem

"Imagine that you are a post office worker in a foreign country. Part of your job is to check letters for postage. The country's postal regulation is that *if a letter is sealed, then it must carry a 20-cent stamp.* The rationale for this regulation is to increase profit from personal mail, which is nearly always sealed. Sealed letters are defined as personal and must therefore carry more postage than unsealed letters. In order to check that the regulation is followed, which of the following four envelopes would you turn over? Turn over only those that you need to check to be sure." Cards show:

> *Back of sealed envelope*
> *Back of unsealed envelope*
> *20-cent stamp*
> *10-cent stamp*

modest improvement—21% correct, compared to 9% for the letter-number task. Using concrete terms has not always led to better performance. For example, Manktelow and Evans (1979) found no difference between using letter-number cards versus cards describing drinks and foods (and a more thematic rule form)—for example, "If I eat fish, then I drink gin." Other variations in card content with arbitrary rules will be discussed in a later section.

Pollard and Evans (1987) showed that deleting concrete terms from the drinking-age problem impaired performance. In the usual version of this problem, the cards show, say, beer, coke, 22 years old, 16 years old. In the letters version, the cards showed B, C, 22, 16. Subjects were told what the letters and numbers stood for—that B was for beer and C was for coke, and that the numbers referred to the ages of the people in the bar. With the scenario otherwise intact, using letters and numbers yielded lower performance compared to the complete version (43% correct selections vs. 71%). Dominowski (1990b) replicated this finding, obtaining solution rates of 55% and 82% for the letter and complete versions, respectively.[1] This result is somewhat surprising, in that the letters and numbers could be mapped on to meaningful terms, and subjects were aware of the relation. The finding suggests that some subjects had difficulty making or maintaining the mapping during work on the problem.

True-false Versus Violation Instructions
Considerable attention has been directed towards the difference between asking subjects to "determine if the rule is true or false" versus "check to see if any cards violate the rule". With true-false instructions, the status of the rule is uncertain, whereas the status of the cards is uncertain with violation instructions. Griggs (this volume, Chapter 2) provides a thorough discussion of instructional effects on the selection task; here we may note that instructions partially contribute to content effects. Two manipulations can be considered—deleting violation instructions from thematic versions, or adding violation instructions to the abstract version. Violation instructions are usually combined with a scenario and role, so the manipulation involves multiple components.

Several researchers have tried deleting violation checking from a thematic problem, substituting true-false testing. For example, both Chrostowski and Griggs (1985) and Yachanin (1986) used the drinking-age problem (Table 3.1) as the violation version. To create a true-false version, the scenario was altered to indicate that the policeman was out of state and was unfamiliar with the state's drinking laws. The subject was told that the four people were drinking legally, and thus the task was to determine if the stated drinking-age rule was true or false. Performance was much better for the violation version compared to the true-false version—88% vs. 42% correct in Chrostowski and Griggs (1985), 100% vs. 30% and 85% vs. 50% in 2 experiments by Yachanin (1986). The implication is that the violation orientation is an important contributor to high levels of performance. Even with true-false instructions, however, performance on the drinking-age version was higher than that usually found for the abstract version.

The influence of violation instructions on the letter-number task has been studied with the widgit problem. The subject is asked to adopt the role of an inspector of widgits, each of which has a letter and a number on it. Given a rule such as "If a widgit has an A on one side, then it must have a 3 on the other side", the task is to select the card(s), representing widgits, that need to be checked to determine if the rule is being violated. Neither Chrostowski and Griggs (1985) nor Yachanin (1986) found any facilitation with this violation version of the letter-number task. Dominowski (1989) used a labels version in which the subject was inspecting labels with letters on one side and numbers on the other, as well as a standard letter-number task. In this study, subjects in the violation condition first indicated which of a selection of fully described cards (e.g. "a card with A on one side and 7 on the other side") would violate the stated rule, and then completed the selection task.[1] Selections averaged 32% correct in the violation condition for the label and basic letter-number versions (which did not differ), compared to 14% in the control condition. Platt and Griggs (1993) found a substantial effect of violation instructions (37% improvement) with a modified version of a letter-number rule. It is important to note that, where violation instructions facilitated performance on a letter-number problem, the procedure required subjects to give reasons for their selection decisions. Griggs (this volume, Chapter 2) discusses violation instructions in greater detail.

Scenarios and Roles
As we have already seen, adding the widgit inspecting scenario and role to the letter-number task did not aid performance. Similarly, Pollard and Evans (1987) found no facilitation from using the drinking-age scenario with letter-number cards (43% correct with the scenario vs. 36% without it). Dominowski (1990b) observed modest improvement—55% vs. 38%, respectively. Pollard and Evans (1987) also found that deleting the scenario from the usual drinking-age problem reduced performance. That is, subjects were shown cards having "number of years old" on one side and names of drinks on the other, and were asked to check cards for violation of the rule "If there is beer on a card then the number of years old is over 18." The result was very little success, comparable to that seen with letter-number cards. The implication is that a scenario will aid performance only if it is familiar and incorporates concrete, meaningful terms (this remark will be qualified later).

Rationales and Plausibility
Regardless of the level of performance they induce, thematic problems typically have been presented without any explicit rationale or justification for the rule. Providing an explicit rationale has proved helpful when

subjects are unfamiliar with the rule given in the problem. Using the postage problem, Cheng and Holyoak (1985) found that presenting the rationale shown in Table 3.1 improved solution rates about 30% for United States subjects, who had no experience with the stated rule. Hong Kong subjects, who were familiar with a rule relating postage to sealing vs. not sealing a letter, had high solution rates whether or not the rationale was provided. Both groups of subjects performed better with an unfamiliar rule concerned with checking immigration documents when a rationale for the rule was included.

Dominowski (1989; 1990a) attempted to justify the letter-number rule. The problem statement included the following: "Because we don't want to bias people by using some familiar rule, the rule you will be given is arbitrary—it's about letters and numbers. Even though this is an arbitrary rule, the issues are the same—how do you check to see if a rule is true or false? Please think carefully about this task and go about checking the letter-number rule the same way you would check the accuracy of any rule you encountered in everyday life." Subjects were asked the question, "Why is a letter-number rule being used in this task?" This attempt at justification, however, was a failure, with solution rates of 10% for both the standard and justified letter-number tasks.

Girotto et al. (1989) gave various forms of the selection task to children of 10 to 14 years old. When no rationale was provided, the children performed better with familiar rules than with unfamiliar rules. Giving the children a rationale for an unfamiliar rule raised performance to the level seen with a familiar rule. These researchers concluded that the plausibility of a rule, rather than direct familiarity with it, is a key feature. French children, who were familiar with a rule requiring one who sits in the front seat of a car to wear a seatbelt, achieved 80% correct selections; however, Italian children, who were unfamiliar with the rule, performed comparably (70% correct). In contrast, both groups performed poorly when given implausible rules (e.g. "If one drives under 100km/h, then one must have a fluorescent car").

Other research has shown that the meaningfulness of the relation between the antecedent and consequent of a rule is important. Ward and Overton (1990) gave selection tasks to sixth- to twelfth-grade students (mean ages = 11–17 years), using rules of high or low relevance (degree of meaningful connection). For example, a high-relevance statement would be, "If you are caught running in the halls, then you will be punished", whereas the following statement has low relevance: "If you are caught running in the halls, then you are wearing sneakers." Performance with high-relevance rules was superior for the older students; sixth-graders performed poorly at both relevance levels, whereas twelfth-graders showed substantial facilitation (around 75% vs. 35% for high vs. low relevance).

Ward and Overton stressed that the sixth-graders scored poorly even though the high-relevance rules were familiar to them. Based on these and other findings (e.g. Overton et al., 1987) showing effects of rule content for older adolescents, they concluded that relevance facilitates reasoning when logical competence is sufficiently developed. Their association of thematic effects with logical ability makes their position noticeably different from other interpretations that have been offered (e.g. Evans, 1989).

To summarise, the abstract, letter-number version of the selection task has proved to be both difficult and hard to facilitate in its original form. Some, but clearly not all, thematic problems have high solution rates. Facilitation is more likely with violation instructions, a familiar scenario, an explicit justification of the rule, or a plausible, high-relevance rule, and the inclusion of concrete terms. In the next section, I will consider the extent to which these factors can help to account for variation in the effectiveness of thematic content.

DIFFERENCES AMONG THEMATIC PROBLEMS

Facilitation of selections through the use of thematic content presumably occurs because the problem makes contact with knowledge possessed by the subject. There is continuing debate over the nature of that knowledge—whether it is experience with the specific content of the problem (Griggs, 1983; Griggs & Cox, 1982), pragmatic reasoning schemas (Cheng & Holyoak, 1985; 1989), procedures for dealing with social exchanges (Cosmides, 1989), or a system of deontic thinking incorporating mental models (Manktelow & Over, 1991). Issues related to these proposals will be discussed in other chapters; the debate could not be resolved here. Consequently, this presentation will focus on empirical results for thematic problems that have been studied with some frequency. Examination of the collection of findings might identify strengths and weaknesses in the empirical foundation and in theoretical accounts.

At the outset, I will concede that thematic versions eliciting good performance include some form of violation instructions. The subject is required not to determine if the given rule is true or false, but to check cards for compliance with the rule—to see if the rule is violated. As Wason (1983) pointed out, using the same type of instruction with non-thematic materials allows a fair comparison. Violation instructions seem more appropriate for thematic problems, and their consistent use would help with comparing thematic versions.

Two thematic problems presented in Table 3.1 have consistently yielded high levels of performance—namely, the drinking-age problem and the sales receipts problem. Correct selection rates of 70% or more for the drinking-age problem have been obtained by many researchers (Cox & Griggs, 1982; Dominowski, 1990b; Griggs & Cox, 1982; 1983; Overton et al., 1987; Pollard & Evans, 1987; Ward & Overton, 1990). With respect to the sales receipts problem, Mandler (1983) informally reported solution rates of 70–75%; Griggs and Cox (1983) obtained 85% solutions; and Dominowski (1989; 1990a; 1992) found solution rates from 62–83%. It is not necessary to mention violations to obtain good performance; asking subjects to "check to see that the rule is being followed" is sufficient.

The postage rule problem (Table 3.1), without explicit rationale, has had an uneven record. Although initially yielding a high solution rate (see Wason & Johnson-Laird, 1972), Griggs and Cox (1982) found no facilitation whatsoever. Combined with Golding's (1981) result of facilitation only for older subjects, the pattern of findings suggested that only people having experience with the rule would score well on the postage problem (Griggs, 1983). More recently, relatively good performance has been observed. Cheng and Holyoak (1985) found 58% correct responses for US subjects without the rationale (vs. 88% with the rationale), and Dominowski (1989; 1990a; 1990b; 1992) obtained solution rates averaging 44% (compared to 11% for the letter-number task). It appears that US subjects are showing modest facilitation with the postage rule, despite the absence of any experience with the rule.

Manktelow and Evans (1979) repeatedly failed to observe facilitation for a food and drink rule (e.g. "If I eat haddock, then I drink gin"), a result which was confirmed by Yachanin & Tweney (1982). Dominowski (1989; 1990a; 1990b) tried a food rule (e.g. "If you eat beef, then you must eat a green vegetable") with mixed results ranging from modest improvement to performance at the level of the letter-number task. These problems, however, have a number of deficiencies—no scenario, no plausible rule, no justification. Dietary rules have not had much of a chance.

The initial facilitation found with a transportation rule (e.g. "If I go to Manchester, then I travel by train") was followed by a series of failures to replicate the result. This problem has the same weaknesses regarding scenario, plausibility, and rationale as the food rules just discussed. Recently, Dominowski (1990b) tried a more thematic travel problem. The scenario referred to a company rule for business trips, with the subject asked to play the role of an office worker with the job of checking travel vouchers for compliance. The rule was given as "If the distance was 150 miles or less, then the trip must be made by car", and the four cards showed distances above and below the target figure, car, and plane, respectively. The solution rate was 38%—i.e. higher than that for the letter-number version (12%), but far below that regularly seen for the sales receipt problem, which it matches in form.

A thematic problem for which Dominowski (1989; 1990b) has obtained good performance with violation instructions (68% correct) includes a scenario about making cards for a children's board game; the problem description includes the following material:

> This problem concerns the manufacture of cards for a children's board game. There are two kinds of cards, those with red tops and those with blue tops. The red-topped cards are "ordinary" cards that players get as they go around the board, and these cards can have positive or negative outcomes. In contrast, the blue cards are bonus cards which are supposed to have only positive outcomes (a player gets these only by landing on special "bonus" squares). So the rule for making the game cards is: *If the card has a blue top, then it must have a positive outcome on the other side.*

This description explicitly states that not-p (red-topped cards) may occur with either q or not-q (positive or negative game outcomes); Hoch and Tschirgi (1985) found that such information facilitates performance. Platt and Griggs (1993) found that explicating a letter-number rule, combined with violation instructions and reason-giving, substantially improved performance (see Griggs, this volume, Chapter 2). This result suggests that clarifying the rule will aid performance whether or not thematic content is involved.

Ward and Overton's (1990) adolescent subjects achieved high success rates (up to 87% correct) with a motor vehicle problem using the rule, "If a person is driving a motor vehicle, then the person must be over 16" (see also Overton et al., 1987). Yachanin (1986) gave subjects the role of a foreman checking for violations of a risk rule, "If a worker's risk factor is 7 or more, then the worker must wear a hard hat", obtaining 85% correct selections. Whereas Yachanin asked subjects to check for violations, Dominowski (1990b) used what seems a milder checking instruction—"to see if the rule is being followed"—with a result of 46% correct. Although performance was lower than in Yachanin's (1986) experiment, it was still clearly higher than that for the letter-number task (12%).

The final thematic version to be considered here is the abstract permission problem created by Cheng and Holyoak (1985). Subjects were given the role of an authority checking whether or not people are obeying certain regulations of the form, "If one is to take action A, then one must first satisfy precondition P." The problem was solved by 61% of their subjects when it was first presented (55% overall); in two attempts to replicate the finding, Dominowski (1989; 1990a) obtained lower performance levels (34% and 29%).

Jackson and Griggs (1990) investigated both the permission problem and an obligation problem related to the obligation schema proposed by

Cheng et al. (1986). For this problem the rule was, "If situation I comes about, then one is obliged to complete action C." With violation instructions, selections were 53% correct for the permission problem and 35% for the obligation problem. Jackson and Griggs identified an important limitation, namely that performance on these problems surpassed that for the abstract letter-number task only when the cards representing not-p and not-q contained explicit negatives—e.g. "has not taken action A", "has not fulfilled precondition P". In one all-positive version, subjects were told that each person had taken one action (A or B) and fulfilled one precondition (P or Q). The rule was as given above, linking action A with precondition P, and the cards showed "has taken action A", "has taken action B", "has fulfilled precondition P", and "has fulfilled precondition Q". With all positive descriptions, performance on the permission and obligation problems was poor (less than 10%); Jackson and Griggs (1990) obtained this result repeatedly in their series of experiments.

Accounting for results with thematic versions is not easy. Clearly, some versions that have not produced good performance (e.g. meat-vegetable rules) are questionably thematic, as they do not seem to have a theme. Requiring direct experience with problem content for high success rates encounters difficulty because facilitation has been obtained without it; Cosmides' (1989) social exchange theory is too narrow to fit a number of thematic problems that yield good performance (see, for example, Cheng & Holyoak, 1989; Manktelow & Over, 1991). A number of high-performance problems fit either the permission or obligation schema as described by Cheng and Holyoak (1985; 1989; Cheng et al., 1986). However, several versions that yield less facilitation also seem to fit such schemas, and fragile performance on the permission (or obligation) problem raises questions about the viability of schemas as the reason for good performance on related thematic problems. Furthermore, one can question the need to attribute completely separate processes to thematic and arbitrary problems. Dominowski and Dallob (1991) found that performance on thematic and arbitrary problems was highly correlated, and that success on both kinds of problems was related to scores on several general reasoning tests.[1] The implication is that a common set of processes—indeed, reasoning processes—applies to selection problems with differing content.

DIFFERENCES AMONG ARBITRARY PROBLEMS

Relatively little attention has been given to varying the content of arbitrary, non-realistic problems. By virtue of unsystematic accrual across studies, information about some variations is available. For example, equivalent, low levels of performance have been obtained repeatedly with

"If a card has a vowel, then it has an even numbᵥr" and with rules naming specific values—for example, "If a card has an A, then it has the number 4". Wason (1968) used a specific letter-number rule in one experiment, then used shape-colour cards in the next ("If there is a square on one side of the card, then there is a red scribble on the other side"); performance was equally poor for the two cases. In Dominowski's (1990b) study, a colour-shape problem and the vowel-even number version produced equivalent, low success rates (6% and 12%).

As noted in the preceding section, simply using concrete terms has not often produced facilitation. For example, results with location-mode of transportation rules have been inconsistent, and food and drink content did not help (e.g. Manktelow & Evans, 1979). Most of this research, however, has involved true-false instructions, which have been found to yield poor performance even with thematic content (e.g. Yachanin, 1986). We have already seen that a checking scenario by itself does not aid performance with the letter-number rule, as in the widgit-inspector problem (e.g. Chrostowski & Griggs, 1985) or the label problem (Dominowski, 1989; 1990a). These results none the less leave open the question of whether other arbitrary content might yield facilitation with a checking context.

Griggs (1989) tested a proposal by Margolis (1987) that poor performance with the abstract letter-number task stemmed in part from scenario ambiguity (see also Griggs, this volume, Chapter 2). In the remedial version, subjects were told that the cards had been picked from a mixed deck (some red backs, some blue backs), and that the person picking the cards was told to obey the rule, "Pick any four cards, except that if a card has a red back, it must be at least a 6." The four cards showed red back, blue back, 7 of hearts, and 5 of clubs. Griggs obtained very high success rates for this problem (69–80% correct), compared to 27% when the sentence about the mixed deck was omitted, or 23–27% when the problem allowed matching of the q card with the q term in the rule. (In the remedial version above, the q card (7) does not match the q term (6) in the rule.) Dominowski (1990b) did not replicate the finding of high success with the remedial version, obtaining success rates of 29–33% for the several versions he included. There is no apparent reason for the lack of replication regarding the remedial version; however, another aspect of the results supports the idea that the nature of the consequent in the rule is important.

Problem versions which contained a numerical inequality in the consequent of the rule consistently yielded better performance (average = 36% over 7 versions) than the vowel-even number task (12%). The best performance occurred with flower-number cards and the rule "If a card says rose then it must have a number greater than 10" (54%). These results are consistent with findings by Hoch and Tschirgi (1985) as well as some findings of Griggs (1989). Poor performance with Pollard and Evans' (1987) beers problem, which contained an inequality, might have been due to ambiguity regarding the rule's status. (The beers problem concerned an arbitrary rule: e.g. "If a person is drinking Bass, then the person is over 40 years old.") Several reasons have been offered for the advantage seen with consequents having numerical inequalities: preventing matching, seeing the choice of the q card as unnecessary, or drawing attention to the status of the not-q card. These ideas are not incompatible; current data do not allow them to be distinguished.

There are a few other arbitrary contents that have yielded better performance than the letter-numerical equality (or vowel-even number) task, but systematic investigation is needed. It seems clear that the original letter-number rule, which has served as the comparison for many thematic problems, is particularly difficult. None the less, high success rates have been obtained with arbitrary, non-thematic content. A spectacular result was reported by Platt and Griggs (1993). Using vowel-even number content, they found that presenting the "if ... then" form of the rule depressed performance. Substituting an explicated version was better: "A card with a vowel on it can only have an even number, but a card with a consonant on it can have either an even or odd number." Using this rule version with violation instructions and reasons required, Platt and Griggs obtained 81% correct solutions! It seems clear that performance on arbitrary problems has been, until recently, understudied and underestimated. Good performance with arbitrary content raises anew questions concerning the extent of logical responding (Hoch & Tschirgi, 1985), or analytic processing (both Griggs and Evans discuss this issue, this volume, Chapters 2 and 7).

PROCESSING CONSIDERATIONS

In research on the selection task, analyses are typically restricted to subjects' choices of cards. These might be analysed in different ways (e.g. as patterns of choices, in terms of choice frequencies for individual cards), but card selections remain the sole data source. In a similar fashion, theoretical accounts tend to consider task behaviour in whole packages. For example, facilitation of selections by appropriate thematic content is assumed to reflect directly people's interpretation of the given rule (perhaps rule + scenario). Evans' two-factor theory (e.g. 1989) is an exception in that it includes an initial intuitive stage that might be followed by analytic processing under some circumstances. In this section, attention will be directed towards the use of additional types of data that might help with understanding selection task behaviour.

Violation Checking

One reasonable way to assess a person's understanding of a rule is to find out what the person considers to be inconsistent with the rule. Wason (1968) obtained data suggesting slippage between rule understanding and selection behaviour. Using a colour-shape problem, he asked subjects to indicate which one of four completely described cards (representing, p q, p not-q, not-p q, and not-p not-q) would falsify the rule, and all subjects picked p not-q. Yet when given the selection task to test the rule, only one person chose the not-q card.

In the violation condition of Dominowski's (1989) study, subjects were asked to identify those fully described cards that would violate the given rule without being restricted to picking only one card. Thus the pattern of their choice of violations could be used as an indicator of their interpretation of the rule. Following the identification of violators, subjects were given the selection task and asked to indicate which cards had to be turned over to see if the rule was violated. Data were obtained for nine problem contents, including both thematic and arbitrary versions.

Subjects nearly always (98%) picked p not-q as violating the rule. Because it has been suggested that subjects might interpret the rule as applying only in the direction from p to q, a reversed description, not-q p, was included. The order of description did not matter, as not-q p was picked as a violator 97% of the time (to simplify discussion, I will refer henceforth only to p not-q). Overall, subjects picked only p not-q as violating 69% of the time, thus exhibiting a conditional interpretation of the if, then rule. The percentage of subjects picking only p not-q varied across problems, from 43% for the vowel-even number rule to 93% for the children's game card problem. Performance on the selection task also varied across problems, from 27% correct for the vowel-even number problem to 83% for the sales receipts problem. The relations between violation checking and choices on the selection task proved interesting.

Subjects who picked only p not-q as violating the rule produced the vast majority of solutions (89%) to the selection task. There was in this regard one anomaly: for the sales receipts problem, 51% of subjects picked only p not-q as violating, but 34% picked both p not-q and not-p q, a biconditional interpretation. However, 70% of the latter group correctly chose p and not-q on the selection task; this association of biconditional violation checking with correct (conditional) card selections occurred only for this problem. For the other 8 problems, those picking only p not-q as violating accounted for 94% of selection task solutions.

The violation-selection relation can also be examined in the opposite direction: given that subjects picked only p not-q as violating, what percentage correctly chose the p and not-q cards on the selection task? The overall answer was 64%, with a range from 54% for the vowel-even number problem to 93% for the sales receipts problem. Most of the problems were clustered between 54–74%.

The data do not support Johnson-Laird and Byrne's (1991) proposal that subjects will select the p card and the q card when they interpret the rule as biconditional. Only 9% of p and q selections were made by subjects who picked violations in accordance with a biconditional interpretation. More often (41%), subjects selecting p and q had identified only the p not-q example as a violator. Another 39% of p and q selectors had picked everything but p q as violating the rule (a conjunctive interpretation).

These data imply that success on the selection task has two major components: the likelihood that the rule will be given a conditional interpretation (only p not-q falsifies), and the probabilty, given that interpretation, that the p card and not-q card will be selected. The content of the problem affects both of these factors. As suggested by the analyses summarised above, the inclusion of subjects' identification of violators helps to delineate the processes affecting selection task performance.

Processing Times

A recent experiment involved an attempt to study processing times at different stages of the four card task (Dominowski, 1992). To do this, a computer was used to present problem information and record subjects' responses and processing times. The information used to describe a problem to a subject was separated into four distinct sections, as shown in Fig. 3.2.

Each section was presented separately on the screen. The subject was allowed as much time as desired to study the section, and the time taken was recorded. When the subject had finished the Task Instructions section, he or she was given the opportunity to take a second look at any of the sections. Which sections were re-read, and second reading times, were recorded. Next the four cards were presented, one at a time, with the subject indicating by button press whether or not the card needed to be turned over, and response time was recorded. After the fourth card, a summary of the subject's choices was presented, with the subject given the opportunity to revise any choice (which cards were revised and second response time were recorded).

Two thematic and two arbitrary problems were included: sales receipts, postage, flower-number, and vowel-even number. Each subject attempted all four problems, with different orders used to counterbalance problems with ordinal position. Computer presentation of the problems yielded the expected pattern of results with respect to solution rates: sales receipts,

1. Introduction

Assume that you are a postal clerk working in some foreign country. Part of your job is to examine letter-size envelopes to check the postage. You will soon see "boxes" on the screen; each box represents an envelope. You will see one side of each envelope but would have to turn the envelope over to see the other side.

2. Card Description

Each envelope has a stamp on the front side, while the back has a flap that can be either sealed or unsealed. Thus, the envelope below that shows "10-cent stamp" has a sealed or unsealed flap on the back, while the envelope showing "Back of sealed envelope" has some stamp on the other side.

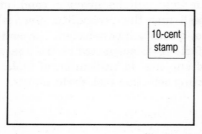 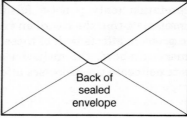

3. Rule Description

The country's postal regulation requires that: *If an envelope is sealed, then it must carry a 20-cent stamp.*

4. Task Instructions

Your job is to check envelopes to make sure that the regulation is being followed, checking no more envelopes than is absolutely necessary.

   You will now be shown some envelopes, one at a time.Your task is to indicate, for each envelope, whether or not you would have to turn it over to make sure the regulation is being followed. Check no more cards than is absolutely necessary.

FIG. 3.2. Division of selection task instructions into four sections.

62%; postage, 35%; flower-number, 29%; and vowel-even number, 12%. (As subjects were not required to give reasons for their selections, somewhat reduced success rates were anticipated, and obtained.)

   Let me turn to some of the results concerning processing times. Subjects took more time on the introduction and card descriptions for the thematic problems. The total times for the first two sections averaged just under 50 sec for the sales receipts problem, over 53 sec for the postage problem, just over 41 sec for the flower-number problem, but less than 32 sec for the vowel-number problem—not much over half the time taken for the thematic problems. To an extent, longer times reflect difficulty; for example, for the card description section, the postage problem had the longest initial study times, the highest rate of review, and the longest re-inspection times. These data suggest that subjects had trouble comprehending the postage cards. However, it is unlikely that people would have greater difficulty comprehending the more meaningful text of the thematic problems; rather, the short time for the vowel-number problem suggests shallow processing of the material. It should also be noted that these differences occurred before any conditional rule was given to the subjects.

The Rule Description section contained only the statement of the rule, and reading times were short, although at the slowest reading rate of all the sections. More time was spent on arbitrary rules (mean = 11.9 sec) than on thematic rules (mean = 10.5 sec). The task instructions were virtually the same across problems and had the fastest reading rate, with no differences among problems.

Response times to the four cards in the selection task were separated on the basis of the nature of the selection decision (yes or no). Some of the data are shown in Fig. 3.3. Overall, correct responses of "yes" for the p card were faster (6.7 sec) than wrong "no" responses (7.9 sec); responses to p were slowest for the postage problem. The not-p card was seldom selected; correct "no" decisions were faster (7.8 sec) than "yes" errors (10.4 sec), with only minor variation across problems (data not included in Fig. 3.3).

Responses to the q card tended to be slow, and there was high variability. For the two thematic problems, correct "no" responses were slightly faster than "yes" responses, whereas "no" responses were noticeably slower than "yes" responses for the arbitrary problems. Incorrect selections of q were numerically fastest for the vowel-number problem.

Correctly selecting the not-q card was relatively infrequent behaviour; response times were slow (overall, 10.5 sec) and (except for the sales receipts problem) significantly longer than "no" responses to not-q (overall, 8.8 sec). The vowel-number problem had the fastest time for incorrect "no" responses.

Comparison of the response times for the four correct responses is informative. Selecting p occurrred most quickly (6.7 sec); saying "no" for selecting the not-p card was next (7.8 sec); saying "no" for q (10.6 sec), or selecting not-q (10.5 sec), took longer. It is interesting that rejecting q was slower for the arbitrary problems, but there were no problem differences in time to select not-q. The idea that people solve thematic problems when an appropriate schema is triggered (e.g. Cheng & Holyoak, 1985) would seem to imply that not-q should be selected more quickly for thematic problems.

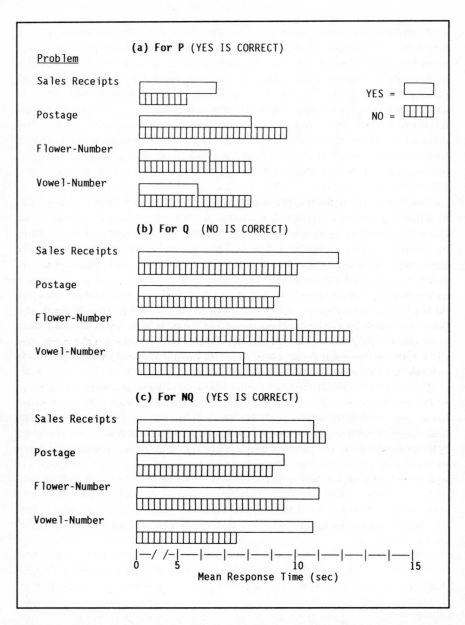

FIG. 3.3. Response times for "Yes" and "No" selection decisions for cards representing different logical cases (p, q, not-q), for thematic and arbitrary problems.

A card may be selected, or not, for any of several reasons. For example, Evans (e.g. 1989) argues that, for arbitrary problems, subjects' attention is automatically fixed on p and q, with no analytic processing added on. The implication is that p and q should be selected very quickly. Selecting p and not-q, however, presumably is based on analytic processing and should be slower. What might happen when a "good" scenario is added to the problem? If people select p and not-q because the problem evokes a schema they possess, a schema which includes "what to do", the implication would seem to be that they should select p and not-q quickly. If, however, meaningful content encourages analytic processing, it would seem that response times should be slower. Some of the data already presented do not fit these expectations. Table 3.2 contains data allowing a closer look at these issues.

The cases in which people selected p and q were identified, as were the cases in which p and not-q were selected. Relevant response times were examined for only these cases. The two left columns contain mean response times when p and q were selected. Subjects took longer to select q than to select p; this does not seem consistent with the idea that subjects select p and q because their attention is automatically drawn to p and q, full stop. At the least, an additional principle is needed. Selection times for p and q were shortest for the vowel-number problem, which might mean that subjects were (closer to) simply matching for this problem. Of course, the difference in times for p and q still requires some account, as do the slower selections of p and q for the other problems.

The two right columns show that subjects selecting p and not-q were much quicker to select p than to select not-q. This difference does not seem consistent with the notion that, for some thematic problems, these cards are selected because the content evokes a schema, and because subjects "already know what to do". The consistency of the difference across problems suggests that a common set of processes leads to these choices, regardless of problem content.

TABLE 3.2

Mean Response Times (sec) for Subjects Selecting p and q and for Subjects Selecting p and not-q

Problem	When Selecting p & q		When Selecting p & not-q	
	q Time	p Time	p Time	not-q Time
Charge slips	11.2	7.0	6.5	10.6
Postage	9.3	8.7	7.8	8.9
Flower-number	9.1	6.1	6.3	11.8
Vowel-number	7.2	5.5	6.5	13.2

The two internal columns contain times to select p for those selecting p and q, versus times to select p for those selecting p and not-q. Suppose that p and q selectors are responding automatically, whereas those selecting p and not-q are responding analytically. The implication would be that p and q selectors should select p more quickly. This might be true for the vowel-number problem, but it is not true for the other problems.

The results described here show that changing problem content affects processing at multiple stages of work on the selection task. The patterns of response times for making selection decisions raise interesting questions about theories of selection task behaviour. Evans (this volume, Chapter 7) presents an alternative approach to measuring processing times; because of differences in procedure, comparing Evans' findings with the present data is problematic. None the less, both data sets show that processing times constitute a rich and useful data source that can sharpen theoretical efforts.

FINAL COMMENTS

The content of a selection task affects performance, but making sense of the collection of research findings is difficult. Three modifications of research practices should help produce more systematic data and theoretical progress. First, the characterisation of problem content needs greater attention; as noted earlier, some so-called thematic problems have been merely arbitrary, non-thematic versions with concrete terms. A number of components contribute to the effective task content, including the nature of the terms found in the rule and on the cards, the relation between the antecedent and consequent, the scenario, and justification of the rule (or lack thereof). Regular attention to such components will facilitate the identification of critical factors.

Secondly, variation in procedures could be curtailed, to our advantage. To a degree, variation in content has been confounded with procedural differences; in addition, researchers employ different procedures such that integrating findings becomes problematic. Very brief task instructions increase the chances that subjects will not understand what they should do. I would propose that studies of content effects employ a checking orientation rather than true-false instructions (which it seems that subjects have trouble comprehending—the difference between the two orientations is not a content issue). I would further advocate that subjects receive clear descriptions of the cards, be asked to make an explicit decision about each card, and be asked to give reasons for their decisions, all with the intent of encouraging subjects to get involved in the task, regardless of its specific content.

Finally, there is a need for data in addition to card selections. As I have tried to show for subjects' identification of violators and processing times, such data enrich our understanding of selections and constrain theory in productive ways. People's behaviour on the selection task is not simple; they engage in multiple stages of processing that lead to a set of selection decisions. Those final selections will be better explained if we attend more closely to the activities involved in their production.

NOTE

1. In the Dominowski (1989) study, subjects worked on a booklet containing a number of problems; each page contained one problem and displayed both instructions and four boxes representing cards. Subjects were asked to make a yes/no decision about each of the four cards and to briefly write a reason for their decision. This procedure was also used in Dominowski (1990b) and in Dominowski and Dallob (1991).

REFERENCES

Ceraso, J., & Provitera, A. (1971). Sources of error in syllogistic reasoning. *Cognitive Psychology, 2*, 400–410.

Cheng, P.W., & Holyoak, K.J. (1985). Pragmatic reasoning schemas. *Cognitive Psychology, 17*, 391–416.

Cheng, P.W., & Holyoak, K.J. (1989). On the natural selection of reasoning theories. *Cognition, 33*, 285–313.

Cheng, P.W., Holyoak, K.J., Nisbett, R.E., & Oliver, L.M. (1986). Pragmatic versus syntactic approaches to training deductive reasoning. *Cognitive Psychology, 18*, 293–328.

Chrostowski, J.J., & Griggs, R.C. (1985). The effects of problem content, instructions, and verbalisation procedures on Wason's selection task. *Current Psychological Research and Reviews, 4*, 99–107.

Cosmides, L. (1989). The logic of social exchange: Has natural selection shaped how humans reason? Studies with the Wason selection task. *Cognition, 31*, 187–276.

Cox, J.R., & Griggs, R.A. (1982). The effects of experience on performance in Wason's selection task. *Memory and Cognition, 10*, 496–502.

Dominowski, R.L. (1977). Reasoning. *Interamerican Journal of Psychology, 11*, 68–77.

Dominowski, R.L. (1989, September). *Success and failure on the four card problem*. Paper given at the sixth Annual Conference of the Cognitive Psychology Section, British Psychological Society, Cambridge, England.

Dominowski, R.L. (1990a). Problem solving and metacognition. In K.J. Gilhooly, M.T.G. Keane, R.H. Logie, & G. Erdos (Eds.), *Lines of thinking (Vol. 2)*. Chichester: Wiley.

Dominowski, R.L. (1990b, September). *Arbitrary and thematic versions of the four card problem*. Paper given at the seventh Annual Conference of the Cognitive Psychology Section, British Psychological Society, Leicester, England.

Dominowski, R. L. (1992, July). *The multiple effects of changing content on Wason's four card task*. Paper given at the Second International Conference on Thinking, Plymouth, England.

Dominowski, R.L., & Dallob, P. (1991, September). *Reasoning abilities, individual differences, and the four card problem*. Paper given at the Eighth Annual Conference, Cognitive Psychology Section, British Psychological Society, Oxford, England.

Evans, J.St.B.T. (1989). *Bias in human reasoning: Causes and consequences*. Hove, UK: Lawrence Erlbaum Associates Ltd.

Evans, J.St.B.T., Barston, J., & Pollard, P. (1983). On the conflict between logic and belief in syllogistic reasoning. *Memory and Cognition, 11*, 295–306.

Gilhooly, K.J., & Falconer, W.A. (1974). Concrete and abstract terms and relations in testing a rule. *Quarterly Journal of Experimental Psychology, 26*, 355–359.

Girotto, V., Gilly, M., Blaye, A., & Light, P. (1989). Children's performance in the selection task: Plausibility and familiarity. *British Journal of Psychology, 80*, 79–85.

Golding, E. (1981, April). *The effect of past experience on problem solving*. Paper presented at the annual conference of the British Psychological Society, Surrey, England.

Griggs, R.A. (1983). The role of problem content in the selection task and in the THOG problem. In J.St.B.T. Evans (Ed.), *Thinking and reasoning: Psychological approaches*. London: Routledge & Kegan Paul.

Griggs, R.A. (1989). To "see" or not to "see": That is the selection task. *Quarterly Journal of Experimental Psychology, 41A*, 517–529.

Griggs, R.A., & Cox, J.R. (1982). The elusive thematic-materials effect in Wason's selection task. *British Journal of Psychology, 73*, 407–420.

Griggs, R.A., & Cox, J.R. (1983). The effects of problem content and negation on Wason's selection task. *Quarterly Journal of Experimental Psychology, 35A*, 519–533.

Hoch, S.J., & Tschirgi, J.E. (1985). Logical knowledge and cue redundancy in deductive reasoning. *Memory and Cognition, 13*, 453–462.

Jackson, S.L., & Griggs, R.A. (1990). The elusive pragmatic reasoning schemas effect. *Quarterly Journal of Experimental Psychology, 42A*, 353–373.

Johnson-Laird, P.N., & Byrne, R.M.J. (1991). *Deduction*. Hove, UK: Lawrence Erlbaum Associates Ltd.

Mandler, J.M. (1983). Structural invariants in development. In L.S. Libaen (Ed.), *Piaget and the foundations of knowledge*. Hillsdale, NJ: Lawrence Erlbaum Associates Inc.

Manktelow, K.I., & Evans, J.St.B.T. (1979). Facilitation of reasoning by realism: Effect or non-effect. *British Journal of Psychology, 70*, 477– 488.

Manktelow, K.I., & Over, D.E. (1991). Social roles and utilities in reasoning with deontic conditionals. *Cognition, 39*, 85–105.

Margolis, H. (1987). *Patterns, thinking and cognition: A theory of judgment*. Chicago: University of Chicago Press.

Markovits, H., & Nantel, G. (1989). The belief-bias effect in the production and evaluation of logical conclusions. *Memory and Cognition, 17*, 11–17.

Overton, W.F., Ward, S.L., Noveck, I.A., Black, J., & O'Brien, D.P. (1987). Form and content in the development of deductive reasoning. *Developmental Psychology, 23*, 22–30.

Platt, R.D., & Griggs, R.A. (1993). Facilitation in the abstract selection task: The effects of attentional and instructional factors. *Quarterly Journal of Experimental Psychology, 46A*, 591–613.

Pollard, P., & Evans, J.St.B.T. (1987). Content and context effects in reasoning. *American Journal of Psychology, 100*, 41–60.

Revlis, R. (1975). Two models of syllogistic reasoning: Feature selection and conversion. *Journal of Verbal Learning and Verbal Behavior, 14*, 180–195.

Ward, S.L., & Overton, W.F. (1990). Semantic familiarity, relevance, and the development of deductive reasoning. *Developmental Psychology, 26*, 488–493.

Wason, P.C. (1968). Reasoning about a rule. *Quarterly Journal of Experimental Psychology, 20*, 273–281.

Wason, P.C. (1983). Realism and rationality in the selection task. In J.St.B.T. Evans (Ed.), *Thinking and reasoning: Psychological approaches.* London: Routledge & Kegan Paul.

Wason, P.C., & Johnson-Laird, P.N. (1972). *Psychology of reasoning: Structure and content.* Cambridge, MA: Harvard University Press.

Wilkins, M. (1928). The effect of changed material on ability to do formal syllogistic reasoning. *Archives of Psychology, 16*, No. 102.

Yachanin, S.A. (1986). Facilitation in Wason's selection task: Content and instructions. *Current Psychological Research and Reviews, 5*, 20–29.

Yachanin, S.A., & Tweney, R.D. (1982). The effects of thematic content on cognitive strategies in the four card selection task. *Bulletin of the Psychonomic Society, 19*, 87–90.

CHAPTER FOUR

Pragmatic Reasoning about Human Voluntary Action: Evidence from Wason's Selection Task

Keith J. Holyoak and Patricia W. Cheng

University of California, Los Angeles, USA

INTRODUCTION

For over a quarter of a century, researchers on reasoning have struggled to understand people's performance on variations of the classic four card selection problem introduced by Peter Wason in 1966. The fascination this paradigm has evoked is in large part due to the contrast between the apparent simplicity of the task and the extraordinary difficulty people encounter in finding the solution seemingly dictated by elementary propositional logic.

The selection task involves giving subjects a conditional rule in the form "if p then q". Subjects are shown one side of each of four cards, which respectively show the cases corresponding to p, not-p, q, and not-q. They are told that the cards show the value of p on one side and the value of q on the other. Their task is to decide which of the cards must be turned over to determine whether the rule is false. The "correct" choice, according to standard propositional logic, is to select the p card (which might have not-q on its back) and the not-q card (which might have p on its back), because these are the only two possibilities that would falsify the rule. Subjects seldom make the correct choice when the conditional rule has arbitrary content (e.g. "If a card has an A on one side, then it must have a 4 on the other"). Rather, they tend to make various errors, of which the most common is to select the cards corresponding to p and q (i.e. A and 4).

Many theories have been advanced to account for people's performance on the selection task (for reviews see Evans, 1989, and Wason, 1983). Early observations of people's puzzling failures to solve the problem correctly with an arbitrary rule were soon compounded by equally puzzling successes observed when the rule was made more familiar or meaningful. The first evidence that content strongly influences reasoning in the selection paradigm emerged from studies by Wason and Shapiro (1971) and Johnson-Laird, Legrenzi, and Legrenzi (1972). The best-documented effects of content have been observed for conditional rules that can be interpreted as expressing deontic relations of permission or obligation, such as "If a person is to drink alcohol, then they must be at least 18 years old", for which the p and not-q cases are selected much more frequently (see, for example, Cheng & Holyoak, 1985; Cosmides, 1989; D'Andrade, 1982; Girotto, Gilly, Blaye, & Light, 1989; Johnson-Laird et al., 1972; Light, Girotto, & Legrenzi, 1990; Manktelow & Over, 1990; 1991; Politzer & Nguyen-Xuan, 1992). Work by Girotto and his colleagues has demonstrated that children as young as six years old can solve simplified versions of the selection task when the rule is interpreted deontically (Girotto, Light, & Colburn, 1988; Light, Blaye, Gilly, & Girotto, 1990), while children as young as nine years old can solve the full selection task given deontic content (Girotto et al., 1989). An earlier study suggests that 6–7-year-old children can solve a complete selection task based on a rule interpretable as an obligation (Legrenzi & Murino, 1974).

Our own interest in the selection paradigm has focused on its utility as a tool for investigating how people reason about general but none the less pragmatically constrained domains, of which regulations governing human voluntary action have been studied most intensively. In this chapter we will briefly describe our theory of pragmatic reasoning schemas (PRS), and review two lines of recent research that bear upon it—studies of reasoning with abstract deontic rules, and studies of the influence of perspective on the interpretation of regulations.

PRAGMATIC SCHEMAS FOR PERMISSION AND OBLIGATION

To explain the influence of content on reasoning in the selection paradigm, as well as in other tasks (such as linguistic rephrasing) involving inference with conditionals, Cheng and Holyoak (1985; Cheng, Holyoak, Nisbett, & Oliver, 1986) suggested that deontic inferences about actions which concern what ought to be done, are governed by schemas specialised for situations involving permission and obligation. Typically both permissions and obligations involve preconditions that serve to trigger the regulation of voluntary action in a manner governed by the goals of an authority empowered to create regulations. In a conditional permission, satisfaction of the precondition bestows a *right* to take a regulated action, typically conveyed by the modal *may*:

If <precondition> then <may take action>.

In a conditional obligation, on the other hand, satisfaction of the precondition imposes a *duty* to take the relevant action, as conveyed by the modal *must*:

If <precondition> then <must take action>.

Although these regulations are stated as conditionals, in many contexts they can be interpreted as being pragmatically biconditional at the deontic level. That is, unless the context suggests some alternative precondition that would also trigger the right or duty, conditional regulations are likely to be interpreted as if the precondition is necessary as well as sufficient to establish the right or duty introduced in the consequent. It is important to distinguish the deontic level (rights and duties) from the level of overt action. A rule that is pragmatically biconditional at the deontic level can none the less be conditional at the level of action, because in a conditional permission the action need not be taken even if the precondition is satisfied, and in a conditional obligation the action may be taken even if the precondition is not satisfied. Furthermore, in no case of a permission or obligation is it certain that the regulated action will in fact be taken. It is the nature of voluntary action that rules can be violated: people can take actions they have no right to take, while failing to perform their duties. Deontic regulations fundamentally govern the creation of rights and duties, and only indirectly influence the actions taken by those subject to the regulations.

PRS theory postulates that for both permissions and obligations, four possible situations can be defined in terms of whether or not the precondition is satisfied and whether or not the action is to be taken. Corresponding to each situation is a rule that comprises part of the relevant schema. The theory predicts that performance on the selection task will be facilitated (i.e. be in accord with standard logic) when the stated rule has content that evokes a schema, and the correspondence between the stated rule and the schema rules is such that the latter map on to rules of standard logic. For example, the "drinking-age" rule will tend to evoke a permission schema, the core of which can be represented in terms of the following rules, P1–P4 (Cheng & Holyoak, 1985, p. 397):

P1: If the action is to be taken, then the precondition must be satisfied.

P2: If the action is not to be taken, then the precondition need not be satisfied.

P3: If the precondition is satisfied, then the action may be taken.

P4: If the precondition is not satisfied, then the action must not be taken.

Note that the above drinking-age rule is in the form of Rule P1, the antecedent of which is matched by the p case. Since the consequent of this rule makes a definite prediction, it indicates that someone who drinks alcohol should be checked to be sure the age precondition has been met. The antecedent of Rule P4 matches the not-q case. The consequent of P4 also makes a definite prediction, indicating that someone who is under age should be checked to be sure they are not drinking alcohol. The antecedents of Rules P2 and P3 respectively match the not-p and q cases. Because the consequents of these rules do not make any definite predictions, they indicate that no violation is possible given the not-p and q cases, thereby blocking the errors that correspond to the selection of these cases.

Corresponding to Rules P1–P4 for the permission schema are Rules O1–O4 for the obligation schema (from Holyoak & Cheng, in press, as adapted from Politzer & Nguyen-Xuan, 1992):

O1: If the precondition is satisfied, then the action must be taken.

O2: If the precondition is not satisfied, then the action need not be taken.

O3: If the action is to be taken, then the precondition may have been satisfied.

O4: If the action is not to be taken, then the precondition must not have been satisfied.

Cheng and Holyoak (1985) found that people were able to select the p and not-q alternatives even for unfamiliar rules as long as the context led subjects to interpret the rule as a conditional permission (matching Rule P1 of the permission schema) or a conditional obligation (matching Rule O1 of the obligation schema). Cheng et al. (1986) found that a brief training session explaining permissions led to further improvement in performance for rules that were interpretable as permissions. In the remainder of this chapter we will review two other lines of evidence that have emerged from more recent research.

FACILITATION WITH ABSTRACT DEONTIC RULES

In addition to explaining patterns of facilitation for rules with concrete thematic content, Cheng and Holyoak (1985) demonstrated that facilitation could be obtained even for an abstract permission rule, "If one is to take action A, then one must first satisfy precondition P". Similarly, Cheng and Holyoak (1989) found that selection performance was significantly better for an abstract statement of a conditional precaution (a form of permission in which the precondition for engaging in a hazardous activity is to take a prudent precautionary measure) than for an arbitrary rule. Although devoid of specific thematic content, such abstract rules appear to evoke regulation schemas that guide reasoning. These demonstrations of selective facilitation for non-arbitrary but abstract rules are not readily explicable either by alternative accounts of human reasoning based on memory for specific counter-examples (e.g. Griggs & Cox, 1982), by current proposals involving content-free, proof-theoretic inference rules (e.g. Braine & O'Brien, 1991), or by current proposals involving content-free, model-theoretic procedures (e.g. Johnson-Laird & Byrne, 1991).

Criticisms of the PRS Interpretation

Recently, Jackson and Griggs (1990) argued that Cheng and Holyoak's (1985) demonstration of facilitation for the abstract permission rule was not due to evocation of a permission schema, but rather resulted from a combination of two "presentation factors": (a) providing explicit negatives in the statement of cases, and (b) providing a violation-checking context. For the rule, "If one is to take action A, then one must first satisfy precondition P", Jackson and Griggs (Experiment 2) compared performance in a condition that employed the cases used by Cheng and Holyoak, which included explicit negatives for the not-p and not-q cases—"has not taken action A" and "has not fulfilled precondition P", respectively—to performance in a condition for which these two explicitly negative cases were replaced by "has taken action B" and "has fulfilled precondition Q", respectively. Jackson and Griggs found that facilitation was eliminated when the latter wording, which did not include explicit negatives, was used. Similarly, these investigators also found (Experiment 4) that facilitation was eliminated when the instructions did not orient subjects to check whether the rule was violated, but rather "to find out whether a certain regulation is being followed". On the basis of these results, Jackson and Griggs argued that performance on the abstract permission rule can be explained by these two presentation factors, without postulating any role for pragmatic schemas. More specifically, they suggested that the overall pattern is consistent with Evans' (1983) general two-stage model of reasoning.

Their conclusion raises the issue of the level of abstraction of inferential rules. If Jackson and Griggs (1990) were correct, then the content effects demonstrated for abstract situations would not be due to people's knowledge about types of situations such as permissions and obligations. Instead, content effects would be attributable to more general heuristics for assessing relevance and for checking violations—heuristics that are not tied specifically to deontic content. The data and conclusions of Jackson and Griggs (1990) have figured prominently in recent critical discussions of the theory of pragmatic reasoning schemas (Johnson-Laird & Byrne, 1991; Rips, 1990).

The Basis for Facilitation of Abstract Deontic Rules

In fact, however, the observed impact of the two presentation factors on facilitation for the abstract permission rule, rather than contradicting PRS theory, is actually explained by it (Kroger, Cheng, & Holyoak, 1993). PRS theory postulates that a context encouraging checking for rule violations constitutes a major cue for evocation of the deontic concepts of permission and obligation that underlie the regulation schemas, as Cheng and Holyoak pointed out: "The core of the permission schema, as well as of similar schemas for other types of regulations, indeed consists of procedural knowledge for assessing whether a type of rule is being followed or violated" (1985, p. 410). The alternative context tested by Jackson and Griggs (an hypothesis-testing context) will presumably lead subjects to interpret the conditional not as an established rule against which compliance is to be assessed, but rather as an hypothesised rule that requires confirmation. As Yachanin and Tweney (1982) and Cheng and Holyoak (1989) have shown, an hypothesis-testing context tends to elicit a very different pattern of choices in the selection task than does a deontic context.

The basis for the impact of explicit negatives in evoking the permission schema is similarly clear. Rule P4 above, which is required to cue selection of the case in which the precondition has not been satisfied (i.e. not-P), has an explicitly negative antecedent, "If the precondition is not satisfied ... ." Jackson and Griggs' implicit negation of the precondition was "has fulfilled precondition Q", whereas the explicit negation was "has not fulfilled precondition P". The explicit version of the negative case thus matches directly with the antecedent of Rule P4, permitting correct selection of this case. In contrast, a subject presented with the implicit version of the negative case must first infer that having fulfilled precondition Q implies that the person has not fulfilled precondition P before they can match the negation to the antecedent of Rule P4 so as to determine that the precondition has not been fulfilled. It should be noted that this inference requires a presumption that only P or Q, and not both, is fulfilled. If for any reason the necessary inference is not reliably made, the probability that Rule P4 will be matched will be reduced when the implicit version of the negative case is presented. Indeed, this consideration guided the construction of materials in Cheng and Holyoak's (1985) original study of performance with the abstract permission rule.

There is, however, a key prediction that distinguishes between the theory of pragmatic schemas and Jackson and Griggs' adaptation of Evans' two-stage model: if a combination of the presentation factors are themselves sufficient to determine reasoning performance, without involving evocation of a permission schema, then a violation-checking context coupled with explicit negatives should facilitate performance for arbitrary rules just as well as for the abstract permission rule. In contrast, "... the schema approach predicts that violation checking will only lead to accurate performance if the problem evokes a schema specifying those situations that in fact constitute violations. Asking subjects to check for violations in an otherwise arbitrary problem would not suffice ..." (Cheng & Holyoak, 1985, p. 410).

Jackson and Griggs did not test whether the combination of the two proposed presentation factors benefits arbitrary rules as much as it benefits permission rules. In particular, the instructions in their "violation" conditions did not clearly establish a violation-checking context for the subjects in the arbitrary condition, because Jackson and Griggs' instructions asked subjects to check whether the rule was "being followed". For the permission materials, because subjects were asked to assume the role of an authority ensuring that people obey the rule, subjects might have understood the task to imply checking for violations. For the arbitrary materials, however, no analogous cue was given.

A further methodological problem with some of Jackson and Griggs' (1990) experiments, which they themselves noted (as did Girotto, Mazzocco, & Cherubini, 1992), is that the implicit negative cases they presented to subjects were not, in fact, logically equivalent to the explicit negative cases they replaced. The rule presented in their Experiment 2 was, "If one is to take action A, then one must first satisfy precondition P". The case negating the consequent was "has not fulfilled precondition P", whereas the supposedly equivalent form without an explicit negative was "has fulfilled precondition Q". However, without additional information that preconditions P and Q are mutually exclusive, there is no logical basis for relating "has fulfilled precondition Q" to the precondition stated in the rule; accordingly, the correct response would be to refrain from checking it, just as Jackson and Griggs' subjects did. In a replication of Experiment 2, Jackson and Griggs added the statement, "Each person has taken one action and fulfilled one precondition" in an attempt to eliminate any misconception that both preconditions could have been satisfied simultaneously. However, this sentence appeared in a separate paragraph from the presentation of the rule, possibly leading to subjects being confused or forgetting to consider this additional constraint when choosing cards. As Girotto et al. (1992) observed, Jackson and Griggs' subjects, when given permission or obligation rules without explicit negatives, tended to make the apparent error of selecting only the "has taken action A" case (the case matching the antecedent), whereas when given arbitrary rules they tended to make the error of selecting both "has taken action A" and "has fulfilled precondition Q". In fact, selection of the A case alone would be the logically correct response if the Q case were not actually interpreted by subjects as a denial that P was fulfilled.

There is evidence that when the interpretation of the case in which the consequent is negated is made unambiguous to subjects, even without an explicit negative, facilitation for the abstract permission rule can in fact be obtained. Girotto et al. (1992) demonstrated that when several possible preconditions are explicitly listed on the response page, along with marks indicating which subset of these had been fulfilled, and the P precondition is not marked, then subjects correctly select this case for the abstract permission rule. In addition, Girotto et al. found substantial facilitation using Jackson and Griggs' non-negative cases when the permission rule was rephrased into an "only if" form—"One can take action A only if one has first satisfied precondition P". This result is consistent with Cheng and Holyoak's (1985) finding that subjects can readily rephrase permission rules (but not arbitrary rules) from "if" to "only if" form, where the latter form serves to emphasise the necessity of the consequent, mitigating against an interpretation under which some precondition other than P might also allow action A (Evans, 1977).

Kroger et al. (1993) performed a set of experiments designed to provide a direct comparison of the effects of a violation-checking context and explicit negatives for arbitrary and abstract permission rules stated in "if" form, with instructions that clarified the logical status of the case corresponding to denying the consequent when explicit negatives were not used. The statement of the problem clearly implied that the implicit version of the case indicating failure to fulfil the relevant precondition is in fact logically equivalent to that case. The form of the implicit negative cases was identical to that employed in the experiments of Jackson and Griggs. PRS theory predicts that a violation-checking context provides an important cue to evoke deontic schemas, and that explicit negatives will make it easier to match the case of denying the consequent to Rule P4 of the permission schema. Accordingly, removing either of these two factors should diminish facilitation for the abstract permission rule. However, if the mutual exclusivity of the complementary cases is clearly conveyed to subjects, some facilitation may be observed for the abstract permission rule, relative to an arbitrary rule, even when explicit negatives are removed. In contrast, even inclusion of both of the favourable presentation factors should provide no facilitation for an arbitrary rule, which will not evoke a deontic schema under any of the presentation conditions.

The results obtained by Kroger et al. disconfirmed Jackson and Griggs' (1990) interpretation of facilitation in the selection task, instead supporting the predictions of PRS theory. Contrary to the implication of Jackson and Griggs' proposal, the presentation factors to which they assigned credit for facilitation of the abstract permission rule proved completely ineffective in enhancing accuracy for an arbitrary rule. Even when the arbitrary rule was clarified to eliminate a possible biconditional interpretation, performance was not improved. In contrast, even when the cards presented to subjects did not include explicit negatives, a small but reliable facilitation effect was still obtained for an abstract statement of the permission rule (22% of subjects selected the case stating the action was taken together with the case stating that a precondition other than the one mentioned in the rule had been fulfilled) relative to an arbitrary rule (6%). Thus, the fact that reliable facilitation can be obtained even for abstract deontic rules (as recently confirmed by Griggs & Cox, 1993) provides strong support for the view that the content effects consistently observed for conditional regulations in the selection task are due to the evocation of pragmatic schemas.

PERSPECTIVE EFFECTS IN DEONTIC REASONING

Another aspect of deontic content effects that has recently been a focus of attention in evaluating alternative theories has been the influence of subjects' perspectives on performance on the selection task. Conditional regulations typically involve interactions between two parties who have distinct points of view. Manktelow and Over (1991) investigated selection performance using a conditional permission statement said to be made by a mother to her young son—"If you tidy your room then you may go out to play"—which pragmatically corresponds to the deterministic conditional "If you go out to play then you must have tidied your room". Here "going out to play" is the p case and "tidying the room" is the q case. The mother plays the role of the permittor who grants conditional permission, while the boy plays the role of the corresponding permittee. As Manktelow and Over observed, the goals of the two parties are likely to differ. The mother's goal is to have the boy tidy his room; thus she is likely to be concerned with the possibility that the boy "cheats" by violating his side of the implicit contract, going out to play without tidying his room. In a selection task, someone taking the mother's point of view would therefore tend to select the p and not-q cases (i.e. a card indicating the boy went out to play and one indicating he did not tidy his room). This is the so-called "logical" pattern often observed for selection problems with deontic content.

It is possible, however, to instead consider the situation from the perspective of the son. He also has an interest in the actions regulated by the contract. In particular, his goal is to go out to play; thus his interests would be ill-served if he tidied up his room but was none the less prevented from playing. From the son's point of view, then, it would be sensible to examine the not-p and q cases (i.e. a card indicating the boy did not get an opportunity to play and a card indicating he did tidy his room). In fact, Manktelow and Over (1991) found that the dominant response pattern could be reversed by instructions that manipulated the subjects' point of view concerning the regulation. Subjects who were led to take the mother's (permittor's) perspective tended to select the p and not-q cases, whereas those led to take the son's (permittee's) perspective tended to select the not-p and q cases.

Similar perspective effects in selection tasks have been reported by Politzer and Nguyen-Xuan (1992) and Gigerenzer and Hug (1992). For example, the latter investigators gave subjects the rule:

(A) If an employee works on the weekend, then that person gets a day off during the week.

Two context stories were used, one of which cued subjects into the employee's perspective, and one that cued the employer's perspective. Those subjects who were encouraged to take the employee's perspective tended to select the p and not-q cases ("worked on the weekend" and "did not get a day off "). In contrast, subjects who were led to take the employer's perspective tended to select the opposite cases, not-p and q ("did not work on the weekend" and "did get a day off ").

Gigerenzer and Hug's (1992) results, like those of Manktelow and Over (1991), reveal that the dominant selection pattern for a deontic rule can systematically deviate from that supported by the standard logic of the material conditional. But as Cheng and Holyoak (1985) noted, evocation of a pragmatic schema will not necessarily lead to selection of the "logically correct" cases, both because different schemas will suggest different relevant inferences, and because the inferences based on any particular schema will vary depending on the mapping between the stated rule and those associated with the schema. For example, a stated rule that can be interpreted as a permission will lead to selection of the "logically correct" cases only if it maps on to Rule P1 of the permission schema. Politzer and Nguyen-Xuan (1992), who also obtained perspective effects in a selection paradigm, showed that an analysis in terms of an integrated combination of schemas for permission and obligation can account for the pattern observed in their own study and those of Manktelow and Over (1991) and Gigerenzer and Hug (1992). Holyoak and Cheng (in press) generalised Politzer and Nguyen-Xuan's analysis by relating it more explicitly to the concepts of rights and duties as they have been used in legal theory, and used this analyis to derive and test a novel prediction from PRS theory. In the next section we review their analysis and findings.

The Complementarity of Permission and Obligation

The explanation provided for perspective effects by PRS theory hinges on the recognition that rights and duties are complementary and interdefinable concepts. This complementarity, noted by Politzer and Nguyen-Xuan (1992), corresponds to fundamental legal conceptions of rights and duties. The most thorough treatment of rights and duties from a legal perspective was provided by Hohfeld (1919), who referred to these concepts as "jural correlates". Hohfeld quotes from a 1894 legal decision in the case of *Lake Shore & M.S.R. Co. v. Kurtz*: "'Duty' and 'right' are correlative terms. When a right is invaded, a duty is violated." Hohfeld then gives the illustration, "... if X has a right against Y that he shall stay off the former's land, the correlative (and equivalent) is that Y is under a duty toward X to stay off of the place" (p. 38).

We can formalise the equivalence noted by Hohfeld by stating the relations of "right" and "duty" as predicate-argument structures. Each relation has three arguments, corresponding to the two parties to a regulatory agreement and the action that is regulated. A right has the general form,

right (of X, against Y, re A),

that is, X has a right against Y with respect to action A (e.g. if X is a property owner, X has the right that Y should remain off of X's land). Similarly, a duty has the form,

duty (of Y, towards X, re A),

that is, Y has a duty towards X regarding action A (e.g. Y has a duty to X to stay off X's land). It should be noted that this type of complementarity is by no means specific to rights and duties. Many pairs of converse relations, such as "left of" versus "right of", and "parent of" versus "child of", have a similar semantic structure, in which the meaning of the paired relations is equivalent (except for pragmatic focus) when their argument fillers are interchanged. For example, parent of (Mary, Sam) is equivalent to child of (Sam, Mary).

The general complementarity of rights and duties gives rise to special cases in which the schemas for permission and obligation are interdefined. The key to this connection hinges on the fact that the "precondition" either to X's right against Y (a permission) or to Y's duty towards X (an obligation) may be the fulfilment of a duty of X to Y. Thus we can state a specific version of Rule P3 of the permission schema, in which the precondition is a fulfilled duty, as:

P3': If duty (of X, towards Y, re A1) is fulfilled, then right (of X, against Y, re A2) is acquired.

where A1 and A2 are regulated actions. Similarly, we can state a specific version of Rule O1 of the obligation schema as:

O1': If duty (of X, towards Y, re A1) is fulfilled, then duty (of Y, towards X, re A2) is incurred.

Note that the antecedents of P3' and O1' are identical, and the consequents of these rules express complementary rights and duties.[1] Conditional permissions and obligations are thus interdefinable.

This analysis of the relationship between the permission and obligation schemas provides a straightforward explanation of the perspective effects observed by Manktelow and Over (1991) and others. We need only assume that people focus on whichever interpretation of the stated rule yields a definite conclusion about their own rights and the duties of others (rather than their own duties and the rights of others). That is, people's selections will be primarily focused on the cases related most directly to their own goals. For example, the rule used by Gigerenzer and Hug (1992),

(A) If an employee works on the weekend, then that person gets a day off during the week,

is, from the perspective of the employee, a conditional obligation imposed on the employer (i.e. a description of a regulation of the employer's duty towards the employee). The employee's goal is to have a day off during the week. A subject taking the employee's perspective would therefore represent this "day off" rule as something like:

(A-O1) If an employee works on the weekend, then the employer must grant a day off during the week.

Under this interpretation, the stated rule thus matches Rule O1 of the obligation schema. Once the schema is evoked, the entire set of rules will apply, encouraging selection of the p ("worked on the weekend") and not-q ("did not get a day off") cases.

The employer, on the other hand, has the goal of getting employees to work on weekends. Therefore, from the employer's perspective the rule is likely to be interpreted as a conditional permission, equivalent to,

(A-P3) If an employee works on the weekend, then that person may take a day off during the week,

a form that matches Rule P3 of the permission schema. Once the permission schema is evoked, the stated rule can be recast in the form of Rule P1, which provides a definite consequent,

(A-P1) If an employee takes a day off during the week, then that person must have worked on the weekend.

That is, the rule is interpreted as regulating a duty of the employee towards the employer. If we consistently notate "worked on the weekend" as p and "did get a day off" as q (as in the original stated rule), the result will be a preference for selection of the not-p ("did not work on the weekend") and q ("did get a day off") cases, just as Gigerenzer and Hug observed. In effect, the mapping to the permission schema causes the stated rule to be internally represented in the logical form if q then p. The difference in perspective thus triggers complementary schematic interpretations, reversing the selection preference.

In addition to providing an explanation of previous demonstrations of perspective effects, this analysis makes a novel prediction. A regulation such as Gigerenzer and Hug's "day off" rule is ambiguous in its pragmatic focus, which is why the context story can guide subjects to a particular point of view. From one of these points of view (that of the employer), the permission schema will apply in a manner that supports selection of the two cases (not-p and q) opposite to those licensed by the material conditional. But if our account is correct, subjects' internal representation of the ambiguous rule in the employer context will in fact be equivalent to the representation of an unambiguous rule presented in a form that matches P1—i.e. the form stated above as (A-P1). Because this version explicitly has the logical form if q then p, selection of the not-p and q cases for this rule is in accord with the logic of the material conditional.

Using the selection task, Holyoak and Cheng (in press) performed an experiment that varied the form and context of conditional rules concerning the regulation of voluntary human action. Each subject received a single selection task, with a rule presented in one of three ways. In two conditions, subjects received a rule in the form if p then q which, in isolation, would be ambiguous between a conditional obligation and a conditional permission. The rule was presented along with a context intended to favour one of these two interpretations. The form of the stated rule was such that the obligation interpretation would match Rule O1 of the obligation schema, and hence tend to promote selection of the p and not-q cases. In contrast, the permission interpretation would match Rule P3 of the permission schema, and hence would tend to promote selection of the not-p and q cases. Subjects in the third condition received an unambiguous version of the rule in a form matching Rule P1 of the permission schema (in the form if q then p), with a minimal context. PRS theory predicts that selection performance should be the same for the ambiguous rule in the permission context as for the unambiguous form of the rule.

Two basic problems were constructed by adapting materials used by Gigerenzer and Hug (1992) to investigate perspective effects. One rule was the above "day off" rule, which, in its ambiguous form (without a modal) was stated as (A) above. In the "employee-O1" condition, the rule was embedded in a context designed to encourage subjects to take the perspective of the employee, which would lead to a match to Rule O1 of the obligation schema. The story indicated that an employee was considering working on the weekend, but was concerned because of rumours that the rule had been violated. In the "employer-P3" condition, the context instead oriented subjects to the perspective of the employer, which would lead to a match to Rule P3 of the permission schema. In this version it was the employer who was described as being concerned that the rule was being violated. Finally, in the "employer-P1" condition the context was more neutral in that the violation-checker was not explicitly specified, and the rule was restated as:

(A-P1′) An employee must have worked on the weekend if the person takes a day off during the week.

The statement (A-P1′) is identical to (A-P1) above, except for a syntactic inversion from the form if q then p to the form p if q (given that we consistently denote "works on the weekend" as p and "gets a day off" as q), thus equating the surface order of p and q across versions (A) and (A-P1′) of the stated rule, and hence across all three presentation conditions. In the (A-P1′) form the modal "must" should facilitate matching the stated rule to Rule P1 of the permission schema. In all conditions subjects were asked to select the cases that might reveal violations of the rule from among cards representing four alternatives: "worked on the weekend" (p), "did not work on the weekend" (not-p), "got a day off " (q), and "did not get a day off " (not-q).

PRS theory predicts that the employee-O1 condition should favour selection of the p and not-q alternatives, whereas both the employer-P3 and the employer-P1 conditions should favour selection of the not-p and q alternatives. The latter two conditions are predicted to yield identical response patterns because both should trigger matches to a core rule of the permission schema (P3 or P1, respectively), either of which will enable access to the entire set of schematic inferences. Importantly, although selection of the not-p and q alternatives is opposite to the so-called "logical" answer for the employer-P3 condition (given that the ambiguous rule is nominally in the form if p then q), this same selection is in accord with the material conditional for the employer-P1 condition (since the unambiguous rule has the logical form if q then p). If these two conditions in fact yield comparable patterns of selections, such a result would support a central claim of PRS theory: people's reasoning about deontic relations is not in fact based on anything like the syntactic rules of the material conditional.

Three parallel conditions were generated on the basis of a second problem, in order to provide greater generality for testing the predictions of PRS theory. The basic rule for the second set of materials was the "subsidy" rule:

(B) If a car owner installs a new catalytic converter, then that person gets a subsidy.

The general rationale for this rule was the Greater Los Angeles Air Quality Management District's concern about the pollution caused by the car exhaust generated by older cars. In the "owner-P1" condition subjects were encouraged to take the perspective of the owner of an older car, who was considering installing a catalytic converter, but was concerned by rumours that the rule had been violated. In the "officer-P3" condition subjects instead were encouraged to take the perspective of an officer working for the Air Quality Management District, who was concerned that the rule was being abused. Finally, the "officer-P1" condition used a more neutral context in which the violation-checker was not specified, and restated the rule in a form parallel to the (A-P1') version of the day-off rule, namely:

(B-P1') A car owner must have installed a new catalytic converter if the person receives a subsidy.

The design and predictions for the subsidy conditions were in all respects the same as those for the day-off conditions.

Figure 4.1 presents the percentage of subjects who selected each individual card for the day-off problem, and Fig. 4.2 presents the percentages who selected each of the two critical combinations. PRS theory predicts that the individual p and not-q responses, as well as the p and not-q combination, will tend to be selected more often in the employee-O1 condition than in the employer-P3 or employer-P1 conditions. In contrast,

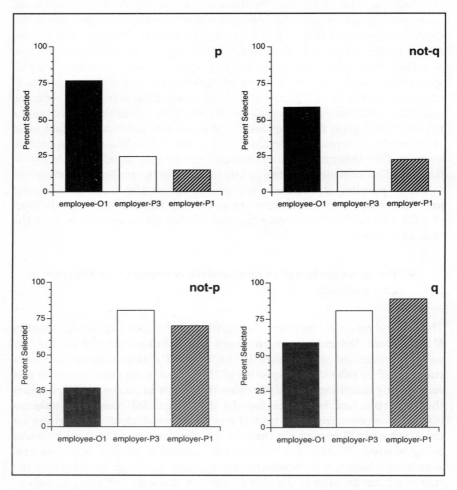

FIG. 4.1. Percentage of subjects in each condition who selected each of the four individual alternatives for the day-off problem. (Adapted from Holyoak & Cheng, in press.)

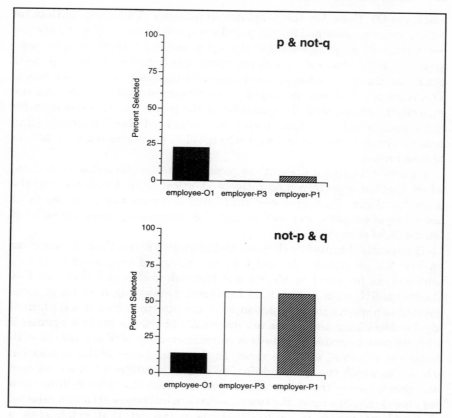

FIG. 4.2. Percentage of subjects in each condition who selected each of the two critical combinations for the day-off problem. (Adapted from Holyoak & Cheng, in press.)

the individual not-p and q responses, as well as the not-p and q combination, were predicted to be selected more frequently in the employer-P3 and employer-P1 conditions. The response patterns for the employer-P3 and employer-P1 conditions were predicted to be the same as each other, because both involve mappings to the permission schema that indirectly (via P3) or directly (via P1) impose the logical form if q then p on the stated rule.

The results were fully in accord with the predictions of PRS theory. For the day-off problem the employer-P3 and employer-P1 conditions did not differ significantly from each other for any individual response or either combination. Tests comparing the O1 condition to the combined P3 and P1 conditions also confirmed the predictions of the theory. The percentage of subjects selecting the p and not-q alternatives were each greater for the employee-O1 than for the employer conditions. The same pattern of differences was obtained for the p and not-q combination. Conversely, the percentage of subjects selecting the not-p and q alternatives were each greater for the combined employer conditions than for the employee-O1 condition; the same pattern was obtained for the not-p and q combination. The response that was predicted to be dominant was in each case the majority response, with the exception of the p and not-q combination for the employee-O1 condition, which was produced less frequently than expected because a substantial percentage of subjects selected q in addition to p and not-q.

Figures 4.3 and 4.4 present the parallel data for the subsidy problem, which yielded a pattern qualitatively identical to that observed for the day-off problem. Each predicted individual response was produced by at least 59% of subjects, and each predicted combination was produced by at least 41% of subjects.

The results obtained by Holyoak and Cheng (in press) thus provide clear support for predictions derived from the theory of pragmatic reasoning schemas, as proposed by Cheng and Holyoak (1985) and elaborated by Politzer and Nguyen-Xuan (1992). In everyday reasoning about regulations governing human voluntary action, as in the interpretation of more formal legal codes, rights and duties are interdefinable: the right of X against Y with respect to action A entails a correlative duty of Y towards X with respect to action A, and vice versa. In the special case of the permission schema in which the "precondition" to a right is fulfilment of a duty, and the special case of the obligation schema in which the "precondition" to a duty is exercise of a right, the two schemas are interconnected by a relation of complementarity. In such situations a context that establishes a particular perspective on an ambiguous rule can trigger a match either to Rule O1 of the obligation schema or Rule P3 of the permission schema. While a match to Rule O1 favours selection of the so-called "logical" alternatives, p and not-q, a match to Rule P3 favours selection of the opposite alternatives, not-p and q. However, in neither case is the selection process actually governed by formal rules of a mental logic equivalent to the material conditional.[2] Rather, a match to Rule P3 implicitly leads subjects to represent the ambiguous stated rule in the logical form if q then p. As our analysis predicted, the same pattern of selections, not-p and q, was also obtained in a more neutral context when the stated rule unambiguously matched Rule P1 of the permission schema with the explicit logical form if q then p.

The results thus support Cheng and Holyoak's (1985, p. 397) claim that the permission schema is not equivalent to the material conditional in standard propositional logic. Rather, the deontic schemas are context-sensitive, and the inferences they will generate will necessarily depend on the specific mapping between the stated rule and the rules of a relevant schema. If a stated rule is matched to Rule P1 of the permission schema or to Rule O1 of the obligation schema, then the so-called "logical" selection of p and not-q will indeed be facilitated. But precisely the opposite selection pattern will be encouraged if the stated rule is instead mapped on to Rule P3 of the permission schema. More generally, of course, other schemas that apply to non-deontic situations, such as causal hypothesis testing, will favour entirely different selection patterns.

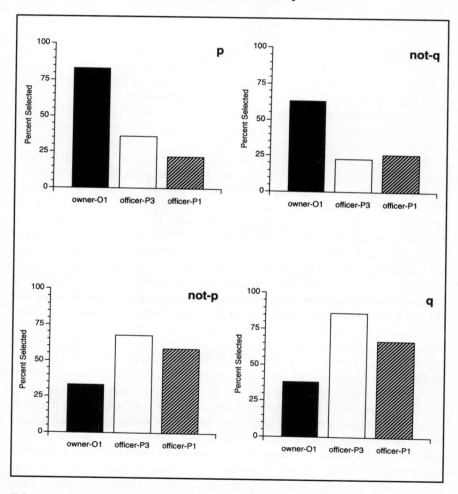

FIG. 4.3. Percentage of subjects in each condition who selected each of the four individual alternatives for the subsidy problem. (Adapted from Holyoak & Cheng, in press.)

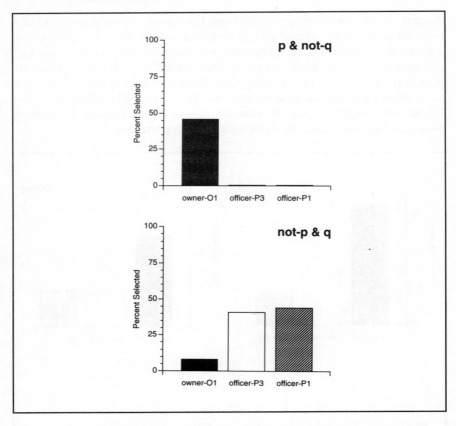

FIG. 4.4. Percentage of subjects in each condition who selected each of the two critical combinations for the subsidy problem. (Adapted from Holyoak & Cheng, in press.)

CONCLUSION

PRS theory was originally supported by a variety of evidence, largely based on content effects observed in Wason's selection task. This evidence included the finding of facilitation for reasoning about abstract regulations, devoid of concrete or familiar content (Cheng & Holyoak, 1985, Experiment 2). Although the interpretation of these results was subsequently challenged, more recent research has confirmed both that facilitation of reasoning with abstract deontic rules is a robust phenomenon, and that PRS theory provides the most complete account of the factors that determine when such facilitation is obtained. In particular, a violation-checking context provides a major cue to interpret the stated rule as a regulation, and explicit negatives describing cases facilitate matching the cases to those schema rules that have explicitly negative antecedents. But when the logical relations between the cases and the stated rule are made clear to subjects, reliable facilitation can be obtained for abstract deontic rules even when the cases are presented without explicit negatives.

A closely related type of evidence originally offered in support of PRS theory emerged from experiments demonstrating the importance of goals and context in the evocation of deontic schemas. For example, Cheng and Holyoak (1985, Experiment 1) found that an identically stated rule either would or would not yield facilitation depending on whether the context made it clear that the rule was an established regulation for which it was necessary to check for possible violations. More recent research on the influence of subjects' perspectives on deontic reasoning has provided a richer and more detailed picture of contextual influences (see Manktelow & Over, this volume, Chapter 5). The findings regarding perspective effects on selection performance have led to a more explicit theoretical integration of the permission and obligation schemas, yielding a new prediction (equivalent performance for stated rules that match either Rule P3 or Rule P1 of the permission schema) that has been confirmed by an experimental test.

PRS theory thus continues to provide a framework for understanding a wide range of evidence concerning the role of content and context in guiding human reasoning about the regulation of voluntary action. More generally, this research area continues to be the focus of a great deal of theoretical and empirical work. (For a recent comparison of PRS theory with alternative accounts, see Holyoak & Cheng, in press.) The developments of recent years owe a large intellectual debt to the foundational contributions of Peter Wason, which include both developing the selection task and initiating investigations of the role of content and context in pragmatic reasoning.

NOTES

1. Alternatively, the precondition to either a permission or an obligation may be the exercise of a right of Y against X.
2. Some theorists have suggested that human reasoning about permissions and obligations might be explained by a model based on some extended formal logic that includes deontic operators (Gigerenzer & Hug, 1992; Rips, 1990). Holyoak and Cheng (in press) describe some of the problems such an approach would have to overcome in order to provide a viable model.

ACKNOWLEDGEMENTS

Preparation of this paper was supported by NSF Grant SBR-9310614 to Keith Holyoak and NSF Grant DBS-9121298 to Patricia Cheng. We thank David Over and Jonathan Evans for helpful comments on an earlier draft. Requests for reprints may be directed to either author at Department of Psychology, University of California, Los Angeles, California 90095-1563, USA.

REFERENCES

Braine, M.D.S., & O'Brien, D.P. (1991). A theory of If: A lexical entry, reasoning program, and pragmatic principles. *Psychological Review, 98*, 182–203.

Cheng, P.W., & Holyoak, K.J. (1985). Pragmatic reasoning schemas. *Cognitive Psychology, 17*, 391–416.

Cheng, P.W., & Holyoak, K.J. (1989). On the natural selection of reasoning theories. *Cognition, 33*, 285–313.

Cheng, P.W., Holyoak, K.J., Nisbett, R.E., & Oliver, L.M. (1986). Pragmatic versus syntactic approaches to training deductive reasoning. *Cognitive Psychology, 18*, 293–328.

Cosmides, L. (1989). The logic of social exchange: Has natural selection shaped how humans reason? Studies with the Wason selection task. *Cognition, 31*, 187–276.

D'Andrade, R. (1982, April). *Reason versus logic.* Paper presented at the Symposium on the Ecology of Cognition: Biological, Cultural, and Historical Perspectives. Greensboro, NC.

Evans, J.St.B.T. (1977). Linguistic factors in reasoning. *Quarterly Journal of Experimental Psychology, 29*, 297–306.

Evans, J.St.B.T. (1983). Linguistic determinants of bias in conditional reasoning. *Quarterly Journal of Experimental Psychology, 35A*, 635–644.

Evans, J.St.B.T. (1989). *Bias in human reasoning: Causes and consequences.* Hove, UK: Lawrence Erlbaum Associates Ltd.

Gigerenzer, G., & Hug, K. (1992). Domain-specific reasoning: Social contracts, cheating, and perspective change. *Cognition, 43*, 127–171.

Girotto, V., Gilly, M., Blaye, A., & Light, P.H. (1989). Children's performance in the selection task: Plausibility and familiarity. *British Journal of Psychology, 80*, 79–95.

Girotto, V., Light, P.H., & Colburn, C.J. (1988). Pragmatic schemas and conditional reasoning in children. *Quarterly Journal of Experimental Psychology, 40A*, 469–482.

Girotto, V., Mazzocco, A., & Cherubini, P. (1992). Pragmatic judgements of relevance in reasoning: A reply to Jackson and Griggs. *Quarterly Journal of Experimental Psychology, 45A*, 547–574.

Griggs, R.A., & Cox, J.R. (1982). The elusive thematic materials effect in Wason's selection task. *British Journal of Psychology, 73*, 407–420.

Griggs, R.A., & Cox, J.R. (1993). Permission schemas and the selection task. *Quarterly Journal of Experimental Psychology, 46A*, 637–652.

Hohfeld, W.N. (1919). Some fundamental legal conceptions as applied in judicial reasoning. In W.W. Cook (Ed.), *Some fundamental legal conceptions as applied in judicial reasoning and other legal essays, by Wesley Newcomb Hohfeld* (pp. 23–64). New Haven, CT: Yale University Press.

Holyoak, K.J., & Cheng, P.W. (in press). Pragmatic reasoning with a point of view. *Thinking and Reasoning.*

Jackson, S.L., & Griggs, R.A. (1990). The elusive pragmatic reasoning schemas effect. *Quarterly Journal of Experimental Psychology, 42A,* 2, 353–373.

Johnson-Laird, P.N., & Byrne, R.M.J. (1991). *Deduction.* Hove, UK: Lawrence Erlbaum Associates Ltd.

Johnson-Laird, P.N., Legrenzi, P., & Legrenzi, S.M. (1972). Reasoning and a sense of reality. *British Journal of Psychology, 63,* 395–400.

Kroger, K.K., Cheng, P.W., & Holyoak, K.J. (1993). Evoking the permission schema: The impact of explicit negation and a violation-checking context. *Quarterly Journal of Experimental Psychology, 46A,* 615–635.

Legrenzi, P., & Murino, M. (1974). Falsification at the pre-operational level. *Italian Journal of Psychology, 1,* 361–368.

Light, P.H., Blaye, A., Gilly, M., & Girotto, V. (1990). Pragmatic schemas and logical reasoning in 6- to 8-year-old children. *Cognitive Development, 5,* 49–64.

Light, P.H., Girotto, V., & Legrenzi, P. (1990). Children's reasoning on conditional promises and permissions. *Cognitive Development, 5,* 369–383.

Manktelow, K.I., & Over, D.E. (1990). Deontic thought and the selection task. In K.J. Gilhooly, M. Keane, R. Logie, & G. Erdos (Eds.), *Lines of thought: Reflections on the psychology of thinking.* Chichester: Wiley.

Manktelow, K.I., & Over, D.E. (1991). Social roles and utilities in reasoning with deontic conditionals. *Cognition, 39,* 85–105.

Politzer, G., & Nguyen-Xuan, A. (1992). Reasoning about promises and warnings: Darwinian algorithms, mental models, relevance judgements, or pragmatic schemas? *Quarterly Journal of Experimental Psychology, 44A,* 402–421.

Rips, L.J. (1990). Reasoning. *Annual Review of Psychology, 41,* 321–353.

Wason, P.C. (1966). Reasoning. In B.M. Foss (Ed.), *New horizons in psychology (Vol. 1).* Harmondsworth: Penguin.

Wason, P.C. (1983). Realism and rationality in the selection task. In J.St.B.T. Evans (Ed.), *Thinking and reasoning: Psychological approaches.* London: Routledge & Kegan Paul.

Wason, P.C., & Shapiro, D. (1971). Natural and contrived experience in a reasoning problem. *Quarterly Journal of Experimental Psychology, 23,* 63–71.

Yachanin, S.A., & Tweney, R.D. (1982). The effect of thematic content on cognitive strategies in the four card selection task. *Bulletin of the Psychonomic Society, 19,* 87–90.

CHAPTER FIVE

Deontic Reasoning

Ken I. Manktelow

University of Wolverhampton, UK

David E. Over

University of Sunderland, UK

INTRODUCTION: CONTENT EFFECTS AND
THE DEONTIC CONTEXT IN REASONING

The study of the effects of content has been the prime concern of researchers on reasoning for 20 years or more. Indeed, a quick glance at the chapter headings for this volume will confirm that observation: several chapters are devoted to various aspects of the issue, and this is one of them. Our topic is deontic reasoning, which actually has its own special logical form as well as content. We shall begin by tracing how this topic emerged out of the general background of research on content effects, though it is not a topic which should only be of interest to a narrow range of reasoning researchers. It is one of fundamental importance for understanding human thought and behaviour.

Deontic thinking is what we are doing when we are trying to decide which actions we must (should or ought to) or may perform. The deontic reasoning we shall be concerned with here is a case of what philosophers call practical reasoning (about actions) as distinct from so-called theoretical reasoning (about states of affairs). You are engaged in theoretical reasoning when you are considering evidence about cigarette smoking and health, with a view to having some well-confirmed belief on the matter. You are engaged in deontic reasoning when you are trying to infer whether you ought to give up cigarette smoking, in the light of moral rules (you should set a good example for your children), social rules (the university has banned smoking on its premises), or prudential ones (you must give up smoking for the sake of your health). Much deontic reasoning takes place in a social context, which needs to be taken into account for a full explanation of it.

A moment's reflection tells us that in everyday life we do an awful lot of this kind of thinking. Indeed most of the "theoretical" reasoning we do has the object of helping us with our practical reasoning, and so it is remarkable that the psychological study of deontic reasoning is of quite recent origin. (The philosophical study of practical thought, particularly of what is called the practical syllogism, goes back to Aristotle; see Audi, 1989.) The reasons for this need not detain us; our purpose here is to give an account of the contemporary state of this now vigorous area of research (but see Evans, Over, & Manktelow, 1993, on the fundamental importance of practical reasoning and a concept of rationality that is suitable for evaluating it).

We don't have to go back very far to begin this survey. As we mentioned at the beginning, the field developed as an outgrowth of research into the effects of content on reasoning, or more precisely, responses on Wason's (1968) selection task. Some people are becoming uneasy about the reliance which psychologists place on this problem, but it is at present unmatched as an instrument for turning intuitions into behaviour in controlled settings, and so has become the foremost technique in the psychology of deontic reasoning. Because other authors in this volume will be looking at other aspects of the task, we shall not give any general background here, but instead pick out those studies that have provided turning points for deontic research.

The first deontic selection task, though it was not presented as such, can in retrospect be seen to be that reported by Johnson-Laird, Legrenzi, and Legrenzi (1972) (see Fig. 5.1). In this experiment, subjects were given four selection tasks, two "symbolic" (i.e. testing conditional statements about letters and numbers), and two "realistic". The two versions of each type were that the target conditional was in "If then" or "Only if" form. The realistic content is what is important here, and we shall deal only with the "If then" form, since most subsequent research has employed this. Subjects were presented with the rule, "If a letter is sealed then it has a 5d stamp on it", together with 5 envelopes, showing them to be sealed, unsealed, bearing a 5d stamp, a 4d stamp, and no stamp. They were asked to imagine they were post office workers sorting letters, and were instructed to "select those envelopes that you definitely need to turn over to find out whether or not they violate the rule". The correct answer is to select the sealed letter and the understamped (and unstamped) ones, because only a sealed letter without the right stamp on it would violate the rule. In this condition, 21 out of 24 subjects produced the correct selection, compared with 2 out of 21 in a corresponding symbolic condition.

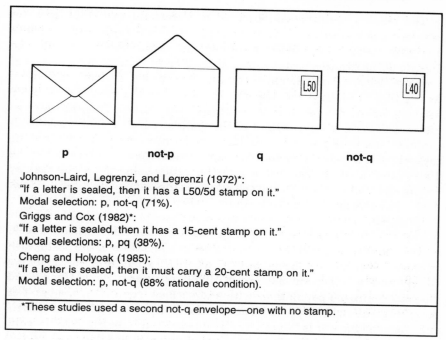

p   not-p   q   not-q

Johnson-Laird, Legrenzi, and Legrenzi (1972)*:
"If a letter is sealed, then it has a L50/5d stamp on it."
Modal selection: p, not-q (71%).

Griggs and Cox (1982)*:
"If a letter is sealed, then it has a 15-cent stamp on it."
Modal selections: p, pq (38%).

Cheng and Holyoak (1985):
"If a letter is sealed, then it must carry a 20-cent stamp on it."
Modal selection: p, not-q (88% rationale condition).

*These studies used a second not-q envelope—one with no stamp.

FIG. 5.1. The postal task, devised by Johnson-Laird et al. (1972), and its later adaptations. (After Johnson-Laird et al., 1972.)

It is worth pausing to draw attention to several aspects of this experiment which make it so noteworthy in the history of research on deontic reasoning. First, the conditional in the realistic case really was a rule, in the sense of a regulation. It would have been familiar to the (British) subjects of the time, as a similar regulation had recently been in operation in the UK. It did not contain the deontic modal operator "must", but the context of the task made it clear that it was to be read this way by the subjects. Secondly, as the original authors correctly pointed out, in this realistic case the subjects' task was to search for violations of a rule the truth of which was not in question, and not, as in the symbolic case, to search for counter-examples in order to test the truth value of a conditional. Thirdly, the result was unfortunately interpreted as an example of the facilitation of correct responding on a task logically equivalent to a symbolic one. We can now see that this was misleading. The logical form of conditional deontic reasoning cannot be adequately represented in extensional propositional logic, but only in some deontic logic. Conditionals in deontic tasks do not have the same logical form as ones in "symbolic", "abstract", or "indicative" tasks.

The level of performance observed by Johnson-Laird et al. was not repeated a few years later when the experiment was replicated by Griggs and Cox (1982). They used an American population which had no experience of two-tier postal rates, with different charges for sealed and unsealed letters, but otherwise the experiment was a close replication, except that "15 cents" was the amount stated in the rule. Only 2 of 24 subjects selected the correct envelopes this time. This result was interpreted as a demonstration of the general effect of familiarity with content; later work has shown that it is the deontic form and content of the task which is the crucial factor. Two experiments from the literature of the 1980s illustrate this. The first is a further study using the postal task by Cheng and Holyoak (1985), and the second is the unpublished "Sears" task devised by D'Andrade (see Rumelhart, 1980).

Cheng and Holyoak were the first researchers to test explicitly the role of a deontic context in facilitating performance on the Wason selection task, and in one of their experiments they used an adaptation of the postal task to do so. As with the Johnson-Laird et al. (1972) study, it is worth looking closely at the important aspects of this experiment. First, Cheng and Holyoak compared populations with and without experience of a two-tier postal regulation, from Hong Kong and the United States. Secondly, their rule included the words "must carry" instead of "has" (see Fig. 5.1). Thirdly, they compared a condition in which a rationale for the regulation was given with one in which it was absent. The rationale was as follows:

The rationale for this regulation is to increase profit from personal mail, which is nearly always sealed. Sealed letters are defined as personal and must therefore carry more postage than unsealed letters.

In both conditions the following instruction was given:

In order to check that the regulation is followed, which of the following four envelopes would you turn over? Turn over only those you need to check to be sure.

For the Hong Kong subjects, the presence of the rationale made no difference: over 80% chose the correct envelopes both with and without it. For the US subjects, those given the rationale performed as well as the Hong Kong subjects, but those not given the rationale produced significantly lower performance. D'Andrade's "Sears" task (see Fig. 5.2) had produced similar high levels of performance among US subjects, and in fact it can be reliably used in classroom demonstrations of the effect.

Why should one group of subjects from a population perform differently compared to another (and compared to a group from another population)

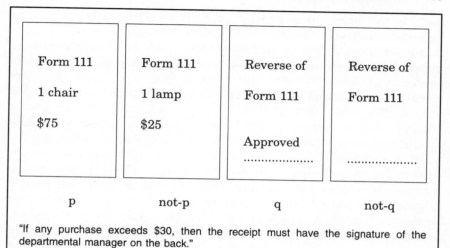

FIG. 5.2. The Sears task, devised by D'Andrade. (Adapted from Rumelhart, 1980.)

on ostensibly the same task? Much recent work has gone into answering this question. Early on, researchers had proposed a rather vague "familiarity" effect, without stating precisely what it consisted of. For instance, do people perform well on the Sears task because they are familiar with shops, or because they are familiar with regulations? Cheng and Holyoak's work strongly indicates the latter.

People have been found to perform well on the postal task either when they are culturally familiar with its content, or when they are provided with a rationale for the regulation, or of course both. When they have neither the familiarity nor the rationale, they perform badly. What counts is that the task is seen by the subjects as a sensible deontic task. If the content taps the subjects' culture, that is sufficient; if not, information must be provided, by the scenario and the wording of the rule, so that an understandable context is constructed into which the task content can be fitted. Deontic reasoning does have its own logical form, displayed using a strong deontic operator ("must", "should", or "ought to") and a weak one ("may"), but just using these operators in a rule does not facilitate performance in a selection task. If people do have a mental version of deontic logic—a set of cognitive algorithms corresponding to the tenets of such a logic—it is insufficient for solving problems like a deontic selection task (see Manktelow & Over, 1992). Deontic reasoning has no point unless it is aimed at inferring "sensible" or "reasonable" actions for people to perform. We hold that these words are to be explained in terms of people's goals in the actions they perform, or more precisely, in terms of their subjective preferences among the options before them.

The strongest possible test of these ideas would be for an almost pure deontic logical form, with a minimal scenario specifying a simple goal, to produce high levels of correct performance, and that is just what was reported by Cheng and Holyoak (1985) in a second experiment. They used the rule, "If one is to take action A then one must first satisfy precondition P", and asked subjects to imagine themselves as an authority checking whether regulations were obeyed. This critical experiment displayed the heart of most deontic selection tasks. Notice that this conditional does not refer to a supposed relationship between states of affairs of "theoretical" interest. It does not state that proposition A truly describes the world when proposition P does—it refers, however abstractly, to an action A that someone is to perform. Its scenario also refers to a generally familiar social situation in which there is an authority who lays down a rule to achieve some end, and who can check whether violations of it have occurred and presumably punish the violators. As we shall see, these elements of deontic selection tasks were to prove important. (See also Kroger, Cheng, & Holyoak,1993, for more on "abstract" deontic tasks.)

We have therefore seen how one particular pathway out of the study of content effects on reasoning has led to the opening up of an area of research into a neglected problem of great interest—that of accounting for deontic thinking. We have also seen the establishment of a stable pattern of empirical findings. Now we shall pass on to the central concern of this chapter, which is the theoretical characterisation of deontic thought that arises from this and later work. To do this, we first need to consider some of the more recent empirical findings.

RECENT EXPERIMENTS: SUBJECTIVE UTILITY AND SOCIAL PERSPECTIVE

To account for their subjects' performance, Cheng and Holyoak (1985) introduced the theory of pragmatic reasoning schemas. This theory is discussed in detail in Chapter 4, but for our purposes its approach can be summarised briefly. The theory proposed sets of content-bound production rules for various contexts (see also Cheng, Holyoak, Nisbett, & Oliver, 1986). For instance, in the case of the schema for permission, one such rule would read: "If the precondition has been satisfied, then the action may be taken." These schemas were said to be abstracted from experience. A problem which contained sufficient cues for a certain context, such as permission, would evoke the attendant schema, whereupon the set of rules would be activated to yield the appropriate inferences.

This theory was soon challenged by Cosmides (1985; 1989). She was generally concerned to argue for an evolutionary perspective in the study of human reasoning, which is a deep topic we cannot go into here. Cosmides specifically claimed that facilitation in the selection tasks she reviewed was the result of an innately given mental structure she labelled a "Darwinian algorithm". This algorithm concerned social exchange, and was encapsulated in the rule, "If you take a benefit then you pay a cost". People were said to be innately sensitive to the possibility of "cheaters"—those who take their benefit without paying any cost. In a postal type task, a cheater would be someone who had the benefit (achieved the goal) of privacy by sealing a letter, but who did not then pay the appropriate cost by putting a high value stamp on it. Cosmides held that subjects would pick out sealed letters and ones with low value stamps because the context would evoke a Darwinian algorithm that had a routine for spotting or uncovering cheaters. A vigorous debate between these two factions ensued, but we will not go into the full details in this chapter (see Cheng & Holyoak, 1989, and Cosmides & Tooby, 1992.) Here our aim is to discuss what we think are the underlying limitations of pragmatic reasoning schemas and Darwinian algorithms.

Consider pragmatic schema theory first. One advantage this proposal has which has received little comment so far lies in its production rules. These specify actions which are taken under certain conditions to achieve presupposed goals. Thus this theory seems well placed to account for any type of practical reasoning, which is essentially aimed at inferring which actions to perform (see Chapter 4 for more on the importance of goals in practical reasoning). However, these schemas are only designed for pragmatic inference, and contain unanalysed deontic terms, such as "must" and "may". This means that the theory cannot be a full explanation of deontic reasoning. To provide that, we need a semantics and epistemology to explain how such terms are used, why sentences containing them are asserted as true or acceptable, and how such sentences are justified. In our view, this can only be done by taking into account people's preferences among states of affairs, which must be done anyway to explain why an outcome of some action is thought of as a "goal". Authorities, for example, have certain preferences and so lay down regulations to try to ensure that other people bring about the preferred states of affairs—i.e. the goals of the authorities. Given what an authority prefers, others would probably prefer that as well, out of respect or fear, and would justify their deontic statements and their actions accordingly.

There is also a problem with Cheng and Holyoak's taxonomy of deontic rules. Conditionals of the above abstract form, about action A and precondition P, they called "permissions". But these are really a type of conditional obligation, which state that before one takes action A precondition P ought to be satisfied. In many contexts in which such conditionals are used, one can *pragmatically* infer that one has permission to do A once P is satisfied. Cheng and Holyoak were themselves aware that one cannot always do this, as sometimes there can be more than one precondition for getting permission to perform an action. Permission and obligation differ at the deepest logical and semantic level, and we should not make pragmatic distinctions which potentially confuse them.

A deontic logician would point out that in most deontic logics obligation and permission are taken as duals of each other, like necessity and possibility in alethic modal logic (see Chellas, 1980). In other words, that we are obliged to do something logically implies that we do not have permission not to do it; and that we have permission to do something logically implies that we are not obliged not to do it. Moreover, in most deontic logics, that we are obliged to do something logically implies that we have permission to do it. Of course, these logical relations seem obvious for most of our uses of deontic terms, and presumably ordinary people more or less conform to them most of the time. But these relations do not follow from schema theory as it stands, for to repeat, it was designed to be a pragmatic theory and has not so far been supplemented by a semantic one. This is its main limitation as we see it.

As we have already said, our view is that the semantics of deontic statements should ultimately be given in terms of people's preferences among states of affairs. Now to talk about these preferences is just to talk about subjective utilities in the technical sense of decision theory. Technically as well, to say that we get a benefit, or suffer a cost, in a state of affairs is just to say that we prefer it to our present state, or vice versa.

This brings us back to Cosmides. By emphasising the prime role of social exchange in a certain kind of deontic context, she introduced reciprocal benefits and costs for the first time into the explanatory field. However, we cannot on that basis subscribe to her original theory. For one thing, it is false to claim, as she seemed to do, that only selection tasks with rules asserting her benefit/cost relation reliably lead to facilitation: the Sears rule (see Fig. 5.2) is not of this kind (Wason made this point to us in a personal communication in 1987), and neither is the "AIDS" rule we used to demonstrate this problem in one of our early experiments (see Manktelow & Over, 1990). In this experiment, people were given the following conditional prudential obligation, so called because it prescribes prudent action: "If you clean up spilt blood, then you must wear rubber gloves." Four record cards were provided, showing on one side whether or not a person had cleaned up blood, and on the other side whether they had worn gloves. Most subjects chose the correct cards, the one showing "cleaned up blood" and the one showing "did not wear gloves".

To explain this performance, we can hardly describe cleaning up blood as a benefit in a social exchange for which one has to pay the cost of wearing rubber gloves. Of course, one can argue on evolutionary grounds that people should be fairly good at prudential reasoning, at least if this is about matters which would have affected their reproductive success under primitive conditions. They should have some ability to spot and then avoid what threatens their lives. Cosmides has indeed moved on to study the special characteristics of this kind of reasoning (see Cosmides & Tooby, 1992). Even so, her Darwinian algorithms are at least like pragmatic schemas in that they do not explain why people consider deontic statements true or acceptable.

We cannot go into the full details of our approach to the semantics of deontic statements here (see Manktelow & Over, 1991 and 1992, and Over & Manktelow, 1993 for more details). But we can reveal more about it by fleshing out a little what we have said about authorities that lay down regulations. Suppose we are university authorities considering stating certain regulations about smoking on campus. We construct a mental model in which students smoke in lectures and compare it to one in which they do not do so. We much prefer the type of state of affairs modelled in the latter to that modelled in the former. Perhaps our preference is purely prudential—we are worried about being sued by non-smokers. Perhaps it is moral—we are thinking of the rights of non-smokers. For the semantics, it does not matter why we have this preference, but on the basis of it, we assert that students must not smoke in lectures. If we had been indifferent as between what the two mental models represented, or preferred a type of state in which students smoke in lectures, then we would have asserted that students may smoke in lectures.

Considering some conditional regulation—e.g. "If a lecture hall is well ventilated then students may smoke in it"—we would have compared a mental model of students smoking in a well-ventilated lecture hall with one of students not smoking in such a hall. Under this condition, our original preference might have changed for whatever reason, and then we would have given students permission to smoke in a well-ventilated hall. To make an informed judgement in this case, we would need to know how the ventilation referred to in the antecedent of this conditional would affect the smoking referred to in the consequent. This might in turn require us to represent possible causal relations between ventilation and smoking, and even to have a model of the particular ventilation system in our university. No matter how far we went into the question, our object would be to assess the conditional probability that some student smoking is safe for non-smokers given that it takes place in a well-ventilated hall. Making good deontic statements, whether conditional or not, does call for some knowledge of causal relationships, but we cannot say more about this here.

We do, however, point out below that subjective probability judgements are necessary for all deontic statements.

Simplifying and being more schematic, we assert that students *ought* to perform action A (whether this is expressed linguistically as a "positive" one like "smoking" or as a "negative" one like "not smoking") rather than not-A if and only if we prefer their performing A to their performing not-A. We assert that they *may* perform A rather than not-A if and only if we are either indifferent between their performing A and their performing not-A, or even prefer that they perform A to not-A. From this it follows in our simple example that, if students are under an obligation not to smoke, then they have permission not to smoke; and if they do not have permission to smoke, then they are obliged not to smoke. So this illustrates how one can get these and the other logical relations right using this kind of semantics.

There is, however, much more to explaining deontic discourse and reasoning than presenting the underlying semantics. Subtle pragmatic and social factors must also be taken account of, but our use of mental models can naturally be extended, as we shall show, to help us to do this. Cheng and Holyoak (1985, p. 398) pointed out that "permissions and obligations are typically imposed by an authority to achieve some social purpose." This does not actually apply to prudential deontic statements we make about ourselves, such as when we say that we really ought to go jogging more often. Some philosophers, it is true, have spoken as if such statements were made by our "stronger selves" and aimed at our "weaker selves" to try to help us overcome weakness of the will. But the analogy with a proper social authority is certainly stretched. It would be good to see experimental investigations of prudential deontic reasoning and weakness of the will, but most published work has so far concentrated on the kind of truly social case Cheng and Holyoak drew attention to. (We say more about deontic reasoning and weakness of the will in Over & Manktelow, 1993.)

In our work on social examples, we wanted to study proper permission statements, which are expressed using "may", and to get underneath talk of goals or purposes by considering people's subjective preferences. This allows us to make use of technical notions from decision theory, particularly those of subjective utility and benefits and costs and, as we shall see, subjective probability. In turn, this allows us to explain why an outcome is a goal for a person—it has some utility for that person greater than other presupposed outcomes. Let us then consider the following conditional permission: "If you tidy your room, then you may go out to play." Suppose this is spoken by a mother to her son in the standard kind of case we are all so familiar with. The mother would not assert this if she was not indifferent to whether her son went out or not, or preferred him to go out, given that he tidied his room. So much follows from the semantics. But now there is much to say about the pragmatics and social context of this utterance. The mother has to be an authority over the son if the utterance is to be felicitous (the son cannot be an adult, or even a young adolescent in our experience). If that is so, the mother can usually supply benefits to the son, or extract costs from him, and this affects the deontic statements he will accept or assert.

In the standard case, the mother prefers tidy to untidy rooms, and the son prefers going out to not going out. If either of these preference relations does not hold, then the utterance is again infelicitous, and will not perform its intended function; it would be strange, in the first place, for the mother to come out with it, and in the second place, it would not bring about the desired behaviour. In most cases, the son could infer pragmatically from his mother's utterance that the only way he can get permission to go out is by tidying his room. The mother could cancel this suggestion with further utterances, but without these the son's pragmatic inference would be justified.

We can now see that, in this kind of example, there are four basic ways in which the mother or the son could produce an outcome which was a cost to just one of them. The son could tidy the room, but the mother could refuse to allow him to go out. The son might not tidy his room but his mother might allow him to go (perhaps the mother suffers from weakness of the will: she cannot face a row with her son). The son could tidy his room and yet not go out. (This could again be weakness of the will: the son does want to go out but is afraid to do so for some reason. Another possibility is that the son could forget that he can go out once he tidies his room.) Finally, the son could go out without tidying his room.

Let us call someone occupying the social role or "perspective" illustrated by the mother the *agent*, and someone occupying that illustrated by the son the *actor*. In our type of example, the agent will utter a rule for the actor having the general form, "If p is made true by the actor then the actor may make q true". Then we can state more abstractly, for the kind of cases we have been describing, the following four ways in which just one of the two roles suffers a cost or a loss:

1. The agent sees that p is true but does not allow q to be made true.
2. The agent sees that p is not true but still allows q to be made true.
3. The actor makes p true but does not make q true.
4. The actor does not make p true but still makes q true.

In various experiments, we constructed selection tasks in which the rule was a permission of the form just given in the kind of context just described. One scenario was actually based on the mother/son example, but another concerned a shop (the agent), which was offering free gifts to customers (the actors). The shop rule read, "If you spend more than £100, then you may take a free gift". Not only does this clearly refer to subjective utilities for the two parties, but the accompanying scenario stated that laying down the rule was an attempt to increase sales. The utility of this possible outcome for the shop gave the rule a purpose. Now the subjects were queried in four different selection tasks to see if they could pick out cards which would reveal the four cases above. They were asked to select cards which reveal whether the shop had not given the customers what they were entitled to (case 1), had given customers more than they were entitled to (case 2), and so on. Thus for the four tasks, the predictions were that subjects would select cards showing, in case 1, p and not-q; in case 2, not-p and q; in case 3, p and not-q; in case 4, not-p and q. In all cases these predictions were strongly confirmed (see Manktelow & Over, 1991).

Other researchers have reported similar results; the role of social perspective has been independently studied by several groups. In fact, it was implicit in Cosmides' (1989) work: her "social law" rules (e.g. in Experiment 1) specified violation on the part of the actor, while her "private exchange" rules (e.g. in Experiment 2), which she considered identical (p.209) except that they were private and not social, specified violation on the part of the agent. Social perspective takes a much more prominent role in Cosmides' other writings than it did in her original *Cognition* paper (1989; see e.g. Cosmides & Tooby, 1989; 1992).

Politzer and Nguyen-Xuan (1992) used a very similar (and independently devised) content about shops and gifts to that above in order to explore perspective effects in assessing potential breaches of what they termed conditional promises. The rule in this case was, "If the purchase exceeds 10,000 francs, then the salesman must stick on the back of the receipt a voucher gift for a gold bracelet", and Politzer and Nguyen-Xuan had subjects assess whether the rule had been "honestly applied" from the perspective of the promiser (the agent, in our terms), the promisee (the actor), and a neutral third party. Their results were not as clear-cut as ours (most probably because their scenarios did not state precisely what the utilities were for each party, and their instructions did not cue their subjects as strongly), but were nevertheless consistent with them: the promiser condition corresponds with our case 1 above, yielding a high proportion of p, not-q selections, and the promisee condition corresponds with our case 4, yielding a high proportion of not-p, q selections.

Gigerenzer and Hug (1992) similarly distinguished the two roles of agent and actor, which they refer to as Party A and Party B in a social contract (following Cosmides' scheme). They link this notion with that of social contracts having what they describe as unilateral and bilateral cheating options. The postal task has only a unilateral cheating option:

you, the sender (i.e. actor), can try to cheat the post office (agent) by understamping a sealed letter, but the post office cannot cheat you (as far as this rule is concerned) in any way. On one level, the shop rules are examples of bilateral cheating options. The shop and the customers can cheat each other, by taking or spending the right money without supplying or receiving the gifts, or by taking or issuing the gifts without paying or receiving the right money. Gigerenzer and Hug used different contents which served the same purpose. They spelt out in the accompanying scenarios what the benefits and costs were for both agent and actor. Once again, their results were consistent with ours and with Politzer and Nguyen-Xuan's, and were stronger than the latter's: a case 1 scenario produced a high rate of p, not-q selections, and a case 4 scenario produced a high rate of not-p, q selections. One might, however, wonder how far even this generalised notion of cheating can explain what is going on in these cases. At a higher level (in our scenario at least), the shop will eventually suffer a cost, by losing sales, if it takes the right money without supplying the gifts.

Light, Girotto, and Legrenzi (1990) have demonstrated that the ability to switch one's social perspective in a deontic context is present in children. They used the permission rule (though they termed it a promise), "If you get more than ten housepoints in a week then you can have a sweet", uttered by a teacher to some pupils. Most were able to select the instance showing a potential cheater from the pupils' perspective (not-p, q). When the scenario was modified to allow for the possibility of cheating on the part of the teacher, children were also able to adopt this perspective, though with some understandable difficulty, given their greater experience in the role of pupil rather than teacher: it would have been easier for them to construe clear preferences in the former case. This is just one of a striking series of demonstrations of children's general proficiency at deontic reasoning given to us by Girotto and his colleagues.

SCHEMAS AND MODELS IN THE EXPLANATION OF DEONTIC REASONING

The majority view among researchers in this area at present is that deontic thinking is mediated by some kind of schema—that is, by domain-specific rules which, when evoked by the content of a problem, deliver appropriate inferences algorithmically. We have seen that there are two major factions of schema theory: Cheng and Holyoak's and its descendants (e.g. in the work of Politzer and Nguyen-Xuan and Girotto and colleagues), and Cosmides' Darwinian algorithms (see also the work of Gigerenzer and Hug). Our approach by no means rejects these ideas completely, and in general we think the mind will be found to contain a miscellany of representations, including different types of schemas and of mental models. Certainly much deontic thought seems "schematic" or "stereotyped" by falling into fixed, almost automatic patterns in certain contexts; for example, our use of traffic regulations to infer what we should do when we are driving.

However, we hold that the notion of mental models is of basic importance in deontic thought. Someone must think up possible traffic regulations in the first place, and by comparing different possible states of affairs decide which ones to adopt. Sometimes we are presented with a new regulation and have to decide whether to accept it. Then we need to compare the result of acting on the regulation with the result of not doing this (so perhaps defying an authority), and see which possible outcome we prefer. Sometimes we face a new deontic problem and have to make our own deontic statements about it, and be prepared to justify these in terms of which states are to be preferred to others. We take these points to indicate that mental models are needed to account for the logic, semantics, and epistemology of deontic discourse.

In addition, we would argue that mental models are used by people to understand the kind of relationships they are presented with in deontic selection tasks. That is, people construct models in these cases, from pragmatic information as well as the semantics of the rules, to represent the different parties and their benefits and costs in the possible outcomes. To illustrate how this may be done, we use a notation adopted from Johnson-Laird and Byrne (1991) to represent what follows from the semantics and pragmatics of a deontic utterance in the kind of social context we have investigated.

Take the specific type of two-party conditional permission uttered in a context like that of our experiments—i.e. "If you do make p hold then you may make q hold". For this utterance to do its job in this kind of case, the actor (that is, the person to whom it is directed) must prefer q to not-q; in our experiments, we also specified that the party uttering the rule (the agent) preferred p to not-p. Without at least the first of these assumptions, the utterance will be infelicitous, and misunderstanding could occur. Each party to this relation, or a third party from the outside who wants to understand it, needs to have the following initial structure to their mental models:

From agent's perspective: *From actor's perspective:*
p+   q   +   p   q+   +
. . .   . . .

The + sign against either component, p or q, denotes a benefit from that instance. The + signs to the right show each party's utility for that particular outcome: the agent prefers outcomes where p is fulfilled, the actor prefers outcomes where q is fulfilled, so both will be happy if both p and q are fulfilled. The three dots indicate possible further, implicit contingencies, in which the preferred or non-preferred situations may arise. These contingencies will only be "fleshed out"—explicitly represented—when the task demands it. Fully fleshed out models would look like this:

From agent's perspective:			*From actor's perspective:*		
p+	q	+	p	q+	+
p+	¬q	+	p	¬q	–
¬p	q	–	¬p	q+	+
¬p	¬q	–	¬p	¬q	–

The – sign denotes a cost; ¬ denotes "not". The cost may come, for example, from being "cheated", from having an expectation unfulfilled, or from having one's authority defied. In experiments, subjects are placed in the perspective of agent or actor by the surrounding story and will readily consider the following models when explicitly cued to do so (see Manktelow & Over, 1991):

Case 1:

p	q	+ for both agent and actor
p	¬q	– for actor, + for agent
. . .		

Case 2:

p	q	+ for both
¬p	q	– for agent, + for actor
. . .		

Case 3:

p	q	+ for both
p	¬q	– for actor, + for agent
. . .		

Case 4:

p	q	+ for both
¬p	q	– for agent, + for actor
. . .		

In our own and others' experiments, which we reviewed earlier, subjects were successfully cued to look for outcomes in which there was a cost for one party or the other: these are the outcomes denoted by the – signs in the four cases above. The – signs in these representations lead directly to predictions about choices in selection tasks. The actor in cases 1 and 3 decides to select the p card and the not-q card because there is some chance that these will reveal that the actor has suffered a loss. Similarly, the agent decides to select the not-p card and the q card in cases 2 and 4 because there is some chance that these cards will reveal that the agent has suffered a loss. Obviously, people need to become aware of outcomes which cost them something in order to take corrective action immediately or in the future. Our supposition then is that there are procedures for identifying representations of possible costs and benefits in mental models.

Several points are worth noting about this formulation. First, note that there are two routes to each empirical prediction in selection tasks. Other approaches do not make this explicit, and have always only tested cases 1 and 4. We tested all four cases in the shop example. Secondly, it reveals another non-preferred situation which people should be sensitive to: when neither p nor q is fulfilled (e.g. the room is not tidied and the son did not go out). Both parties will be unhappy with this outcome, and it should be possible to show that people can be cued to an awareness of it in experiments: subjects should pick the not-p and not-q cards in a selection task. However, as far as we know no one has tested for it. Thirdly, where the cues to perspective are weak, subjects will waver between them, or cover them both (i.e. choose all four cards in the selection task), and when cues to utility are weak there will be no strong response tendency, either toward the p, not-q or not-p, q selection. The research literature confirms both these predictions (see e.g. Manktelow & Over, 1991, Experiment 1 and Politzer & Nguyen-Xuan, 1992 on the first, and Cosmides, 1989 and Manktelow & Over, 1992 on the second).

Fourthly, this way of using mental models departs from that of its progenitors, as they have pointed out (Johnson-Laird & Byrne, 1992). They offer an interpretation-based alternative consistent with their original exposition in which the perspective effects are tied to biconditional readings of the rule and to cues to what is "not permissible". Utilities are excluded. We think this misses the essence of deontic thinking about actions, which centres on preferences between states of affairs brought about by people. The subjects' search for counter-examples in the original theory of mental models (see Chapter 6 in this volume) is replaced in deontic selection tasks by outcomes which should not occur, because other outcomes are preferred to them by at least one party. That is what being not permissible means, semantically. Cognitions of utility are central to deontic thinking (see Manktelow & Over, 1992).

Using mental models to explain deontic reasoning yields certain advantages over present schema theories. Johnson-Laird and Byrne's construct of implicit models seems particularly useful in this context, because of the richness and complexity of deontic thought which the experiments have begun to reveal, and which rigid schema theories alone cannot account for. Perhaps the most promising way of generalising schema theory would be to give the schemas "slots" in which preferences, or benefits and costs, could be inserted from contextual information. We think that something can be done along these lines which would be interesting to compare with mental models theory. In fact, when both theories are fully worked out, the differences between them might be shown to be more apparent than real.

DEONTIC REASONING AND DECISION MAKING

Deontic reasoning and decision making are deeply related to each other, and this is well illustrated in deontic selection tasks. The subjects are asked, in effect, to take a role or perspective in these tasks, and then to make decisions which will possibly reveal violations of the rules, or at least of understandings between the different parties based on the rules. In all deontic selection tasks so far studied, the cards correctly chosen are ones which could show that the role or perspective of the subject was suffering a cost. That is, in this role or perspective, one prefers one's current state of affairs to the outcome that might be revealed by the cards. One has to have some ability to make decisions which could reveal serious costs to avoid the risk of suffering them continually.

It should, however, be possible to demonstrate people's sensitivity to the possibility of a gain, as well as a loss, but producing such demonstrations has not been so straightforward. In one experiment in Manktelow and Over (1990), we investigated a case in which the p, not-q outcome would mean missing out on a benefit rather than suffering a cost. The rule we used was, "If you have a winning line then you must shout BINGO to win a prize". To have a winning line but not to shout BINGO is to fail to get a benefit, rather than to suffer a cost. But we did not find significant facilitation in this task: not enough subjects chose just the p and not-q cards. This suggests that costs may be weighted more heavily than benefits in deontic selection tasks, and that it may be possible to measure the extent to which this is so. Finding that this held and measuring it would enable us to make a specific connection with what descriptive decision theories imply about loss aversion, such as the classic prospect theory of Kahneman and Tversky (1979).

The two fundamental concepts of decision making are subjective utility and subjective probability. The fact that one outcome is preferred to another is not enough in itself to make us pursue the former rather than the latter. For successfully securing the latter outcome may be much more probable than securing the former. Combining subjective probability and utility we get subjective *expected* utility, and it is really this, rather than just utility judgements alone, which should affect deontic reasoning as well as decision making. However, only very recently have researchers started to manipulate probability judgements in deontic selection tasks. Kirby (1994) has reported some interesting results on this and also on the possibility that subjects may weight losses more heavily than gains in deontic selection tasks.

Kirby modifies the well-known drinking-age task of Griggs and Cox (1982). Here the rule is, "If a person is drinking beer then the person must be over 21 years of age". Kirby's scenario asks subjects to imagine that they are a security guard who has the job of making sure that people conform to rules like this. The significant change is that Kirby then presents the subjects with six cards: one showing "drinking beer"; one "drinking ginger-ale"; one "22 years of age"; one "19 years of age"; one "12 years of age"; and one "4 years of age". This means the subjects see a p card, a not-p card, a q card, and three not-q cards. The subjects should grasp that the probability of finding an under-age drinker declines with the age of the possible violator, and this probability judgement should affect the cards it is worth examining. In line with a decision theoretic account of this task, Kirby does find a decline in the proportion of subjects who select each of the three not-q cards, with the highest proportion selecting the "19 years" card, the next highest the "12 years" card, and the lowest the "4 years" card.

Along with this manipulation, Kirby makes use of three special conditions, separately added to the baseline of a standard drinking-age task. The DON'T CHECK condition states that the subjects' employer does not want them to offend innocent customers, and that they will be fired if they do so. The DON'T MISS condition states that their employer is very concerned about illegal drinking, and that they will be fired if they miss a guilty person. The CHECK condition states that their employer is very concerned about illegal drinking, and that they will get a bonus if they catch a guilty person. Given everything we have said in this chapter about subjective utility judgements and deontic tasks, we would predict significantly fewer card selections in the DON'T CHECK condition than in the baseline, but more in the DON'T MISS condition than in the baseline. This is just what Kirby predicted and found.

There was no significant difference in Kirby's results between the CHECK condition and the baseline. Now note that this condition tells subjects that they will get a benefit (a bonus) if they catch guilty people, rather than suffer a cost (getting fired) if they miss a guilty person as in the DON'T MISS condition. Again, this result suggests that people weight costs more heavily than benefits; but Kirby's tasks are really too rich in pragmatic suggestions, like our bingo example, for us to be sure that this difference in weighting has been found in deontic selection tasks. More work needs to be done to confirm the presence of this in deontic tasks and to measure the extent of it. (For more on this, and the important points Kirby makes about abstract selection tasks, see Over & Evans, 1994.)

We have also been exploring the relation between subjective probability and utility in deontic reasoning, using an extended version of the selection task. We adapted another of Cheng and Holyoak's problems from their original 1985 paper (the immigration task). The rule they used was, "If the form says ENTERING on one side, then the other side includes cholera among the list of diseases." Cards showed ENTERING (p), TRANSIT (not-p), and "cholera" either present in (q) or absent from (not-q) the list of diseases. Nearly all subjects given the role of an immigration officer and an appropriate rationale successfully selected the potential violating cases—i.e. just the p card and the not-q card.

We adapted the content for our British subjects and used a larger array of cards (20 in all), with repeated instances of each logical case. This enabled the insertion of a simple probability manipulation, by adding information on the p and not-p cards about the countries of origin of the passengers they referred to. Half had a tropical country named on them, and half a European country, and the scenario gave a simple rationale for the problem. Part of this stated, in effect, that there would be a serious cost if people with cholera were allowed to enter the country. Another part was aimed at people's probability judgements, and pointed out that cholera was common in tropical countries. Neither piece of information would have any effect if subjects did strictly what they were asked to, which was to look for violators of the rule—i.e. people entering the country without "cholera" on their inoculation list. However, we found that while 98% of subjects chose the "tropical" p cards, only 57% chose the European ones (Over, Manktelow, & Sutherland, 1994).

Further experiments with the large array but without the information about country of origin clearly showed that its effect was to suppress selection of the European cards: the name of a European country thus acted as a "disabling condition" (cf. Cummins, Lubart, Alksnis, & Rist, 1991) which caused these cards to be seen as less relevant to the goal of keeping cholera out the country (see Chapter 7 of this volume for an extended discussion of relevance in reasoning). The goal was given by relative utility judgements—i.e. that it is preferable to keep cholera out of the country than to let it in. What was relevant to attaining it was based on comparing conditional probability judgements: it is less probable that people have cholera given that they come from a European country than given that they come from a tropical country.

Again consistent with a decision theoretic analysis of deontic tasks, card selections are based on judgements, not only of the utility of possible outcomes, but also on how probable certain outcomes are. One should note that a card with the name of a European country on it is more likely to reveal a violation than one with a name of a tropical country. The point is that people entering from a European country are less likely to bring cholera with them, even if they are not inoculated against it, and so the expected cost of missing such people is low. Furthermore, one might also note that a person entering from Europe without inoculation is "cheating" in Cosmides' sense; however, this behaviour is apparently unimportant (from the agent's perspective) because such a person is thought unlikely to be carrying the disease. Cheating is thus overridden by considerations of probability with utility: the notion of cheating itself is not sufficient to determine choices in such a context.

The founders of normative decision theory were well aware that they were specifying the principles of an idealised notion of rationality (see particularly Savage, 1954). In the light of the work of Simon (1957; 1983) we can now describe their theory as one of "unbounded" rationality, whereas actual human reasoning is very much "bounded". We cannot always ensure that our probability judgements are coherent and that a preference relation satisfies the axioms of normative decision theory. One of these axioms states that, for any possibilities x and y, we prefer x to y, prefer y to x, or are indifferent between x and y. But ordinary deontic conflicts and dilemmas show that we cannot always conform to this axiom. Even a relatively simple moral question, such as whether we should lie to spare the feelings of a friend, can illustrate this. Do we prefer lying to hurting our friend, hurting our friend to lying, or are we indifferent between these? Such questions can be too difficult for us to answer in the "bounded" time given to us. Researchers on decision theory and game theory have long been aware of the importance of studying deontic conflicts and dilemmas. Even so, actual deontic reasoning in these cases has not yet been properly investigated by reasoning researchers. This is another topic on which we hope to see much more work in the future. (Over & Manktelow, 1993, have more on these conflicts and dilemmas, and point out that these have raised questions even about deontic logical relations.)

Our descriptive approach to deontic reasoning goes most naturally with the version of normative decision theory formulated by Jeffrey (1983). We can illustrate this kind of theory by considering two "positive" actions and their "negations", expressed in propositions. There are the actions we perform when making true or making false the proposition that we take up jogging, and the actions we perform when making true or making false the proposition that we give up smoking. To apply the theory as a normative one, we construct what might be called a generalised truth table (Jeffrey, 1983, Chapter 5). In it there are four rows indicating the four possible combinations of the actions:

we take up jogging and we give up smoking;
we take up jogging and we do not give up smoking;
we do not take up jogging and we do give up smoking; and
we do not take up jogging and we do not give up smoking.

Each of these rows represents a "generic" state of affairs under which many more specific ones fall. For example, the first row covers both states in which we perform the two "positive" actions and our health improves, as well as ones in which we perform both these actions and we are run over by a bus while out jogging. Finally, we assign numbers to these rows representing their subjective expected utilities.

The final step is the really difficult one. To take it, we obviously need some idea of how much we prefer health to illness, but we would also like to know the probability that we will have good health and the probability that we will be run over by a bus, in each of the generic states of affairs. Assuming we can make all the relevant preference and probability judgements, we have ideal grounds for making a rational decision, and saying which actions we *ought to* perform and *may* perform. The former are those performed in all the generic states of affairs with the highest expected utility, and the latter are those performed in at least one of these states. For example, suppose in our list above that the first row and the third come out equal in expected utility, with the other two rows lower. Then we ought to give up smoking and may take up jogging.

What we have just sketched is very much an ideal way of making decisions about what we ought to do and may do. We agree with Johnson-Laird and Byrne (1991) that people do not construct mental truth tables in their ordinary reasoning, let alone work out numbers for the rows representing their expected utilities. Truth tables are an ideal system for extensional propositional reasoning, while the mental model theory of Johnson-Laird and Byrne is a "bounded" system people could use for the same purpose in a rough and ready way. By constructing mental models to evaluate a propositional argument, people are, in effect, looking for a row of a truth table in which the premises are true and the conclusion false. In our view, there must be a similar relation between the ideal tables of a Jeffrey-type decision theory and the actual, "bounded" mental models used for ordinary deontic reasoning. The latter will not always yield perfect deontic reasoning and the maximising of subjective expected utility, but may still be a serviceable system for doing reasonably well. We make a couple of suggestions about how it is "bounded" before concluding this chapter.

When people are thinking about whether they ought to take up jogging, they generally construct a mental model of their taking up jogging and compare it with one of their not doing so. They do not normally express the advantages or disadvantages of an activity like jogging in quantitative terms, to the extent that normative decision theorists would recommend, but often just represent a preference one way or the other. This is why we have merely used + or − in our examples of deontic mental models above. Often people do not even break down their mental model of not taking up jogging into ways they could satisfy this, such as by doing some other sport or by inactivity. Following Legrenzi, Girotto, and Johnson-Laird (1993) we would say that they "focus" on the advantages or disadvantages of jogging, and will only "defocus" and consider not jogging in detail under special circumstances. Moreover, people will not usually attempt to model more than one pair of alternatives at the same time—it will seem too difficult, under the constraints of working memory, to model together jogging and not jogging and smoking and not smoking. They will tend to construct models of the latter alternative separately, if they want to think about whether they ought to give up smoking. All this means that they will sometimes miss the very best overall course of action for them to take, since this can be some combination of specific actions, such as going for long walks and giving up smoking.

CONCLUSIONS

In this chapter we have looked at a field of research, deontic reasoning, which has only recently become highly active, in spite of the ubiquity of deontic thought in everyday cognition. On the basis of our own and others' research, we consider that this form of thought is best explained in terms of mental representations of benefits, costs, probability, and social role. The richness and diversity of deontic thinking seem hard to reconcile with the kinds of schema theories which have dominated contemporary psychological research on reasoning. However, one positive consequence of the view we have urged here should be to bring about a convergence of interest between the fields of reasoning and decision making.

Deontic reasoning is so fundamental for human thought and action that it has been studied for a long time non-experimentally in moral philosophy and the law, and yet as we have seen in this chapter, there is obviously much to learn through its controlled experimental study. Deontic versions of Wason's selection task have played a large part in the beginning of this enterprise, and will surely continue to do so.

REFERENCES

Audi, R. (1989). *Practical reasoning*. London: Routledge & Kegan Paul.

Chellas, B.F. (1980). *Modal logic: An introduction*. Cambridge: Cambridge University Press.

Cheng, P.W., & Holyoak, K.J. (1985). Pragmatic reasoning schemas. *Cognitive Psychology, 17*, 391–416.

Cheng, P.W., & Holyoak, K.J. (1989). On the natural selection of reasoning theories. *Cognition, 33*, 285–313.

Cheng, P.W., Holyoak, K.J., Nisbett, R.E., & Oliver, L.M. (1986). Pragmatic versus syntactic approaches to training deductive reasoning. *Cognitive Psychology, 18,* 293–328.

Cosmides, L. (1985). *Deduction or Darwinian algorithms? An explanation of the "elusive" content effect on the Wason selection task.* Unpublished PhD thesis, Harvard University.

Cosmides, L. (1989). The logic of social exchange: Has natural selection shaped how humans reason? Studies with the Wason selection task. *Cognition, 31,* 187–316.

Cosmides, L., & Tooby, J. (1989). Evolutionary psychology and the generation of culture, Part II: A computational theory of social exchange. *Ethology and Sociobiology, 10,* 51–97.

Cosmides, L., & Tooby, J. (1992). Cognitive adaptations for social exchange. In J.H. Barkow, L. Cosmides, & J. Tooby (Eds.), *The adapted mind.* Oxford: Oxford University Press.

Cummins, D.D., Lubart, T., Alksnis, O., & Rist, R. (1991). Conditional reasoning and causation. *Memory and Cognition, 19,* 274–282.

Evans, J.St.B.T., Over, D.E., & Manktelow, K.I. (1993). Reasoning, decision making, and rationality. *Cognition, 49,* 165–187.

Gigerenzer, G., & Hug, K. (1992). Domain-specific reasoning: Social contracts, cheating, and perspective change. *Cognition, 43,* 127–171.

Griggs, R.A., & Cox, J.R. (1982). The elusive thematic materials effect in Wason's selection task. *British Journal of Psychology, 73,* 407–420.

Jeffrey, R. (1983). *The logic of decision.* Second Edition. Chicago: University of Chicago Press.

Johnson-Laird, P.N., & Byrne, R.M.J. (1991). *Deduction.* Hove, UK: Lawrence Erlbaum Associates Ltd.

Johnson-Laird, P.N., & Byrne, R.M.J. (1992). Modal reasoning, models, and Manktelow and Over. *Cognition, 43,* 173–182.

Johnson-Laird, P.N., Legrenzi, P., & Legrenzi, M.S. (1972). Reasoning and a sense of reality. *British Journal of Psychology, 63,* 395–400.

Kahneman, D., & Tversky, A. (1979). Prospect theory: An analysis of decision under risk. *Econometrica, 47,* 263–291.

Kirby, K.N. (1994). Probabilities and utilities of fictional outcomes in Wason's four card selection task. *Cognition, 51,* 1–28.

Kroger, K., Cheng, P.W., & Holyoak, K.J. (1993). Evoking the permission schema: The impact of explicit negation and a violation-checking context. *Quarterly Journal of Experimental Psychology, 46A,* 615–635.

Legrenzi, P., Girotto, V., & Johnson-Laird, P.N. (1993). Focusing in reasoning and decision making. *Cognition, 49,* 37–66.

Light, P.H., Girotto, V., & Legrenzi, P. (1990). Children's reasoning on conditional promises and permissions. *Cognitive Development, 5,* 369–383.

Manktelow, K.I., & Over, D.E. (1990). Deontic thought and the selection task. In K.J. Gilhooly, M.T.G. Keane, R.H. Logie, and G. Erdos (Eds.), *Lines of thinking: Reflections on the psychology of thought, Vol. 1.* Chichester: Wiley.

Manktelow, K.I., & Over, D.E. (1991). Social roles and utilities in reasoning with deontic conditionals. *Cognition, 39,* 85–105.

Manktelow, K.I., & Over, D.E. (1992). Utility and deontic reasoning: A reply to Johnson-Laird and Byrne. *Cognition, 43,* 183–188.

Over, D.E., & Evans, J.St.B.T. (1994). Hits and misses: Kirby on the selection task. *Cognition, 52*, 235–243.

Over, D.E., & Manktelow, K.I. (1993). Rationality, utility, and deontic reasoning. In K.I. Manktelow & D.E. Over (Eds.), *Rationality: Psychological and philosophical perspectives*. London: Routledge & Kegan Paul.

Over, D.E., Manktelow, K.I., & Sutherland, E.J. (1994, January). *Subjective probability and conditionals*. Paper presented at the London meeting of the Experimental Psychology Society, University College London.

Politzer, G., & Nguyen-Xuan, A. (1992). Reasoning about conditional promises and warnings: Darwinian algorithms, mental models, relevance judgements, or pragmatic schemas? *Quarterly Journal of Experimental Psychology, 44A*, 401–421.

Rumelhart, D.E. (1980). Schemata: The building blocks of cognition. In R.J. Spiro, B.C. Bruce, and W.F. Brewer (Eds.), *Theoretical issues in reading comprehension*. Hillsdale, NJ: Lawrence Erlbaum Associates Inc.

Savage, L. (1954). *The foundations of statistics*. New York: Wiley.

Simon, H.A. (1957). *Models of man: Social and rational*. New York: Wiley.

Simon, H.A. (1983). *Reason in human affairs*. Stanford: Stanford University Press.

Wason, P.C. (1968). Reasoning about a rule. *Quarterly Journal of Experimental Psychology, 20*, 273–281.

CHAPTER SIX

Inference and Mental Models

Philip N. Johnson-Laird

Department of Psychology, Princeton University, USA

INTRODUCTION

Suppose that the facts are:

> The defendant left town before the restaurant closed. The arsonist put a match to the cooking oil in the kitchen after the restaurant closed.

What conclusion would you draw? Probably, you would infer that the defendant could not have started the fire because, barring some remote scenario, the culprit must have been there to start the fire. The question for psychologists is: what mental process enabled you to reach your conclusion? In principle, it could be syntactic or semantic. Most psychologists who have studied the topic favour syntactic theories, but over the past decade a growing number have entertained the possibility of a semantic theory. My plan in this chapter is to describe one particular semantic theory—the theory of mental models—and to illustrate its power by applying it to three areas of reasoning: first, a hitherto uninvestigated area (temporal reasoning), secondly an established area (reasoning with sentential connectives), and thirdly the most studied area of all (Peter Wason's selection task).

Before we can compare syntax and semantics, we need to be clear about the difference between them. The clearest distinction has been drawn by 20th century logicians. Syntax concerns the form of expressions. Thus, a syntactic process operates on the form of expressions represented in some medium, such as marks on paper. Such a process occurs in constructing a well-formed expression according to the rules of a grammar. It also occurs in deriving a conclusion from a set of premises according to formal rules of inference. The power of syntactic processes is that they apply to any content provided that it is expressed in the appropriate form. Semantics, in contrast, concerns the relations between expressions in a language and some domain outside the language—e.g. the relation between names in the language and the entities in the domain that they name. In a natural language, it is possible to use names, predicates, and other parts of speech to construct expressions that correspond to states of affairs in the world. The process is probably compositional with each syntactic rule in the grammar having an associated semantic rule that specifies how to combine the meanings of constituents according to the syntactic relations captured by the grammatical rule. In this way, the semantics of the language specifies the conditions in which a sentence would be true, and the actual state of affairs in the domain renders the sentence true or false depending on whether it satisfies these so-called "truth conditions". Of course, this picture is simplistic. Sentences in natural language do not have truth conditions, but rather their use in context has them. Similarly, certain aspects of idiomatic meaning are not compositional, and many speech acts do not seem to have truth conditions. We can be sure, however, that some assertions have truth conditions—otherwise, we should never be able to judge truth or falsity.

Syntax concerns form; semantics concerns truth. The burden of certain theorems in meta-logic is that an unbridgeable gulf exists between them (*pace* those theorists who seek to reduce meaning to syntax). As Gödel showed, there are truths in arithmetic that cannot be proved by any consistent syntactic method of inference. Now we can pose our central question—is the human inferential system syntactic or semantic? Does it manipulate expressions in a mental language according to purely syntactic principles akin to those of formal proofs, or does it proceed in a semantic way? And if the latter, what could the method be? Most theories of deductive reasoning have postulated a syntactic system of rules of inference (e.g. Braine & O'Brien, 1991; Macnamara, 1986; Osherson, 1974–76; Rips, 1983). Yet, for reasons that will become clear, the present paper defends the semantic theory developed originally by Johnson-Laird (1983) and later by Johnson-Laird and Byrne (1991).

THE THEORY OF MENTAL MODELS

A valid deduction, by definition, is one in which the conclusion must be true if the premises are true. What we need is a semantic method to test for this condition. Unfortunately, assertions can be true in indefinitely many different situations, and so it is out of the question to test that a conclusion holds true in all of them. If, *per impossible*, it could be done, then there would be a general semantic method for evaluating deductions.

Here is how it could be done for certain everyday inferences. Consider, again, the opening example about the temporal order of events, which can be abbreviated as follows:

a before b
c after b

where "a" stands for "the defendant left town", "b" stands for "the restaurant closed", and "c" stands for "the arsonist put a match to the cooking oil in the kitchen". The assertions say nothing about the actual durations of the events or about the intervals between them. Instead of trying to build models of all the different possible situations that satisfy these premises, let us build a "partial" model that leaves open the details and that captures only the structure that all the different situations have in common:

a   b   c

where the left-to-right axis corresponds to time, but the distances between the tokens have no significance. This model represents only the sequence of events, and it is the only possible model of the premises—i.e. no other model corresponding to a different sequence of the three events satisfies the premises.

Now consider the further assertion:

a before c.

It is true in the model, and, because there are no other models of the premises, it must be true given that the premises are true. The deduction is valid, and because reasoners can determine that there are no other possible models of the premises, they can not only make this deduction but also know that it is valid (see Barwise, 1993). The same principles allow us to determine that an inference is invalid. Given, say, the following inference:

a happens before b
c happens before b
∴ a happens before c

the first premise yields the model:

a   b

but now when we try to add the information from the second premise, the relation between a and c is uncertain. One way to respond to such an indeterminacy is to build separate models for each possibility:

a   c   b   c   a   b   a   b
                                                                         c

where the third model represents a and c as contemporaneous. The first of these models shows that the putative conclusion is possible, but the second and third models are counter-examples to it. It follows that event a may happen before event c, but it does not follow that event a must happen before event c.

One disadvantage of this procedure is that as the number of indeterminacies in premises increases so there is an exponential growth in the number of possible models. The procedure is intractable for all but small numbers of indeterminacies. Yet, even though the human inferential system is bounded in its powers (Simon, 1959), it may use an intractable procedure. Consider the following premises, which go beyond the simple transitive inference illustrated above:

a happens before b
b happens before c
d happens while a
e happens while c
What's the relation between d and e?

The premises call for the construction of a single model:

a   b   c
d   e

which supports the conclusion:

d happens before e.

The model theory predicts that this one-model problem should be easier than a similar inference that contains an indeterminacy. For example, the following premises call for several models:

a happens before c
b happens before c
d happens while b
e happens while c
What's the relation between d and e?

The premises are satisfied by the following models:

a	b	c		b	a	c		a	c
d	e			d		e		b	
								d	e

In all three models, d happens before e, and so it is a valid conclusion. The model theory also predicts that the time subjects spend reading the second premise, which creates the indeterminacy leading to multiple models, should be longer than the reading time of the second premise of the one-model problem. Recently, Walter Schaeken and the present author have corroborated both these predictions: subjects took reliably longer (about 2 sec) to read an indeterminate premise, and made reliably more errors (about 10%) with such problems (see Schaeken, Johnson-Laird, & d'Ydewalle, 1993; and for similar results with spatial inferences, Byrne & Johnson-Laird, 1989).

Systems based on formal rules of inference make exactly the wrong predictions about these domains. The one-model problem above calls for a transitive inference to establish the relation between a and c, which is a precursor to establishing the relation between d and e. In contrast, the multiple-model problem does not need to derive the relation between b and c, because it is directly asserted by the second premise. Hence, the one-model problem has a longer formal derivation than the multiple-model problem, and so according to rule theories the one-model problem should be harder than the multiple-model problem. The irrelevant premise in the multiple-model problem cannot be responsible for its greater difficulty, because one-model problems with an irrelevant premise remain reliably easier than multiple-model problems, and no harder than one-model problems without irrelevant premises. In short, multiple models do cause problems for the human inferential system.

MODELS AND SENTENTIAL REASONING

If a speaker tells you:

Both the alarm light came on and the bell sounded.

you can imagine the two events in a single model:

a   b

where "a" denotes a representation of the alarm light coming on and "b" denotes a representation of the bell sounding, and the two are combined in a single model in which the left–right axis has no temporal significance. Suppose that instead of a conjunction, the speaker asserts:

The alarm light came on or the bell sounded.

how are you likely to represent this assertion? An obvious answer is that you construct two models, one for each possibility:

a

      b

The further assertion:

In fact, the alarm light did not come on.

rules out the first model to leave only the second, from which it follows:

The bell sounded.

There are three points to note about this inference. First, it was made without relying on a syntactic rule of inference, such as:

p or q, or both
not q
∴ p

Secondly, it was made without any decision about whether the disjunction was inclusive (the alarm light came on or the bell sounded, or both) or exclusive (the alarm light came on or the bell sounded, but not both). The advantage of moving straight to the deduction is that it saves time, and here it does not matter which interpretation is correct. Indeed, the speaker may not have had a particular interpretation in mind. Thirdly, the models are partial in that the first model does not represent explicitly that "not b" holds in this situation, and the second model does not represent explicitly that "not a" holds in this situation.

Now let us consider how this approach might be extended to deal with the most puzzling of sentential connectives, "if". Imagine that the speaker asserts:

If the alarm light came on then the bell sounded.

Despite many pages of philosophical and linguistic analysis, there is no consensus about the meaning of conditionals. Yet children appear to master them without too much difficulty. So what does this conditional mean, and how is it likely to be mentally represented? Granted that the conditional is true, it allows that one possible state of affairs is that the alarm light came on and so the bell sounded too. This possibility calls for a model akin to the one above for a conjunction:

    a   b

But, clearly, the conditional differs in meaning from the conjunction. The "if" clause refers to just one possibility, and another possibility is that the alarm light did not come on. Hence, the representation must allow for this other possibility. But, if the alarm light did not come on, what then? Did the bell sound, or not? Before you get too embroiled in this question, bear in mind that individuals may not have to answer it in order to understand the rest of the discourse. They need not make the possibilities explicit if they do not matter. In short, the following models of the conditional can serve as an initial representation of its meaning:

    a   b
    . . .

where the ellipsis represents the other possibilities. Of course, individuals ought to make a mental note that one event which cannot occur as an alternative possibility is that the alarm light came on, because this possibility is already represented in the explicit model. How this mental note is actually represented is by no means certain.

There is a well-known indeterminacy in the meaning of conditionals. An assertion such as:

If you eat your semolina, then you can have a chocolate.

naturally suggests that if you don't eat your semolina then you won't get a chocolate. This interpretation is equivalent to a bi-conditional:

If you eat your semolina, then you can have a chocolate, and if you don't eat your semolina, then you cannot have a chocolate.

Or, more succinctly:

If, and only if, you eat your semolina, then you can have a chocolate.

In contrast, the following conditional:

If you eat your semolina, then you will stay healthy.

has an interpretation that is not so strong. You may stay healthy even if you abstain from semolina. This interpretation is equivalent to a one-way conditional:

> If you eat your semolina, then you will stay healthy, and if you don't eat it you may or may not stay healthy.

In daily life, people often seem to understand conditionals without worrying about whether they are one-way or bi-conditionals — just as they interpret disjunctions without worrying about whether they are inclusive or exclusive. In the laboratory, experimental subjects similarly vacillate in their interpretations of conditionals and disjunctions, though a specific content or context can bias their interpretations (see e.g. Legrenzi, 1970).

The initial models of the conditional, "If the alarm light came on then the bell sounded", are:

> a   b
>   . . .

and it may not be clear whether the conditional should be interpreted as a one-way or bi-conditional. But it may not matter. If you learn as a definite categorical fact:

> The alarm light came on.

then you can forget about the implicit alternatives. They are eliminated to leave only the explicit model that supports the conclusion:

> ∴ The bell sounded.

Once again, you have made a deduction without fixing the precise interpretation of a premise and without using the relevant formal rule, which is known as *modus ponens*:

> if p then q
> p
> ∴q.

Other inferences may cause reasoners to make a fuller interpretation of a conditional of the form "if a then b". Its initial models, as we have seen, take the form:

        a   b
        . . .

If reasoners bear in mind that the implicit model corresponds to the situations in which the antecedent, a, does not hold, then there are several ways in which they could represent this information. For instance, they could indicate that the antecedent is exhaustively represented in the explicit model—i.e. it cannot occur in the implicit model (see Johnson-Laird and Byrne, 1991). But, they could do the same job by storing a footnote with the implicit model. The explicit model captures what happens when the antecedent is true, and so the footnote (shown here in parentheses) represents that the antecedent does not occur:

        a   b
        {¬a} . . .

where "¬" signifies negation. Similarly, the models of a bi-conditional are as follows:

        a   b
        {¬a   ¬b} . . .

The computations required to combine models are simple with footnotes, and they could be treated as merely a notational variant of the method using exhaustion.

A computer program recently devised by the author implements several levels of expertise in sentential reasoning according to the model theory. Here, we will consider three such levels. At a simple level (level 1), the program represents a conditional premise:

        if p then q

as having the following models:

        p   q
        {¬p} . . .

The explicit model captures what happens when the antecedent occurs, and the footnote in parentheses represents that the antecedent does not occur in the implicit model (the ellipsis). At this level, the program similarly represents an inclusive disjunction:

p or q, or both

by the following models:

   p

       q

   p   q

in which the first model does not make explicit that q does not occur, and the second model does not make explicit that p does not occur. The computations required to interpret compound premises are simple with footnotes. Thus, given the premise:

if p then q, *and* p

the program combines each of the models for the conditional with the model for p using a semantic procedure for "and". According to this procedure, two explicit models combine to yield an explicit model that avoids unnecessary duplications:

p   q   *and* p yield p   q

If one explicit model is inconsistent with another, or with the content of a footnote on an implicit model, then no new model is formed from them—i.e. the output is the null model:

{¬p} . . . *and* p yield nil

where "nil" represents the null model, which is akin to the empty set. The procedure for conjoining two sets of models thus multiplies each model in one set by each model in the other set according to the following principles:

1. If the two models are explicit, then they are joined together eliminating any redundancies, unless one model contradicts the other—i.e. one represents a proposition and the other represents its negation, in which case the output is the null model. When people combine two separate premises, they tend to drop propositions that they know categorically. For example, if they know that p is the case, then the model:

    p   q

combines with the model of the categorical premise:

p

to yield the following model:

q

2. If one model is explicit and the other model is from the footnote on an implicit model, then the result is the explicit model unless its content contradicts the model in the footnote, in which case the output is the null model.
3. If both models are implicit, then the result is an implicit model, which conjoins the footnotes on the two implicit models unless the two footnotes contradict one another, in which case the output is the null model.

As an illustration, consider the conjunction of two conditionals, "if a then b", and "if b then c", with the following respective models:

   a   b
{¬a} . . .

and:

   b   c
{¬b} . . .

The conjunction of the two sets of models yields:

a	b	c	(rule 1)
	b	c	(rule 2)
{¬a	¬ b} . . .		(rule 3)

The conjunction of:

   a   b   and   {¬b} . . .

yields the null model according to rule 2. Although conjunction is guided by the content of footnotes, their content does not surface in any explicit models. Hence, at this stage, it is still impossible to make certain inferences, such as *modus tollens*.

In contrast, at the next level up in competence (level 2), the content of footnotes is made explicit in any models resulting from the conjunction of implicit and explicit models. The previous premises accordingly yield the models:

```
   a       b      c
  ¬a       b      c
 {¬a     ¬b} . . .
```

One consequence is that at this level the program is able to make a *modus tollens* deduction. Given the premises:

> if a then b
> not b

the conjunction of the two sets of models proceeds as follows:

```
   a    b  and  ¬b  yields  nil
 {¬a} . . .  and  ¬b  yields  ¬a
```

from which it follows:

> not a.

Performance at this level also yields negated models in disjunctions, and indeed is probably as accurate as possible given the use of implicit models.

At its highest level of performance (level 3), the program fleshes out the contents of implicit models wholly explicitly. For example, fleshing out the implicit model of a conditional:

```
   p     q
 {¬p} . . .
```

calls for ¬p to occur in every new model, whereas separate models need to be made for q and ¬q because the footnote does not constrain them. The result is accordingly:

```
   p      q
  ¬p      q
  ¬p     ¬q
```

With such wholly explicit models, the program needs only rule 1 to combine sets of models. When the models of a set of premises are wholly explicit, there are as many of them as there are rows that are true in a truth table of all the premises. Footnotes are accordingly a device that allows the inferential system to represent certain information implicitly—it can be made explicit but at the cost of fleshing out the models. The notation can be used recursively—as it is in the computer program—to accommodate propositions of any degree of complexity.

How, in fact, do logically naive individuals reason? The data do not allow us to pin down a precise answer. What we do know, however, is that the principal predictions of the model theory are correct. When individuals reason, the greater the number of explicit models that they have to construct, the harder the task is—they take longer, they make more errors, and their erroneous conclusions tend to be consistent with the premises. Thus, for example, reasoning from inclusive disjunctions is harder than reasoning from exclusive disjunctions, reasoning from disjunctions is harder than reasoning from conditionals, and reasoning from conditionals is harder than reasoning from conjunctions (see e.g. Johnson-Laird, Byrne, & Schaeken, 1992; Bauer & Johnson-Laird, 1993). Conclusions that are merely consistent with the premises are not valid deductions, but the theory predicts such errors. They occur because reasoners construct some, but not all, of the models of the premises.

WHEN "OR" MEANS "AND": AN UNEXPECTED PREDICTION

Readers may find the account of temporal reasoning plausible, but have doubts about the extension of the model theory to sentential connectives. The apparatus of implicit models and footnotes seems implausible at first, yet, the underlying intuition is simple. Given a conditional, such as:

If the alarm light came on then the bell sounded.

individuals grasp that both events may have occurred, but defer a detailed representation of what happens if the alarm light did not come on. One striking and unexpected piece of evidence in favour of the theory was discovered from observing the performance of the computer program outlined in the previous section. Before I describe this phenomenon, however, readers might like to think for themselves about the following question: in what sorts of assertions does "or" tend to mean the same as "and"? Many people suppose the answer has to do with the specific lexical content of the assertions, but the phenomenon in question applies to neutral content about letters and numbers. In testing the program, I noticed that at level 1, an inclusive disjunction of the form:

If A then 2, *or* if B then 3.

elicited the following set of models:

```
A      2
              B     3
A      2      B     3
       . . .
```

But, the program also produced exactly the same set of models for a conjunction of the two conditionals:

If A then 2, *and* if B then 3.

It seemed at first sight that there might be a "bug" in the program (or the theory), but a closer inspection revealed that the interpretations were a consequence of an interaction between two components of the theory: the use of an implicit model in representing conditionals, and the use of partial models of disjunctions. A further test revealed that a disjunction of two conjunctions:

A and 2, *or* B and 3.

also yielded the same explicit models as those above (though no implicit model).

In order to test these predictions, we have recently carried out two experiments (Johnson-Laird & Barres, 1994). For each assertion, the subjects wrote down a list of the possible circumstances in which the assertion would be true—i.e. pairings of letters and numbers, such as "A 2". The results reliably corroborated the predictions. Many individuals do interpret a disjunction of conditionals in the same way as a conjunction of conditionals (and in the same way as a disjunction of conjunctions). Which assertions do subjects erroneously interpret? The answer is that the disjunction of the conditionals is true in many more cases than the models above allow, the conjunction of the conditionals is true in some more cases than the models above allow, but the disjunction of conjunctions is accurately represented by the models above (though they do not enumerate the different ways in which each conjunction can be false). Individuals untrained in logic therefore do seem to represent conditionals using implicit models and disjunctions using partial models.

SOME APPARENT DIFFICULTIES FOR THE THEORY OF CONDITIONALS

Despite the successes of the theory, there are certain aspects of it to which sceptics take exception (see the commentaries accompanying Johnson-Laird and Byrne, 1993). They object to the theory's account of the meaning of one-way conditionals, which it treats as equivalent to what logicians refer to as "material implication"—i.e. to the following truth table:

p	q	p *implies* q
T	T	T
T	F	F
F	T	T
F	F	T

The first two rows in this truth table are obvious: if the antecedent is true, the consequent has to be true, and if it is false then so too is the conditional as a whole. But the second two rows raise problems. In daily life, one does not treat a conditional as true merely because its antecedent is false. Indeed, subjects in experiments often judge that a conditional is "irrelevant" in such cases (see Johnson-Laird & Tagart, 1969; Evans, Newstead, & Byrne, 1993). Conditionals, the sceptics say, seem to go beyond a mere relation between the truth values of their antecedents and consequents—they convey a connection between the two events, such as a cause or a reason.

In fact, these objections to the model theory are not decisive. People judge a conditional as irrelevant when its antecedent is false, because such cases do not correspond to anything that they have made explicit in their initial models of the conditional. If they do flesh their models out explicitly, however, then they will realise that a conditional is certainly not falsified by a case where the antecedent is false. Such cases are entirely consistent with the conditional. In other words, the following possibilities are all allowed by the respective interpretations of the conditional:

One-way conditional		*Bi-conditional*	
p	q	p	q
¬p	q	¬p	¬q
¬p	¬q		

Hence, a one-way conditional is true in cases where the antecedent is false, and in cases where the consequent is true. These facts lead on to the so-called "paradoxes of material implication". They are not real paradoxes, but merely valid inferences that seem strange at first:

The alarm light did not come on.
∴ If the alarm light came on then the bell sounded.

and:

The bell sounded.
∴ If the alarm light came on then the bell sounded.

The reason they are odd is because they throw semantic information away—i.e. the premises convey more information than the conclusions (see Johnson-Laird & Byrne, 1991). Similar oddities can be constructed using disjunctions—e.g.

The alarm light came on.
∴ The alarm light came on *or* the bell sounded, or both.

This deduction is also valid, but logically untrained individuals balk at it, finding it improper. It too throws semantic information away.

While it is true that the antecedent and consequent of a conditional are often connected causally or in some other way, the conditional *per se* does not convey the connection. It makes sense to conjoin a conditional with a denial of any such over-arching connection—e.g.

If the alarm light came on then the bell sounded, though there was no causal or other connection between the two events.

This case contrasts with the use of the connective "because". An analogous assertion with this connective is manifest nonsense:

Because the alarm light came on, the bell sounded, though there was no causal or other connection between the two events.

Sceptics also object to our account of reasoning with conditionals. They argue that it makes the wrong predictions about certain conditional inferences. Thus, the initial models of a conditional allow an inference of the form known as "affirmation of the consequent":

If a then b
b
∴ a

that is valid only if the "if" premise is interpreted as a bi-conditional. But the initial models do not allow an inference of the form known as "denial of the antecedent":

If a then b
not a
∴ not b

that is also valid only if the "if " premise is interpreted as a bi-conditional. The critics say that both these inferences occur with comparable frequencies (Evans, 1993; O'Brien, personal communication). In fact, the only safe generalisation is that the frequencies of the two inferences are remarkably labile. Some studies do indeed report that affirmation of the consequent occurred more often than denial of the antecedent. There is now known to be a marked "figural effect" in propositional reasoning—that is, individuals tend to frame conclusions in the same order as the information in them entered working memory (see Bauer & Johnson-Laird, 1993). This effect may depress the frequency of affirmation of the consequent (and *modus tollens*). Once reasoners flesh out their models more explicitly, they will affirm the consequent and deny the antecedent only if they make the bi-conditional interpretation.

Another objection concerns inferences of the following form:

> If p and either q or r then s or both t and u
> p and either q or r
> ∴ s or both t and u.

This deduction calls for many models, and so it ought to be difficult. Clearly, it is not difficult, and so the model theory seems to be wrong. In fact, the theory allows that reasoners can construct a representation of the meaning of premises—indeed, the theory needs such a representation so that the manipulation of models can occur without losing track of the meaning of the premises. This representation enables reasoners to notice the match between one proposition and another. Indeed, just such a process was part of the first attempt to devise a semantic account of reasoning (see Johnson-Laird, 1983, p. 46 *et seq*.). If reasoners notice such a match, as in the premises above, they do not have to construct detailed models of the premises. They need only make an inference of the form:

> If A then B
> A
> ∴ B

where A = "p and either q or r", and B = "s or both t and u". There is no reason to suppose that they will use the formal rule of *modus ponens*. The standard model-theoretic machinery will do as well. What would challenge the model theory is a case where an easy inference can be made only by constructing many models. So far, no such cases have been forthcoming.

THE PHENOMENA OF THE
SELECTION TASK

The aim of this section is to describe one particular reasoning task, which has probably attracted more competing explanatory hypotheses than any other. The task was invented by Peter Wason (1966), investigated by Wason and the present author, and has inspired many subsequent investigations (for a review, see Evans et al., 1993). This section will describe five of the task's main phenomena, and the next section will show how the model theory accounts for them.

In an early version of the selection task, Wason laid four cards on the table:

A   B   2   3

and the subjects knew that every card had a letter on one side and a number on the other side. Their task was to select those cards that needed to be turned over to find out whether the following conditional rule was true or false:

If there is an "A" on one side of a card, then there is a "2" on the other side.

The materials do not engage any existing knowledge about the relation at stake. With such "neutral" materials, most subjects selected the "A" card alone, or the "A" card and the "2" card. Only a few subjects selected the "3" card. Yet, if this card were turned over to reveal an "A" on the other side, it would falsify the rule. The failure to select the card corresponding to the false consequent of the conditional is robust, and it is the first phenomenon of the selection task.

An experimental manipulation pioneered by Evans (e.g. Evans & Lynch, 1973) is to use conditionals with negative constituents in the selection task. Given the conditional:

If there is an "A" on one side, then there is *not* a "2" on the other side.

subjects perform much better. They tend to select the "A" card and the card that falsifies the consequent—i.e. the "2" card. But, this gain in performance may not reflect a better insight into the task. Evans (1989) argues that subjects are not really reasoning at all, but are guided by two heuristics that lead them merely to select whatever card makes the antecedent true (the "if" heuristic), and whatever card is mentioned in the consequent, whether or not it is negated (the "matching" heuristic). Thus, given the conditional:

If there is *not* an "A" card on one side, then there is a "2" card on the other side.

the subjects select the card that makes the antecedent true (i.e. the "B" card), and the card mentioned in the consequent (i.e. the "2" card). The tendency to ignore negations in the consequent of conditionals and to select whatever card is mentioned in them is the second phenomenon of the selection task.

Anyone with a syntactic conception of deductive reasoning is likely to be puzzled by the subjects' failure to select a potentially falsifying card. That arch-formalist, Jean Piaget, wrote that "reasoning is nothing more than the propositional calculus itself" (Inhelder & Piaget, 1958, p. 305), and that faced with verifying whether x implies y, a subject "will look in this case to see whether or not there is a counter-example x and non-y" (Piaget, in Beth & Piaget, 1966, p. 181). It seems that adult subjects in the selection task have not reached the Piagetian level of formal operations. Yet they are supposed to have attained it around the age of 12. There is a still more striking effect. By changing the content of the selection task, subjects' performance was strikingly enhanced. They tended to make the correct selections with a rule such as "Every time I go to Manchester I travel by train" (Wason & Shapiro, 1971), and with the deontic task of checking for violations to a postal regulation, such as: "If an envelope is sealed, then it must have a 5d stamp on it" (Johnson-Laird, Legrenzi, & Legrenzi, 1972). These results were not so robust, however, and some studies failed to replicate them. One sort of content did yield a reliable improvement in performance. As Griggs and Cox (1982) showed, deontic conditionals, such as:

If a person is drinking beer then the person must be over 18.

tended to elicit correct selections (the card corresponding to a beer drinker, and the card corresponding to someone less than 18). This finding is the third robust phenomenon of the selection task. It has led some theorists to postulate a special role for knowledge of the relevant situation. Others argue that deontic contents trigger special "pragmatic reasoning schemas" (Cheng & Holyoak, 1985), such as:

If the precondition is not satisfied (e.g. not over 18 years) then the action (e.g. drinking beer) must not be taken.

And still others argue for the relevance of social contracts and particularly for a procedure for checking for cheaters that has evolved as a result of natural selection (see Cosmides, 1989; Gigerenzer & Hug, 1992).

The hypothesis about checking for cheaters has led to the discovery of quite different patterns of selections in the task. Cosmides (1989) told subjects a story about a fictitious tribe that culminated in a statement of the condition governing the right to eat cassava root:

If a man has a tattoo on his face then he eats cassava root.

The subjects tended to check for those who might be cheating—i.e. they selected the card corresponding to the *false* antecedent (man with no tattoo) and a *true* consequent (eats cassava root). Given the following conditional used by Manktelow and Over (1991):

If you tidy your room then you may go out to play.

the subjects' selections depended on whether they were asked to take the point of view of the mother, who laid down the condition, or the point of view of the child, who was on the receiving end of it. The mother is presumably concerned that her child does not cheat, and subjects who take her point of view tended to select the following cards:

did not tidy   (false antecedent)
went out to play   (true consequent)

The child is presumably concerned that the mother does not renege on the deal, and the subjects who took the child's point of view tended to select the following cards:

tidied the room   (true antecedent)
did not go out to play   (false consequent)

Politzer and Nguyen-Xuan (1992) demonstrated similar effects with a conditional of the form:

If the purchase exceeds 10,000 francs, then the salesman must stick on the back of the receipt a voucher gift for a gold bracelet.

The selections depended on whether the subjects took the point of view of a manager checking for cheating customers or the point of view of a customer checking the deal. Subjects with a neutral point of view tended to select all four cards. Manktelow and Over argue that subjects assess the utilities of the outcomes in ways that go beyond social contracts or checking for cheaters. Politzer and Nguyen-Xuan defend a revised version of pragmatic reasoning schemas. The selection of false antecedent and true consequent cards, and sometimes of all four cards, is the fourth phenomenon of the selection task.

There are many other findings on the selection task, but one other phenomenon is often lost sight of in the controversies over pragmatic reasoning schemas, social contracts, and utilities: the task can be made easier by changing the form of the rule. Wason and Johnson-Laird (1969) observed an improved performance with a disjunction instead of a conditional. Likewise, Wason and Green (1984) showed that subjects performed more accurately with a rule concerning a single sort of entity and its property:

All the circles are black.

than with a rule interrelating two entities. Such improvements are the fifth phenomenon of the selection task.

The five phenomena are accordingly:

1. With neutral conditionals of the form, if p then q, subjects tend to select the p card alone, or the p and q cards.
2. With neutral conditionals containing negations, subjects tend to select the card that makes the antecedent true and the card mentioned in the consequent, whether or not the consequent is negated—e.g. with "if p then not q", subjects tend to select the p card and the q card.
3. With a realistic content, subjects carry out the task more accurately.
4. Depending on the subjects' point of view about a deontic rule of the form if p then q, they tend to select the p and not-q cards, or the not-p and q cards, or all four cards.
5. A change in the form of the rule can yield a greater number of correct selections.

One final word of warning before we turn to the explanation of these phenomena. It is tempting to suppose that an experimental manipulation either yields insight into the task or not—indeed, papers on the selection task often adopt this dichotomous point of view. In fact, the range of performance covers the entire spectrum. Experimenters typically report reliable improvements in performance above the level with a neutral conditional, but the degree of the improvement varies considerably from one manipulation to another. No manipulation yields perfect selections in one condition and wholly erroneous selections in another.

HOW THE MODEL THEORY EXPLAINS THE SELECTION TASK

Some authors doubt whether the selection task engages any process of reasoning at all: it may just elicit biases or trigger relevant knowledge. Or, say others, it may engage a process of decision making in which subjects compute the expected utilities of different outcomes. Or it may engage special mental procedures with which evolution has equipped human beings to enable them to live a rich social life. The diversity of phenomena is matched by the diversity of explanations. Many of the explanations, however, have little psychological justification from outside the selection task; and none of them explains all five of the phenomena. According to the model theory, however, subjects *do* reason in the selection task—albeit not always successfully, and the theory does provide a unified explanation of the five phenomena (Johnson-Laird & Byrne, 1991).

When people reason, as we have seen, they can do so only on the basis of what is explicit in their models of the premises. This principle applies to the selection task too: people reason only about what is explicit in their models of the rule. The task requires subjects to select those cards that they need to turn over to determine whether an indicative rule is true or false, or whether a deontic rule has been violated. Hence, the model theory predicts that subjects will apply these constraints but only to those cards that they have explicitly represented in their models of the rule. A one-way interpretation of the neutral conditional:

If there is an "A", then there is a "2".

yields the models:

    A   2
    {¬A} . . .

and a bi-conditional interpretation yields the models:

    A   2
    {¬A ¬2} . . .

Subjects should therefore select the "A" card alone in the one-way case, and the "A" card and the "2" card in the bi-conditional case. The theory accordingly accounts for the first phenomenon of the selection task: these are the predominant selections for neutral conditionals. The theory goes beyond the phenomenon to make a further prediction: there should be a correlation between the interpretation of the conditional (as a one-way or bi-conditional) and the pattern of selections. This correlation has been recently confirmed by Francesco Cara and Stefana Broadbent (personal communication).

When do people use negative assertions? The answer according to Wason (1965) is in order to correct misconceptions—e.g. "A spider is not an insect". Hence, the proposition to be corrected is ordinarily one that the listener or reader has in mind—that is, it should be separately represented in a mental model. This assumption also applies to the interpretation of conditionals with negative constituents. With the conditional:

If there is an "A", then there is not a "2".

if subjects tend to represent both the consequent and the proposition that it negates, they will construct the following models for a one-way interpretation:

A   ¬2
    2
{¬A} . . .

Likewise, for a one-way conditional with a negated antecedent:

If there is not an "A", then there is a "2".

they will tend to construct the following models:

¬A   2
A

Reasoners may even omit the negative propositions from these models. In any case, their models of the first of these conditionals, though not the second, should include the negated consequent, and so they should consider this card in carrying out their selections. It bears on the truth or falsity of the conditional, and so they should tend to select it. The card corresponding to the true antecedent, which is also explicitly represented, bears on the truth or falsity of the conditional and so subjects should also tend to select it. The model theory thus accounts for the second phenomenon of the selection task. But, it makes an additional prediction: negating the antecedent of a conditional should yield a proposition that can be paraphrased by a disjunction, whereas negating the consequent should not. Thus, the second of the two conditionals above, but not the first, can be paraphrased as:

Either there is an "A" or there is a "2".

There are no experimental data, but the equivalence was noted by Stoic logicians long ago (see Kneale & Kneale, 1962, p. 162).

When should subjects get the selection task right? One necessary condition according to the model theory is that they represent the negated consequent in their models of the conditional. But, as Johnson-Laird and Byrne (1991, p. 80) write: an insightful performance may further depend on an explicit representation of what is not possible—i.e. the real impossibility given the rule [if "A" then "2"] of:

A   ¬2

This idea relates to the model theory's treatment of counter-factual conditionals, such as:

If there had been an "A" then there would have been a "2".

which should normally elicit the following models:

Actual state: ¬A   ¬2
Counter-factual states: A   2
                             {¬A} . . .

The epistemic status of the different models has to be represented, as the labels show.

The models of an indicative conditional, such as:

If there is an "A" then there is a "2".

are represented as real possibilities. This apparatus also allows a model to be represented as impossible. And, in order to test the truth of a conditional, it may be necessary to focus on what it rules out as impossible. It follows that any experimental manipulation that leads individuals to flesh out their models of the conditional should tend to improve performance in the selection task. One such manipulation is the use of a content that is likely to make violations of the rule salient, either by triggering specific memories or by eliciting a framework in which such violations are highlighted. The model theory therefore accounts for the third phenomenon of the selection task—the enhanced performance with realistic materials and especially those of a deontic sort—without invoking permission schemas (Cheng & Holyoak, 1985) or special procedures for checking for cheaters (Cosmides, 1989). However, the theory goes beyond these findings to make a general prediction. Any manipulation that draws attention to counter-examples should improve performance even if the materials are not deontic (Johnson-Laird & Byrne, 1991, p. 80–81). This prediction has been corroborated recently by two unpublished studies. Daniel Sperber and Vittorio Girotto (personal communication) have established the point using several domains. For example, they told their subjects that a certain machine generated cards according to the rule:

If a card has an "A" on one side, then it has a "2" on the other side.

The machine went wrong and ceased to obey the rule, but it has been repaired, and the subjects have to check that the job has been done properly. They are thus likely to represent the machine's potential error explicitly: A ¬2. The subjects in this condition and other similar ones carried out the selection task more accurately.

Roberta Love and Claudius Kessler (personal communication) have obtained similar results. For example, in a science fiction domain, they used the conditional rule:

If there are Xow then there must be a force field.

where Xow are strange crystal-like living organisms who depend for their existence on a force field. In a context that suggested the possibility of counter-examples—mutant Xows who can survive without a force field—the subjects carried out the selection task more accurately than in a control condition that did not suggest such counter-examples. As Fillenbaum (1977) and others have argued, many conditional promises in daily life call for a bi-conditional interpretation. For example, the conditional:

If you tidy your room then you can go out to play.

is taken to imply:

If you don't tidy your room then you cannot go out to play.

When the models for such a bi-conditional are fleshed out in a fully explicit way, they are as follows:

```
  t       p
 ¬t      ¬p
```

where "t" denotes tidying your room and "p" denotes going out to play. There are two potential counter-examples in this case:

```
  t      ¬p
 ¬t       p
```

Hence, a proper test of the conditional calls for selecting all four cards (as a neutral point of view elicits from subjects). If subjects focus on the first counter-example, they will select the t and not-p cards; if they focus on the second counter-example, they will select the not-t and p cards.

One way that experiments have manipulated the focus is by asking subjects to take a particular point of view. In conditional promises, there is usually an asymmetry between the violations. On the one hand, for the mother the salient interpretation of the conditional is:

If you don't tidy your room, then you cannot go out to play.

and the salient violation is that you don't tidy your room but nevertheless go out to play:

```
 ¬t      p
```

On the other hand, for the child the salient interpretation is:

If I tidy my room, then I can go out to play.

and the salient violation is, I tidy my room and yet I don't get out to play:

```
  t      ¬p
```

The model theory accordingly explains the fourth phenomenon of the selection task: when deontic rules are interpreted as bi-conditionals, instructions can make salient one or other (or both) of the counter-examples.

Once again, the theory goes beyond the obtained results to make a further prediction. With a factual conditional that strongly suggests a bi-conditional interpretation, such as:

If candidates are qualified, then they passed the exam.

the same phenomena should occur as with the deontic conditionals. When counter-examples are made salient, subjects with a neutral point of view should tend to select all four cards. The suggestion that some candidates may have qualified improperly should make salient the counter-example:

qualified   ¬passed exam

In contrast, the suggestion that some candidates may have been improperly debarred should make salient the counter-example:

¬qualified   passed exam

Such a result would show that a deontic content is not essential to the phenomenon.

The explanation of the fifth phenomenon should now be obvious. The purpose of implicit models is to minimise the load on working memory. Manipulations that lead to explicit models, or that minimise load, should improve performance on the selection task. Hence, the task should be easier with disjunctions, which have no wholly implicit models, and with conditionals about single entities rather than two entities. Any manipulation that reduces the memory load should be effective, and indeed this prediction has also been corroborated (see e.g. Oakhill & Johnson-Laird, 1985). Most theories of cognition are likely to allow for such effects, but they are a natural consequence of the model theory with its emphasis on minimising explicit representations.

CONCLUSIONS

There is a gulf between formal and semantic methods in logic. The two sorts of psychological theories of reasoning similarly differ so much that experimental evidence should enable us to decide between them. In practice, it has not been easy. There are many different rule theories, and several of them are still under active development: theorists continue to modify the rules of inference and the strategies that deploy them. The model theory also continues to develop—the version for propositional reasoning described here differs from previous accounts. It postulates slightly different models and the principles for combining them. Hence, if the controversy is to be resolved, then empirical results need to contravene the fundamental principles of a theory rather than just a specific version of it.

Formal rule theories apply to only limited domains of deductive reasoning. They predict that the difficulty of a deduction depends on the length of the derivation and the accessibility or ease of use of the particular rules on which it depends. The rules and the strategy differ from one version of a theory to another, and it is therefore hard to specify what could strike at the heart of rule theories—perhaps no experiment can do better than to test a specific rule theory. In contrast, the model theory is easy to refute in principle. It applies to all domains of deduction, and it makes two general predictions. The first prediction is that erroneous conclusions will tend to be at least consistent with the premises. This prediction can be tested without any account of the particular models for the domain: it is necessary to test merely that the erroneous conclusions tend to be consistent with the premises rather than inconsistent with them. The prediction has been corroborated in all the main domains of deduction (see e.g. Johnson-Laird & Byrne, 1991). The second prediction is that the greater the number of models on which an inference depends, the harder it will be—it will take longer, and it will be more likely to go wrong. In temporal reasoning, the number of models is easy to assess and, as shown in the "Theory of mental models" section above, it correctly predicts difficulty. In other domains, such as syllogisms, the prediction requires a detailed account of the models constructed from premises. Sentential reasoning stands somewhere between these two domains. As the "Models and sentential reasoning" section above showed, a conjunction (a and b) calls for one model; an exclusive disjunction (a or else b) calls for two models; and an inclusive disjunction (a or b, or both) calls for three models. No version of the model theory could realistically change these numbers, and they make the correct predictions about inferential difficulty (see Johnson-Laird et al., 1992).

What complicate matters are conditionals. The "Models and sentential reasoning" section defended the view that they tend to be interpreted by one explicit model and one implicit model with an attached mental footnote. The next section in this chapter ("When 'or' means 'and': an unexpected prediction") showed that this hypothesis leads to the correct prediction that logically untrained individuals will interpret a disjunction of conditionals:

If A then 2, or if B then 3.

as true in the same cases as the conjunction of the conditionals:

If A then 2, and if B then 3.

The next section ("Some apparent difficulties for the theory of conditionals") defended the theory against some potential objections, and the final two sections showed how it elucidates the main phenomena of Wason's selection task.

In conclusion, there are three crucial distinctions between formal rule theories and the mental model theory. First, the rule theories lack a decision procedure whereas the model theory has a simple one. In contrasting a semantic and a syntactic method in logic, Quine (1974, p. 75) wrote: "[The syntactic method] is inferior in that it affords no general way of reaching a verdict of invalidity; failure to discover a proof for a schema can mean either invalidity or mere bad luck". The same problem vitiates the psychological theories based on formal rules: "The 'search till you're exhausted' strategy gives one at best an educated, correct guess that something does not follow" (Barwise, 1993). A conclusion is valid if, and only if, it holds in all models of the premises, and so the model theory provides a simple decision procedure in many domains of deduction.

The second comparison concerns predictive power. Rule theories exist for spatial and sentential reasoning. Unlike the model theory, they have nothing to say about temporal or modal reasoning, or reasoning with quantifiers such as "most" or "more than half " that do not correspond to those of formal logic. Even within sentential reasoning, current formal rule theories give no account of several robust phenomena, including the nature of erroneous conclusions, or the results of Wason's selection task.The model theory explains these phenomena, and it goes beyond deduction to suggest a unified account of different modes of thought—for example, induction and creation depend on adding semantic information to models (e.g. Johnson-Laird, 1993). It also yields a foundation for probabilistic thinking and informal reasoning: the strength of such inferences depends on the proportion of possible states of affairs consistent with the premises in which the conclusion is true, and subjects can estimate this proportion by constructing models, which each correspond to an infinite set of possibilities (or, in some cases, a set of infinite sets of possibilities, Johnson-Laird, 1994).

The third point concerns falsifiability. There seem to be no experiments on verbal reasoning that could contravene the fundamental principles of formal rule theories, whereas experiments can in principle refute the fundamental principles of the model theory. One way in which formal rule theories might be refuted is to consider inferences based on visual perception. A rule theory posits the extraction of logical form from an internal description of the percept, whereas the model theory assumes that vision leads directly to a mental model (Marr, 1982). The two sorts of theories therefore diverge on the matter of diagrams. According to the model theory, it should be easier to reason from a diagram making explicit the alternative possibilities than from logically equivalent verbal premises. With a diagram, reasoners do not need to engage in the process of parsing and compositional semantic interpretation. Formal rule theories, however, have no grounds for such a prediction. With a diagram, reasoners have to construct an internal description from which they can extract a logical form, and there is no reason to suppose that the process should be easier than the extraction of logical form from verbal premises. In fact, a recent study has shown that subjects reasoned reliably faster (about 30 sec) and considerably more accurately (30% increase in the number of valid conclusions) when the premises were diagrams rather than sentences (Bauer & Johnson-Laird, 1993). This result corroborates the model theory and perhaps contravenes the rule theories.

ACKNOWLEDGEMENTS

Ruth Byrne is a co-author of the model theory of sentential reasoning, and the work on temporal reasoning was carried out in collaboration with Walter Schaeken. I am also grateful to them and to the following colleagues for ideas and for help: Malcolm Bauer, Bruno Bara, Patricia Barres, Vittorio Girotto, Alan Garnham, Jung Min Lee, Paolo Legrenzi, Rick Lewis, Juan Garcia Madruga, Jane Oakhill, Victoria Shaw, and Patrizia Tabossi. The present research was carried out with support from the James S. McDonnell Foundation. My thanks to the editors for their advice on an earlier version of the chapter. Finally, I am greatly indebted to Peter Wason for originally exciting my interest in the psychology of reasoning—a field that he almost single-handedly created—and for much advice over the years.

REFERENCES

Barwise, J. (1993). Everyday reasoning and logical inference. (Commentary on Johnson-Laird & Byrne, 1991.) *Behavioral and Brain Sciences, 16*, 337–338.

Bauer, M.I., & Johnson-Laird, P.N. (1993). How diagrams can improve reasoning. *Psychological Science, 4*, 372–378.

Beth, E.W., & Piaget, J. (1966). *Mathematical epistemology and psychology*. Dordrecht: Reidel.

Braine, M.D.S., & O'Brien, D.P. (1991). A theory of If: A lexical entry, reasoning program, and pragmatic principles. *Psychological Review, 98*, 182–203.

Byrne, R.M.J., & Johnson-Laird, P.N. (1989). Spatial reasoning. *Journal of Memory and Language, 28*, 564–575.

Cheng, P.N., & Holyoak, K.J. (1985). Pragmatic reasoning schemas. *Cognitive Psychology, 17*, 391–416.

Cosmides, L. (1989). The logic of social exchange: Has natural selection shaped how humans reason? Studies with the Wason selection task. *Cognition, 31*, 187–276.

Evans, J.St.B.T. (1989). *Bias in human reasoning: Causes and consequences*. Hove, UK: Lawrence Erlbaum Associates Ltd.

Evans, J.St.B.T. (1993). The mental model theory of conditional reasoning: Critical appraisal and revision. *Cognition, 48*, 1–20.

Evans, J.St.B.T, & Lynch, J.S. (1973). Matching bias in the selection task. *British Journal of Psychology, 64,* 391–397.

Evans, J.St.B.T., Newstead, S.E., & Byrne, R.M.J. (1993). *Human reasoning: The psychology of deduction.* Hove, UK: Lawrence Erlbaum Associates Ltd.

Fillenbaum, S. (1977). Mind your p's and q's: The role of content and context in some uses of and, or, and if. In G.H. Bower. (Ed.), *Psychology of learning and motivation, Vol. II.* New York: Academic Press.

Gigerenzer, G., & Hug, K. (1992). Domain-specific reasoning: Social contracts, cheating, and perspective change. *Cognition, 43,* 127–171.

Griggs, R.A., & Cox, J.R. (1982). The elusive thematic-materials effect in Wason's selection task. *British Journal of Psychology, 73,* 407–420.

Inhelder, B., & Piaget, J. (1958). *The growth of logical thinking from childhood to adolescence.* London: Routledge & Kegan Paul.

Johnson-Laird, P.N. (1983). *Mental models: Towards a cognitive science of language, inference and consciousness.* Cambridge: Cambridge University Press.

Johnson-Laird, P.N. (1993). *Human and machine thinking.* Hillsdale, NJ: Lawrence Erlbaum Associates Inc.

Johnson-Laird, P.N. (1994). Mental models and probabilistic thinking. *Cognition.*

Johnson-Laird, P.N., & Barres, P.E. (1994). When "or" means "and": A study in mental models. *Proceedings of the Sixteenth Annual Conference of the Cognitive Science Society.* Hillsdale, NJ: Lawrence Erlbaum Associates Inc., pp. 475–478.

Johnson-Laird, P.N., & Byrne, R.M.J. (1991). *Deduction.* Hove, UK: Lawrence Erlbaum Associates Ltd.

Johnson-Laird, P.N., & Byrne, R.M.J. (1993). Precis of "Deduction", and authors' response: Mental models or formal rules? *Behavioral and Brain Sciences, 16,* 323–333, 368–376.

Johnson-Laird, P.N., Byrne, R.M.J., & Schaeken, W. (1992). Propositional reasoning by model. *Psychological Review, 99,* 418–439.

Johnson-Laird, P.N., Legrenzi, P., & Legrenzi, M.S. (1972). Reasoning and a sense of reality. *British Journal of Psychology, 63,* 395–400.

Johnson-Laird, P.N., & Tagart, J. (1969). How implication is understood. *American Journal of Psychology, 82,* 367–373.

Kneale, W., & Kneale, M. (1962). *The development of logic.* Oxford: Clarendon Press.

Legrenzi, P. (1970). Relations between language and reasoning about deductive rules. In G.B. Flores D'Arcais, & W.J.M. Levelt (Eds.), *Advances in psycholinguistics.* Amsterdam: North-Holland.

Macnamara, J. (1986). *A border dispute: The place of logic in psychology.* Cambridge, MA: Bradford Books, MIT Press.

Manktelow, K.I., & Over, D.E. (1991). Social roles and utilities in reasoning with deontic conditionals. *Cognition, 39,* 85–105.

Marr, D. (1982). *Vision: A computational investigation into the human representation and processing of visual information.* San Francisco: W.H. Freeman.

Oakhill, J.V., & Johnson-Laird, P.N. (1985). Rationality, memory, and the search for counter-examples. *Cognition, 20,* 79–94.

Osherson, D.N. (1974–76). *Logical Abilities in Children, Vols. 1–4.* Hillsdale, NJ: Lawrence Erlbaum Associates Inc.

Quine, W.V.O. (1974). *Methods of logic*. Third edition. London: Routledge & Kegan Paul.

Politzer, G., & Nguyen-Xuan, A. (1992). Reasoning about conditional promises and warnings: Darwinian algorithms, mental models, and relevance judgements or pragmatic schemas. *Quarterly Journal of Experimental Psychology, 44,* 401–412.

Rips, L.J. (1983). Cognitive processes in propositional reasoning. *Psychological Review, 90,* 38–71.

Schaeken, W., Johnson-Laird, P.N., & d'Ydewalle, G. (1993). *Mental models and temporal reasoning*. Unpublished paper, Department of Psychology, Princeton University.

Simon, H.A. (1959). Theories of decision making in economics and behavioral science. *American Economic Review, 49,* 253–283.

Wason, P.C. (1965). The context of plausible denial. *Journal of Verbal Learning and Verbal Behavior, 4,* 7–11.

Wason, P.C. (1966). Reasoning. In B.M. Foss (Ed.), *New horizons in psychology*. Harmondsworth: Penguin.

Wason, P.C., & Green, D.W. (1984). Reasoning and mental representation. *Quarterly Journal of Experimental Psychology, 36A,* 597–610.

Wason, P.C., & Johnson-Laird, P.N. (1969). Proving a disjunctive rule. *Quarterly Journal of Experimental Psychology, 21,* 14–20.

Wason, P.C., & Shapiro, D. (1971). Natural and contrived experience in a reasoning problem. *Quarterly Journal of Experimental Psychology, 23,* 63–71.

CHAPTER SEVEN

Relevance and Reasoning

Jonathan St.B.T. Evans

Department of Psychology, University of Plymouth, UK

Research on deductive reasoning has proceeded rapidly in the past decade. Work on conditional reasoning has accounted for many of the studies and, to cover adequately, required a full three chapters in the recent review of the field by Evans, Newstead and Byrne (1993). Progression in empirical findings has not, however, led to a convergence of theoretical opinion—in fact, quite the reverse. Since the earlier review by Evans (1982) we have seen the development of a host of new theories which have been applied to the findings of reasoning experiments, as well as significant development of the older theory that people reason by mental logics comprising general purpose inference rules (e.g. Rips, 1983, 1989; Braine & O'Brien, 1991). New theories include the mental model theory of reasoning (Johnson-Laird, 1983; Johnson-Laird & Byrne, 1991), heuristic-analytic theory (Evans, 1984; 1989), the theory of pragmatic reasoning schemas (Cheng & Holyoak, 1985) and social contract theory (Cosmides, 1989). The last two, however, have been applied only to the findings of work on a particular paradigm—the Wason selection task, discussed later in this chapter.

Recently, I have bemoaned this fragmentation of reasoning theory (Evans, 1991) and, as explained shortly, have made some attempt to integrate my own heuristic-analytic theory with that of mental model theory. However, the principal focus of this chapter is on relevance effects in reasoning. I intend to concentrate on the idea that people reason with a selective representation of problem information which appears to them to be relevant. Relevance is assumed to be determined by rapid, preconscious processes. I will first discuss some theoretical background for the idea, showing its origin and its connection with other theoretical approaches, especially the mental model theory of reasoning. In the latter part of the chapter I present a review of evidence for relevance effects in reasoning, including an informal report of a number of my own recent experiments.

THEORETICAL BACKGROUND

The Heuristic-analytic Theory

Evans (1984; 1989) proposed a heuristic-analytic theory which has roots in the earlier dual process theory of Wason and Evans (1975; see also Evans & Wason, 1976; Evans, 1982, Chapter 12). The dual process theory arose from an attempt to explain a discrepancy between observations of bias and introspective reports on the Wason selection task (Wason, 1966). Both the selection task itself and the matching bias effect which concerned Wason and Evans will be described later in this chapter. Suffice it to say for the present that subjects' choices on the task could be predicted by a bias of which subjects showed no awareness in their verbal reports. Wason and Evans argued that subjects were biased by an unconscious, non-verbal type 1 process (subsequently termed heuristic), whereas their verbalisations served to rationalise choices in the context of the instructions using type 2, verbal thought processes (subsequently termed analytic).

The heuristic-analytic theory of Evans (1989) incorporates these ideas but also develops them. The motivation for the theory was primarily to account for biases in reasoning, especially where subjects can be shown to possess the relevant logical knowledge but still persist in error. It provides an essentially representational account of bias in which it is supposed that reasoning proceeds in two stages: a heuristic stage in which preconscious heuristics serve to select aspects of the problem information as "relevant", and an analytic stage in which deductions are made based on the selected information. Biases occur according to this view because logically relevant information fails to get represented at the heuristic stage or because logically irrelevant information is included. In essence, people make mistakes in reasoning because they think selectively.

A key concept in this theory is that of relevance. Let us consider the example of chess. It is well known that experienced chess players look at a chess position and "see" that a small number of moves (out of many more legal possibilities) need to be considered. Similarly, when analysing possible replies of the opponent, only a few moves appear to be relevant. Thus it is possible to analyse a position to a reasonable depth without hitting the problem of "combinatorial explosion" which has bedevilled attempts to produce strong chess playing computer programs. Of course, stronger players see better moves. It is this rapid, perceptual-like identification of relevance which both constitutes the intelligence of the human player and also marks its tacit nature. These rapid, preattentive processes—heuristic in my terminology—are by definition unreportable, and as a result cannot be described to the computer programmer. Of course, analysis of relevant moves also takes place, with plausible moves being refuted and so on. This corresponds to what I call the analytic stage of reasoning.

The chess example is useful because it shows that heuristic processes serve intelligence by reducing large search spaces or by retrieving relevant prior knowledge. Nevertheless, the preconscious selection of information can clearly be a cause of bias since logically irrelevant information may get included, or logically relevant information omitted. Evans (1989) discusses a number of phenomena in inductive, deductive and statistical reasoning which are attributed to misrepresentation of problem information. The approach is particularly useful in explaining what Kahneman and Tversky (1982) call errors of application (as opposed to errors of understanding) where people apparently know the relevant principle but fail to apply it. Of course, if the critical piece of information is not encoded as relevant, then the principle cannot be applied to it at the analytic stage. If a chess player fails to consider the best move in a position then her powers of analysis are of no avail.

Some authors have been puzzled by my characterisation of the heuristic stage as rapid and preconscious. For example, since I argue that linguistic and pragmatic factors (of which more later) act as cues to relevance, some think that this must involve some deliberative process of reasoning such as that which I assume occurs at the analytic stage. However, I am proposing nothing different from that required to explain relevance in other types of cognitive activity. Consider, for example, the extraordinarily complex processes involved in comprehending discourse. The listener must immediately and effortlessly retrieve associated knowledge, expand the context, and derive inferences in order to understand the simplest of utterances. The discussion of relevance in pragmatics and communication offered by Sperber and Wilson (1986) has close connections with my own use of the term in the context of understanding explicit inference and decision tasks. Relevance in language comprehension is also immediate, given, and non-introspectible.

I have discussed some of the cues or heuristics which appear to determine relevance in reasoning tasks but I have not provided a specific theory of the nature of the cognitive processes involved. However, their rapid, unconscious (and generally very efficient) nature is clearly consistent with ideas of connectionist or "neural" networks of the kind proposed to account for a variety of cognitive phenomena such as associative memory, pattern recognition, and language comprehension (see McClelland & Rumelhart, 1986). The idea of a neural network taking a particular series of inputs and "relaxing" into a given stage is consistent with the idea of relevance "popping out" into consciousness. We are already accustomed to the idea that associated knowledge can be rapidly retrieved in this way. We also accept that only the product of rapid, parallel pattern recognition processes becomes conscious. So why should pragmatically relevant information not pop out to the reasoner in just the same way?

The analytic stage in the theory is there to reflect the idea that in explicit reasoning and decision-making tasks, the reasoner does some active thinking about the relevant information. In most reasoning tasks—for example, with classical syllogisms (see Evans et al., 1993, Chapter 7)—people succeed in solving logical problems at well above chance rates. Hence any theory of reasoning must account for competence as well as bias (Evans, 1991). However, this is the weaker part of the theory presented by Evans (1989) because the nature of the analytic processes (and hence the basis for deductive competence) was left unspecified. For this reason, I have recently attempted to reconcile the proposals of the heuristic-analytic theory with those of the mental model theory of deduction proposed by Johnson-Laird and Byrne (1991). It is to this endeavour that I now turn.

Relevance and Mental Models

Of the various reasoning theories mentioned at the outset, there are several which aim to provide an account of deductive competence (for critical discussions of the rival accounts, see Evans, 1991; Oaksford & Chater, 1993). The theory of pragmatic reasoning schemas attempts to explain deduction but only in semantically rich contexts to which reasoners can bring prior experience. The two more general theories are (a) that reasoners possess a mental logic comprising a set of general purpose inference rules, and (b) that people reason by manipulation of mental models representing possible world states. An intense debate has been conducted between the advocates of mental logic and mental models, which is reviewed in some detail by Evans et al. (1993, Chapter 3).

The mental model theory is an attractive candidate for the analytic reasoning mechanism of the heuristic-analytic theory, because it also proposes that people think selectively about the problem information. The general theory (Johnson-Laird, 1983) proposes that people represent possible states of the world by the use of models which incorporate tokens to represent classes or propositions and their relation to one another. In contrast with formal rule theories, such as those of Rips (1983), the method of deduction is semantic, not syntactic. There are three main steps in the process:

1. Reasoners construct a model of a possible state of the world in which the premises are true.
2. Next, they form a putative conclusion which is true in the model and which is informative—i.e. not a repetition of a premise or a trivial inference.
3. Finally, they search for counter-examples—i.e. they try to build a model in which the premises hold but the putative conclusion does not. If no such counter-example is found then the conclusion is declared as a valid consequence of the premises.

Early work on this theory involved reasoning with syllogisms and quantified statements (e.g. Johnson-Laird & Bara, 1984). However, Johnson-Laird and Byrne (1991) recently put forward a model theory of conditional reasoning. In this theory, a conditional, "if p then q" is represented initially by a partial model such as:

[p]   q
. . .

where the square brackets mean that p is exhaustively represented in the model, and the ellipsis represents an implicit model meaning that other states of the world (as yet unspecified) may exist. Under some circumstances, the model may be fleshed out explicitly to include the other possibilities consistent with the conditional statement, such as:

p   q
¬p   q
¬p   ¬q

where ¬p represents not-p and so on. As an example, Johnson-Laird and Byrne discuss the *modus ponens* and *modus tollens* inferences:

If p then q
p
Therefore, q   *Modus ponens*

If p then q
not-q
Therefore, not-p   *Modus tollens*

It is a common finding that people draw the first of these (valid) inferences significantly more often than the second. In the theory, this is explained on the grounds that *modus ponens* can be drawn from the initial representation—which includes only the affirmative p and q values—whereas *modus tollens* requires fleshing out of the model to include the case:

¬p   ¬q

Neither inference will be blocked by discovery of a counter-example (stage 3 of the general theory) because subjects' understanding of the truth conditions of the conditional statement precludes them from constructing:

p   ¬q

as a possible state of affairs.

The heuristic-analytic and mental models accounts can be linked by equating my own concept of "relevance" with the notion of explicit representation in a mental model. The fused theory combines complementary strengths. The heuristics proposed by Evans (1989) help to explain which items of information are explicitly represented in the models. The model theory then provides the missing account of how reasoning proceeds on the basis of the representation thus formed. Recently, model theorists have started to talk of "focusing effects" (Legrenzi, Girotto, & Johnson-Laird, 1993) which are closely related to, if not identical with my notion of relevance. In stating that "individuals are likely to restrict their thoughts to what is explicitly represented in their models", Legrenzi et al. (1993, p. 37) are effectively endorsing my assertion that relevance corresponds to explicit representation. Their focusing account of choices in the selection task is very similar to my own relevance account (Evans, 1989) described later in this chapter (see also Johnson-Laird in Chapter 6 of this volume for further discussion of the model theory of the selection task).

There is, however, a complication. On close inspection of the model theory of conditionals I found the proposals of Johnson-Laird and Byrne (1991) to be somewhat unsatisfactory with regard to (a) the specification of the formation of representations and the deduction of inferences from them, and (b) the extent to which the theory was able to account for a number of the established phenomena of conditional reasoning. My criticisms of the theory are expounded in detail in Evans (1993) together with a number of suggestions for revisions and improvements to the theory. Perhaps the most important difference concerns the mechanism by which an inference is drawn. For example, Johnson-Laird and Byrne suggest that a conditional may be initially represented by a model in which p is not exhaustively represented:

p   q
. . .

supporting both the inferences *modus ponens* (p, therefore q) and affirmation of the consequent (q, therefore p). However, such inferences could be refuted by expanding the implicit model and discovering a counter-example. Hence, I propose that an inference is drawn only if the premise is exhaustively represented in a model, or if all possible models have been fleshed out. Thus, I suggest that the initial representation of a conditional is usually:

[p]   q
. . .

from which *modus ponens* follows but affirmation of the consequent does not. Both inferences, however, follow if the subject represents the statement as a bi-conditional:

[p]   [q]
. . .

There are many other points of detail, especially concerning the account of various phenomena in the literature, which are expounded by Evans (1993). Johnson-Laird and Byrne (personal communication) accept some of my points but dispute a number of others. Hence, my attempt at theoretical integration has, for the time being, generated some new controversy.

For the purposes of this chapter, however, I am happy to report that we do agree on the central idea that what I have termed relevance and what Legrenzi et al. call focusing effects arise from selective attention to that which is explicitly represented in a model. This equation also requires development of the original notion of relevance as applied in the heuristic-analytic theory. If a model can be fleshed-out—for example, in response to a question asked—this implies that new information can become relevant in the course of attending to the problem; a very reasonable assumption.

For the rest of this chapter I will concentrate mostly on the evidence for relevance effects in one particular problem: the Wason selection task. After a brief review of existing evidence in the literature I will present informal discussion of a number of my own recent experiments designed to test the theory.

RELEVANCE IN THE WASON SELECTION TASK

The Abstract Task: If- and Not-heuristics

A typical standard abstract version of the Wason selection task is shown in Fig. 7.1. With the affirmative conditional "if p then q", most people choose p or p and q, whereas the correct answer is p and not-q. In terms of the example shown, the rule can only be falsified if a card is found which has an A on one side and does not have a 3 on the other side, so the cards that need be turned are the A and the 7. Few subjects choose the 7 (not-q) however. The failure to select this card is of great psychological interest. We know from research on conditional reasoning using other paradigms that subjects have the necessary understanding of logical principles (see Evans et al., 1993, Chapter 2). For example, most subjects can make the *modus tollens* inference that if there is not a 3 on the back then there cannot be an A on the front. Equally, the evidence of truth table tasks is

---

Subjects are shown a set of cards, each of which are seen to have a capital letter on one side and a single figure number on the other side. The experimenter then hides the cards and selects four which are placed on the table. The subject can then see the four facing sides as follows:

The subject is then told that "the following rule applies to these four cards and may be true or false": *If there is an A on one side of the card, then there is a 3 on the other side of the card.*
The subject is then asked to decide which of the four cards would need to be turned over in order to decide whether the rule is true or false.

Typical choices
A alone, or A and 3

Correct choice
A and 7, because the rule can only be falsified if a card is found which has an A on one side and does not have a 3 on the other side.

FIG. 7.1. The Wason selection task: standard abstract presentation. (Adapted from Evans, Newstead, & Byrne, 1993.)

that most subjects understand that a card with an A on one side and a number other than a 3 on the back falsifies the rule. And yet, on the selection task very few subjects choose the not-q card. Why?

In order to answer this I must first review an effect called "matching bias" initially demonstrated on the selection task by Evans and Lynch (1973) and replicated many times since (see Evans et al., 1993, Chapter 4 for a detailed review of selection task experiments). Table 7.1 shows the four logical choices on the selection task with negative components permuted. We now refer to the four cards in terms of the logical cases as true antecedent (TA), false antecedent (FA), true consequent (TC) and false consequent (FC). The correct choice is TA and FC on all rules. Notice that according to the rule used, each logical case can be represented by either an affirmed (matching) or negated (mismatching) value. For example, when the antecedent of the rule is affirmative, the TA case is produced by matching the card to value in the rule and the FA card by altering it (e.g. a D is FA because it is a letter which is not an A).

Figure 7.2 shows some typical selection task frequencies for rules with and without negations in either component. There are two effects present. First, if we average over the matching status of the cards, then their logical ordering appears to be TA>TC ≈FC>FA. So the first effect to be explained is why TA is the most frequent and FA the least frequent choice regardless

TABLE 7.1

The Four Logical Choices on the Wason Selection Task with Negative Components Permuted and with Concrete Examples of Letter–Number Rules

Rule	Logical Case			
	TA	FA	TC	FC
If p then q	p	not-p	q	not-q
If there is a T on one side then there is a 7 on the other side	T	Y	7	5
If p then not q	p	not-p	not-q	q
If there is a B on one side then there is not a 2 on the other side	B	D	4	2
If not p then q	not-p	p	q	not-q
If there is not an M on one side then there is a 3 on the other side	S	M	3	9
If not p then not q	not-p	p	not-q	q
If there is not a J on one side then there is not a 6 on the other side	G	J	1	6

Note: TA = true antecedent; FA = false antecedent; TC = true consequent; and FC = false consequent. (Adapted from Evans, Newstead, & Byrne, 1993.)

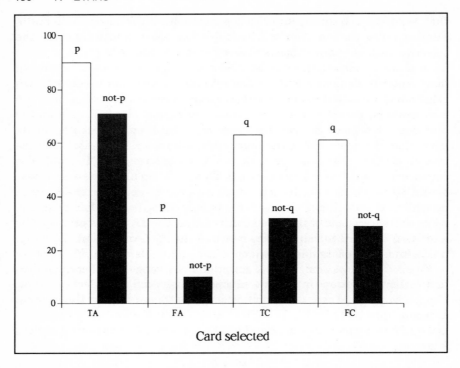

FIG. 7.2. Percentage frequency selections of the four cards where they do and do not match the items in the rules, aggregated from four experiments. (Adapted from Evans, Newstead, & Byrne, 1993.)

of matching. However, if we now examine each logical case in turn we can compare the frequency of selection on rules where the card matches (p or q) and those where it does not match (not-p or not-q). These correspond to the white and black bars respectively in the figure. In each case there are substantially (and significantly) more selections when the case matches than when it does not—the so-called matching bias effect. (In replication studies, the consequent matching bias is almost always observed; the antecedent matching effect, which is weaker, sometimes falls short of significance.)

Evans (1989) explains these two findings on the assumption that card selections reflect perceived relevance at the heuristic stage rather than analytic reasoning. Since the task is abstract, linguistic rather than pragmatic factors determine relevance—specifically an if-heuristic and a not-heuristic. The linguistic function of "if" is to direct the listener's attention to the possible state of affairs in which the antecedent condition holds true. "Not" on the other hand is used to deny presuppositions so that the proposition denied is still the topic of the sentence and the focus of attention. The statements "I watched television today" and "I did not watch television today" both concern the topic of watching television; the latter does not invite attention to all of the other possible activities I may have indulged in. The if-heuristic explains the high selection of TA and low selection of FA, whereas the not-heuristic explains matching bias.

Some evidence that choices in the selection task reflect an attentional bias of the kind envisaged by this theory was presented by Evans, Ball, and Brooks (1987). They used a computer-presented version of the task with a button underneath each card. In contrast with standard procedure, subjects had to indicate a decision for each of the four cards which was either YES (it needs to be turned over) or NO (it does not need to be turned over). What this method permitted was measurement of the order in which decisions were made about the four cards. It was predicted that the attentional bias would lead subjects to make decisions about matching cards before mismatching cards and about TA cards before FA cards. In other words subjects were expected to think about "relevant" cards, select them, and then reject others as an afterthought. This is precisely what happened—there was a strong correlation between selection order and YES decisions throughout.

Matching bias is also demonstrated on a related reasoning problem known as the conditional truth table task (see Evans et al., 1993, Chapter 2). Evans (1972) asked subjects to construct cases which could make conditional rules true and, separately, to construct cases which could make them false. Consider the case where the antecedent is false but the consequent is true (FT). On a rule of the form "if not p then q" such as:

If there is not a blue circle on the left then there is a red triangle on the right.

the FT case is constructed by a double match—i.e. placing a blue circle to the left of a red triangle. Many subjects constructed such a case when asked to falsify the rule. When the rule has the form "if p then not q", however, i.e.

If there is a blue circle on the left then there is not a red triangle on the right.

the FT case can only be constructed by a double mismatch—e.g. by placing a green square to the left of a blue circle. Evans found that few subjects construct this case either when verifying or falsifying the rule. Oaksford and Stenning (1992, Experiment 1) recently replicated this experiment with similar findings. In other research, subjects have been presented with truth table cases and asked to evaluate them as either conforming to the rule, contradicting it, or being irrelevant. In this task, subjects describe as irrelevant precisely the cases which they fail to select in the construction version of the task described above (see Evans et al., 1993). While this provides further evidence for the not-heuristic, the operation of the if-heuristic in the truth table task is also observable in the form of the almost universal construction/evaluation of the TT (true-antecedent, true-consequent) case as conforming to the rule, regardless of matching.

Further evidence in favour of the not-heuristic explanation of matching bias has been presented by Evans (1983) using a truth table evaluation task. In the normal task negations are implicit, produced by using an alternative value which does not match the item in the rule. A modified version of this was used in a control group. The following example is for the TF case on an affirmative conditional:

RULE:
If the letter is H then the number is 4.
INSTANCE:
The letter is H and the number is 7.

In the experimental group, however, all negations were explicit. Hence the last statement would read:

The letter is H and the number is not 4.

With this format, all cases to be evaluated matched—i.e. referred to the same letters and numbers. A substantial and significant reduction in the size of the matching bias effect was observed in the experimental group, although the effect was not eliminated.

Explicit negation should similarly reduce matching bias on the Wason selection task. This idea was picked up by Jackson and Griggs (1990) who argued that the facilitation observed by Cheng and Holyoak (1985) in support of their pragmatic schema theory could be due to the inclusion of explicit negatives for the not-p and not-q cases in their thematic versions of the task. The substantive issue so far as schema theory is concerned is not relevant here, but has been the subject of several successive papers by Girotto, Mazzocco, and Cherubini (1992), Kroger, Cheng, and Holyoak (1993) and Griggs and Cox (1993). What is relevant here is that in the course of these papers abstract task control groups showed that use of explicit negatives does not facilitate logically correct selection rates on the selection task—a finding in apparent contrast with that of Evans (1983). I say "apparent" because (a) the absence of matching does not necessarily imply the presence of logical facilitation and (b) it is not possible to measure matching bias except in an experiment in which all four rules with rotation of negative components are used. No one has yet run this experiment. In the meantime, however, the findings of Jackson and Griggs, replicated by Griggs and Cox (1993) do raise an unresolved question for the theory.[1]

The heuristic-analytic account of matching bias has been disputed in the recent paper of Oaksford and Stenning (1992). Part of their argument rests on an alternative method of analysis of "matching" which seems to me to alter the definition of what the bias is. Oaksford and Stenning do, however, offer an interesting argument that matching might reflect difficulty in the construction of contrast classes—i.e. in identifying what is referred to by a statement such as "there is not a red circle". Although offered as a critical alternative to my account, this idea relates to what I have termed a general positivity bias, or an aversion to thinking in terms of negatively defined information (Evans, 1989). Oaksford and Stenning also show in their experiments that manipulations which facilitate the construction of contrast classes (e.g. by providing binary materials in which there is a single propositional alternative to the negative), tend to suppress the matching bias effect. I do not, however, agree with their claim that this refutes my account. If subjects are able to avoid the difficulty of negation by recoding the negative as an equivalent affirmative, then the not-heuristic will no longer apply.

The account of the abstract selection task offered in terms of the heuristic-analytic theory by Evans (1984; 1989) implies that choices reflect heuristic processes only, with no analytic reasoning involved. This is certainly consistent with the data in Fig. 7.1 which seem to require no explanation beyond the if- and not-heuristics. The supposition of analytic process is, however, required to account for data on the truth table task where matching is shown to affect relevance, but not the classification of a relevant card as either true or false. It is not clear why subjects should not also apply analytic reasoning on the selection task. It is indeed possible that they do so, but that this reasoning fails to affect the decision to select the card. In other words, subjects apply analytic processes to "relevant" cards but always convince themselves that these cards need selecting. I will later present some evidence consistent with this hypothesis.

In recent years I have conducted a number of experiments in order to test the relevance theory of the selection task, which will be reported briefly and informally here. For the sake of clarity I will number the entire sequence of experiments, although they fall into two distinct studies.

Reasoning Versus Judgement: Experiments 1 and 2

In the first study, the manipulation of interest was the instruction given to the subject. In each experiment, one group of subjects was given the standard presentation of the selection task as a reasoning problem, while the other was instructed to make judgements of relevance. In Experiment

1, abstract letter-number rules of the kind shown in Table 7.1 were used. Each subject was given four problems corresponding to the four rules produced by permuting negations in either component of the rule. The instructions used were as follows:

REASONING GROUP ONLY
This experiment is concerned with people's logical reasoning ability. You will be given four problems which can be solved by reasoning.

JUDGEMENT GROUP ONLY
This experiment is concerned with people's understanding of natural language. You will be given four problems on which you must make a set of judgements.

Each of the problems concerns a deck of cards which always have a capital letter on one side and a single digit number on the other side. On each problem you will be shown:

(a) a diagram of four such cards;
(b) a rule which applies to these cards and may be true or false.

REASONING GROUP ONLY
Your task, in each case, is to decide which of the four cards must be turned over in order to decide whether the rule is true or false. Please place a tick under any card which you select.

JUDGEMENT GROUP ONLY
Your task, in each case, is to decide to which of the four cards the rule appears to be relevant. Please place a tick under any card which you select.

The problems are on the attached sheets. Please attempt them in order and when you have finished one problem proceed to the next without referring back to your previous answers.

Each page consisted of a diagram of four cards showing a letter and a number that were referred to in the rules (p and q) and a letter and number not referred to (not-p and not-q), followed by the rule and with a small prompt printed underneath. The prompt for the Reasoning group was "Please tick those cards you would need to turn over in order to check whether the rule is true or false"; for the Judgement group it was "Please tick those cards to which the rule appears to be relevant."

The reason for conducting this experiment was to see if instructions to judge relevance led to the same choices as normal reasoning instructions.

This seemed a reasonable prediction, especially since judgements of "irrelevance" on the truth table task correspond to the predictions of relevance theory. However, the results (Table 7.2) came as a nasty surprise! Looking at the column of frequencies for the Reasoning group across the four rules, one can see that the normal pattern illustrated in Fig. 7.2 is present. Subjects are choosing far more TA than FA cards on each rule and also choosing more cards which match (p or q) than which do not match (not-p or not-q). However, inspection of the column of frequencies for the Judgement group shows something quite different. There is no matching bias at all and a marked tendency to choose the TA and TC cards on all rules.

How can we explain this? Well I suppose the relevance theory could just be wrong and that people do reason about the cards in order to select them. But if the relevant cards are what Judgement subjects select, why is there not a verification bias on the reasoning task also; and if subjects do reason on the selection task, why do they match? The alternative possibility is that the instructions to make judgements change what is relevant in the task. Lest the reader suspects me of wriggling, I should say that some evidence will be presented shortly (Experiments 3–5) which lends strong support to the relevance theory of the selection task. In fact, there is an account of the data shown in Table 7.2—admittedly post hoc—which is consistent with other data. In the truth table study of Evans (1972, and the replication by Oaksford & Stenning, 1992) matching bias was found only when subjects were asked to construct cases which made the conditional false. On the verification task subjects almost universally construct the TT case (i.e. TA and TC) regardless of negations in the rules. Suppose, then, that subjects in my Experiment 1 interpret the instruction as that of finding cases which conform to the rule? This would account for the verification pattern and lack of matching bias.

TABLE 7.2

Card Selection % Frequencies for Reasoning (n=34) and Relevance (n=33) Groups in Experiment 1

Averaged by logical case	TA	FA	TC	FC
Reasoning	81	21	46	38
Judgement	76	13	76	11
Averaged by matching case	p	not-p	q	not-q
Reasoning	62	44	61	33
Judgement	43	46	45	42

Experiment 2 used a computer-presented version of the task in which subjects chose cards by pointing to them on the screen and clicking the mouse button. This experiment also used the four rules with rotated negations but on this occasion they were placed in arbitrarily thematic contexts. By this I mean real world scenarios lacking any of the pragmatic cues that might be expected to assist subjects in solving the task. (For a detailed review of the kinds of thematic materials that alter performance on the selection task see Evans et al., 1993, Chapter 4). There were four contents used which were randomly assigned to each of the four rule types separately for each subject. Here is an example:

You visit a friend of yours, Sarah, who is an art student. "I have just been working on my Christmas cards", she says. "I thought I would economise this year by making my own cards with my friend's names written on one side and an illustration of my own on the back." You look at four cards that she has just finished.

"I have decided that it would be a good idea to stick to the following rule: *If a card has [does NOT have] a male name on one side then it has [does NOT have] a red flower on the other side.*"
CARD DISPLAY
Four cards showing "Paul", "Mary" and pictures of a red and a yellow flower.

There were four groups in this experiment in a 2 by 2 design. One variable was the use of reasoning versus judgement instructions as in the previous experiment. The other concerned the use of a preceding scenario. Scenario groups had the problems in the form shown above. No scenario groups had the first paragraph removed and replaced by a single sentence. In the case of the example shown, this was:

Each of the four cards shown below has a person's name drawn on one side and a drawing on the other side. The following rule applies to these four cards and may be either true or false.

The scenario manipulation was introduced to resolve a discrepancy in the findings of a pilot study and those of Experiment 1 (Table 7.2). The data are summarised in Table 7.3. Experiment 2 replicated the finding of a verification pattern TA and TC in the two Judgement groups when data were analysed by logical case. As intended, introduction of the scenarios did not facilitate correct TA and FC choices in any condition. However, the scenario manipulation did produce several surprising results as follows:

- A verification pattern, TA and TC, was also found for the Reasoning-Scenario group.
- Matching bias was observed for Reasoning-No Scenario groups, but not in the Reasoning-Scenario group.
- Matching bias was observed in the Judgement-No Scenario group but not in the Judgement-Scenario group.

In all cases, trends reported as present were highly statistically significant. Assuming that No Scenario groups are roughly equivalent to abstract tasks, then the findings are not inconsistent with Experiment 1. They are, however, very surprising. In effect, introducing scenarios has removed matching bias on the reasoning task, but introduced matching bias into the judgement task. The former of these two findings, however, is not without precedent and has significance for the theory of relevance in reasoning. Reich and Ruth (1982), Griggs and Cox (1983), and Oaksford and Stenning (1992) have all reported suppression of matching with realistic content.

Griggs and Cox (1983, Experiment 1), for example, introduced negative components into one of the most reliable facilitatory contents—the Sears problem—complete with scenario. The rule to be tested was thus of the form: "If a purchase exceeds [does not exceed] $30 then the receipt must have [not have] the signature of the department manager on the back." Although facilitatory in the affirmative form, the presence of negations changes the logical relationships so that they no longer correspond with the subjects' experience, thus rendering the rules effectively arbitrary. Griggs and Cox's findings are very similar to those of Experiment 2. There

TABLE 7.3
Card Selection % Frequencies for Reasoning (n=34) and
Relevance(n=33) Groups in Experiment 2

Averaged by logical case	TA	FA	TC	FC
Reasoning-Scenario	69	31	60	33
Reasoning-No scenario	64	25	17	23
Judgement-Scenario	63	21	63	13
Judgement-No scenario	62	13	50	19
Averaged by matching case	p	not-p	q	not-q
Reasoning-Scenario	48	52	48	44
Reasoning-No scenario	48	33	31	10
Judgement-Scenario	50	35	46	31
Judgement-No scenario	37	38	29	40

was no facilitation on the arbitrarily realistic negative rules, but also no matching bias either (abstract controls showed normal trends). In their second experiment where negative thematic rules were made to correspond with subjects' experience, facilitatory effects were demonstrated.

In summary, the use of realistic, but non-facilitatory content and scenarios normally eliminates matching bias. (The one apparent exception in the literature—the study of Manktelow & Evans, 1979—is discussed below.) This trend is consistent with the view that realistic content causes switching from linguistic to pragmatic cues to relevance even though the pragmatic cues do not assist the subject in solving the task. I will present further evidence for this argument below.

A Study of Card Inspection Times:
Experiments 3 to 5

The second study developed from the use of computer presentation in the experiment last described above. It occurred to me that since subjects were in any case using a mouse pointer to select cards, a slight modification to the program would allow me to measure the length of time at which a card was pointed prior to selection. Subjects were instructed to point at any card they were considering, which resulted in the word "Considering" being flashed beneath the card. As soon as the mouse was clicked on the card this changed to a steady "Selected". Card inspection times were recorded as the cumulative time spent pointing to a card which had not yet been selected. Of course, subjects might point at a card and then not select it. However, the argument of the relevance theory is that people will only think about the cards which they end up selecting. Hence, I predicted that inspection times would be longer for selected than non-selected cards.

Experiment 3 used 4 rules and tested 30 naive undergraduate student subjects. An abstract affirmative rule was expected to give the usual pattern, while an abstract negative "if p then not-q" was expected to give many correct TA and FC choices due to matching bias. I also used two thematic versions: a strong facilitator and a weak facilitator. The notion that selection task responses can be "facilitated" by realistic material has been around for a long time (Wason & Johnson-Laird, 1972). While some versions do facilitate, others do not, and still others cue alternative patterns which are neither the logically correct nor the kind of choices normally seen on abstract tasks (see Evans et al., 1993, Chapter 4 for a detailed review and discussion). Hence, it is more accurate to describe the effects of content as providing pragmatic cues to selection that may or may not facilitate the TA/FC choice. Where the effect does coincide with the logically correct choice, however, I use the conventional term of "facilitation".

The weak facilitator was the towns and transport rule of Wason and Shapiro (1971), which has only been replicated in about half of later studies using it, and the strong facilitator was the very strong and reliable drinking-age rule of Griggs and Cox (1982). All problems produced the expected patterns of selection. This permitted testing of the first and weaker of two hypotheses derived from the relevance theory. Those cards which were chosen more often were also associated with higher mean inspection times. The correlation between mean selection frequency and mean inspection latency was significant (r = 0.785, p < 0.001).

The second and stronger hypothesis was that, for any given card, the subjects who choose it should spend longer inspecting it than those who do not. This pattern was found on almost every card. In Fig. 7.3, the mean time spent inspecting selected and non-selected cards is shown aggregated across the four cards on each of the four rules. The differences are extremely striking and of course highly statistically significant. The next experiment (4) used 4 thematic rules which included a non-facilitator (the food and drinks rule of Manktelow & Evans, 1979), a different strong facilitator (D'Andrade's Sears problem described by Griggs, 1983), and both a

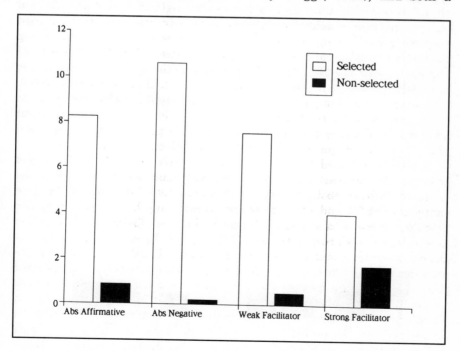

FIG. 7.3. Mean inspection times for selected and non-selected cards on each rule in Experiment 3 (n = 30).

standard and switched social contract rule based on that of Manktelow and
Over (1991; see also Manktelow & Over, this volume, Chapter 5). The
former facilitates TA and FC choices, while the latter tends to encourage
an FA and TC pattern. Once again, selection frequencies conformed broadly
to expectations and there was a significant, though weaker correlation with
mean inspection times ($r = 0.478$, $p < 0.05$).

Figure 7.4 shows the mean inspection times of selected and non-selected
cards in this experiment. Again, the subjects who chose a given card spent
considerably longer looking at it than those who did not. The relationship
is thus shown to hold for thematic as well as abstract rules. This is
important with respect to the application of relevance theory to thematic
versions of the selection task, on which there is more than one possible
view. My own belief (Evans, 1989) is that the reason that facilitation (TA
and FC) and other patterns (e.g. FA and TC) are elicited by thematic content
is because the basis of subjects' choices switch from pragmatically to
linguistically cued relevance. A similar argument has been made by
Girotto, Mazzocco, and Cherubini (1992). However, an alternative
application of the heuristic-analytic theory might involve the proposal that

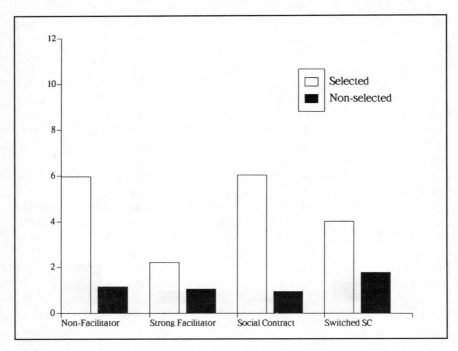

FIG. 7.4.   Mean inspection times for selected and non-selected cards on each rule
in Experiment 4 (n = 30).

subjects switch from heuristic to analytic reasoning. Platt and Griggs (1993) have introduced a manipulation into an abstract task which they argue may cause this to occur.

The idea of a switch from linguistic to pragmatic relevance helps, of course, to explain why a thematic content and context can override matching bias, as appears to be the case in the data of Experiment 2 (Table 7.3) and in other studies discussed earlier. An apparently discrepant finding is reported by Manktelow and Evans (1979): this study's totally non-facilitatory thematic content showed typical matching bias patterns. It could, however, simply be that this content, which arbitrarily linked eating and drinking with such rules as "Every time I eat haddock then I drink gin" was so semantically impoverished as to function effectively as an abstract content. Consistent with this is the fact that when we did not include the scenario paragraph in the reasoning task of Experiment 2, the matching bias effect was retained (see Table 7.3). Scenarios we know can be critical in providing pragmatic cues. For example, Pollard and Evans (1987) showed that facilitation disappears on the drinking-age rule when the usual scenario paragraph is removed.

When I show people the data in Figs. 7.3 and 7.4, the question they usually ask is, "What are subjects thinking about for all that time, and why think about the card if you are going to select it anyway?" My answer is that subjects are effectively rationalising a choice already made. We know from the study of Evans and Wason (1976) that people can convince themselves that almost any card is part of the correct solution if they are cued to think about it. Evans and Wason presented their subjects with the selection task and one of four common answers presented as the "solution". In compliance with the instructions all subjects happily provided explanations as to why their randomly allocated solution was correct and none protested that they had been given the wrong answer.

There is also evidence from verbal protocol analyses. For example, Beattie and Baron (1988) reported that subjects did not consider alternatives to the cards they chose. In Experiment 5, verbal protocol analysis was conducted which replicated and extended the findings of Beattie and Baron. This experiment used the same four groups as in Experiment 2—i.e. Reasoning and Judgement groups with and without scenarios—and employed both the inspection time method as well as the collection of verbal protocols. Inspection times were again longer for selected cards on Judgement as well as Reasoning groups—a useful generalisation of the finding. Protocols were analysed on two measures, the first similar to that of Beattie and Baron. First, the protocols were scored for mentions of the facing sides of cards. The percentage mentions were then divided according to whether the subject selected the card or not. The protocols were also scored for mention of the hidden sides of cards, and

TABLE 7.4

Results of Protocol Analyses in Experiment 5

Group	% Reference to Facing Side			% Reference to Hidden Sides		
	Selected	Not Selected	χ^2	Selected	Not Selected	χ^2
RS (n=4)	66	9	43.6	52	6	25.4
RN (n=5)	78	6	22.8	53	4	17.2
JS (n=3)	83	25	9.1	71	8	6.9
JN (n=3)	71	26	16.4	65	26	19.6

Notes: Each subject contributes 16 data points; subjects who produced no useful verbalisations were excluded from the analysis; and χ^2 tests compare reference rates between selected and non-selected cards on frequencies pooled across the subjects in each group, and all are significant at $p < 0.01$.

again broken down according to whether the card was selected or not. The results of the protocol analyses are summarised in Table 7.4.

What these analyses show is, first, that in all groups there is a significant and substantial tendency to refer to the facing sides of the cards that will be selected more often than those that will not be selected. There are, however, more references to non-selected cards in the Judgement groups. What is particularly interesting, however, is that there is a similar tendency to refer also to the hidden sides of cards that will be selected: again significant in all groups. The latter finding is of particular interest because it shows that subjects *do* think about the hidden sides of the cards, and so presumably are attempting to analyse the consequence of turning over the cards. This contrasts with the finding (Fig. 7.4) that their selections are entirely predictable on the basis of relevance cues on the facing sides. What appears to be happening is that (a) subjects only think about some cards and not others, and (b) thinking about the hidden sides of such cards mostly confirms a decision to choose those cards. So it appears that analytic reasoning does occur after all, but on this particular problem—the selection task—serves only to rationalise or justify a choice already cued by relevance.

CONCLUSIONS

In this chapter I have developed some of the evidence for the heuristic-analytic theory of Evans (1984; 1989). In essence, what I have argued is the following:

- With abstract conditional reasoning, relevance is cued by heuristics deriving from the linguistic function of "if " and "not". These heuristics are sufficient to explain card choices on the selection task, and the rating of some cards as irrelevant on the truth table task. Analytic reasoning accounts for why relevant cards are regarded as either true or false on the truth table task.

- On the abstract Wason selection task, analytic reasoning (while present) does not alter the choices made and serves only to rationalise or confirm them. In support of this claim, evidence based on both card inspection times and on verbal protocols has been presented to show that subjects think only about the cards they choose.

- On thematic forms of the selection task, especially when a scenario is present, card choices are still determined by relevance, but relevance is now cued pragmatically and not linguistically. Evidence for this claim is based upon (a) the finding that matching bias does not occur with scenario-based thematic material, and (b) the finding of the same sources of evidence of selective thought—in the inspection times and protocol analyses—as presented for abstract tasks. In other words, no matter how pragmatic cues alter selection patterns, the findings remain that subjects think much longer about the cards they choose and are much more likely to mention such cards while thinking aloud.

NOTE

1. Since writing this chapter I have run some relevant experiments in collaboration with John Clibbens and Ben Rood in which negated components were rotated in the conditionals. In the first experiment we replicated and extended the Evans (1983) finding that explicit negation reduces matching bias on the truth table task. In two further experiments we showed that explicit negation in the cases entirely removes the matching bias effect on the selection task without, at the same time, increasing the frequency of correct solutions.

REFERENCES

Beattie, J., & Baron, J. (1988). Confirmation and matching biases in hypothesis testing. *Quarterly Journal of Experimental Psychology, 40A*, 269–297.

Braine, M.D.S., & O'Brien, D.P. (1991). A theory of If: A lexical entry, reasoning program, and pragmatic principles. *Psychological Review, 98*, 182–203.

Cheng, P.W., & Holyoak, K.J. (1985). Pragmatic reasoning schemas. *Cognitive Psychology, 17*, 391–416.

Cosmides, L. (1989). The logic of social exchange: Has natural selection shaped how humans reason? Studies with the Wason selection task. *Cognition, 31*, 187–276.

Evans, J.St.B.T. (1972). Interpretation and matching bias in a reasoning task. *British Journal of Psychology, 24*, 193–199.

Evans, J.St.B.T. (1982). *The psychology of deductive reasoning*. London: Routledge & Kegan Paul.

Evans, J.St.B.T. (1983). Linguistic determinants of bias in conditional reasoning. *Quarterly Journal of Experimental Psychology, 35A,* 635–644.

Evans, J.St.B.T. (1984). Heuristic and analytic processes in reasoning. *British Journal of Psychology, 75,* 451–468.

Evans, J.St.B.T. (1989). *Bias in human reasoning: Causes and consequences.* Hove, UK: Lawrence Erlbaum Associates Ltd.

Evans, J.St.B.T. (1991). Theories of human reasoning: The fragmented state of the art. *Theory and Psychology, 1,* 83–105.

Evans, J.St.B.T. (1993). The mental model theory of conditional reasoning: Critical appraisal and revision. *Cognition 48,* 1–20.

Evans, J.St.B.T., Ball, L.J., & Brooks, P.G. (1987). Attentional bias and decision order in a reasoning task. *British Journal of Psychology, 78,* 385–394.

Evans, J.St.B.T., & Lynch, J.S. (1973). Matching bias in the selection task. *British Journal of Psychology, 64,* 391–397.

Evans, J.St.B.T., Newstead, S.E., & Byrne, R.M.J. (1993). *Human reasoning: The psychology of deduction.* Hove, UK: Lawrence Erlbaum Associates Ltd.

Evans, J.St.B.T., & Wason, P.C. (1976). Rationalisation in a reasoning task. *British Journal of Psychology, 63,* 205–212.

Girotto, V., Mazzocco, A., & Cherubini, P. (1992). Pragmatic judgements of relevance and reasoning: A reply to Jackson and Griggs. *Quarterly Journal of Experimental Psychology, 45A,* 547–574.

Griggs, R.A. (1983). The role of problem content in the selection task and in the THOG problem. In J.St.B.T. Evans (Ed.), *Thinking and reasoning: Psychological approaches.* London: Routledge & Kegan Paul.

Griggs, R.A., & Cox, J.R. (1982). The elusive thematic materials effect in the Wason selection task. *British Journal of Psychology, 73,* 407–420.

Griggs, R.A., & Cox, J.R. (1983). The effects of problem content and negation on Wason's selection task. *Quarterly Journal of Experimental Psychology, 35A,* 519–533.

Griggs, R.A., & Cox, J.R. (1993). Permission schemas and the selection task. *Quarterly Journal of Experimental Psychology, 46A,* 637–652.

Jackson, S.L., & Griggs, R.A. (1990). The elusive pragmatic reasoning schemas effect. *Quarterly Journal of Experimental Psychology, 42A,* 353–374.

Johnson-Laird, P.N. (1983). *Mental models.* Cambridge: Cambridge University Press.

Johnson-Laird, P.N., & Bara, B.G. (1984). Syllogistic inference. *Cognition, 16,* 1–62.

Johnson-Laird, P.N., & Byrne, R. (1991). *Deduction.* Hove, UK: Lawrence Erlbaum Associates Ltd.

Kahneman, D., & Tversky, A. (1982). On the study of statistical intuition. *Cognition, 12,* 325–326.

Kroger, J.K., Cheng, P.W., & Holyoak, K.J. (1993). Evoking the permission schema: The impact of explicit negation and a violation-checking context. *Quarterly Journal of Experimental Psychology, 46A,* 615–636.

Legrenzi, P., Girotto, V., & Johnson-Laird, P.N. (1993). Focusing in reasoning and decision making. *Cognition, 49,* 37–66.

Manktelow, K.I., & Evans, J.St.B.T. (1979). Facilitation of reasoning by realism: Effect or non-effect? *British Journal of Psychology, 70,* 477–488.

Manktelow, K.I., & Over, D. (1991). Social roles and utilities in reasoning with deontic conditionals. *Cognition, 39,* 85–105.

McClelland, J.M., & Rumelhart, D. (Eds.) (1986). *Parallel distributed processing: Experiments in the microstructure of cognition. Volume 2: Psychological and biological models.* Cambridge, MA: MIT Press.

Oaksford, M., & Chater, N. (1993). Reasoning theories and bounded rationality. In K.I. Manktelow & D. Over (Eds.), *Rationality.* London: Routledge & Kegan Paul.

Oaksford, M., & Stenning, K. (1992). Reasoning with conditionals containing negated constituents. *Journal of Experimental Psychology: Learning, Memory and Cognition, 18,* 835–854.

Platt, R.D., & Griggs, R.A. (1993). Facilitation in the abstract selection task: The effects of attentional and instructional factors. *Quarterly Journal of Experimental Psychology, 46A,* 591–614.

Pollard, P., & Evans, J.St.B.T. (1987). On the relationship between content and context effects in reasoning. *American Journal of Psychology, 100,* 41–60.

Reich, S.S., & Ruth, P. (1982). Wason's selection task: Verification, falsification, and matching. *British Journal of Psychology, 73,* 395–405.

Rips, L.J. (1983). Cognitive processes in propositional reasoning. *Psychological Review, 90,* 38–71.

Rips, L.J. (1989). The psychology of knights and knaves. *Cognition, 31,* 85–116.

Sperber, D., & Wilson, D. (1986). *Relevance.* Oxford: Basil Blackwell.

Wason, P.C. (1966). Reasoning. In B.M. Foss (Ed.), *New horizons in psychology, I.* Harmondsworth: Penguin.

Wason, P.C., & Evans, J.St.B.T. (1975). Dual processes in reasoning? *Cognition, 3,* 141–154.

Wason, P.C., & Johnson-Laird, P.N. (1972). *Psychology of reasoning: Structure and content.* London: Batsford.

Wason, P.C., & Shapiro, D. (1971). Natural and contrived experience in a reasoning problem. *Quarterly Journal of Experimental Psychology, 23,* 63–71.

CHAPTER EIGHT

The Abstract Selection Task: Thesis, Antithesis, and Synthesis

David W. Green

Department of Psychology, Centre for Cognitive Science, University College London, UK

The thesis of the original research on the abstract selection task was that the task required reasoning and that individuals varied in their ability to reason effectively. On this view, the reasons individuals gave reflected their analysis and hence could be used to infer psychological process. The antithesis proposed, on the contrary, that individuals were not reasoning at all and that card selection reflected preconscious processes of relevance. On this proposal, reasons were merely rationalisations for actions already chosen and could not therefore be used to infer anything about the psychological processes preceding action. Despite its undoubted successes this chapter questions some aspects of the latter proposal and some of the evidence adduced in support of it. It moots a synthesis in which card selection is the result of an internal process of argumentation. In essence, it proposes that selections reflect a competition between alternative courses of action. The actions chosen are the ones that make most sense to the individual. Such a view connects individual cognition to the social context in which cognitive processes operate.

The first part of the chapter reviews data in support of the thesis and the nature of the evidence adduced in support of the antithesis. It also references data showing that performance in the abstract selection task can be remarkably good. Such data indicate the importance of specifying an analytic process. Much of the research used outcome measures (e.g. percentage of correct selections) but such measures alone are insufficient to determine the various processes of selection. Accordingly, the second part of the chapter considers some task variants which do offer a more detailed picture of the psychological processes. Such data support some aspects of the antithesis but are incompatible with other aspects. The third part explores these and other problematic features of the antithesis and describes the synthesis which treats thinking as a process of argumentation.

THESIS AND ANTITHESIS

Wason (1968, Experiment 1) required subjects to read a conditional sentence of the form, "If there is a D on one side of any card, then there is a 3 on the other side". Subjects were told the sentence referred to four cards, each of which had a letter on one side and a number on the other side. They were required to decide which of the four cards would enable them to determine whether the sentence was true or false, if they were to know the values on the back of the cards. These four cards, corresponding to a vowel, consonant, even number, and odd number are designated p, not-p, q, and not-q, or, by logical case, true antecedent, false antecedent, true consequent, and false consequent, respectively.

Subjects had to decide what evidence was relevant to the claim. (The term "claim" will be used in preference to the term "rule" in order to distinguish the abstract task from selection tasks with deontic content such as permissions or obligations—see Manktelow & Over, 1990.) The task appears simple: select those cards which are potential counter-examples to the claim; cards, that is, which could yield a combination of the true antecedent, p (e.g. a consonant), and the false consequent, not-q (e.g. an even number). Given this goal, the analysis required is straightforward. For each card, project two alternatives on to the hidden side and consider the implications of each for the truth or falsity of the claim. Most subjects, as is well known, choose the true antecedent (p) alone, or the true antecedent and the true consequent (pq), and typically only 10% select correctly. This pattern of results was obtained for a wide range of different claims (see Wason & Golding, 1974).

Wason (1968) explored many possible sources of difficulty. For instance, he showed that when presented with a counter-example, subjects were able to recognise it. However, they do not use this prior experience to select correctly. He also found that some subjects who failed to select correctly, failed to envisage that p could be associated with not-q even when explicitly required to project falsity on to the cards (see also George, 1990, Experiment 3).

Early research also established some conditions for improving performance on the abstract task. Mosconi and D'Urso (1974) argued that only a plausible and established claim can be submitted to the operation of falsification. They tested this supposition by varying the experience of subjects before the selection task. In Experiment 1, one group of subjects was presented with four cards and was asked to select cards which could demonstrate that a particular claim was true. Having completed this task, subjects were presented with another set of four cards and given the same instructions. In both cases, there were no counter-examples to the claim. For the third series, the instructions were different. Subjects were asked to check that the claim is always true. The result was that 75% of subjects (8/12) selected not-q, compared to 8% (1/12) in a group that experienced only the third series of cards.

The notion that it is easier to falsify a claim once its plausibility or validity has been established is also consistent with the results of an experiment by Legrenzi (1971). Legrenzi (Experiment 2) first asked individuals to discover a rule about a set of cards and then to express it as an indicative conditional. When subjects were subsequently presented with the same rule in the selection task, all of them selected correctly. Clearly, individuals can appreciate the logic of the selection task given certain conditions. They reason but do not always appreciate the need to identify the counter-example.

The information-processing model of Johnson-Laird and Wason (1970a) captures the essence of the thesis. They considered that most subjects rather than seeking disconfirming evidence that could falsify the claim, sought confirming or verifying evidence and selected p and q. Such subjects showed no insight into the nature of the inference. Others—those who selected p, q, and not-q—showed partial insight because they recognised the significance of the not-q card. Subjects who selected p and not-q showed full insight into the nature of the inference required. Goodwin and Wason (1972) provided corroborating evidence by analysing the reasons subjects gave for their selections.

The challenge to this thesis came from the finding that subjects in the standard task seemed to match the terms mentioned in the claim with those marked on the cards (Evans, 1972; Evans & Lynch, 1973; Manktelow & Evans, 1979). Consider a conditional claim such as, "If p then not-q"; matching would predict the selection of p (the true consequent) and q (the false consequent) (see Evans, this volume, Chapter 7) whereas verification would predict the selection of p and not-q. Most subjects selected the matching cards and hence selected correctly. Wason and Evans (1975) also showed that they provided apposite reasons.

The fact that this result was interpreted as evidence for matching and rationalisation requires comment. On the face of it, the result is compatible with the thesis that subjects show insight with the negative conditional. This interpretation was rejected because it seemed difficult to imagine how insight could be shown for the negative but not for the affirmative conditional. In fact, there is one possibility: the negative conditional ensures that the counter-example is mentally represented. In contrast, for an affirmative conditional further mental work is required in order to identify it (cf. Oaksford & Stenning, 1992).

Clearly, if subjects are matching in the task then the processes of selection and the process of providing reasons for those selections are entirely distinct (Wason & Evans, 1975). If so, reasons cannot be used to provide corroborating evidence for a process theory of the selection task. This position was bolstered by the findings of a study in which subjects were presented with a "solution" to the selection task and asked to justify it (Evans & Wason, 1976). In fact, the correct solution plus three common wrong solutions were given to different groups of subjects. A majority of subjects provided an explanation for whatever solution they were given and expressed high confidence in it (see also Evans, 1989).

The antithesis was captured in the heuristic-analytic proposal (Evans, 1984; Evans, 1989; Evans, this volume, Chapter 7). For present purposes two aspects of the proposal are pertinent. First, card selection is attributed to "a preconscious heuristic judgement of relevance" whereas subjects' reasons are attributed to an explicit analytic process which rationalises selections made on other grounds (Evans, 1989, p. 106; this volume, Chapter 7). Secondly, until recently (Evans, 1991; 1993a; this volume) the nature of the analytic mechanism was not spelled out. Hence, it was not clear how the antithesis could account for correct selection on affirmative conditionals. By proposing a mental models account of performance in the selection task (see Johnson-Laird & Byrne, 1991; Johnson-Laird, this volume, Chapter 6, for the basis of Evans' account), Evans can explain a wider range of data.

One issue which has to be faced in examining the evidence for either the thesis or the antithesis is the fact that subjects do not all make the same selections. Hence it is not at all clear whether or not one can give a single account of performance in the selection task. A more immediate problem is to understand why a subject selects a particular card. Consider the selection of p and q given an affirmative conditional. In the information-processing model of Johnson-Laird and Wason (1970a) it was presumed that selection was an attempt to verify (i.e. subjects must have expected to find q on the other side). But it may not have meant that at all. In principle, the selection of p allows the subject to discover a counter-example (i.e. to discover the presence of not-q). According to the heuristic-analytic proposal the selection of p and q indicates matching. Does this mean that subjects who match never consider not-q?

In the 1970s a range of outcome criteria were proposed in an effort to determine whether individuals were verifying, matching, or falsifying. Evans and Lynch (1973), for instance, recognised verification as operating when the selection of the true consequent cards exceeded the selection of false consequent cards. However, this ignores the possibility that verification and falsification may both be operating. Reich and Ruth (1982) proposed an alternative. They examined evidence for each strategy in isolation by looking for predictions which were exclusive. Given a rule such as "If not-p then not-q", matching should lead to the selection of p and q; verifying to the selection of not-p and not-q; and falsifying to the selection of not-p and q. On this basis they discovered that when the thematic value of the material was low, matching was the most popular strategy (see also Griggs & Cox, 1983; Oaksford & Stenning, 1992). In contrast, when thematic content was high, verification and falsification were the most popular strategies. However, this technique, as the authors acknowledged, neglects a lot of the data. It does not permit a direct estimate of the proportion of responses attributable to each strategy.

Other indices have also been developed. Pollard and Evans (1987) devised two indices—a matching index and a logic index. The matching index scored +1 for a selection of p or q and −1 for a selection of not-p or not-q. It yielded a scale of 5 points running from +2 (selection of p and q) to −2 (selection of not-p and not-q). A logic index was constructed in a similar fashion in which +1 was scored for p or not-q and −1 for not-p or q. However, a problem of determinacy remains. For instance, in the matching index a score of 1 is derivable in various ways (e.g. p alone, q alone, or p, q, and not-q). On affirmative conditionals, the matching selections are potential verifiers and the selection of p alone is potentially falsifying. Outcome measures alone, however subtly constructed, are insufficient to permit a unique determination of the process of selecting a given card.

In summary so far, the thesis and antithesis promote radically different views of the nature of cognitive processes in the selection task. The thesis promotes the view that individuals may try to reason but often fail, whereas the antithesis promotes the view that selections are made before any thinking occurs and that it is only in exceptional circumstances that appropriate analytic processes are engaged. However, the fact that performance can reach 100% in the abstract selection task requires some account. One problem in assessing these alternative theses is the reliance on outcome measures. In order to know what subjects are doing when they are selecting cards we need to devise special tasks. A number of variants of the selection task which do provide information on psychological processes are considered in the next section.

TASK VARIANTS

Three ways of exploring the process of selection are considered: card specification; thinking-aloud protocols (combined with temporal measures); and externalisation. Each of these variants point to the subtleties of the selection process.

In order to examine what subjects had in mind, Beattie and Baron (1988) required subjects to specify *both* the number and the letter when selecting cards. In this version, selected cards are no longer ambiguous as to whether they were selected with the intention to verify or to falsify the rule.

Beattie and Baron showed subjects a pack of cards that had both symbols—i.e. a number (1, 2, or 3) and a letter (A to G)—on the same side. Four of these cards, the identities of which were not known, were put in a bag. A subject was then given a claim about only those four cards (e.g. "If there is an A on a card, then there is also a 2 on that card") and was instructed to ask about all cards (and only those cards) that would be informative in deciding whether the claim was true or false of the cards in the bag. To be correct, subjects should ask about all cards with an A and a number other than 2 (assuming the one-way conditional interpretation).

Subjects completed both the "multi-card" task and the 4 card task, once each with an affirmative rule and with a negated rule ("If A then not-2"), and 61% of subjects (11/18) selected correctly in the multi-card task (unnegated rule). None did so in the 4 card task. The respective figures for the negated versions were 61% and 50% (9/18). Negated rules provided the main discrimination between confirming and matching. Two subjects just selected A1 and A3 cards in the negated multi-card version, and such subjects were confirming. In addition, 11 subjects matched in the multi-card negated task—i.e. chose A2. As found by others (e.g. Van Duyne, 1973), subjects matched more on task materials in which matching led to a correct solution. This variant tells us what values a subject is selecting but it still does not go far enough. The matching selection could have been selected because it is logically correct.

The second variant requires subjects to think aloud while solving the problem. In contrast to the negative conclusion drawn by Nisbett and Wilson (1977, p. 246) to the effect that people have "little ability to report accurately on their cognitive processes", Ericsson and Simon (1980, p. 247) argued that verbal reports, "elicited with care and interpreted with full understanding of the circumstances under which they were obtained, are a valuable and thoroughly reliable source of information about cognitive processes." For instance, Kellogg (1982) showed that when a task prompts intentional hypothesis testing, introspective reports are accurate (see Berry, 1990). Thinking-aloud protocols should therefore be a valid way to explore performance on the selection task.

Beattie and Baron (1988, Experiment 2) asked subjects to think aloud while solving the 4 card selection task and the multi-card selection task. They checked to establish whether subjects classified by the experimenters at the time as confirmers actually believed that confirming evidence would prove the rule true despite the existence of potentially falsifying cards. Using protocols in this way, 50% of subjects (8/16) were classified as confirming on the unnegated 4 card task, compared with only 2 subjects in the unnegated multi-card task. Beattie and Baron suggested that such subjects were seeking corroborating evidence for the claim. Such a view is consistent with the experimental evidence cited earlier (Legrenzi, 1971; Mosconi & D'Urso, 1974).

Beattie and Baron also classified subjects in terms of matching. In true matching a subject only considers one hypothesis—the matching solution. In Experiment 2, 6/16 subjects were categorised in this fashion for the negated multi-card task compared with 1/16 subjects in the affirmative multi-card task. Hence true matching occurred more commonly when matching yielded the correct solution. Furthermore, there were some subjects (pseudo-matchers) who produced the matching response but who considered alternative hypotheses. Such a finding is inconsistent with the heuristic-analytic proposal. Card specification provides further information on the meaning of certain card choices. Protocols afford an even richer picture which is only partially supportive of the antithesis.

In a recent study, Evans (1993b, Experiment 5; this volume, Chapter 7) combined thinking-aloud protocols with an on-line methodology in which four-card versions of the selection task were presented via a computer screen. On-line presentation methods have been used before (Evans, Ball, & Brooks, 1987; Dominowski, 1992) but Evans' methodology sought to record the times subjects spent inspecting the cards as well as their protocols. Subjects used a "mouse" to indicate which one of the four cards they were currently inspecting or considering and the computer recorded the cumulative inspection times up to the moment that the subject actually selected the card using the same device. Subjects who eventually selected a card spent longer inspecting it compared to subjects who did not select it. Such a result is consistent with the heuristic-analytic proposal but does not refute the alternative possibility that inspection time reflects the time needed to reach a decision. In fact, some cards were not mentioned at all by some subjects in their protocols, consistent with a rapid judgement of relevance. On the other hand, subjects did think about the hidden side of the cards—especially about those that they were going to select. Although data concerning pseudo-matching have not been reported, the protocols do not support a simple matching process. The use of eye movement recordings together with protocol analysis may offer one way to increase the sensitivity of on-line variants.

The above variants help determine which cards and which matters subjects are considering. However, detailed analysis of protocols is needed in order to make full use of their possibilities for identifying the various component processes in the task. Another variant—the externalisation technique (Green, 1992; 1993a)—seeks to examine putative processes more directly.

It was noted earlier that subjects are able to recognise counter-examples when they see them. But do subjects have difficulty envisaging counter-examples as part of the selection task? What is the relationship between envisaging counter-examples and the selection of cards? Is it the case that once a subject has envisaged a counter-example they go on to select it? According to the theory of mental models (Johnson-Laird & Byrne, 1991; p. 80; Johnson-Laird, this volume, Chapter 6), subjects should select not-q whenever their model is fleshed out with an explicit representation of that card. One way to establish that subjects have an explicit representation of that card is to ask them to draw it. It follows from the theory that subjects who have drawn the card should select it.

Green (1992, Experiment 1) used the claim, "All the triangles are darkly shaded". This referred to a set of four cards each of which contained either a triangle or a circle which was either darkly shaded or lightly shaded. In the task, subjects were presented with outline squares depicting each of the four cards. Each card had a different heading—i.e. triangle, circle, darkly shaded shape, lightly shaded shape—corresponding to p, not-p, q, and not-q. Subjects were asked to envisage which combination of shape and shading would be inconsistent with the claim and to draw it on the appropriate card or cards. Green showed that correct performance was reliably associated with the production of counter-examples. The result was that 30% of subjects (12/40) failed to depict a correct counter-example at all, and none of these subjects selected correctly. Whereas only 23% of subjects (3/13) who produced just one counter-example (either drawn on the p card or on the not-q card) selected correctly, 60% of subjects (9/15) who produced both counter-examples (one drawn on the p card and the other on the not-q card) selected correctly.

The production of counter-examples appears necessary but not sufficient for correct selection. Indeed, some subjects who depicted *both* counter-examples selected the matching cards instead. In other words, the production of a counter-example associated with not-q does not guarantee that not-q will be selected. Further, a matching response does not entail a matching process. There were "pseudo-matchers" who explicitly represented the counter-example and drew it on the correct cards but who selected p and q. The externalisation technique provides a useful way to explore the various loci of difficulty in the selection task. Some subjects have difficulty envisaging a counter-example at all, but many do construct it and yet fail to map their understanding on to all the relevant cards.

Variants of the selection task offer a way to explore why a subject selects a particular card. Such detailed consideration is required because the same outcome may be the product of distinct processes. Without such consideration one might be led to believe that individuals in the abstract selection task generally do not envisage counter-examples. The data give evidence for a variety of strategies, some of which are apparently inconsistent with the thesis (matching) and some of which are inconsistent with the antithesis (pseudo-matching). The next section reviews the critical issue and moots a synthesis.

SYNTHESIS

A critical issue requires resolution: what is the relationship between selection and reasons? By seeking to characterise the analytic component of the heuristic-analytic proposal in mental model terms, Evans succeeds, as noted earlier, in increasing the explanatory power of the proposal. However, the consequence of this rapprochement is that enhanced performance can be explained in one of two ways: either the context, instructions, or materials may alter the perceived relevance of the cards, or such manipulations may invoke analytic procedures which override the initial representations constructed. Either of these factors could potentially explain the effects of prior experience shown by Legrenzi (discussed above), or the benefits of instructional changes shown by Platt and Griggs (1993) and Griggs (this volume, Chapter 2), or performance improvements revealed by reducing the number of cards to be considered, as in the reduced array selection task or RAST (Johnson-Laird & Wason, 1970b; Wason & Green, 1984; Wason, this volume, Chapter 13). Evans (this volume, Chapter 7) favours the relevance approach whereas others (e.g. Platt & Griggs, 1993) favour the analytic approach, at least as accounts of enhanced performance in their own studies.

Advocating relevance as the critical factor preserves the claim that reasons are mere rationalisations. But there is a cost to this commitment. For the abstract task, there is no *a priori* reason to predict any association between the nature of selections and the nature of the reasons provided. In fact, such an association was noted in the study by Goodwin and Wason (1972). More recently, Green (1993a) analysed the reasons for card selection provided by a sample of 132 subjects. The reasons given for selecting a particular card depended upon which other cards were also selected. Subjects selecting p and not-q provided logically apposite reasons for selecting these cards and for not selecting not-p and q. Their reasons were implicational—the selection carried implications for the truth or falsity of the claim. In contrast, those who selected p and q generally gave informational reasons for selecting these cards (they needed to know more about them) and they gave relevance reasons for not selecting not-p and not-q (they were not mentioned in the claim). Individuals who selected p, q, and not-q gave implicational or informational reasons for selecting p and not-q, and false implicational or informational reasons for selecting q.

These data show that the reasons for selecting a given card depend on which other cards are selected. They demonstrate specifically that correct selections are associated with logically appropriate reasons.

In order to provide apposite reasons for correct selections, the analytic device is required. To date the mental model account of performance in the selection task has not addressed the question of how to generate accounts of selections. However, one requirement is clear. In order to provide an apposite reason the device must operate analytically. But if it can operate analytically to produce accounts, what reason is there to suppose it cannot do so to provide selections in the first place? This point bears expansion.

Consider the fact that there is a relationship between the production of counter-examples and correct selection for affirmative claims (Green, 1992, discussed above, and Green, in press). According to the heuristic-analytic proposal subjects who select correctly must have overridden an initial matching solution by fleshing-out their model of the claim. If this view is adopted, why is it that subjects who select correctly produce logically apposite reasons? The process could operate as follows: having reasoned analytically, subjects look at their selections and seek to provide an explanation of that selection. But what would they need to do in order to provide such reasons? They would need to reason in such a way that these selections were logically apposite. In other words they would have to recapitulate the analytic process. The question naturally arises, why do it twice?

A comparable oddness arises in seeking to explain the fact that individuals who select correctly with the negative conditional also provide apposite reasons for their selections. If the cause of correct selection is matching, the production of apposite reasons can only occur by the analytic machinery operating analytically. Why is it that the machinery does not produce selections too? In the case of correct selections it would be perverse not to conclude that reasons are based on the internal process used in selecting the cards. But if this is the case for correct selections, is there any reason for refusing to accept its possibility for incorrect selections? Such refusal cannot be based on the view that individuals are only considered to reason if their selections are correct, because this ignores the possibility, and the evidence, that we may reason, but not well enough.

One possible objection to this line of thinking is the evidence that subjects are prepared to generate an account to justify any selection (Evans & Wason, 1976). But this study cannot be used to justify the claim that reasons are mere rationalisations. This study is an example of what Kunda (1990) has termed *directional* reasoning. Motivated to arrive at a particular conclusion, individuals attempt to construct a justification of the desired conclusion. Such reasoning may lead to different information being accessed as well as leading to a truncation of the argument process. The study does not show that directional reasoning occurs universally, or even at all, when subjects have to select cards themselves and write reasons for their selections.

In contrast to directional reasoning, subjects can be motivated to arrive at an accurate conclusion whatever it may be. Work within the social psychological area indicates that subjects motivated to be accurate (e.g. because they expected to justify their beliefs to others), attended to relevant information more carefully and expended greater cognitive effort. Such reasoning may underlie the performance improvements shown by Platt and Griggs (1993) and also by Dominowski (1992).

How then might we reconstrue the relationship between reasons and selections? One way—the essence of the synthesis—is to consider thought as a process of internal argumentation. The grounds for considering thought in this fashion are as follows. The success of the human species arguably depends on the social organisations that have been created rather than on adaptations at the individual level (Bruner, 1972). Hence adaptive success is likely to be dependent upon success in social relationships (cf. Byrne and Whitten, 1988). Language, by rendering thought explicit and verbalisable makes it possible to influence others in symbolic ways and to share and discuss ideas with them. Debate and argument are part of the social process. It is a process in which alternatives are appraised in terms of their sense. To the extent that cognitive abilities are formed and built up as part of social interaction (cf. Vygotsky, 1960), thinking itself can be considered to be a form of internal argument.

Integral to the idea of an argument is the contrast between data and claim (cf. Toulmin, 1956). Many adults (see Kuhn, 1989) appear not to grasp this contrast. Such individuals will have difficulty envisaging the counter-factual possibility that a claim is false. If subjects are unable to distinguish claim and evidence, then they will fail to envisage counter-examples and will fail to select appropriately. Even though they have been arguing, their arguments are flawed. As individuals commence selections, their arguments develop (there are initial matchers who change) and there are pseudo-matchers (individuals who generate counter-examples but who select the matching cards). Such individuals may fail to convince themselves.

Reasons are based on these processes of argumentation. Rather than being constructed *post hoc*, reasons reflect processes integral to selection. The act of explaining is, of course, distinct from the content of the explanation. It may occur after the selection of cards or it may occur as part of a thinking-aloud protocol. Reasons are not rationalisations then. Nor are they the causes of the selections. It is the process of internal debate that elicits selection. Decisions are based on which arguments win and these arguments are output as reasons or accounts of action.

In this synthesis, the process of analysis is replaced by the broader concept of argumentation. Selection always involves argumentation—the subject is attempting to find a choice that makes sense. What counts as sensible may be affected by content and instructions: requirements such as the need to produce reasons, acknowledged prior to the act of selection, can alter performance because they alter the nature of the argumentation. However, argumentation does not entail exclusive reliance on logical appeals. Ultimately, what counts as a selection which makes sense will depend on how the task is construed. It may be construed, for instance, as a task which requires logical analysis or as one in which subjects appraise the probability and utility of different selections (Kirby, 1994; Oaksford & Chater, 1993; Over & Evans, 1994). In each case, it is possible to speak of the strength of an argument for some action.

A possible way forward at this point is to extend the theory of mental models to cover this view of thinking as argument: a token in the model refers to an argument (i.e. to a conceptual-intentional object) rather than to a physical object (Green, 1994). The argument consists of a proposed action with respect to some state of affairs in the world (to select a card or not to select a card) and the grounds for that action. The grounds for an action consist of data and warrants for using that data. Which actions are taken depends on a process of weighing the different arguments. This could be achieved in various ways. It will be illustrated here in a rather simple fashion.

Consider a subject selecting p and q for the affirmative conditional. The internal process of argumentation may run along the following lines where the underlined portion is the action proposed, the bold portion is the data considered and the italicised portion is the warrant:

1. <u>Select p</u> because **it is mentioned in the claim** and *what is mentioned is relevant*; and **q could be on the other side** which *would support the truth of the claim*; and **q may not be on the other side** which *might be relevant*.
2. <u>Select q</u> because **it is mentioned in the claim** and *what is mentioned is relevant* and **p could be on the other side** which *would support the truth of the claim* and **p might not be on the other side** which *might be relevant*.
3. <u>Do not select not-p</u> because **it is not mentioned in the claim** and *what is not mentioned is not relevant*.
4. <u>Do not select not-q</u> because **it is not mentioned in the claim** and *what is not mentioned is not relevant*.

Assume a competitive process that counts each argument supporting a selection as a plus (+) and each argument against a selection as a minus

(–), then the action select p has 3+; select q has 3+; do not select not-p has 1– and do not select not-q has 1–. The result is that p and q are selected on the grounds that they both have arguments for and none against.

Obviously this process of argumentation will be more complex for those who are "pseudo-matchers" because at some point the combination of p and not-q is considered. Certain kinds of argument—for example, those based on what is linguistically relevant—might be weighted more highly by such subjects and lead to a reduced weight being attached to the not-q selection. In contrast to such complexities which must also exist for those selecting p, q, and not-q, the selection of p and not-q, at least for some individuals, will be straightforward. Suppose a subject construed the task as one of determining whether or not a counter-example (p and not-q) existed. In this case, the argumentation process might run on the following lines: select p, **it could have not-q on the other side** which *would prove the claim false*; select not-q, **it could have a p on the other side** which *would prove the claim false*; do not select not-p, **it cannot be a counter-example** and *is not relevant to the truth of the claim*; do not select q, **it cannot be a counter-example** and is *not relevant to the truth of the claim*. In this case, p and not-q both score 1+ whereas not-p and q both score 1– and so p and not-q are selected. The example brings out the fact that the meaning or sense of selecting a card depends upon the argumentation process: the sense of selecting p in the context of also selecting not-q is different from the case where p is selected along with the selection of q.

One consequence of this approach is that the times required to effect a selection will depend upon the complexities of the argumentation process. But the most important consequence for the present is that in this synthesis the basis for selection and the basis for accounts is one and the same. The synthesis avoids the problematic features of the antithesis but is consistent with the evidence showing that the initial representation in the model depends on the nature of the claim. It also suggests a way to explore individual differences in the task: skills in assessing evidence (see Kuhn, 1989) may correlate with performance in the selection task.

CONCLUSION

Science is a social activity that changes its knowledge base as a function of thought processes that occur between persons (Westrum, 1989). The pilot study reported by Peter Wason nearly 30 years ago (Wason, 1966) initiated a debate that still continues. Performance in the selection task may elicit many different kinds of processing. Human rationality may be hybrid (Green, 1993b) relying on the construction of explicit models or being guided by retrieved schema. It may rely sometimes on implicit processes and other times on explicit processes (Evans, 1993c; Holyoak & Spellman, 1993). Nevertheless, this chapter has provided ample evidence that subjects do reason in the abstract selection task. With respect to the reasons subjects provide, we have seen a shift from the assumption that reasons are what they seem to be (reports on the "causes" of actions) to an explicit denial of this assumption. Reasons are mere rationalisations. This chapter has proposed a synthesis: reasons and selections are outcomes of internal argumentation. According to this view, individual cognition emerges out of the context of social cognition. It is suggested that the theory of mental models be extended to treat arguments as tokens. In this way there is a single basis for generating selections and reasons.

ACKNOWLEDGEMENTS

I thank Peter Wason for his insightful comments on an earlier version of this paper, and Jonathan Evans and Richard Griggs for their helpful comments and suggestions.

REFERENCES

Beattie, J., & Baron, J. (1988). Confirmation and matching biases in hypothesis testing. *Quarterly Journal of Experimental Psychology, 40*, 269–297.

Berry, D.C. (1990). Talking about cognitive processes. In K.J. Gilhooly, M.T.G. Keane, R.H.Logie, & G.Erdos (Eds.), *Lines of thinking: Volume 2*. London: John Wiley and Sons.

Bruner, J.S. (1972). Nature and uses of immaturity. *American Psychologist, 27*, 687–708.

Byrne, R.W., & Whitten, A. (1988). *Machiavellian intelligence: Social expertise and the evolution of intellect in monkeys, apes, and humans*. Oxford: Clarendon Press.

Dominowski, R.L. (1992, July). *Changing content on Wason's four card task*. Paper presented to the Second International Conference on Thinking, Plymouth University.

Ericsson, K.A., & Simon, H.A. (1980). Verbal reports as data. *Psychological Review, 87*, 215–251.

Evans, J.St.B.T. (1972). Interpretation and "matching bias" in a reasoning task. *Quarterly Journal of Experimental Psychology, 24*, 193–199.

Evans, J.St.B.T. (1984). Heuristic and analytic processes in reasoning. *British Journal of Psychology, 75*, 451–468.

Evans, J.St.B.T. (1989). *Bias in human reasoning: Causes and consequences*. Hove, UK: Lawrence Erlbaum Associates Ltd.

Evans, J.St.B.T. (1991). Theories of human reasoning: The fragmented state of the art. *Theory and Psychology, 1*, 83–105.

Evans, J.St.B.T. (1993a). The mental model theory of conditional reasoning: Critical appraisal and revision. *Cognition, 48*, 1–20.

Evans, J.St.B.T. (1993b). *Deciding before you think: Relevance and reasoning in the selection task.* Manuscript, Department of Psychology, University of Plymouth.

Evans, J.St.B.T. (1993c). On rules, models, and understanding. *Behavioral and Brain Sciences, 16,* 345–346.

Evans, J.St.B.T., Ball, L.J., & Brooks, P.G. (1987). Attentional bias and decision order in a reasoning task. *British Journal of Psychology, 78,* 385–394.

Evans, J.St.B.T., & Lynch, J.S. (1973). Matching bias in the selection task. *British Journal of Psychology, 64,* 391–397.

Evans, J.St.B.T., & Wason, P.C. (1976). Rationalisation in a reasoning task. *British Journal of Psychology, 67,* 486–487.

George, C. (1990). Dissociation des difficultes dans la tache de selection de Wason. *L'Annee Psychologique, 90,* 169–193.

Goodwin, R.Q., & Wason, P.C. (1972). Degrees of insight. *British Journal of Psychology, 63,* 205–212.

Green, D.W. (1992, July). *Counter-examples and the selection task.* Paper presented to the Second International Conference on Thinking, Plymouth University.

Green, D.W. (1993a). *Mental models, counter-examples, and the selection task.* Manuscript, Department of Psychology, University College London.

Green, D.W. (1993b). Mental models: Rationality, representation, and process. *Behavioral and Brain Sciences, 16,* 352–353.

Green, D.W. (1994). Induction: Representation, strategy, and argument. *International Studies in the Philosophy of Science, 8,* 45–50.

Green, D.W. (in press). Externalisation, counter-examples, and the abstract selection task. *Quarterly Journal of Experimental Psychology.*

Griggs, R.A., & Cox, J.R. (1983). The effects of problem content and negation on Wason's selection task. *Quarterly Journal of Experimental Psychology, 35A,* 519–533.

Holyoak, K.J., & Spellman, B.A. (1993). Thinking. *Annual Review of Psychology, 44,* 265–315.

Johnson-Laird, P.N., & Byrne, R.M.J. (1991). *Deduction.* Hove, UK: Lawrence Erlbaum Associates Ltd.

Johnson-Laird, P.N., & Wason, P.C. (1970a). A theoretical analysis of insight into a reasoning task. *Cognitive Psychology, 1,* 134–148.

Johnson-Laird, P.N., & Wason, P.C. (1970b). Insight into a logical relation. *Quarterly Journal of Experimental Psychology, 22,* 49–61.

Kellogg, R.T. (1982). When can we introspect accurately about mental processes? *Memory and Cognition, 10,* 141–144.

Kirby, K.N. (1994). Probabilities and utilities of fictional outcomes in Wason's four card selection task. *Cognition, 51,* 1–28.

Kuhn, D. (1989). Children and adults as intuitive scientists. *Psychological Review, 96,* 674–689.

Kunda, Z. (1990). The case for motivated reasoning. *Psychological Bulletin, 108,* 480–495.

Legrenzi, P. (1971). Discovery as a means to understanding. *Quarterly Journal of Experimental Psychology, 23,* 417–422.

Manktelow, K.I., & Evans, J.St.B.T. (1979). Facilitation of reasoning by realism: Effect or non-effect? *British Journal of Psychology, 70,* 477–488.

Manktelow, K.I., & Over, D.E. (1990). *Inference and understanding: A philosophical and psychological perspective.* London: Routledge & Kegan Paul.

Mosconi, G., & D'Urso, V. (1974, April). *The selection task from the standpoint of the theory of double code.* Paper presented at the Conference on the Selection Task, University of Trento.

Nisbett, R.E., & Wilson, T.D. (1977). Telling more than we can know: Verbal reports on mental processes. *Psychological Review, 84,* 231–279.

Oaksford, M., & Chater, N. (1993). *A rational analysis of the selection task as optimal data selection.* Manuscript, Cognitive Neurocomputation Unit, Department of Psychology, University of Wales, Bangor.

Oaksford, M., & Stenning, K. (1992). Reasoning with conditionals containing negated constituents. *Journal of Experimental Psychology: Learning, Memory, Cognition, 18,* 835–854.

Over, D.E., & Evans, J.St.B.T. (1994). *Hits and misses: Kirby on the selection task.* Manuscript, University of Sunderland and University of Plymouth.

Platt, R.D., & Griggs, R.A. (1993). Facilitation in the abstract selection task: The effects of attentional and instructional factors. *Quarterly Journal of Experimental Psychology, 46A,* 591–613.

Pollard, P., & Evans, J.St.B.T. (1987). Content and context effects in reasoning. *American Journal of Psychology, 100,* 41–60.

Reich, S.S., & Ruth, P. (1982). Wason's selection task: Verification, falsification, and matching. *British Journal of Psychology, 73,* 395–405.

Toulmin, S. (1956). *The uses of argument.* Cambridge: Cambridge University Press.

Van Duyne, P.C. (1973). A short note on Evans' criticism of reasoning experiments and his matching bias hypothesis. *Cognition, 2,* 129–140.

Vygotsky, L.S. (1960). The development of higher mental functions. Quoted in J.V. Wertsch (1985), *Vygotsky and the social formation of mind.* Cambridge, MA: Harvard University Press.

Wason, P.C. (1966). Reasoning. In B.M. Foss (Ed.), *New horizons in psychology, 1.* Harmondsworth: Penguin.

Wason, P.C. (1968). Reasoning about a rule. *Quarterly Journal of Experimental Psychology, 20,* 273–281.

Wason, P.C., & Evans, J.St.B.T. (1975). Dual processes in reasoning? *Cognition, 3,* 141–154.

Wason, P.C., & Golding, E. (1974). The language of inconsistency. *British Journal of Psychology, 65,* 537–546.

Wason, P.C., & Green, D.W. (1984). Reasoning and mental representation. *Quarterly Journal of Experimental Psychology, 36A,* 597–610.

Westrum, R. (1989). The psychology of scientific dialogues. In B. Gholson, W. Shadish, R. Neiymeyer, & A. Houts (Eds.), *Psychology of science: Contributions to metascience* (pp. 370–382). New York: Cambridge University Press.

CHAPTER NINE

Finding Logic in Human Reasoning Requires Looking in the Right Places

David P. O'Brien

Baruch College and the Graduate School,
City University of New York

Since its introduction (Wason, 1966; 1968) the selection task has been the most investigated logical reasoning problem in the psychological literature, generating richly interesting data and providing evidence in support of several major theoretical proposals. Evans (1982, p. 187) wrote that the selection task "has been more productive of psychologically interesting findings and theories than work with any other reasoning paradigm. The experiments have shown an extraordinary capability for illogical reasoning in intelligent adults." In spite of its prominent role in the deductive-reasoning literature, some leading mental-logic advocates have argued that the selection task is outside the concerns of their theories (e.g. Braine & Rumain, 1983; Rips, 1990). This reluctance by mental-logic advocates to address the selection task has been criticised (e.g. Evans, 1992) as placing mental-logic research outside the mainstream.

Clearly, two separate approaches to the investigation of logical reasoning have developed. Researchers in one approach propose that the repertory of ordinary reasoning skills includes a mental logic, and these researchers have shown little interest in the selection task, or in other similarly complex reasoning tasks. I shall show that mental-logic researchers have been following Popperian principles in not including the selection task in investigations, as failure on the task does not impeach the claims of mental-logic theory. Researchers in a second approach see little evidence for a mental logic, focusing instead on reasoning biases or on content-dependent reasoning processes, and the selection task has played a prominent role in these investigations. Proponents of bias theory have made an appropriate choice in presenting the selection task; finding evidence for biases requires presenting tasks on which errors are committed and biases can be found, and the selection task has proven fruitful for this purpose. Further, use of the selection task is appropriate for those researchers interested in content-dependent effects—interest in the selection task stems largely from findings that the task often is solved when presented with certain kinds of content, but is solved rarely otherwise (e.g. Griggs & Cox, 1982; Johnson-Laird, Legrenzi, & Legrenzi, 1972).

The present chapter argues that mental-logic theory is compatible with the content effects and response biases proposed by its critics. People routinely make many logical inferences, but they also commit many fallacies; sometimes they are able to reason logically, and sometimes they appear befuddled. A psychological theory needs to account both for appropriate logical judgements and for reasoning errors. The solution I propose is that people reason logically, and can be seen to do so, when task demands are within the scope of their basic mental-logic skills, but when the demands of a task exceed their basic skills people must rely on other processes, and can make mistakes and give responses that show no evidence of any use of logic. Finding logic in reasoning requires looking for it in the right places—i.e. on tasks that can be solved by the basic skills of mental logic. The selection task, notwithstanding the logic particle "if" in its rule, is not a good place to look.

The first section of this chapter describes research with the selection task. No attempt is made to be exhaustive—the literature is far too large—and the discussion is limited to the role of the selection task in some arguments against mental logic. The second section describes the mental-logic approach that I advocate. The theory has three parts: (a) a set of inference schemas that provides a repertory of basic inference-making skills; (b) a reasoning program that selects a schema at a point in a line of reasoning; and (c) an independently motivated set of pragmatic principles that influence interpretation of surface-structure cues, can encourage or discourage more sophisticated reasoning strategies, and provide additional inferences that go beyond those of the logical inference schemas. I show why the failure of most subjects to solve the selection task appropriately does not impeach mental logic, and why successful solution on some realistic-content versions of the task is not inconsistent with the claims of mental-logic theory. The third section describes the sorts of tasks that have been of interest in mental-logic research; these are tasks that can be solved by the basic mental-logic skills, and in some cases they investigate differences in predictions made by mental-logic theory and a competing mental models theory. I argue that mental logic can be found not only in reasoning tasks, but also in text comprehension tasks, and that the data both from reasoning tasks and from text comprehension tasks favour mental-logic theory over competing accounts.

WASON'S SELECTION TASK

Wason's selection task presents four cards showing, for example, A, D, 5, and 7, respectively. Subjects are told that each card has a letter on one side and a number on the other side, and are presented with a universally quantified conditional rule for the four cards—e.g. "If a card has an A on one side, then it has a 5 on the other side". Finally, they are told that the rule might be either true or false, and that they are to select those cards, and only those cards, that one would need to turn over for inspection to test the truth status of the rule. Typically, few people choose the two cards showing an A and showing a 7, even though these are the only two cards that potentially can falsify the rule. The response patterns given most often are to select the two cards showing an A and a 5, or to choose only the card showing an A (see reviews by Evans, 1982; 1989).

Evans (1982; 1989) described how the task can be solved. Because the rule is universally quantified, information about a single card cannot verify the rule, but potentially can falsify it, and the task thus requires a strategy of searching for potentially falsifying cards. The truth table for the material conditional shows that a card with an A and not a 5 is the sole falsifying sort of card, and the reasoner must decide for each card whether it could reveal such a case. Thus the card showing an A should be selected because it might show a number other than 5, and the card showing a 7 should be selected because it might show a letter A. The other two cards could not reveal a falsifying case, so they need not be selected.

Early researchers (e.g. Wason & Johnson-Laird, 1970) proposed that subjects fail to solve the task because they are following a confirmation bias rather than applying the appropriate falsification strategy. Note that this account does not imply any lack of understanding of the logic of "if", but rather a failure to appreciate the falsification demands of the rule's universal quantification. This explanation would account for the cards that are selected (as reasonable attempts to find confirming exemplars) and is consistent with subjects' verbal justifications of their selections. Evans (e.g. Evans & Lynch, 1973) has provided a persuasive case against this confirmation bias explanation, however, arguing instead for a matching bias, claiming that subjects simply select those cards with values that are mentioned in the rule. This is a very primitive basis for the responses, and it implies that subjects are not showing any logical appreciation of "if".

The principal evidence for matching bias comes from the experimental manipulation of negatives in the antecedent and consequent terms of the conditional rule. If subjects were following a confirmation strategy, then given a rule, for example, of the form "if p then not q", they should select the cards corresponding to p and to not-q to discover possibly confirming evidence; Evans and Lynch found, however, that subjects still tend to select the cards corresponding to p and to q—i.e. the values mentioned in the rule. Further evidence that these responses result from a non-logical process comes from Wason and Evans (1975), who argued that although verbal justifications appear to reflect some appreciation of the task's logic, they are disconnected from the actual processes leading to the selections. For example, given a rule of the form "if p then q", the selection of q is justified as a search for confirming evidence, whereas given a rule of the form "if p then not q", the selection of q is justified as a search for falsifying evidence. Thus, Evans and his colleagues conclude that although the verbal protocols appear to reflect some logic in reasoning, the actual processes are primitive and non-logical.

Evans (1982, p. 231) concluded that "performance indicates no more than a superficial understanding of the sentence "if p then q", and little evidence of any depth of understanding." More recently Evans (1993a, p. 11) has said that the selection task has "an apparent simplicity of structure and the tendency to invoke almost universal error", and writes of "an apparent mass of evidence for bias and illogicality in human reasoning." Referring both to Rips (1983) and to Braine and O'Brien (1991), he says that "advocates of mental logic persist, however, and contemporary formulations envision a cognitive system consisting of a set of abstract logical rules together with an inferential mechanism for applying them to particular premises in order to draw conclusions." Clearly, Evans interprets failure on the selection task (and on similarly complex reasoning tasks) as counting against mental-logic theories, including the one I advocate. I argue below that primitive non-logical responses on the selection task do not count against mental logic, as the demands of the task exceed the basic skills of mental logic.

Content-dependent Theories

Interest in the selection task stems largely from findings that the logically appropriate responses often are made when the task is presented with thematically realistic content (e.g. Griggs & Cox, 1982; Johnson-Laird et al., 1972). Several investigators have interpreted these findings as counting against mental logic. Writing about their investigations into content effects on the selection task, Cosmides (1989, p. 191) concluded that people rarely reason "according to the canons of logic", and Cheng, Holyoak, Nisbett, and Oliver (1986) speak of their "negative conclusion" concerning a mental logic. Evans (1982, p. 233) says that a competence for formal reasoning "is surprisingly—no doubt to some—depressingly lacking", and "all evidence points to content-dependent thought processes on these tasks."

Although early work on the content effect suggested that familiar content alone might account for task solution, Manktelow and Evans (1979) showed that only some realistic content versions are solved. The task version that has led most reliably to solution is the drinking-age problem of Griggs and Cox (1982). Subjects are told to take the role of a policeman enforcing the rule that "if a person is drinking beer then that person must be over 19 years of age". For 4 instances (a person drinking beer, a person drinking Coke, a person over 19, and a person under 19) subjects are required to select those who could be violating the rule. Subjects almost always select a person drinking a beer and a person under 19.[1]

Cosmides (1989) proposed that task versions that refer to social contracts with their attendant costs and benefits will be solved. In order for the social-contract theory to explain success on the drinking-age version, being over 19 years of age must be considered a cost—something that has struck some commentators as odd (Cheng & Holyoak, 1989; Manktelow & Over, 1990; Pollard, 1990; O'Brien, 1993), and so I shall say no more here about the social-contract theory. Cheng and Holyoak (1985) proposed that reasoning with thematic materials typically proceeds through application of inductively acquired pragmatic schemas, and not through any mental logic. Thus far, only two pragmatic schemas have been described—one for permissions and one for obligations. According to pragmatic schemas theory, a task will be solved when its content triggers the appropriate content-dependent schema. The permission schema, for example, holds that if an action is to be taken, then its precondition must be satisfied, and the theory claims that the drinking-age problem is solved because it triggers the permission schema, with drinking beer as the action taken and being over 19 as the requisite precondition.

The pragmatic schemas theory was received with interest because it provides a theoretical account of the content effect on the selection task, although the theory has made claims about reasoning generally. No empirical evidence has been provided for any reasoning tasks beyond some versions of the selection task, however, indicating at least a tacit claim that the selection task measures what is typical in reasoning—a claim that I shall argue against below.

Cheng and Holyoak (1985, Experiment 2) reported an arbitrary content search-for-violators problem presenting a permission rule that leads to successful solution, whereas a similar arbitrary content control problem presenting a non-pragmatic rule does not. This is the most persuasive evidence for pragmatic schemas theory, because it suggests the possibility that the pragmatic rule alone, without the familiar content, can elicit the appropriate selections. Indeed, the abstract permission problem was the first search-for-violators problem presented with arbitrary content that subjects are able to solve. The abstract permission problem asks subjects to assume the role of an authority checking to be sure that people are obeying the regulation that "If one is to take Action A, then one must first satisfy Precondition P. In other words, in order to be permitted to do Action A, one must first have fulfilled Prerequisite P." The four cards show "has taken Action A", "has not taken Action A", "has fulfilled Precondition P", and "has not fulfilled Precondition P".

Several recent investigations have addressed the extent to which the superior performance on the abstract permission problem is attributable to its permission rule (Girotto, Mazzocco, & Cherubini, 1992; Griggs & Cox, 1993; Jackson & Griggs, 1990; Kroger, Cheng, & Holyoak, 1993). The abstract permission problem differs from Cheng and Holyoak's control problem in several ways that have nothing to do with its permission rule. For example, whereas the original abstract permission problem asks subjects to assume the role of an authority which is seeking violators, the original control problem does not; as Pollard and Evans (1987) noted, role playing may motivate a search for violators, and Politzer and Nguyen-Xuan (1992) reported that changing the perspective of role playing affects which cards are selected. Another difference concerns the way in which negative information presented: the abstract permission problem is consistent in using explicit negatives throughout the problem (e.g. "has not taken Action A" rather than "has taken Action D"), whereas the control problem introduces explicit negatives only parenthetically in the cards. Thirdly, the abstract permission problem adds a clarifying phrase to the rule ("in other words..."), whereas the control problem does not. Fourthly, the two tasks introduce the problem information in different orders: the abstract permission problem introduces the rule first, followed by the cards, whereas the control problem introduces the cards before the rule. Finally, the presentation of the control problem is much more sparse than that of the permission rule problem, which requires almost 50% more words than the control problem. Collectively, these differences confound the variable of interest—the pragmatic rule—and the abstract permission problem has generally richer features than its control problem.

Some of these differences have been investigated. Jackson and Griggs (1990) found that presenting the negatives in the cards implicitly rather than explicitly, or removing the role-playing instruction, is sufficient to depress performance on permission rule problems to the low level usually found on the non-pragmatic rule versions. Thus, at least some of the features of the abstract permission problem that are required for task solution have nothing to do with the permission rule *per se*.

Girotto et al. (1992) argued that these findings do not impeach pragmatic schemas theory, because the pragmatic relevance of the cards is apparent only when such features are present, a position recently endorsed by Griggs and Cox (1993) and Kroger, Cheng, and Holyoak (1993). Further, Griggs and Cox (1993) and Kroger et al. (1993), as well as Girotto et al. (1992) reported that adding explicit negatives and a checking context to the non-pragmatic control problem does not lead to an increase in rates of solution. These findings remain difficult to interpret, though. For example, Kroger et al. presented the information in their permission rule versions in a different order from that in their control problems, and with a generally richer description (the control problems are much shorter). Griggs and Cox presented permission rule and control problems that are comparable to one another in how the information is presented, but both are closer to the relatively impoverished original control problem rather than to the original permission rule problem, resulting in lower rates of solution for the permission rule problem than that reported in the original Cheng and Holyoak (1985) study (35% versus 61%). This reveals that there are task features other than the type of rule (permission versus non-permission), type of negative (implicit versus explicit), and presence versus absence of a checking context, that influence whether a problem will be solved.

In a recent investigation with Ira Noveck (Noveck & O'Brien, submitted) two sets of problems were constructed, one based on the original abstract permission problem with all of its relatively rich features, and one based on the original control problem and containing its relatively sparse features. The result was that 67% of subjects solved the enriched permission problems with explicit negatives, whereas only 42% solved the sparse permission problems with explicit negatives—values roughly equivalent to those of Cheng and Holyoak (1985) and Griggs and Cox (1993); replacing explicit with implicit negatives in the cards lowered solution rates to 17% and 8% for the enriched and sparse problems, respectively. On the non-permission problems, providing explicit rather than implicit negatives in the cards had no effect, replicating earlier findings; presenting enriched non-permission problems, though, led to an increase from 13% to 33% over the sparse problems, with or without explicit negatives.

Several conclusions can be drawn. First, the presence versus absence of a permission rule makes a difference: no problem with a permission rule leads to a majority of subjects solving the task in these studies. Secondly, the permission rule alone is not sufficient for the problem to be solved: not only are explicit negatives and a checking context needed, but so are some other enriching features. Thirdly, some of these features lead to significant increases in rates of solution on non-pragmatic control problems—something that is not captured by the pragmatic schemas theory. As things stand, then, pragmatic schemas theory is required to account for the high rate with which the abstract permission problem is solved, but provides only a partial account, and some of the operative task features have nothing to do with pragmatic schemas.

Pragmatic schemas have not been tested by Cheng and her associates on problems other than the search-for-violators task. Markovits and Savory (1992), however, have presented universally quantified conditional syllogisms with a permission rule as the major premise (drawn from the postal rule problem of Johnson-Laird et al., 1972), and found that the permission rule did not help subjects make the logically appropriate responses. Further, Griggs (1989) and Platt and Griggs (1993) have reported non-pragmatic abstract task versions that are solved by a majority of subjects. To date, then, pragmatic schemas theory has presented only a single schema—the permission rule—that has a reliable beneficial effect, and thus far only on a single task type, and only when other problem-enriching features are present.

This is a weak empirical foundation for a theory to make claims about how people reason typically. To provide an acceptable general account of logical reasoning, pragmatic schemas theory would need to provide more than a single effective schema, to show that the theory makes predictions successfully on something beyond the search-for-violators task, and to account for why some non-pragmatic versions of the search-for-violators task (as well as other tasks) are solved. Advocates of content-dependent processes in reasoning have not yet provided an account of the wide variety of materials about which people reason, nor have they shown that the content-independent processes of a mental logic play little or no role in reasoning.

Kroger et al. (1993) do not mention the earlier claims of pragmatic schemas theory that reasoning typically proceeds with pragmatic schemas, nor do they restate earlier negative conclusions about mental-logic inferences; they argue only that pragmatic schemas theory is needed to account for performance on the abstract permission problem. They point out—correctly I think—that the content-general inference schemas of mental-logic theory do not account for performance on the abstract permission problem. The results provide no reason to reject mental-logic inferences, however, although they do point to some additional content-dependent ones. The pragmatic schemas alone do not provide a complete theory of propositional reasoning, and as I shall argue in the next section, content-specific inferences cohabit easily with the content-general ones of mental logic.

MENTAL-LOGIC THEORY

That people's judgements often differ from the output of a standard-logic system does not impeach mental-logic theory, because mental logic differs from standard logic in several ways. The basic inferences made in mental logic do not include all of those of a standard-logic system, and the basic mental-logic skills are quite limited. Failure to solve a logical reasoning problem would threaten mental-logic theory only if the problem should be solved according to the theory, not simply because it would be solved on some textbook calculus. Furthermore, findings that responses are influenced by extralogical features are not inconsistent with mental-logic theory, which does not claim that logic inferences are the only sorts of inferences people make.

Mental-logic theory begins with the understanding that logical reasoning is propositional (see discussion in O'Brien, 1993). The chief concern of logic is to ensure that an argument with true premises leads only to a true conclusion, and logic thus is propositional in that truth and falsity are properties of propositions rather than of sentences. Note that the sentence "The rate of inflation was 30% last year" cannot be judged true or false until we know the circumstances of its utterance—e.g. in which year it was uttered and about which economy. Once a sentence is interpreted in reference to an intentional state, the proposition can be asserted, denied, inferred, believed, doubted, and so forth. All such propositional activities concern judgements about truth and falsity in reference to some intentional state, and these intentional states can be factual, fictional, or suppositional.

Because propositional activities refer to intentional states, logical inferences co-exist with pragmatic inferences that concern the practical consequences of propositions for the intentional states. Mental-logic theory therefore allows pragmatic inferences as well as logic inferences, and the two sorts cohabit easily within a line of reasoning, with the output of the one sort feeding inferences made by the other sort. In general, an inference does not come marked with the sort of process by which it was generated; although this is of interest to cognitive researchers, ordinarily it is not of interest to the person making the inference. Thus people usually are not aware of whether an inference resulted from a logical process or from another sort of process.

As Macnamara (1986) argued, mental logic need not be complete, so the basic skills of mental logic are not able to derive all of the theorems of a standard-logic calculus. Mental logic is concerned with soundness, however, and mental logic is truth preserving, proceeding from premises assumed true to conclusions that inherit their truth. The truth-preserving procedures are found in a set of inference schemas rather than in some sort of manipulation of truth tables.[2] An inference schema specifies the conclusion that can be drawn from premises of a particular form. The inference schemas of the theory specify how "and", "or", "if ", and negation may be used in reasoning, and they define a repertory of elementary steps available in propositional reasoning. For example, given two premises of the form "p or q" and "not p", one can conclude q, for any p and q, as long as the premises are assumed true (for descriptions of the set of schemas, see Braine, 1990; Lea, O'Brien, Noveck, Fisch, & Braine, 1990). In standard logic an argument is valid as long as there is no assignment of truth values to its atomic propositions such that the premises taken conjunctively are true and the conclusion is false; thus any argument with contradictory premises is valid. In mental logic nothing could be inferred in such a situation except that some assumption is wrong, and the schemas are not applied to premises unless the premises are accepted.

The difference between mental logic and standard logic is illustrated by the schema for conditional proof (see discussion in Braine & O'Brien, 1991), which states that to infer or to evaluate "if p then ...", first suppose p; for any proposition q that follows from the supposition of p taken together with other information assumed, one may assert "If p then q". In other words, when a consequent can be derived from a set of assumptions and a supposition, the conditional can be asserted on the assumptions alone. The schema for conditional proof in mental logic differs from that in standard logic in two ways. First, there is no requirement in mental logic that the derivation of the consequent is on logical grounds; it could be the result of pragmatic inferences. Only the person engaged in the line of reasoning, and any interlocutor, would decide on the adequacy of the derivation. Secondly, because of the mental-logic principle that nothing follows from a contradiction except that some assumption is wrong, a supposition can be the antecedent of a conditional only if it is consistent with premise assumptions and any prior suppositions.[3] Thus, any assumption reiterated into a conditional proof cannot contradict the supposition that is to be the antecedent of that conditional. Put simply, one cannot suppose something and rely on information incompatible with that supposition, even when that information is true. This constraint on suppositional arguments is not a feature of standard-logic systems, which explains why the material conditional of standard logic leads to conclusions that strike ordinary intuitions as paradoxical—e.g. "If not p, then if p then not p" is necessarily true in standard logic.

Note that the schema for conditional proof does not govern when suppositions are made—only how they are used. More generally, a set of inference schemas alone could not account for how inferences are made or conclusions are judged; a reasoner also needs a reasoning program that selects the schemas to be used at a particular point in a line of reasoning. The reasoning program of mental-logic theory includes a direct reasoning routine and some more sophisticated strategies. The direct reasoning routine is claimed to be universally available, but the more sophisticated strategies are not similarly claimed to be so, and their acquisition may require some reflection or tuition. The direct reasoning routine simply applies any schema that can be applied to the set of available assumptions (with constraints to prevent infinite loops), adds the inference(s) to the set of assumptions, and either recycles or evaluates a conclusion.

The direct reasoning routine provides only a single situation in which a supposition will be made—when a conditional conclusion is to be evaluated. Clearly, though, people make suppositions in other situations, and they occur when more sophisticated strategies are known or when knowledge about the intentional state suggests them. Complex logical reasoning tasks, such as the selection task, require subjects to orchestrate the schemas in complex lines of reasoning, and knowledge of the requisite strategies is far from universal—indeed, few people acquire this sort of strategic sophistication. A basic prediction of mental-logic theory is, therefore, that those reasoning tasks that can be solved on the direct reasoning routine generally will be solved, but those tasks that require the orchestration of a sophisticated strategy are relatively unlikely to be solved. On problems where nothing follows on the direct reasoning routine, subjects often might respond that nothing follows. Whether they do or not often depends on whether the task circumstances lead them to understand that "nothing follows" is a fully acceptable response. (O'Brien, Braine, Connell, Noveck, Fisch, & Fun, 1989, discussed a bias against "can't tell" responses.) Otherwise, unless subjects have knowledge of sophisticated reasoning strategies they must rely on non-logical resources such as pragmatic inferences, heuristics, or response biases. Note that Evans (1989) reports that responses based on reasoning biases generally occur on invalid problems (where nothing would follow on the direct reasoning routine) much more often than on valid problems (where the correct answer often follows on the direct reasoning routine).

Mental-logic theory proposes that the lexical entry for a logic particle, such as an English word like "if", "and", "not", or "or", consists of the basic inference schemas for that particle. How any particular proposition is construed on a particular occasion, however, depends on many factors other than the lexical entry, such as knowledge of the subject matter, conversational or text comprehension processes, and the plausibility of particular interpretations. A complete inventory of such factors would be a general theory of pragmatic comprehension processes, and would go well beyond mental-logic theory *per se*. (See Sperber & Wilson, 1986, for a major proposal of this sort.)

Braine and O'Brien (1991) discussed three sorts of pragmatic principles. One concerns how the content of propositions influences how they are construed. An example is Bever's plausibility strategy (Bever, 1970), and subjects should prefer semantic plausibility over local syntactic cues. For example, "If I put up my umbrella it starts to rain" is likely to be interpreted (particularly by children) as "If it starts to rain, I'll put up my umbrella" (Emerson & Gekoski, 1980). Another example includes the influence of things like the permission rule of pragmatic schemas theory. Such pragmatic interpretations enrich what is available on the mental-logic inference schemas alone without contradicting anything that could be inferred from them. The permission schema, for example, would add a *modus tollens* inference for certain deontic conditionals to those available from the inference schemas of mental logic, and would be consistent with the two schemas for conditionals available from the mental-logic repertory (i.e. *modus ponens* and a schema for conditional proof). The theoretical advantage of viewing pragmatic inferences as extending what is provided by the logic schemas is that the theory can account for content-specific effects without requiring that content-dependent schemas do all the work in reasoning. This explains why the logic particles are used across a wide variety of sorts of content, most of which could not be captured by any particular sort of content-dedendent schema. The general principle is that propositions are interpreted in reference to intentional states, and knowledge about the intentional states will be used to judge the plausibility of particular interpretations, and to extend the available inferences.

A second sort of pragmatic principle concerns the Gricean co-operative principle—listeners assume that a speaker is being relevant, informative, truthful, and so forth. The conversational implicatures that are made on the co-operative principle can lead to errors on reasoning tasks because laboratory tasks often flout the co-operative principle. A third sort of pragmatic principle, which may be reducible to the co-operative principle, concerns invited inferences (e.g. Fillenbaum, 1977; Geis & Zwicky, 1971). For example, a proposition of the form "if p then q" invites the inference of "if not p then not q". Such inferences are unlike those of the logic schemas because they are non-necessary and can be countermanded. Geis and Zwicky, and Fillenbaum, proposed that such invited inferences are made unless they are countermanded, although the first principle just discussed would cause the invited inferences to be encouraged or discouraged by certain sorts of materials. Sperber and Wilson (1986) subsume the co-operative principle in their principle of relevance.

Inferences from the mental-logic schemas co-exist in a line of reasoning with inferences from other sources. Mental-logic theory has argued consistently that logic inferences cohabit with inferences from a variety of sources, such as those made from scripts, case inferences, causal inferences, trait inferences, inferences from story grammars, and so forth (Braine, 1990; Braine & O'Brien, 1991; submitted; Lea et al., 1990; Noveck, Lea, Davidson, & O'Brien, 1991; O'Brien, 1987; 1991; 1993). Finding an influence of subject matter on logical reasoning is consistent with mental-logic theory, which does not claim that the logic schemas are exclusive.

What sorts of tasks ought to be of principal interest to mental-logic theorists? A Popperian view is provided by thinking of the question as a sort of Wason's selection task, with the hypothetical rule, "If a task can be solved by the basic mental-logic skills, it will be". Only two situations could falsify this hypothesis: a mental-logic researcher would need to select (a) those tasks that can be solved on the direct reasoning routine of mental logic, to ensure that they are solved, and (b) those tasks that are not solved, to ensure that they would not be solved on the direct reasoning routine. Wason's selection task usually is not solved, and I turn now to whether it should be. The final section addresses whether people solve those tasks that can be solved on the direct reasoning routine.

The Logic of Wason's Selection Task

Suppose, as mental-logic theory does, that in ordinary reasoning people do not have access to truth tables, but rather that their mental logic provides inference schemas. Without the truth table for the material conditional, how would one know that turning over the card showing an A might reveal a falsifying card, given a rule to be tested of the form "If A then 5"? Mental logic provides only two schemas directly relevant to conditionals—*modus ponens* and a schema for conditional proof—and these are not sufficient to solve the task. Consider the sorts of arguments that would be required for task solution when one uses the usual inference schemas of a first-order predicate calculus found in standard-logic textbooks. The only certain information is that the card has an A, so neither the rule nor the number on the other side of the card can be a premise. A suppositional argument is required, beginning either with a supposition about the rule or about the number on the other side of the card. Given that the task requires a judgement about the truth of the rule, a reasonable starting point is to suppose that the rule is true. One such possible line of reasoning is shown in Table 9.1 as Argument 1.

The premise that there is an A on this card is on Line 1. (The notation Ai includes an indexical for "this card has an A".) The argument then supposes that the rule is true (Line 2), instantiates the rule for this card (Line 4), applies *modus ponens* to infer that "this card has a 5" (Line 5), and discharges the supposition to infer that "if the rule is true, then this card has a 5" (Line 6). Note that at this point in the argument there is as

TABLE 9.1

Some Sample Arguments for Wason's Selection Task for the Card Showing an A When the Rule is "If a Card Has the Letter A On One Side Then it Has the Number 5 On the Other Side"

Argument 1

1.	Ai	(premise)
2.	(⊃x)(Ax → 5x)	(supposition)
3.	Ai	(reiteration, 1)
4.	Ai → 5i	(universal instantiation, 2)
5.	5i	(*modus ponens*, 3, 4)
6.	(⊃x)((Ax → 5x) → 5i)	(conditional proof, 2–5)
7.	~5i	(supposition)
8.	(⊃x)(Ax → 5x)	(supposition)
9.	(⊃x)(Ax → 5x) → 5i	(reiteration, 6)
10.	5i	(*modus ponens*, 8–9)
11.	~5i	(reiteration, 7)
12.	~(⊃x)(Ax → 5x)	(negation introduction, 8–11)
13.	~5i → ~(⊃x)(Ax → 5x)	(conditional proof, 7–12)

Argument 2

1.	Ai	(premise)
2.	~5i	(supposition)
3.	(⊃x)(Ax → 5x)	(supposition)
4.	Ai	(reiteration, 1)
5.	~5i	(reiteration, 2)
6.	Ai → 5i	(universal instantiation, 3)
7.	5i	(*modus ponens*, 4, 6)
8.	~(⊃x)(Ax → 5x)	(negation introduction, 3–7)
9.	~5i → ~(⊃x)(Ax → 5x)	(conditional proof, 2–8)

Note: Ai = "This card has an A;" (⊃x)(Ax → 5x) = "If a card has an A, then it has a 5;" ~(⊃x)(Ax → 5x) = "It is false that if a card has an A, then it has a 5."

yet no reason to turn the card over, for the rule is merely the antecedent of a conditional; one needs to establish the conditional's contrapositive.

The argument in Lines 7–13 establishes that "If this card does not have a 5, then the rule is false". This part of the argument is a conditional proof, with a subordinate *reductio ad absurdum* on the supposition in Line 8 that "the rule is false". Only at Line 13 does the argument provide a reason to turn over the card; a sophisticated reasoner now could realise that were the card turned over and a number other than 5 found, then by *modus ponens* the rule would be false.

A slightly shorter argument (Argument 2 in Table 9.1) that leads to the same final conclusion is possible when one begins with the supposition that the card does not have a 5. As with Argument 1, the proof of the theorem that "If this card does not have a 5, then the rule is false" (Line 9) requires a subordinate *reductio ad absurdum* argument. Other similar arguments can be constructed—e.g. Line 1–8 in Argument 1 could be followed by Lines 4–9 in Argument 2. Note that these sorts of complex lines of reasoning go well beyond anything that could be done with the basic skills of mental logic, and it is unlikely that the vast majority of subjects who select the card showing an A are doing so on the basis of such arguments.

The sorts of lines of reasoning that are required to know that the card showing a 7 needs to be selected are quite similar to Arguments 1 and 2 for the card showing an A. For example, Argument 3 in Table 9.2, like Argument 1 in Table 9.1, begins by supposing that the rule is true, which leads on Line 9 to the realisation that "If the rule is true, then there is not an A". Two features of this argument make it more complex than Argument 1. First, it requires an additional *reductio* to establish that a consequence of supposing that the rule is true is that there is not an A on the card. Secondly, introducing the negative requires recognition of the contradiction between 5i in Line 6 and 7i in Line 7, a realisation that is not represented in the predicate calculus, but comes from knowledge about the nature of the cards—a sort of pragmatic inference from local world knowledge. This suggests that making 7i clearly equivalent to ~5i could influence performance on this card, a task feature that has nothing to do with logic *per se* (see the discussion above of explicit negatives on the abstract permission problem). The decision to turn over the card showing a 7 can be made more easily with Argument 4, shown in Table 9.2, which is more difficult than Argument 2 only in the need to notice the contradiction between 7i and 5i. Note that there is no single way to decide whether any particular card should be turned over, and the length of the derivation required for any card is a matter of luck, should any acceptable argument be constructed at all.

The principal conclusion to be drawn from this exercise is that whether one thinks that a logical reasoning problem is simple depends on which logic one has in mind. If mental logic included the truth table for the material conditional, people might find the selection task simple.[4] From the perspective of mental-logic theory, however, the selection task is a very difficult problem indeed, and few people should be able to appreciate its logical structure. Nothing in the two schemas for conditionals, nor in the direct reasoning routine, suggests which suppositions should be made, and few people have the sophistication to orchestrate such complex lines of reasoning; the almost universal failure to solve the selection task thus does not weigh against mental-logic theory. Because the task is so difficult,

TABLE 9.2

Some Sample Arguments for Wason's Selection Task for the Card
Showing a 7 When the Rule is "If a Card Has the Letter A On One Side,
Then it Has the Number 5 On the Other Side"

Argument 3

1.	7i	(premise)
2.	$(\supset x)(Ax \to 5x)$	(supposition)
3.	Ai	(supposition)
4.	$(\supset x)(Ax \to 5x)$	(reiterations, 2)
5.	Ai $\to$ 5i	(universal instantiation, 4)
6.	5i	(*modus ponens*, 3–5)
7.	7i	(reiteration, 1)
8.	~Ai	(negation introduction, 3–7)
9.	$(\supset x)(Ax \to 5x) \to$ ~Ai	(conditional proof, 2–8)
10.	Ai	(supposition)
11.	$(\supset x)(Ax \to 5x)$	(supposition)
12.	$(\supset x)(Ax \to 5x) \to$ ~Ai	(reiteration, 9)
13.	~Ai	(*modus ponens*, 11, 12)
14.	Ai	(reiteration, 10)
15.	~$(\supset x)(Ax \to 5x)$	(negation introduction, 11–14)
16.	Ai $\to$ ~$(\supset x)(Ax \to 5x)$	(conditional proof, 10–15)

Argument 4

1.	7i	(premise)
2.	Ai	(supposition)
3.	$(\supset x)(Ax \to 5x)$	(supposition)
4.	Ai	(reiteration, 2)
5.	Ai $\to$ 5i	(universal instantiation, 3)
6.	5i	(*modus ponens*, 4, 5)
7.	7i	(reiteration, 1)
8.	~$(\supset x)(Ax \to 5x)$	(negation introduction, 3–7)
9.	Ai $\to$ ~$(\supset x)(Ax \to 5x)$	(conditional proof, 2–8)

Note: Ai = "This card has an A;" $(\supset x)(Ax \to 5x)$ = "If a card has an A, then it has a 5;"
~$(\supseteq x)(Ax \to 5x)$ = "It is false that if a card has an A, then it has a 5."

however, it provides an ideal vehicle for investigating response biases,
which should occur when the task demands exceed the skills of the direct
reasoning routine, as the demands of the selection task clearly do.

SOME EMPIRICAL SUPPORT FOR
MENTAL-LOGIC THEORY

Evans (1982, p. 255) wrote that "there is little evidence of a general competence to perform any given inference". In the years following this assessment, evidence for a competence to make a variety of logic inferences has been gathered; the primary goal of mental-logic research has been to establish that people make the inferences predicted on the direct reasoning routine, and several studies find that they do (e.g. Braine, Reiser, & Rumain, 1984; Lea et al., 1990). The reasoning problems in our investigations have presented propositions referring to letters on an imaginary blackboard (e.g. "On the blackboard there is either a D or a Q") or to toy animals and fruits in a box (e.g. "In the box there is either a lion or an elephant"). These sorts of materials allow subjects to refer the propositions to an intentional state, but not to one that would provide the information needed for task solution. We have found, for example, that people routinely introduce and eliminate conjunctions, and they cancel double negatives; given premises of the form "p or q" and "not p", people routinely infer q, and from premises of the form "not both p and q" and "p" they routinely infer not q; they routinely make *modus ponens* inferences, and infer r from "if p or q then r" and "p"; when a set of premises together with a supposition entail a proposition, people infer a conditional with the supposition as its antecedent and the entailed proposition as its consequent. (See Braine, 1990 and Braine & O'Brien, submitted, for reviews of the basic mental-logic inferences that people make routinely.) Because so much of the empirical work in the literature has reported errors on complex reasoning tasks, it has been easy to overlook that there is a body of simple sound inferences that people make routinely. Other valid inferences that could be made on a standard-logic calculus, but not on the basic mental-logic skills, generally are not made. On problems that present premises together with a conclusion to be evaluated, both the number and the difficulty of the reasoning steps on the direct reasoning routine predict errors, response times, and perceived problem difficulty. The direct reasoning routine also predicts the inferences people write down when given a set of premises without any conclusion to be evaluated. Note that such findings are not explained by a theory that relies solely on content-dependent processes or on heuristics and reasoning biases.

A recent focus of our mental-logic work has been motivated by a debate between mental-logic and mental models advocates. Mental models theory (e.g. Johnson-Laird & Byrne, 1991; Johnson-Laird, Byrne, & Shaeken, 1992) provides a competing account of how people reason on problems with propositional connectives such as "if", "and", "not", and "or", and like mental-logic theory it does not rely on problem content. According to models theory, mental models are constructed as premises are encountered, with the set of models adjusted with each additional premise. A conclusion is formulated from the final model set, following two guidelines: first, semantic information should not be thrown away; secondly, a categorical premise will not be restated as a conclusion.[5] In addition, modelers have proposed a figural effect, such that conclusions are made most easily when their order corresponds to the order in which information was received.

According to models theory, the principal source of difficulty stems from the limited capacity of working memory, and so initial model sets will represent as little information as possible explicitly, leaving open the possibility that the model sets might be fleshed out. As Evans (1993b) noted, the presentation of the mental models theory for propositional reasoning has been ambiguous. In particular, models theory has been presented in three different versions. One is known as the psychological algorithm, and is a computer implementation that is simpler than the "full theory", and uses only initial (unfleshed) model sets. A second computer implementation is referred to as the AI algorithm; it is more sophisticated than the full psychological theory, and makes no claims to psychological reality. The third version is the full theory—although it has not been presented in full, so one must refer to the two algorithms and inspection of examples to glean how the full theory works. The way(s) in which models are combined as new premises are encountered has not been specified for the full theory, leaving us with only the description of the psychological algorithm.

Recently, my colleagues and I have been investigating some predictions of mental-logic theory concerning the order in which inferences are made in a line of reasoning (Braine, Noveck, Samuels, Fisch, Lea, Yang, & O'Brien, submitted; Fisch, 1991; Lea et al., 1990; O'Brien, Braine, & Yang, 1994). The problems are of intrinsic interest to mental-logic theory because, in general, mental-logic theory predicts that inferences will be made as schemas are activated by the available assumptions, including the premise assumptions and any prior inferences. They are also of interest because mental models theory provides no reason to expect the same order of inferences predicted on mental-logic theory. Consider the premises of a problem presented by O'Brien et al. (1994) of the form "n or p, not n, if p then h, if h then z", and "not both z and q". According to mental-logic theory, a disjunction-elimination schema will be applied to the first two premises, yielding p, which together with the third premise yields h by *modus ponens*, which feeds a *modus ponens* inference on the following premise, which combines with the last premise to yield "not-q" by a schema to eliminate "not both". The problem is simple because each inference immediately feeds another schema when the next premise is read. Subjects were required to write down everything they could figure out from the premises in the order in which the inferences occurred to them. Almost all subjects wrote down the inferences in the predicted order. Another group of subjects were presented the same premises and instructions, but with the premises in the reverse order. Mental-logic theory predicts that the same order of inferences will be made on the two problems, because the inferences are governed by the applicability of the inference schemas, and not by the order of presentation of the premises. Again, almost all subjects wrote down the inferences in the predicted order. Braine et al. (submitted) also presented several problems investigating the order of inferences, and subjects almost always made the inferences in the order predicted by mental-logic theory.

How any competing theory could account for this sort of order-of-inferences effect is unclear. Models theory is unable in its present form to account either for the inferences made on these problems, or for the order in which the inferences are made. On the first of the two problems just described, the final model from the psychological algorithm is:

p ~n h z ~q

and on the second problem the final model is:

z ~q h p ~n

According to the psychological algorithm, then, on the first problem subjects should respond "p and h and z and not q", whereas on the second problem they should respond "z and not q and h and p" (~n is not included in either conclusion because it corresponds to a categorical premise). Models theory thus accounts neither for the responses that subjects made on these problems, nor for the order in which the inferences were made.

In principle, I see no reason that models theory could not be revised to provide some predictions about the order in which inferences are made, perhaps by the addition of some new principles while providing a completely specified algorithm for the full theory by which model sets for premises are combined. The descriptions of the psychological algorithm and of the AI algorithm provide details about how premises are combined as they are encountered, but neither of these algorithms provide any reason to expect these order-of-inference effects. Johnson-Laird and his associates say that the full psychological theory differs both from the psychological algorithm and from the AI algorithm, but they have said little about how it differs. The models advocates will need to describe how the full theory works in a detail that has thus far been missing if they are to show how the theory might account for such findings.

Although the psychological algorithm fails to account for the order-of-inference data, clearly the models advocates intend for it to have some psychological reality. The largest data set in the literature for simple propositional reasoning problems is in Braine et al. (1984), who presented 61 direct reasoning problems. Johnson-Laird et al. (1992) and Johnson-Laird (1992) argued that the models theory provides as good a fit for these data as does mental-logic theory, and their argument relies on how the psychological algorithm treats the problems. O'Brien et al. (1994) provide a detailed discussion of the treatment of these problems by the two theories, and here I shall provide only a single illustration of the inadequacy of the mental models account: the psychological algorithm, as presented by Johnson-Laird et al. (1992), makes a rather odd prediction of a sort of fallacy that people simply do not make. Consider how the two premises "If P and Q then R" and "P" are combined:

P Q R; P; P Q R
. . .

where the models for the two premises and then for their combination are separated by semicolons. Suppose now that one is asked whether R follows on the two premises; the answer would be "yes", for the sole final model includes R. O'Brien et al. report several such problems, and find that people do not accept such fallacious conclusions. Clearly, the psychological algorithm is not a serious candidate as an account of what people are doing on these tasks. This means, of course, that the mental models account of the 61 direct reasoning problems cannot be taken seriously, because it relies entirely on the predictions of the psychological algorithm.

Models theory in its present form provides one way in which such fallacies can be avoided—it can assume that subjects are fleshing out the models for the premises. O'Brien et al. describe in detail how this leads to model sets that are extremely large, which should make resisting the fallacies extremely difficult. Even though models theory holds that problem difficulty primarily is a function of the number of explicit models that a problem requires, Johnson-Laird and his associates have not provided clear guidance concerning how many models make a problem difficult. In their description of some "double-disjunction" problems they say that three or more models makes a problem almost impossibly difficult, and I can find nothing in their work to suggest otherwise for problems like those described here, so the fleshed-out model sets required to block these fallacies should be almost impossibly difficult. Of course, in principle models theory could be revised, or the algorithm(s) for the full model could be worked out in sufficient detail in such a way that the fallacies are not made. In its present form, however, models theory does not account for the order-of-inferences data and does not provide an account of the direct reasoning problem data except in a form that predicts odd fallacies that people do not make.

Even on problems for which the two theories predict the same responses, there are reasons to prefer the mental-logic account. For example, both the mental-logic and mental models theories predict that *modus ponens* inferences will be made routinely; the two theories differ, however, on the basis for the inference. According to mental-logic theory, *modus ponens* is a basic inference in that given premises of the form "if p then q" and "p", people will straightforwardly infer q, as long as the premises are held together in working memory, the subject is motivated to consider their meaning, and they are taken as true. According to mental models theory, the two premises lead to a final model that includes both p and q, and only the constraint against restating a categorical premise leads to the conclusion q. The difference between the two theories is apparent when one considers a problem with the same premises as the *modus ponens* argument, but requiring instead evaluation of the conclusion "not both p and q". According to mental models theory, subjects should straight-forwardly evaluate the conclusion as false, because the final model supports "both p and q". Mental-logic theory, however, predicts that the two premises will lead by the *modus ponens* schema to q, and only then will consideration of the conclusion to be evaluated activate a conjunction-introduction schema to infer "p and q", leading then to the response that the conclusion is false. Mental-logic theory thus predicts an intermediate conclusion of q that is not predicted on any version of mental models theory. Braine et al. (submitted) presented several such problems, requiring subjects to write down everything they figured out on the way to evaluating the conclusion, and found that almost all subjects wrote down the intermediate inference predicted on mental-logic theory, even though mental models theory provides no reason for them to do so. I find it hard to imagine what sort of revision of models theory could account for such intermediate conclusions. The data clearly favour the mental-logic over the mental models account.[6]

Another area of empirical work on mental-logic theory has been concerned with the role of mental logic in text comprehension, and this work provides additional support for mental-logic theory, and raises another reason to doubt the mental models theory. Lea et al. (1990) presented short story vignettes and asked subjects to judge whether or not the last sentence in each story made sense. The judgements require inferences that would be made on the basic mental logic, and subjects showed little difficulty in making the appropriate judgements, showing that the inferences are made during text comprehension. After each story, an additional sentence was provided—either a paraphrase of information that was given in the story, or an inference that would be made on the basic mental-logic schemas, or an inference that would be made on standard logic but not on mental logic. Subjects had little difficulty judging the paraphrases as being paraphrases, and the standard-logic inferences as being inferences, but they judged the mental-logic inferences as being paraphrases. Thus, in text comprehension the mental-logic inferences were made so easily that subjects did not even judge them as requiring inferences.

Mental-logic theory predicts that the mental-logic inferences are made whenever the requisite propositions are in working memory, whether or not the inferences are bridging—i.e. necessary for textual coherence. In a text comprehension investigation both of a disjunction-elimination schema and of *modus ponens*, Lea (in press) used an on-line priming paradigm measuring reaction time on a lexical decision task. Short story vignettes were presented on a computer screen, one sentence at a time. The stimulus words for the lexical decision task were semantic associates of the output of the inference schemas. For example, one story about Amanda stated that "If this is a Halloween party, then I'll wear black." In the inference condition the story said that Amanda discovered that it was in fact a Halloween party; the control condition said that there was nothing to indicate whether or not it was a Halloween party. Subjects responded faster on the subsequent lexical decision task on the inference condition than on the control condition to the associate "white", even though "black" was mentioned only once in both conditions. This finding indicates that the inference schemas are applied as the propositions are read. Note that mental models theory does not account for this finding; "black" would be contained in the final model set both in the inference condition and in the control condition, and thus there is no reason in models theory to expect a faster response time in the inference condition.

In summary, the data both from simple reasoning problems and from text comprehension tasks show that people make the basic inferences of the direct reasoning routine easily and routinely—so easily that in text comprehension subjects do not even notice that they are making inferences. Other inferences that could be made on standard logic, but not on mental-logic theory, are not made. Mental logic accounts for findings that seem inexplicable otherwise, for these findings can be accounted for neither by content-dependent theories, nor by bias theories, nor by mental models theory.

CLOSING COMMENTS

Evans (1993) described formal logic as providing an inaccurate and unnatural representation of reasoning in natural languages and with real-world concepts. I agree. Mental logic, however, provides an accurate and natural representation that is not equivalent to a standard formal system of the sort found in a logic textbook. On the one hand, mental logic makes only some of the inferences that are sanctioned in standard-logic systems; on the other hand, mental-logic inferences cohabit easily in a line of reasoning with pragmatic inferences that go beyond those of a standard-logic system.

Evans (1989) argued that for mental-logic theory to account for content effects, it requires complex encoding and decoding mechanisms, which severely compromises its apparent parsimony, whereas pragmatic schemas theory accounts for content effects directly, and mental models theory permits in principle construction of models that are influenced by prior knowledge of the content domain. Note, however, that neither pragmatic schemas theory nor mental models theory are adequate to account for the available logical reasoning data; further, because mental-logic theory includes both pragmatic comprehension processes and extralogical pragmatic inferences, it provides a way for interpreting content effects.

Pragmatic schemas theory has provided an extremely limited account of content effects (only the permission rule has been reliably effective, and as yet only on a single type of task and only when other extraneous features are present), and it as yet provides no explanation of the wide variety of situations in which people reason. Pragmatic schemas theory thus consists largely of a promissory note of wide scope. One way to redeem this promissory note is to view the content-dependent inferences made on pragmatic grounds as complementary to those made on the content-general schemas of mental logic; the permission schema, for example, includes a contrapositive inference that is not available on mental logic alone, and is quite consistent with the inferences available on mental logic. Mental models theory is unable to account for a variety of data for which mental-logic theory accounts (e.g. the order of inferences and intermediate inferences described above), and provides a less plausible account than does mental-logic theory of how logical inferences are made (e.g. the *modus ponens* inference form described above). Further, mental models theory would need to provide encoding and decoding mechanisms that are just as complex as those Evans requires of mental-logic theory, both to account for how different materials lead to different models, and for how conclusions are formulated from final model sets, neither of which have been provided by models theory as yet. Mental-logic theory uses general principles from cognitive psychology to account for content effects, as well as for responses on tasks whose demands exceed basic mental-logic skills. A complete inventory of the sorts of inferences made in discourse processing and in problem solving would include logical inferences, pragmatic inferences, and inferences resulting from heuristics and response biases, and would constitute a large part of a general theory of cognitive psychology, of which mental logic would be only a part.

The advantages of including mental-logic inferences in cognitive psychology are both theoretical and empirical. Mental-logic schemas constrain the inferences that can be drawn on pragmatic grounds in that pragmatic inferences do not contradict logic principles. The logical inference schemas provide a natural explanation of sound inferences and provide a way of checking inferences made on other grounds. Of particular importance, mental-logic theory explains data that remain inexplicable on competing theories. One will not find evidence for logic in human reasoning, however, unless one looks in the right places—i.e. on tasks that are within the basic skills of mental logic.

NOTES

1. Two features of tasks such as the drinking-age problem make them *sui generis* with respect to the original selection task. First, these problems present a true rule, and subjects are asked to identify which individuals might be rule violators. The title of Wason's seminal article introducing the selection task (Wason, 1968) is "Reasoning about a rule", signalling that the task concerns reasoning about the conditions in which the truth status of a rule can be assessed, and not merely reasoning from a rule that is given as true. The logical structure of the search-for-violators sort of task thus is much simpler than that of the selection task. I know of no thematic task version that is solved reliably when subjects are required to test a rule rather than merely to search for violators, so facilitation of the selection task has not yet occurred reliably. Secondly, the sorts of rules presented in these tasks do not lend themselves to rule testing; ordinarily, finding a rule violator does not falsify such a rule—we all know of under-age drinkers, but we do not think that this falsifies the drinking regulation. Manktelow and Over (1991) have made a similar point about differences in truth conditions among various deontic and indicative conditionals.

2. Truth tables have been worked out by professional logicians, but are not available in the ordinary reasoning of mental logic.

3. When a contradiction is discovered under a supposition, assuming the premises are consistent, the supposition is negated, which is, of course, a *reductio ad absurdum*. See Braine and O'Brien (1991) for a discussion of deliberately counter-factual suppositions.

4. One still would require some sort of reasoning program to know how to use the information in the truth table.

5. The second guideline contradicts the first; their examples show that modelers intend the second guideline to take precedence over the first, although the first is more basic to models' principles.

6. For additional reasons that the mental models theory provides flawed predictions about the conditional syllogisms, see Evans (1993b) and O'Brien, Avaltroni, Borg, and Dias (submitted). For further comparison of mental logic and mental models, see Braine et al. (submitted) and O'Brien, Braine, & Yang (1994).

ACKNOWLEDGEMENTS

The author expresses appreciation to Peter Wason for constructing the tasks that have provided so much fun to a cottage industry of logical reasoning researchers, to Martin Braine for several years of collaboration in developing mental-logic theory, and to Steve Newstead, David Over, and Maria Dias for comments on an earlier manuscript that resulted in a better chapter.

REFERENCES

Bever, T. (1970). The cognitive basis for linguistic structures. In J.R. Hayes (Ed.), *Cognition and the development of language.* New York: Wiley.

Braine, M.D.S. (1990). The "natural logic" approach to reasoning. In W.F. Overton (Ed.), *Reasoning, necessity, and logic: Developmental perspectives.* Hillsdale, NJ: Lawrence Erlbaum Associates Inc.

Braine, M.D.S., Noveck, I.A., Samuels, M., Fisch, S.M., Lea, R.B., Yang, Y., & O'Brien, D.P. (submitted). *Predicting intermediate inferences in propositional reasoning.*

Braine, M.D.S., & O'Brien, D.P. (1991). A theory of If: A lexical entry, reasoning program, and pragmatic principles. *Psychological Review, 98,* 182–203.

Braine, M.D.S., & O'Brien, D.P. (submitted). *There is a mental logic, what some of it is like, and some consequences for cognitive theory.*

Braine, M.D.S., Reiser, B.J., & Rumain, B. (1984). Some empirical justification for a theory of natural propositional logic. In. G. Bower (Ed.), *The psychology of learning and motivation: Advances in research and theory. Vol. 18.* New York: Academic Press.

Braine, M.D.S., & Rumain, B. (1983). Logical reasoning. In J.H. Flavell & E. Markman (Eds.), *Handbook of child psychology. Vol. 3.* New York: Wiley.

Cheng, P.W., & Holyoak, K.J. (1985). Pragmatic reasoning schemas. *Cognitive Psychology, 17,* 391–416.

Cheng, P.W., & Holyoak, K.J. (1989). On the natural selection of reasoning theories. *Cognition, 33,* 285–313.

Cheng, P.W., Holyoak, K.J., Nisbett, R.E., & Oliver, L.M. (1986). Pragmatic versus syntactic approaches to training deductive reasoning. *Cognitive Psychology, 18,* 293–328.

Cosmides, L. (1989). The logic of social exchange: Has natural selection shaped how humans reason? Studies with the Wason selection task. *Cognition, 31,* 187–276.

Emerson, H.F., & Gekoski, W.L. (1980). Development of comprehension of sentences with "because" or "if". *Journal of Experimental Child Psychology, 28,* 202–224.

Evans, J.St.B.T. (1982). *The psychology of deductive reasoning.* London: Routledge & Kegan Paul.

Evans, J.St.B.T. (1989). *Bias in human reasoning: Causes and consequences.* Hove, UK: Lawrence Erlbaum Associates Ltd.

Evans, J.St.B.T. (1992, July). *The Wason selection task: An appreciation.* Paper presented to the Second International Conference on Thinking, Plymouth, UK.

Evans, J.St.B.T. (1993a). Bias and rationality. In K.I. Manktelow & D.E. Over (Eds.), *Rationality: Psychological and philosophical perspectives*. London: Routledge & Kegan Paul.

Evans, J.St.B.T. (1993b). The mental model theory of conditional reasoning: Critical appraisal and revision. *Cognition, 48*, 1–20.

Evans, J.St.B.T., & Lynch, J.S. (1973). Matching bias and the selection task. *British Journal of Psychology, 64*, 391–397.

Fillenbaum, S. (1977). Mind your p's and q's: The role of content and context in some uses of "and", "or", and "if". In G. Bower (Ed.), *The psychology of learning and motivation. Vol. 11*. New York: Academic Press.

Fisch, S.M. (1991). *Mental logic in children's reasoning and text comprehension*. Unpublished PhD thesis. New York University.

Geis, M., & Zwicky, A.M. (1971). On invited inferences. *Linguistic Inquiry, 2*, 561–566.

Girotto, V., Mazzocco, A., & Cherubini, P. (1992). Judgements of deontic relevance in reasoning: A reply to Jackson and Griggs. *Quarterly Journal of Experimental Psychology, 45A*, 547–574.

Griggs, R.J. (1989). To "see" or not to "see": That is the selection task. *Quarterly Journal of Experimental Psychology, 41A*, 517–529.

Griggs, R.J., & Cox, J.R. (1982). The elusive thematic-material effect in Wason's selection task. *British Journal of Psychology, 73*, 407–420.

Griggs, R.J., & Cox, J.R. (1993). Permission schemas and the selection task. *Quarterly Journal of Experimental Psychology, 46A*, 637–651.

Jackson, S.L., & Griggs, R.J. (1990). The elusive pragmatic reasoning schemas effect. *Quarterly Journal of Experimental Psychology, 42A*, 353–373.

Johnson-Laird, P.N. (1992, July). *Mental models or mental logic?* Paper presented to the Second International Conference on Thinking, Plymouth, UK.

Johnson-Laird, P.N., & Byrne, R.M.J. (1991). *Deduction*. Hove, UK: Lawrence Erlbaum Associates Ltd.

Johnson-Laird, P.N., Byrne, R.M.J., & Shaeken, W. (1992). Propositional reasoning by model. *Psychological Review, 99*, 418–439.

Johnson-Laird, P.N., Legrenzi, P., & Legrenzi, S. (1972). Reasoning and a sense of reality. *British Journal of Psychology, 63*, 395–400.

Kroger, J.K., Cheng, P.W., & Holyoak, K.J. (1993). Evoking the permission schema: The impact of negation and a violation-checking context. *Quarterly Journal of Experimental Psychology, 46A*, 615–635.

Lea, R.B. (in press). The time course of propositional logic inferences in text comprehension. *Journal of Experimental Psychology: Learning, Memory, and Cognition*.

Lea, R.B., O'Brien, D.P., Noveck, I.A., Fisch, S.M., & Braine, M.D.S. (1990). Predicting propositional logic inferences in text comprehension. *Journal of Memory and Language, 29*, 361–387.

Macnamara, J. (1986). *A border dispute: The place of logic in psychology*. Cambridge, MA: MIT Press.

Manktelow, K.I., & Evans, J.St.B.T. (1979). Facilitation of reasoning by realism: Effect or non-effect? *British Journal of Psychology, 70*, 477–488.

Manktelow, K.I., & Over, D.E. (1990). Deontic thought and the selection task. In K.J. Gilhooly, M. Keane, R.H. Logie, & G. Erdos (Eds.), *Lines of thinking*. Chichester, UK: Wiley.

Manktelow, K.I., & Over, D.E. (1991). Social rules and utilities in reasoning with deontic conditionals. *Cognition, 39*, 85–105.

Markovits, H., & Savory, F. (1992). Pragmatic schemas and the selection task: To reason or not to reason? *Quarterly Journal of Experimental Psychology, 45A*, 133–148.

Noveck, I.A., Lea, R.B., Davidson, G.M., & O'Brien, D.P. (1990). Human reasoning is both logical and pragmatic. *Intellectica, 11*, 81–109.

Noveck, I.A., & O'Brien, D.P. (submitted). *To what extent do pragmatic reasoning schemas affect performance on Wason's selection task?*

O'Brien, D.P. (1987). The development of conditional reasoning: An iffy proposition. In H. Reese (Ed.), *Advances in child development and behavior. Vol. 18*. New York: Academic Press.

O'Brien, D.P. (1991). Conditional reasoning: Development. In R. Dulbecco (Ed.), *Encyclopedia of human biology*. San Diego, CA: Academic Press.

O'Brien, D.P. (1993). Mental logic and irrationality: We can put a man on the moon, so why can't we solve those logical reasoning problems? In K.I. Manktelow & D.E. Over (Eds.), *Rationality: Psychological and philosophical perspectives*. London: Routledge & Kegan Paul.

O'Brien, D.P., Avaltroni, J., Borg, D., & Dias, M. (submitted). *Mental models and the conditional syllogisms: The predictions are wrong.*

O'Brien, D.P., Braine, M.D.S., Connell, J., Noveck, I.A., Fisch, S.M., & Fun, E. (1989). Reasoning about conditional sentences: Development of understanding of cues to quantification. *Journal of Experimental Child Psychology, 34*, 274–290.

O'Brien, D.P., Braine, M.D.S., & Yang, Y. (1994). Propositional reasoning by model? Simple to refute in principle and in practice. *Psychological Review, 101*, 711–724.

Platt, R.D., & Griggs, R.A. (1993). Facilitation in the abstract selection task: The effects of attentional and instructional factors. *Quarterly Journal of Experimental Psychology, 46A*, 637–651.

Politzer, G., & Nguyen-Xuan, A. (1992). Reasoning about conditional promises and warnings: Darwinian algorithms, mental models, relevance judgements, or pragmatic schemas? *Quarterly Journal of Experimental Psychology, 44A*, 401–421.

Pollard, P. (1990). Natural selection for the selection task: Limits to social exchange theory. *Cognition, 36*, 195–204.

Pollard, P., & Evans, J.St.B.T. (1987). On the relationship between content and context effects in reasoning. *American Journal of Psychology, 100*, 41–60.

Rips, L.J. (1983). Cognitive processes in propositional reasoning. *Psychological Review, 90*, 38–71.

Rips, L.J. (1990). Reasoning. *Annual Review of Psychology, 41*, 321–353.

Sperber, D., & Wilson, D. (1986). *Relevance: Communication and cognition*. Cambridge, MA: Harvard University Press.

Wason, P.C. (1966). Reasoning. In B.M. Foss (Ed.), *New horizons in psychology.* Harmondsworth: Penguin.

Wason, P.C. (1968). Reasoning about a rule. *Quarterly Journal of Experimental Psychology, 20,* 273–281.

Wason, P.C., & Evans, J.St.B.T. (1975). Dual processes in reasoning? *Cognition, 3,* 141–154.

Wason, P.C., & Johnson-Laird, P.N. (1970). A conflict between selecting and evaluation of information in an inferential task. *British Journal of Psychology, 61,* 509–515.

CHAPTER TEN

Hypothesis Testing

Michael E. Gorman

*School of Engineering and Applied Science,
University of Virginia, USA*

One of Peter Wason's classic heuristics for stimulating thought was to pose a problem by inventing a task. Most of the papers in this volume focus on his selection task. A few mention his THOG problem. In this chapter, I am going to use his 2-4-6 task as a vehicle for raising questions about hypothesis testing.[1]

WASON'S 2-4-6 TASK

The 2-4-6 task, like most of Wason's problems, appears to be devilishly simple. You are told the number triple "2,4,6" is an instance of a rule the experimenter has in mind; to discover the rule, you must propose additional triples. Each time you propose a triple the experimenter tells you whether or not it is an instance of the rule.

Wason's particular interest was in "the logical fallacy of induction by simple enumeration" (Wason & Johnson-Laird, 1972, p. 205). This fallacy is illustrated by the typical behaviour of Wason's (1960) subjects; they tended to propose triples like "6, 8, 10" and "12, 14, 16" and, after being told that these were correct, stopped and announced a rule like "numbers must go up by twos". In other words, they searched for positive instances of their hypotheses, and when they found several—the amount of enumeration varied from subject to subject—they concluded they had found the rule. Wason referred to this strategy as verification, to distinguish it from two alternatives. Subjects could instead have adopted a Popperian approach and tried to falsify their hypotheses, deliberately generating instances that were inconsistent with their hypotheses, or they could have used a more Kuhnian approach and tried to vary their current hypothesis. "When hypotheses are varied the work involved in discovery is internalised; but when hypotheses are only verified on the basis of confirming evidence the subject is forced to appeal to an external authority (the experimenter) to find out if his conclusions are correct" (Wason & Johnson-Laird, 1972, p. 207).

When a subject followed a verification strategy and announced a guess like "numbers ascending by twos" Wason told them that this was not the rule. The actual rule was "numbers increasing in order of magnitude". In his first study, only 21% of the subjects announced this rule on the first guess, and most of those followed the "vary hypothesis" strategy; the unsuccessful subjects typically followed the verification strategy. Furthermore, more than half the triples proposed after an incorrect announcement were consistent with the old hypothesis the experimenter had said was wrong, and further announcements were typically either restatements of the original hypothesis or new guesses which varied in small ways from the initial hypothesis—e.g. replacing "numbers go up by twos" with "adding a number, always the same one, to form the next number."

Wason argued that his subjects were displaying a "verification bias", in that verification appeared to be the only strategy they could use. Indeed, some subjects had trouble understanding alternative strategies even when they were explained to them.

The 2-4-6 and Selection Tasks Compared

Wason found a similar verification bias in his initial studies with the selection task. There were a number of important differences between these tasks. In hypothesis-testing terms, the two most important were, first, that subjects were given an hypothesis to test in the selection task. In the 2-4-6 task, they were given a triple which suggested a number of possible hypotheses; they had to decide which to pursue. Secondly, the type of hypothesis being tested was different in the two tasks. To illustrate this point, we need to imagine converting the 2-4-6 task into a selection task. Suppose one were asked to select the minimum number of cards sufficient to test the rule, "If there are consecutive even numbers on one side of the card, the other side will have 'Correct' written on it", and the four cards were as follows:

2,4,6   Correct   1,2,3   Incorrect

In this case, the first and fourth cards are the necessary and sufficient choices. But supposing one reworded the task to sound more like the sort of problem subjects confront on the 2-4-6 task: "Select the minimum number of cards necessary to test whether the rule is 'consecutive even numbers'". Now all four cards are essential.

It would be interesting to see how subjects actually performed on these two versions of the selection task, but it is clear that they are quite different because the rule, in the first case, does not say that *only* consecutive even numbers will be correct, whereas in the second it does. The first case corresponds to the solution many subjects reach on the 2-4-6 task; once they have determined that a rule like "consecutive even numbers" always produces a correct response, they stop without checking whether other triples might also have produced correct responses. The second case corresponds to the typical sort of rule on the 2-4-6 task which demands that subjects consider the equivalent of all four alternatives on the selection task.

The third important difference was that subjects on the 2-4-6 task had to generate their own instances,[2] whereas subjects on the selection task were given evidence. The selection task focuses on hypothesis justification, whereas the 2-4-6 task could be used to study the relationship between discovery and justification. Wason, for example, was interested in whether the investment involved in discovering an hypothesis would make subjects more likely to adhere to it. A task that asks subjects both to discover and justify hypotheses could potentially be used to simulate aspects of scientific reasoning—a point that occurred to a number of researchers who developed more complicated tasks that resemble the structure of the 2-4-6.

Tasks That Simulate Scientific Reasoning

When I first encountered this problem, I had been working independently with a similar task called Eleusis. The goal in Eleusis is to discover the rule that determines how one can place cards in a sequence—e.g. alternating colours, or odds and evens, or suits—and/or far more complicated rules. For example, one rule I experimented with was "odd and even cards must alternate". All cards that fit this alternating pattern would be laid out in a straight line; all cards that violated it would be placed at right angles. Subjects could therefore always see a complete record of their previous experiments (see Fig. 10.1).

What intrigued me about Eleusis was that its creator, Robert Abbott, intended it to model the search for truth—scientific, mathematical, or religious (see Gardner, 1977). Each of the card plays could be viewed as a kind of experiment and the rule as analogous to a scientific law. Similarly, the 2-4-6 task gave students the opportunity to conduct experiments by

Rule 3:	AD	2D	3D	4D	KS	QH	7C	10S	3S	8D	AS	QH
						10H	3C	2C	7C	QD		
						5D	6H	JD				

FIG. 10.1. An example of a New Eleusis rule (where D = Diamond, H = Heart, C = Club, S=Spade, J = Jack, Q = Queen, K = King, and A = Ace). Adapted from Gorman (1992) with the permission of the Indiana University Press.

proposing triples as they searched for an underlying rule or pattern. Eleusis had the advantage of being a multi-dimensional task: the rule could involve colour, number, suit and/or a variety of other dimensions or features. This seemed more like the noise and confusion of actual science to me.

An even more realistic task was the artificial universe developed by Mynatt, Doherty, and Tweney (1977; 1978). Subjects fired particles at shapes on a screen to determine the rules governing their behaviour. This task included even more distracting dimensions than Eleusis; indeed, one version of it was so complicated that after ten hours, no subject had solved it!

I found that instructions to falsify greatly improved group performance on Eleusis (Gorman, Gorman, Latta, & Cunningham, 1984). In contrast, Mynatt, Doherty, and Tweney (1977) found that disconfirmatory instructions did not improve performance on an artificial universe, and Tweney et al. (1980) obtained a similar result on the 2-4-6 task. In the former study, subjects instructed to disconfirm had difficulty following their strategy; in the latter, disconfirmatory subjects clearly tried to follow their strategy, but it did not significantly improve their performance.

Why had I been the only one to get this effect? Was it because I used groups? Eleusis? So I decided to run a replication of sorts, using individuals and the 2-4-6 task. When I got a similar effect with a few subjects, I shipped a paper off to the *British Journal of Psychology*. At the same time, I was trying to get down to Bowling Green to consult with Ryan Tweney. Only one problem with your dates, he said, "You'll be arriving at the same time as Peter Wason". Happy coincidence, I thought, and jumped at the prospect. Right after we met, Peter took me aside for a little chat. He had my *British Journal* manuscript and—although he knew I would get his written comments—took the time to go over it with me personally, a courtesy I greatly appreciated.

In the course of our conversation, Peter pointed out that he was less interested in whether subjects solved the rule than how they tried to solve it. He was also less willing to generalise from the task to scientific reasoning. I would restate these two issues as follows: (1) Is it really useful to give subjects instructions to perform according to a strategy on the 2-4-6 and analogous tasks ? (2) To what extent can such tasks simulate scientific reasoning?

Should Subjects Be Instructed to Adopt a Strategy?

D.D. Tukey (1986) has objected to instructions with particular vehemence: "Rather than legislating what subjects should be doing in this task and then trying to evoke that behaviour, the present research suggests that psychologists learn from subjects which methods or strategies are easily and/or beneficially used" (p. 30). The original motive for using such instructions was to eliminate a problem raised by Wetherick (1962). He argued that Wason confused a confirmatory strategy with a positive test strategy, and disconfirmatory with negative tests. For example, if a subject's hypothesis were "numbers ascend by twos" and she proposed "3-5-7", that would constitute a positive test: the triple is an instance of the rule. But this positive test would not necessarily be confirmatory: she might actually expect that this triple would be wrong and therefore intend it as a disconfirmatory experiment. She might, for example, be testing whether her hypothesis applied only to even numbers. As Wason (1962) pointed out, such a subject is presumably sceptical about his or her hypothesis: "Hence, Wetherick's criterion implies that a subject can only be said to have eliminated a hypothesis if he had believed that this hypothesis was likely to be the rule—i.e. would not be eliminated. And this seems somewhat arbitrary. It makes the criterion of elimination depend on the degree of confidence which is felt about an hypothesis, and it would not count the checking of a dubious hypothesis as being eliminative reasoning at all" (p. 250).

Whether one agrees with his line of criticism or not, Wetherick did suggest a methodological modification. To make certain of subjects' intentions, Wetherick asked them to predict whether each triple would conform to the rule, a procedure I used in several of my studies (see, e.g., Gorman & Gorman, 1984).

Another approach I adopted was to instruct subjects to use strategies like disconfirmation and confirmation and check whether they followed instructions by studying their predictions. Instructions are one way of making sure that subjects are doing what you think they are doing. Gorman and Gorman found, for example, that subjects given instructions to disconfirm predicted significantly more of their triples would be incorrect than subjects in confirmatory or control conditions.

Does this "legislate" the strategy subjects ought to use? Certainly—the goal of an experiment using instructions is to teach strategies and compare the effect. These instruction studies are an excellent way to follow-up on the kind of exploratory, process-oriented study which reveals interesting strategies subjects "naturally" follow—and also to investigate strategies that few or no subjects use naturally. Studies which include instructions are essential if one wants to make normative claims like "disconfirmation is a superior strategy (under specified conditions)". One cannot rely on enough subjects pursuing such a strategy naturally under the specified conditions, nor—as noted above—can one be certain that they are following the normative version of the strategy.

One compromise position I have adopted is to make all strategy instructions suggestions. I try to make these suggestions as compelling as possible, but leave subjects the option of abandoning or altering the suggested strategy. One can always drop such groups or individuals from an analysis based on instructions, but include them in more process-oriented analyses that have to do with how easy such instructions are to follow and whether any groups or individuals created other strategies that might be usefully pursued in future studies.

Can Tasks Like 2-4-6 Simulate Scientific Reasoning?

Houts and Gholson (1989) argued that experiments can play a useful role in studying scientific reasoning. The usual objection is that tasks like the 2-4-6 have low ecological validity—the problem itself does not clearly model the sort of complex, domain-specific task scientists work on, nor are the subjects scientists themselves.

But the value of experiments is their artificiality—the way in which they allow us to study variables in isolation and determine whether they could play a causative role. Consider a disconfirmatory strategy. If it does not work under ideal, isolated conditions on a relatively simple problem, its usefulness as a heuristic in the messier, more confusing world of actual science may be called into question. Indeed, Fuller (1989) has gone so far as to suggest that many philosophical prescriptions regarding science ought to be subjected to experimental test.

So, experimental simulations can test the potential normative value of heuristics like disconfirmation under a variety of controlled conditions, and determine when such a strategy might be effective at changing the way people approach a problem. Note that one cannot be sure working scientists can apply such a heuristic—more ecologically valid studies are required to check this (see Dunbar, in press, for an example).

Ecological features can also be added to experiments. For example, Mynatt, Doherty, and Tweney (1978) designed an artificial universe that included many of the complexities of real scientific problems. Dunbar (1989) has developed a computerised task that simulates important discoveries in genetics. One can also employ scientists as subjects, as Mahoney (1976), Clement (1991) and others have done (see Gorman, in press, for a more detailed review).

In conclusion, experiments can be used to isolate variables that may have an important causal role in science, thereby providing a check on philosophical prescriptions and also highlighting factors that ought to be studied in ecological contexts.

When You Can't Ask God Whether Your Rule is Right

Let me illustrate these important issues by continuing the story of my encounter at Bowling Green. Later, at Ryan Tweney's house, I ran Ryan on Eleusis, and he discovered the reason why disconfirmatory instructions improved performance in my experiments and not in his.

In the classic Wason/Tweney version of the 2-4-6 task, the experimenter provides feedback on both triples and guesses—if a subject announced a guess about the rule, the experimenter told her whether it was right or wrong. Subjects were supposed to withhold any announcement until they had a high degree of confidence in their hypotheses, but it was possible that they sought feedback from the experimenter rather than continuing to conduct tests themselves. Wason saw this as illogical: "In fact, the generation of an instance consistent with a new hypothesis provides more information than announcing the old hypothesis. It would show decisively whether the old hypothesis is incorrect (if the instance is positive), and it would also show whether the new hypothesis is at least on the right lines. Hence, if anything, the announcement of an hypothesis suggests that the subject really believes that it is correct rather than incorrect" (Wason & Johnson-Laird, 1972, p. 210).

In my experiments, I encouraged subjects to write down as many guesses as occurred to them, but made it clear that they would receive no feedback on the correctness of any guess until the entire experiment was over. If at any time a group of subjects—or an individual subject in my 2-4-6 study— asked whether their current hypothesis was correct, I told them it was up to them to decide when they were satisfied with their hypothesis, and that they could continue to propose experiments or stop at any time. My model for this sort of instruction was Popper's emphasis on making bold conjectures and trying to disconfirm them. I wanted subjects to conjecture frequently and boldly, then find ways of testing their own conjectures, without the benefit of any feedback from the experimenter. After all, a scientist can't simply ask God whether her hypothesis is correct or not (though some certainly think they can—witness Einstein's "God does not play dice" remark).

Therefore, a disconfirmatory strategy would only be effective when subjects couldn't get any feedback on the correctness of their announced guesses. Mynatt, Doherty, and Tweney (1978) proposed that a confirmatory strategy is particularly useful early in the inference process, when one is still trying to formulate a promising hypothesis; disconfirmation is useful later, when one has an hypothesis that is worth testing. "Perhaps explicit disconfirmation will be most effective at just the point where subjects have a confirmed hypothesis which they are sure is correct" (Tweney et al., 1980, pp. 115–116).

To test this idea, Tweney et al. (1980, Experiment 2) gave some subjects disconfirmatory instructions after they had announced a guess. These subjects were told they could retract the guess, if they wanted, and keep testing. Even though most disconfirmatory subjects followed their instructions, they were no more successful at solving the rule than subjects who had not been told to disconfirm.

Again, a paradox—disconfirmatory instructions were very effective in one situation where there was no feedback on announced guesses, but not in another. However, there were at least three major methodological differences between my 2-4-6 study and Tweney et al.'s Experiment 2:

1. I emphasised that subjects should "guess early, guess often" in an effort to encourage subjects to conjecture. None of these guesses were announced; subjects always wrote them down, and when they felt satisfied that one was the rule, indicated that fact in writing. Tweney et al.'s subjects still announced guesses and knew that they could, if they chose, receive feedback from the experimenter.
2. In my study, there was no time limit; subjects could take as long as they wanted to test their hypotheses. In Tweney et al.'s study, subjects were limited to 25 minutes.
3. In my study, the traditional "ascending numbers" rule was the first of two rules subjects worked on; when they started the second rule, they still did not know whether they had solved the first. This forced them to test their hypotheses on the first rule very carefully.

It seemed, at any rate, that eliminating the option of asking the experimenter altered the task in a way that made disconfirmation essential. One could not appeal to an outside authority; one had to test one's own hypothesis very thoroughly. Let us relate this finding to the two issues raised above.

Was it useful in this case to give subjects strategy instructions? Yes—disconfirmatory instructions led to a difference in performance that forced Tweney and I to look closely at differences in our methodology. A critic could counter-argue that one could simply have looked at what strategies subjects spontaneously followed under feedback-on-announcements and no feedback conditions. Certainly such a study is worth doing. But the advantage of giving instructions, as noted above, is that one can be a little more precise about what the subjects are doing, and one can also establish that a particular strategy is teachable.

Does this result have any relevance to actual scientific practice? Perhaps. It raises the whole issue of what happens when a scientist can appeal to an outside authority to find out whether he or she is making progress towards a discovery. If my results, combined with Tweney and Wason's, are right, then disconfirmation will be less useful when one can appeal to such an authority. Is there an analogy in science or science education? Perhaps the laboratory exercises done in high-school and college classes come closest. The object of most of these labs is to get the right answer, not explore a novel phenomenon, and frequent appeals to authority in the form of the lab assistant or the instructor can be helpful. In this kind of situation, disconfirmation has little value, which suggests that another, more open-ended kind of exercise might provide better training for future scientists or engineers.[3]

The Relationship Between Representation, Testing Strategy, and Rule

Disconfirmatory instructions dramatically improved performance on Wason's "ascending numbers" rule when subjects wrote down their guesses and could not ask the experimenter whether they were right or wrong. Disconfirmatory subjects obtained significantly more incorrect triples, and obtaining this sort of negative information was a significant predictor of success.[4] In the same study (Gorman & Gorman, 1984), however, we found that the positive effect for disconfirmatory instructions disappeared when subjects were asked to work on a second rule: "The three numbers must be different". We tried reversing the order of the rules, and when the "three different numbers" rule was first, there was still no effect for disconfirmatory instructions.

Therefore, the utility of disconfirmatory instructions depends not only on whether one can appeal to an external authority for feedback on one's hypotheses, but also on the nature of the rule. Klayman and Ha (1987) carried out an excellent analysis of this problem. First of all, they rejected the use of the terms "confirmatory" and "disconfirmatory", substituting the terms "positive" and "negative" test strategy (cf. Wetherick, 1962). They did this because a positive strategy can lead to confirmation or disconfirmation depending on whether the experimenter's rule is more general or less general than the subject's hypothesis. For example, if a subject's hypothesis was "numbers ascending by twos" and the experimenter's rule was "even numbers ascending by twos", then a positive test like "3,5,7" could lead to a disconfirmatory result.

To take this analysis a step further, let us consider the subject's intentions. Naturally, he does not know the target rule—but he could estimate whether it is likely to be more general or narrower than his hypothesised rule. If he thinks it is narrower, then a positive test might be intended as a disconfirmation. But are subjects really thinking about what sort of rule they might be looking for? This question raises the issue of task representation: how do subjects represent the sort of problem they are working on? One can only make indirect inferences about subjects' representations, because these are often hazy, half-formed notions that would be difficult for subjects to describe even if they could be induced to do so.

Here is another advantage of experiment—they allow us to manipulate representations.[5] I did this almost accidentally when I gave up using disconfirmatory instructions and instead tried a manipulation used by Tweney et al. (1980, Experiment 4), following a suggestion from Wason: he suggested that instead of asking subjects to find positive and negative instances of a single rule, they might be asked to try discovering two rules, which he labelled DAX and MED.

Both Tweney et al. and Gorman, Stafford, and Gorman (1987) found subjects perform much better on this DAX-MED version than on the regular version. For example, on "the three numbers must be different" rule, we found DAX-MED subjects proposed more triples, predicted and obtained more MED triples and solved the rule significantly more often than a control group which was told whether their triples were right or wrong, in terms of the rule (see Fig. 10.2). These DAX-MED subjects deliberately sought MED instances, and when they found them, knew that they were clues to a more general rule. In contrast, control subjects had trouble getting any triples wrong, and when they did, they frequently failed to search for other negative instances. For example, when a control subject tried "0,0,0" and found it was wrong, he decided the rule was "any number except 0,0,0". In the same situation, several DAX-MED subjects used "0,0,0" as a clue about a more general MED rule—in good Klayman and Ha fashion, they tried triples at variance with previous instances in an effort to probe the MED problem space.

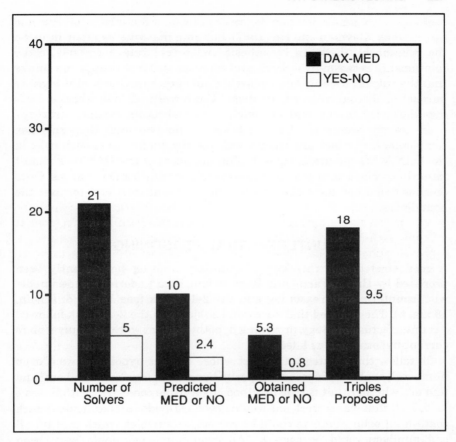

FIG. 10.2. Differences between DAX-MED and YES-NO conditions on the "three different numbers" rule. (Adapted from Gorman, 1992, with the permission of the Indiana University Press.)

In other words, this DAX-MED manipulation changed the way subjects represented the task—instead of looking for a single rule that might have exceptions, they knew they were looking for two rules, probably mutually exclusive and complementary. This altered their search strategy. Subjects told to disconfirm on the "three different numbers" rule did try negative instances, but frequently were unable to get any triples wrong. DAX-MED subjects seemed to try a wider range of instances, eventually trying two or more numbers that were the same.

Therefore, whether and when one ought to use confirmatory or disconfirmatory strategies depends on the relationship between one's current hypothesis and one's representation of the type of rule one is seeking. This generalisation is essentially a restatement of the one proposed by Klayman and Ha (1987), but note that whereas they focus on the relationship between hypothesis and actual rule, I emphasise the relationship between hypothesis and representation of rule. If one thinks that the rule is probably more general than one's hypothesis, one ought to pursue a disconfirmatory strategy. Conversely, if one thinks one's hypothesis is more general, one ought to pursue a confirmatory strategy.

If one represents the task as a search for two mutually exclusive, complementary rules, one should seek positive instances of each rule; in the DAX-MED condition, subjects find instances of the DAX rule almost immediately, but have to search persistently for any MED instances. Once one has found instances of each rule, then one must test to determine the boundaries.

COUNTERFACTUAL REASONING

A good strategy for this sort of boundary hunting has recently been proposed by Hilary Farris and Russ Revlin, who undertook experiments with counterfactual reasoning and the 2-4-6 task (see Farris & Revlin, 1989a, b). They argued that successful subjects on the 2-4-6 task followed a counterfactual strategy, proposing hypotheses that were true only if one's current hypothesis was false.

To follow this strategy, a subject whose current hypothesis was "even numbers", ought to propose an opposite hypothesis like "odd numbers" and find out whether that is true by proposing a triple consistent with it—say, "3, 5, 7". If that was correct, she would now have evidence that triples which contain all even numbers could be correct, and triples which contain all odd numbers could be correct. "All even numbers" would have been falsified; a different hypothesis that included odd numbers would be required.

To an observer, this "3,5,7" might appear to be a confirmatory triple, as it follows the hypothesis "all odd numbers". But in this example, "odd numbers" is a counterfactual hypothesis, generated in an attempt to disconfirm the earlier "all even numbers" hypothesis. "Unfortunately, if the reasoner follows the counterfactual strategy, the substantial frequency of confirming triples can be misinterpreted by the experimenter as a bias to confirm" (Farris & Revlin, 1989b, p. 222). This strategy resembles what subjects do in the DAX-MED version of the 2-4-6 task; instead of looking for evidence that might disconfirm one hypothesis, in the DAX-MED design subjects looked for positive evidence for two complementary hypotheses.

Farris and Revlin argue that their results demonstrate counterfactual reasoning is more effective than simply proposing disconfirmatory triples. Unfortunately, Farris and Revlin's subjects could ultimately appeal to the experimenter to find out whether their announced guesses fit the rule. As noted above, disconfirmation is only an effective strategy when one knows that one can never ask God or the experimenter whether one's rule is right.

One possibility would be to conduct a study in which disconfirmatory and counterfactual instructions would be compared, using the "you can't ask God" design. But why counterfactual instructions? Why not just re-do the original Farris and Revlin design, omitting "God"? It seemed to me Farris and Revlin were claiming that subjects arrive at this counterfactual strategy "naturally". Therefore, it ought to be fairly easy to come up with instructions that would facilitate this "natural" response in more subjects. Furthermore, instructions force one to operationalise a strategy in very much the same way as building a computer simulation: neither computers nor subjects tolerate ambiguity very well, though the latter are perhaps more tolerant than the former. Also, giving instructions is the only sure way of determining whether a strategy can be taught. The problem, of course, is that if the instructions fail, one cannot be sure whether the fault lies in the instructions or the strategy: one has to complement instructions with process measures designed to check whether a strategy is being applied.

It occurred to me that counterfactual instructions might transform the regular 2-4-6 task into a kind of DAX-MED situation. Farris and Revlin suggested that a counterfactual strategy should involve proposing complementary hypotheses, which corresponds to what subjects do when they search for the MED rule. But in fact, the example Farris and Revlin used was an opposite hypothesis: all evens as the counterfactual hypothesis for all odds. The complement for "all evens" is "at least one odd". Constructing an opposite hypothesis is very different from constructing a counterfactual one. Consider an example. Suppose a young cosmologist started with the hypothesis that "the universe is expanding". If she followed a counterfactual-opposite strategy, she would propose "the universe is contracting", and look for evidence that supported that point of view. If she followed a counterfactual-complement strategy, she would also have to consider hypotheses like "the universe is in a steady state" and "the universe alternately expands and contracts".

DAX-MED instructions in the past have encouraged subjects to search for mutually exclusive, complementary hypotheses, although some do begin with opposite hypotheses. Therefore, future research should involve a comparison between DAX-MED and counterfactual conditions, focusing on the types of hypotheses subjects propose in each condition.

Mike Oaksford and Nick Chater (1994) have suggested how the counterfactual strategy might be strengthened. Their analysis differs from Farris and Revlin's at the point where a subject obtains a positive result for a triple that is consistent with his or her counterfactual hypothesis (H').

According to Farris and Revlin, this result makes H′ plausible. But Oaksford and Chater point out that H′ is by definition inconsistent with the pool of triples which support the original hypothesis (H). Therefore, a result consistent with H′ disconfirms H, and H′ is already false. So at this point the subject has to iterate through the strategy again, generating a new H and H′ and a triple consistent with H′ (see Fig. 10.3).[6]

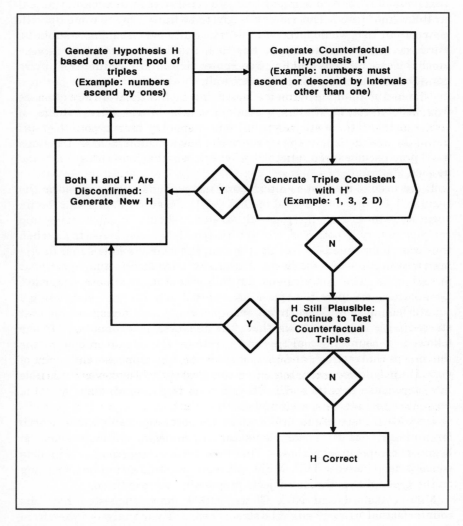

FIG. 10.3. Iterative counterfactual strategy.

This sort of iterative strategy should be useful for exploring the boundaries of one's hypothesis. A counterfactual strategy is really a kind of disconfirmatory heuristic in which the subject not only proposes triples at variance with his hypothesis, but focuses these triples by proposing an H' that targets the space of instances that lie beyond the boundaries of H. One could, for example, begin with "three different numbers" as one's H and propose "two or more the same" as an H'. If one obtained no positive instances of H', then one might stop and conclude H was correct.

But what if the target rule were narrower than H? One would have to propose an H' that was narrower than H, and search the boundaries between this narrower hypothesis and H. Such a strategy might be consistent with Farris and Revlin's fuzzier definition of counterfactual but clearly does not correspond with Oaksford's.

The real value of the counterfactual research, like the work of Wetherick, Klayman, and Ha and others, is that it focuses us on alternative hypotheses and representations subjects consider when they test hypotheses. The common practice of having subjects write down what hypotheses they are testing is not always an effective way of determining how they represent the sort of rule they are seeking; they may be proceeding intuitively, without necessarily having clear hypotheses they can state.

INCREASING ECOLOGICAL VALIDITY

As noted above, the power of experiments is that they allow us to abstract and to simplify, which is the goal of theories and models. But once one has a theory, one can test it under conditions that approximate features of actual science.

For example, rules on the 2-4-6 task involve one dimension: number. What do terms like "narrower" or "more general" mean when the task has several dimensions, as in Eleusis or the artificial universe problems posed by the Bowling Green Group? Consider Eleusis: suppose one's current hypothesis is "alternating colours" and the rule is "odd and even cards must alternate". Hypothesis and rule overlap, in this case; finding the target requires that subjects "switch frame" and attend to another dimension. Kepler's discovery of the three laws of planetary motion required such a frame shift; he had to abandon the idea that planetary orbits were circular and search for alternate geometric regularities (see Gorman, 1992, for a more extended analysis).

Klahr and Dunbar (1988) asked subjects to discover the function of an "RPT" key on a device called a "Big Trak" without giving instructions on what strategy subjects should follow. Subjects had to test hypotheses about how this key functioned by typing programs that told the device where and how far to move. Successful subjects reacted to disconfirmations by developing new hypotheses that represented a "shift in frame" which in turn suggested new areas of the problem space to search for evidence. For example, most subjects began with the idea that the RPT key would specify number of repetitions; an instruction like "RPT 4" might mean "repeat the whole program four times". Typically, they tried initially to confirm this hypothesis and quickly obtained disconfirmatory results. In order to discover the rule, subjects had to change their representation of the function of the RPT key from counting the number of repetitions to selecting the steps to be repeated: "RPT 4" meant "repeat the last four steps".

This is different from searching for a complementary hypothesis, or one that is more general or narrower. To solve this problem, one has to switch frames and consider a different kind of hypothesis. In a more recent study using a version of their RPT task, Klahr, Fay, and Dunbar (1993) established that third, and to a lesser extent, sixth graders had trouble with evidence that disconfirmed counter hypotheses, in part because they could not switch to a selection hypothesis. This result reinforces the importance of considering alternate hypotheses that involve different dimensions or features of the task.

Part of the reason younger children had difficulty with this task is a kind of confirmation bias: "inconsistencies were interpreted not as disconfirmations, but rather as either errors or temporary failures to demonstrate the desired effect" (p. 140).[7] This task, like the 2-4-6 and other tasks discussed in this chapter, included no possibility of error, but in the real world of both childhood and science, errors and exceptions are common. Therefore, another way of building ecological validity into these tasks is to add error to them.

System-failure Error

One type of error that plays an important role in science and technology is what Doherty and Tweney (1988) call "system-failure error". Basically, this is the type of error that makes a disconfirmatory result appear to be confirmatory or vice-versa. A good example is Wilhelm Kaufmann's initial disconfirmation of Einstein's special theory of relativity. Einstein was not concerned by this result; he said that one would have to wait for replication before taking this result seriously. He was right: Kaufmann's result was an error (see Gorman, 1992). This case illustrates the methodological falsificationist's position, as outlined by Lakatos (1978): the way to distinguish between genuine falsifications and errors is to replicate—"it is a matter of convention how many times". Otherwise, the possibility of error could be used to immunise hypotheses from disconfirmation.

To see if the mere possibility of error affected falsification, I told subjects that on anywhere from 0–20% of their trials on Eleusis and the 2-4-6 task, the feedback they received would be an error—i.e. an apparently positive result would actually be a negative one and vice-versa. I felt that this addition added ecological validity to both of these tasks, as scientists always work in environments where error is possible. On Eleusis, I found that the possibility of error removed the positive effect for disconfirmatory instructions I had observed in an earlier study (see Gorman, 1986). Disconfirmatory groups did not solve the "odd-even" rule significantly more often than groups in other conditions, but they were better at establishing that there was no error on the task (see Fig. 10.4). Essentially, they expended so much effort checking for error that they ended up with rules like "cards separated by ones" that were subsets of the actual rule.

I found that the mere possiblility of error made it more difficult to discover the rule when results of the current experiment or observation hinged on a pattern of previous ones—as in investigations of geological strata (Rudwick, 1985) or chromosomal patterns (Keller, 1983). On these sorts of problems, the cost of replication is increased—one has to replicate

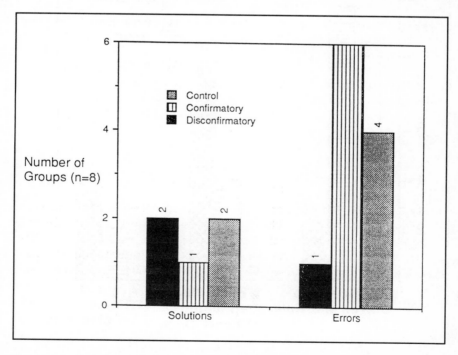

FIG. 10.4. How the possibility of error affects performance on the odd-even rule.

a whole series of experiments or observations to see if an error has occurred.

Actual system-failure error had a highly disruptive effect in situations where the mere possibility of error did not. On Wason's traditional 2-4-6 task, I found that subjects run in a condition where there was actual system-failure (SF) error solved the rule significantly less often than possible-error subjects, despite the fact that significantly more of these actual-error subjects replicated triples (see Gorman, 1989) (see Fig. 10.5). In contrast, Doherty and Tweney (1988) found a far smaller and less reliable disruption when they added SF error to the 2-4-6 task. The key difference is that Doherty and Tweney gave their subjects feedback regarding whether their announced guesses were correct or not, whereas I used the "you can't ask God" manipulation. Doherty and Tweney concluded by recommending that future studies of SF error withhold feedback on rule announcements.[8]

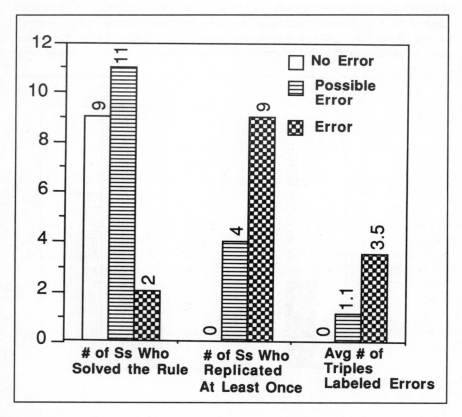

FIG. 10.5. The effect of error on the 2-4-6 Task. (Adapted from Gorman, 1992.)

Future studies of SF error should be run on more complex tasks that would allow subjects to use other means besides replication to check for error. Scientists have the option of improving procedures and replacing or repairing faulty equipment. On an artificial universe or some similar task with SF error, subjects could be given the option of purchasing a new piece of equipment if they thought their current device was providing erroneous information. This replacement would come at a cost—perhaps they would be able to perform fewer experiments with the new device. One could also introduce measurement error and give subjects the opportunity to refine their procedures to reduce this source of variation—again, at a cost.

Future research on error should also incorporate the possibility of negotiations among members of a group, as in Gorman (1986). Recently, Rosenwein, Koenemund, and Gorman (1991) contrasted 40% system-failure error with a no error condition, and found that groups in a no error condition solved a multi-dimensional version of the 2-4-6 task significantly more often than 40% error groups. The multiple dimensions constituted a modification of the 2-4-6 task to make it more like Eleusis: triples could be written in either of two colours, and each triple also had a final letter. Therefore, the rule could involve number, colour and/or letter.

In addition, groups were divided into four-person majorities and one- or two-person minorities, and allowed to exchange information about triples and hypotheses (see Laughlin, 1988, for a similar design). We expected that error would facilitate influence, and indeed minority members were more likely to adopt parts of the majority's hypothesis and to report being influenced by the majority in the error condition. However, the difference is slight, suggesting the need for further, fine-grained analyses of subjects' processes which we are now conducting.

This study illustrates the way in which experimental studies can be used to simulate social aspects of hypothesis testing, including how scientists negotiate meanings when evidence is ambiguous. One could even include instructions designed to facilitate intra- or inter-group negotiations. But this possibility brings us back to the two questions we posed earlier.

CONCLUSIONS

(1) Should instructions be used to compare hypothesis-testing strategies, or should one simply observe the strategies subjects actually use? (2) Can laboratory simulations of scientific reasoning shed light on the way scientists test hypotheses?

The answers to these questions are linked. Instructions are useful if they permit us to manipulate, under ideal circumstances, strategies that ought to be useful in actual science. The task, therefore, must simulate, in an artificial way, the aspect of science that the strategy is supposed to affect.

Once the effect is determined, *ceteris paribus*, one can modify the task to make it more ecologically valid—e.g. by adding error and/or inter-group communication.

I would argue that Wason's 2-4-6 task does simulate the process by which scientists or students decide what part of a space of possible experimental outcomes to search. Furthermore, it allows us to study strategies like falsification and counterfactual reasoning under artificial, controlled conditions where we would expect them to have maximum impact, then gradually to introduce features like system-failure error that increase the ecological validity of the simulation.

Experiments with the 2-4-6 and related tasks are important not just for what they might say about the conduct of science under ideal circumstances. They also provide a kind of microworld in which we can explore issues like the relationship between representations and heuristics.[9] Such experiments sensitise us to similar relationships in the work of scientists and inventors, even if the kinds of representations formed by subjects bear little resemblance to those of scientists.

Therefore, experimental work may give us a perspective from which to analyse cases. Once again, Tweney (this volume, Chapter 11) has led the way in his work on Faraday. Similarly, I am attempting to look closely at the cognitive processes of three telephone inventors, in collaboration with an historian of technology (see Gorman, 1992, for a description of the general approach we are taking).

Kevin Dunbar (in press) provides perhaps the best example of how one can relate experimental and field work on hypothesis testing. His goal was to shift iteratively between what he calls *in vitro* and *in vivo* studies—the former referring to experimental simulations and the latter to field studies. For the *in vivo* part of his project, he studied four molecular biology laboratories, focusing on variables that played an important role in his earlier *in vitro* research (cf. Dunbar, 1989). In terms of falsification, he found that scientists quickly discarded hypotheses in the face of negative evidence. Individual scientists typically made small changes in features of their hypotheses, but in laboratory meetings, the group of scientists tended to consider alternate hypotheses. Indeed, Dunbar detected a "falsification bias" among the senior scientists; they tended to discard data that confirmed their hypotheses. Dunbar inferred that these senior scientists had frequently had the painful experience of being proved wrong, and therefore were more prone to adopt a critical stance towards their own work. Anomalous results also led to hypothesis change, provided the scientist decided that error played no role in the anomaly. "When the researcher believes that the findings are due to error, no amount of challenging, or suggestions of other explanations will result in conceptual change" (p. 14). Dunbar is currently conducting further *in vitro* studies to pursue issues like falsification bias that emerged from his *in vivo* work. Field studies alone are not sufficient to settle issues like the role of error in preventing conceptual change; there are too many confounded variables *in vivo*. Experimental simulations can play an important role in isolating critical factors that can be checked in further field work. The solution is to maintain a constant, iterative dialogue between *in vivo* and *in vitro* research.

NOTES

1. Of course, Wason's was not the first work in the hypothesis-testing area; for example, Bruner, Goodnow, and Austin's (1956) classic studies of concept identification involve the testing of hypotheses.

2. Later versions of the selection task (e.g. the RAST procedure) allowed subjects to generate tests but the test instances are limited to two categories (cf. Wason & Green, 1984; Green, this volume, Chapter 8).

3. In collaboration with several colleagues, I am designing a set of open-ended, exploratory modules in a course on Invention and Design. Interested readers can write for more information.

4. Fenna Poletiek (personal communication, 30th June, 1993) pointed out that, as Wetherick (1962), Klayman and Ha (1987) and Farris and Revlin (1989b) have shown, an incorrect triple is not necessarily an indicator of a disconfirmatory strategy. Poletiek is studying the difference between getting falsifications and searching for them.

5. For a good example from the selection task literature, see Wason & Green (1984): they created a unified mental representation by the way they presented materials in the RAST version of the selection task, and found that improved performance was the result.

6. Mike Oaksford, Mike Guanzon and I found that instructions to follow this iterative counterfactual strategy significantly inhibited performance on the "three different numbers" rule, as compared with disconfirmatory, DAX-MED, and a control no strategy condition. DAX-MED subjects proposed complementary hypotheses about twice as often as counterfactual subjects. Unfortunately, proposing complements is not predictive of success, so this relationship does not explain why counterfactual subjects do significantly worse than subjects in other conditions. For details, see M.E. Gorman,"2-4-6: The Once and Future Task" paper delivered to the Second International Conference on Thinking, Plymouth, UK, 29th July, 1992; a copy can be obtained by writing to me.

7. There is a growing literature on how children deal with falsification; a thorough discussion lies beyond the scope of this chapter (see Brewer & Chinn, 1991 and Brewer & Samarapungavan, 1991).

8. David Penner, in an unpublished PhD thesis at Carnegie-Mellon, conducted studies of SF error with the 2-4-6 task using the no feedback design recommended by Doherty and Tweney, and found that, as in Gorman's studies, SF error-subjects were significantly less likely to solve the rule than subjects in a control, no error condition. He also found that a positive test heuristic was a useful strategy for identifying errors, especially when the

target rule is surrounded by the hypothesis suggested by the seed triple 2,4,6—the rule he used was "positive, sequential even numbers less than or equal to 100".

9. Robert Rosenwein and I are designing a human, experimental simulation environment called "SIMSCI" that would allow one to create a kind of miniature scientific world and introduce variables like error and funding sources and explore their interaction. Those interested should contact the author of this chapter for more details.

ACKNOWLEDGEMENTS

The author is indebted to Ryan D. Tweney and David Penner for their comments.

REFERENCES

Brewer, W.F., & Chinn, C.A. (1991). Entrenched beliefs, inconsistent information, and knowledge change. In L. Birnbaum (Ed.), *Proceedings of the 1991 International Conference on the Learning Sciences*. Charlottesville, VA: Association for the Advancement of Computing in Education.

Brewer, W.F., & Samarapungavan, A. (1991). Children's theories vs. scientific theories: Differences in reasoning or differences in knowledge? In R.R. Hoffman & D.S. Palermo (Eds.), *Cognition and the symbolic processes: Applied and ecological perspectives*. Hillsdale, NJ: Lawrence Erlbaum Associates Inc.

Bruner, J., Goodnow, J., & Austin, G. (1956). *A study of thinking*. New York: John Wiley.

Clement, J. (1991). Experts and science students: The use of analogies, extreme cases, and physical intuition. In J.F. Voss, D.N. Perkins, & D.W. Segal (Eds.), *Informal reasoning and education*. Hillsdale, NJ: Lawrence Erlbaum Associates Inc.

Doherty, M.E., & Tweney, R.D. (1988). *The role of data and feedback error in inference and prediction*. Final report for ARI Contract MDA903-85-K-0193.

Dunbar, K. (1989). *Scientific reasoning strategies in a simulated molecular genetics environment*. Program of the eleventh annual conference of the Cognitive Science Society. Hillsdale, NJ: Lawrence Erlbaum Associates Inc.

Dunbar, K. (in press). How scientists really reason: Scientific reasoning in real-world laboratories. In R.J. Sternberg & J. Davidson (Eds.), *Insight*. Cambridge, MA: MIT Press.

Farris, H., & Revlin, R. (1989a). The discovery process: A counterfactual strategy. *Social Studies of Science, 19*, 497–513.

Farris, H., & Revlin, R. (1989b). Sensible reasoning in two tasks: Rule discovery and hypothesis evaluation. *Memory and Cognition, 17*(2), 221–232.

Fuller, S. (1989). *Philosophy of science and its discontents*. Boulder, CO: Westview Press.

Gardner, M. (1977). On playing New Eleusis: The game that simulates the search for truth. *Scientific American, 237*(4), 18–25.

Gorman, M.E. (1986). How the possibility of error affects falsification on a task that models scientific problem solving. *British Journal of Psychology, 77*, 85–96.

Gorman, M.E. (1989). Error, falsification and scientific inference: An experimental investigation. *Quarterly Journal of Experimental Psychology, 41A*, 385–412.

Gorman, M.E. (1992). *Simulating science: Heuristics, mental models, and technoscientific thinking.* Bloomington: Indiana University Press.

Gorman, M.E. (in press). Psychology of science. In W. O'Donohue & P. Kitchener (Eds.), *Psychology and philosophy: Interdisciplinary problems and responses.* (Allyn & Bacon, forthcoming.)

Gorman, M.E., & Gorman, M.E. (1984). A comparison of disconfirmatory, confirmatory, and a control strategy on Wason's 2-4-6 task. *Quarterly Journal of Experimental Psychology, 36A*, 629–648.

Gorman, M.E., Gorman, M.E., Latta, R.M., & Cunningham, G. (1984). How disconfirmatory, confirmatory, and combined strategies affect group problem solving. *British Journal of Psychology, 75*, 65–79.

Gorman, M.E., Stafford, A., & Gorman, M.E. (1987). Disconfirmation and dual hypotheses on a more difficult version of Wason's 2-4-6 task. *Quarterly Journal of Experimental Psychology, 39A*, 1–28.

Houts, A., & Gholson, B. (1989). Brownian notions: One historicist philosopher's resistance to psychology of science via three truisms and ecological validity. *Social Epistemology, 3*, 139–146.

Keller, E.F. (1983). *A feeling for the organism. The life and work of Barbara McClintock.* New York: W.H. Freeman & Co.

Klahr, D., & Dunbar, K. (1988). Dual space search during scientific reasoning. *Cognitive Science, 12*, 1–48.

Klahr, D., Fay, A., & Dunbar, K. (1993). Heuristics for scientific experimentation: A developmental study. *Cognitive Psychology, 25*, 111–146.

Klayman, J., & Ha, Y.-W. (1987). Confirmation, disconfirmation, and information in hypothesis testing. *Psychological Review, 94*, 211–228.

Lakatos, I. (1978). *The methodology of scientific research programmes.* Cambridge: Cambridge University Press.

Laughlin, P.R. (1988). Collective induction: Group performance, social combination processes, and mutual majority and minority influence. *Journal of Personality and Social Psychology, 54*, 254–267.

Mahoney, M.J. (1976). *Scientist as subject: The psychological imperative.* Cambridge, MA: Ballinger.

Mynatt, C.R., Doherty, M.E., & Tweney, R.D. (1977). Confirmation bias in a simulated research environment: An experimental study of scientific inference. *Quarterly Journal of Experimental Psychology, 29*, 85–95.

Mynatt, C.R., Doherty, M.E., & Tweney, R.D. (1978). Consequences of confirmation and disconfirmation in a simulated research environment. *Quarterly Journal of Experimental Psychology, 30*, 395–406.

Oaksford, M., & Chater, N. (1994). Another look at eliminative and enumerative behaviour in a conceptual task. *The European Journal of Cognitive Psychology, 6*, 149–169.

Rosenwein, R., Koenemund, K., & Gorman, M.E. (1991, November). *Development of group agreement in scientific decision making as the outcome of the interaction between majority and minority positions: An experimental analogue.* Paper presented to the Society for the Social Studies of Science, Cambridge, MA.

Rudwick, M.J.S. (1985). *The great Devonian controversy*. Chicago: University of Chicago Press.

Tukey, D.D. (1986). A philosophical and empirical analysis of subjects' modes of inquiry on the 2-4-6 task. *Quarterly Journal of Experimental Psychology, 38A*, 5–33.

Tweney, R.D., Doherty, M.E., Worner, W.J., Pliske, D.B., Mynatt, C.R., Gross, K.A., & Arkkelin, D.L. (1980). Strategies of rule discovery on an inference task. *Quarterly Journal of Experimental Psychology, 32*, 109–123.

Wason, P.C. (1960). On the failure to eliminate hypotheses in a conceptual task. *Quarterly Journal of Experimental Psychology, 12*, 129–140.

Wason, P.C. (1962). Reply to Wetherick. *Quarterly Journal of Experimental Psychology, 14*, 250.

Wason, P.C., & Green, D.W. (1984). Reasoning and mental representation. *Quarterly Journal of Experimental Psychology, 36A*, 597–610.

Wason, P.C., & Johnson-Laird, P.N. (1972). *Psychology of reasoning: Structure and content*. London: B.T. Batsford.

Wetherick, N.E. (1962). Eliminative and enumerative behaviour in a conceptual task. *Quarterly Journal of Experimental Psychology, 14*, 246–249.

CHAPTER ELEVEN

Scientific Reasoning

Ryan D. Tweney and Susan T. Chitwood

Department of Psychology, Bowling Green State University, USA

It may seem inevitable that the study of reasoning would lead investigators to consider the applicability of their models and results to an understanding of scientific reasoning; natural though the extension may seem, however, it is only very recently that such concerns have been manifest in the cognitive literature. There has been a long period of neglect, and this seems doubly puzzling when one reflects that science is, in the popular view and in that of most working scientists, the domain of reasoned thought *par excellence,* challenged in this role only by mathematics and logic itself.

Perhaps this tells us something about the relative maturity of studies of thinking and reasoning in general: though each is an old topic (harking back at least to Aristotle) only in the past few decades have truly useful explanatory frameworks about thinking and reasoning become available. In no small part, the change is due to exactly those investigators represented in this book, and especially to Peter Wason who, as we shall try to demonstrate, is a leading figure in what we prefer to call the "cognitive psychology of science". In this chapter, we will survey some of the existing literature on scientific thinking and demonstrate that the most recent work is in fact supportive of a strong claim to the vitality of just such a subdiscipline.

We will divide the survey into two parts, the first of which will briefly characterise several historically significant traditions that have led to research directly upon scientific thinking, and the second of which will focus upon the specific contributions of the Wason tradition. By placing the Wason tradition in this larger context, the significance of its contributions should be more clear, as well as some of the future activity that we should expect. In a concluding section of the chapter, we will consider the implications for the future role of the cognitive psychology of science in cognitive psychology on the one hand, and in the broader domain of science studies on the other. Note also that throughout the chapter we will not be making a sharp distinction between "thinking" and "reasoning"; the latter term we will use rather loosely for those instances of thinking in which conscious deliberative processing of a sort representable by logical propositions is dominant. As we will argue, we do not believe the existing evidence permits us to sharply separate the two terms as a reflection of two different "kinds" of thought. Our preference for a fuzzy, rather than sharp, distinction stems, as will become clear, from our view about the limited role of formal logical reasoning in scientific thinking.

TRADITIONS IN THE COGNITIVE PSYCHOLOGY OF SCIENCE

By "tradition", we mean here a set of ideas sharing certain common assumptions about the way in which cognitive considerations ought to motivate research on scientific thinking. In most cases, these traditions are not closely linked by a common heritage in the sense they are grouped within particular institutions, nor are they reflective of "teacher–student" descent in very many cases. As historical descriptive categories, then, the distinctions made would not survive careful historiographic scrutiny. None the less they do focus our attention upon certain presuppositions and certain commonalities of cited works; each tradition is an invisible college.

Kuhn

Thomas Kuhn's *Scientific Revolutions* (1962; second edition, 1970) can be seen as the seminal work for the entire subdiscipline of the cognitive psychology of science, just as it is for certain schools of thought within the history and the philosophy of science (see, for example, Bechtel, 1988.) For the cognitive psychology of science, Kuhn represents a first call to battle— a first claim that the actual conduct of scientific thinking might be understandable using methods derived from disciplines other than logic. His emphasis was primarily on social factors, to be sure, but it is often forgotten that he placed as much emphasis on Gestalt models of insight as on social factors. For Kuhn, it was just as plausible to seek cognitive explanations as social explanations; only an accident of history, as it were, led later commentators to focus more upon the social aspects in Kuhn's writings.

Kuhn himself made clear that a full understanding of science would not be possible unless the full variety of processes by which scientists deal with ideas was appreciated. For Kuhn, a particular scientist's acceptance or rejection of a point of view was not a matter of objective evaluation of evidence according to a logical canon. Instead, Kuhn sensitised his readers to concern themselves with non-logical mechanisms (social consensus formation, the constraints imposed by already accepted formulations, and the like). In the process he opened a new window on all empirical studies of science. And, in the context of the present book, Kuhn's work must be seen as broadening the nature of what is considered to fall within the domain of "reasoning" as such. Kuhn provides us with a first hint that "reasoning" in science cannot be restricted to just those aspects that can be identified with formal logic.

There is a more or less explicitly Kuhnian tradition within the cognitive psychology of science that attempts to understand this variety of non-logical processes and that defines itself, more or less, with reference to his views. The work described here as "Kuhnian" is characterised by two things:

1. A blurring (or merging) of the cognitive and the social, as in Kuhn's own work, but with a principal emphasis on the cognitive dimensions of scientific thought.
2. A focus upon the creation and transformation of scientific meaning, taken here to be a cognitive psychological reflection of Kuhn's notion of the paradigm.

A good example of an explicit Kuhnian focus is DeMey's (1982) book, perhaps the first to clearly advocate a specifically cognitive approach to science. DeMey takes Kuhn's notion of paradigm as a central defining concept. Although Piagetian influences are also strong in DeMey's approach, Kuhn is far more frequently cited and is far more central to the theme of the book. For DeMey, paradigms in the Kuhnian sense are seen as cognitive units: "Paradigms are internal models, cognitive structures which give shape to the specific expectations that guide the research of 'normal' scientists" (DeMey, 1982, p. 89). For DeMey, specific meaning can be given to the cognitive correspondent of a paradigm, a meaning derivable from the concept of "frames" in artificial intelligence.

Following DeMey, we will consider as "Kuhnian" works which use such frame-like approaches to situate scientific thinking within the larger cognitive context. Frequently, this approach to the study of scientific thinking includes an attempt to understand the boundaries of such thought as well as its enabling characteristics. For example, Tweney (1985) attempted to describe Michael Faraday's discovery of electromagnetic induction by constructing a multi-levelled cognitive framework which included scripts and schemata as a way of discussing the coherence of specific ideas. "Cognitivising" Faraday within such a framework is Kuhnian in our sense because the specific movements of Faraday's thought are captured within a cognitive matrix of schemas and scripts which are, in effect, a paradigmatic frame. Similarly, in a later paper, Tweney (1992) examined some of Faraday's research on acoustic vibrations and on optical deceptions as a means of gaining insight into the origins of his discovery of electromagnetic induction. In this paper, the emphasis was on Faraday's sensori-motor interaction with the materials of his research and the cognitive synthesis that Faraday imposed on his materials. This too is Kuhnian in so far as the driving problem implicated by the analysis is the attempt to understand what Faraday construed as the problem space of his work. Kuhnian terminology, though not invoked by Tweney, could have been as easily used, asking, for example, how Faraday's developing paradigm drove his inquiries.

Several investigators can be seen as cognitively Kuhnian in a similar sense. Thus, Nancy Nersessian (1984; 1992) has dealt explicitly with the nature of meaning change in science, basing her work on an extensive analysis of the notion of field in the theoretical physics of Faraday, Maxwell, Lorentz, and Einstein and showing how this analysis can be tied to specific cognitive developmental models of conceptual change on the one hand, and to cognitive conceptions of mental models on the other. In a recent paper, Nersessian (1992) argues that the study of science has been unnecessarily limited by considering only inductive and deductive modes of reasoning; instead, she claims that a detailed analysis of "abstraction techniques" such as analogical reasoning, imagistic analysis, and thought experiments "are strongly implicated in the explanation of how existing conceptual structures play a role in constructing new, and sometimes radically different, structures" (Nersessian, 1992, p. 13). For her, meaning change is the cognitive particularisation of the original questions raised by the notion of a paradigm shift.

Like Nersessian, David Gooding (1990; 1992) has developed an account of the emergence of scientific concepts which relies upon non-propositional aspects of thought. Critical of the exclusively linguistic focus of analytically oriented philopsophy of science, Gooding has emphasised the role of a dynamic interaction between "hand, eye, and brain". Using a detailed reconstruction of Faraday's experimentation, Gooding has produced maps of the process by which vague construals were turned by Faraday into concrete communicable scientific concepts of a formal sort: "Making meaning is a process" (Gooding, 1990, p. 271). For both Nersessian and

Gooding, a cognitive account of science is fundamentally one that accounts for the emergence and transformation of meaning in scientific practice, and their method of analysis is an attempt to show that this can be done within the boundaries of what Kuhn would perhaps call cognitive paradigms (to use DeMey's term, not theirs).

Gorman and Carlson's work on the creative inventions of Thomas Edison and Alexander Graham Bell has a similar character (Carlson & Gorman, 1992; Gorman & Carlson, 1989), as does Lovie's recent book on the way in which commitment to a scientific concept can be shown to drive innovation in a variety of cognitive case histories in science (Lovie, 1992). In the study of Bell, in particular, the focus has been to show how the emergence of particular ideas about mechanical and electrical arrangements can be traced through the series of working drawings made by Bell during the invention of the telephone. Carlson and Gorman thus reveal a sequence of non-verbal "reasonings" used by Bell to concretise, test, and refine his ideas.

All of the work we have identified as Kuhnian has relied heavily upon historical case study analysis. Like Kuhn, all of the authors have been committed to the understanding of science through the use of historical methods of analysis. All thus regard scientific thinking as understandable through careful analysis of the contingent circumstances that surround particular episodes of science. As will be made clear, this partially distinguishes the Kuhnian tradition from most of the work detailed below (although both Gruber and Miller within the Piagetian tradition have shared an historical focus and are an exception to this generalisation). Indeed, Nersessian (1992) has argued explicitly for a new approach to the history of science; one that is grounded in cognitive principles. For cognitive psychology, an appeal to historical case studies is an unusual wrinkle; it is perhaps in this respect that the study of scientific reasoning may serve as an exemplar for cognitive historical investigations in other domains. Consider, for example, the reconstruction given by Arnheim (1962) of the processes by which Picasso developed the famous painting "Guernica". Arnheim's tracing of the problem solving engaged in by Picasso through a series of early sketches, drawings, and paintings could easily be shown to fit within a scripts and schemas analysis (i.e. a paradigmatic framework) of the sort used by Tweney and Gooding and described above.

Piaget

Concern with the cognitive aspects of scientific thought characterised Piaget's own work from an early date. Thus, his *Genetic Epistemology* (1970) argued that the foundations of epistemology must be construed along cognitive developmental lines. For Piaget, understanding how a child conceptualises the world is analogous to understanding the developmental course of scientific concepts: "Genetic epistemology attempts to explain knowledge, and in particular scientific knowledge, on the basis of its history, its sociogenesis, and especially the psychological origins of the notions and operations upon which it is based" (Piaget, 1970, p. 1). In fact there is more than just an analogy here. Piaget regarded a child's knowledge as a construction rooted in actions, a construction which undergoes continual transformation. Such a view places the child's developing notions of, say, time, on a continuum with the development of the scientific conception of time (as in relativity, for example). For Piaget, the task of genetic epistemology includes what we would call the cognitive psychology of science. And, in a theme found in much of the other work described in this chapter, Piaget is explicit in calling attention to the dynamic character of thinking—even at its most abstract, thinking unfolds within time in a rich complexity that is often lost when the products of thought are reduced to static formalisms.

In some respects, Piaget's approach resembles the Kuhnian approach (as manifested, say, in Gooding's work), particularly in its emphasis on historical relevance. It differs in many other respects, however, not least of which is the relative absence of attention to the social and cultural context of scientific thinking. Further, psychological principles were at the very centre of Piaget's effort, whereas they were one among a set of factors considered by Kuhn. Finally, note that Piaget's theory is rooted in a conception of reasoning that attempts to reconcile the adaptive character of thought with the constraints of formal logical analysis; logic *emerges*, via equilibration processes, from the increasingly adaptive efforts of thought to accommodate the constraints of the external world. For Kuhn (or for those we have identified as Kuhnian), no such emphasis is central.

Howard Gruber's (1974; 1989) analysis of the diaries of Charles Darwin was the first demonstration that Piagetian approaches could in fact lead to a deepened understanding of the detailed psychological development of scientific ideas. For Gruber, science can be understood as the unfolding of a network of enterprise in which new ideas emerge, mesh and combine. Gruber's focus on equilibrating mechanisms marks his work as explicitly Piagetian; in his account of Darwin's construction of a theory of evolution by natural selection, Gruber shows how a complex network of interests and a complex series of transactions with external "data" led Darwin to the crucial insights that resulted in the theory of evolution. To understand these processes, Gruber invoked Darwin's personal goals and motivations as well as his intellectual meanderings, arguing for a unity amid the diversity—a unity driven by the processes of equilibration.

Arthur Miller has also used Piagetian ideas as a framework within which he has explored the development of concepts in modern physics

(Miller, 1984). In particular, Miller has argued for the importance of a grand transition in physicists' use of images to represent concepts. Traditionally, images in physics were representations of the things about which physics was concerned: light, for example, was represented as a stream of particles. After 1900, however, Miller documents an increasing use of images as representations of the theoretical concepts of physics, rather than as representations of the things physics is about. Einstein's visualisation of light is presented by Miller as a case in point: such famous visual representations as, say, world-lines, are not pictures of the world as such, they are instead pictures that visualise the relationships between time and space in the theory of relativity. Similarly, the notion of light quanta as simply "pictures" of a physical world misconstrues the nature of quantum theory. Instead, light quanta are an *Anschauung*, an "intuition", roughly, of the dual nature of light as wave and as particle. The emergence in modern physics of such *Anschauungen* is, Miller argues, a crucial turning point in the history of science.

Miller was unable to fit his historical insights into the context of the usual cognitive distinction between imagery and propositional thinking: "The contrast between the simplicity of Einstein's mental images, their theoretical context, and the dazzling theories that they spawned is so startling as to undercut available cognitive scientific models" (Miller, 1984, p. 248). Instead, he accounted for the changed visual role of *Anschauungen* by appealing to Piaget's notion of the developmental emergence of abstract concepts out of more primitive, perceptually rooted cognitions: "The dynamics of scientific progress is driven by the upward spiral of the assimilation / accommodation process resulting in a hierarchical series of structures in which equilibration is achieved only in part" (Miller, 1989, p. 185). In the specific case of Einstein, Miller argued that such partial equilibration drove Einstein to think in ways that proceeded beyond the usual stage of formal operational thinking to a realm which was in fact at a greater level of abstraction than the highest levels previously considered by Piaget.

For both Gruber and Miller, the problem of the origin of scientific concepts is a principal focus (see also Ippolito & Tweney, 1995). Such concern also animates the work of a number of cognitive psychologists who, though they have focused on children's use of scientific concepts, have also had a great deal to say about scientific thinking as such. Thus, Carey (1992) has shown that the developmental course of acquisition of physical concepts (weight, density, and matter) is usefully illuminated by drawing parallels between ontogenetic development in the child and the historical development of formal scientific concepts. Chi (1992) has made similar arguments, using Lavoisier's discovery of oxygen as an exemplar for a more general theory of conceptual change during scientific revolutions. Neither

Carey nor Chi explicitly identifies their approach with Piaget's; we include them in this category, nevertheless, because their accounts of the dynamics of conceptual change resemble Miller's (and hence Piaget's). Like Miller, Chi and Carey seek to explain conceptual change as the result of discrepancies between an existing formulation and the perceptual world, and both identify in spirit with a broader notion of epistemology as essentially developmental in character.

Simon

As he makes clear in his autobiography (Simon, 1991), Herbert A. Simon's research has had a strong focus on the nature of scientific thinking. Most of his work during the 1980s has centred on this issue, supporting, in his words, "the proposition that scientific discovery is achieved by the normal problem-solving processes that have been observed in less formidable problem domains" (Simon, 1991, p. 330). For Simon, problem solving is characterised as a search through a "problem space", the task of psychological explanation being, in part, to account for the nature and use of the specific heuristics that guide that search. Most of the heuristics bear little resemblance to formal logical procedures which, for Simon, represent a late stage in scientific thinking. Instead, his heuristics are extensions of the "rule of thumb" procedures used by limited symbol processing systems (like human minds) to make large problem spaces tractable. Like Polya (1945), to whom Simon attributes this notion of heuristics, formal procedures exceed the capacity of human thinkers and instead are replaced by informal methods of manipulating symbols which can be characterised as symbol transformation procedures applied to mental states.

In the 1980s, Simon and his students produced a series of papers and a book, *Scientific Discovery* (Langley et al., 1987), which sought to document the applicability of his model of problem solving in scientific domains. The most compelling of these efforts is an extensive simulation of a portion of the diary of Hans Krebs—a portion recording Krebs' discovery of the biochemical cycle that now bears his name (Kulkarni & Simon, 1988). Krebs' diary had been described by Holmes (1980), an historian of science who has written extensively about the need for detailed study of scientific diaries (Holmes, 1987). By building upon Holmes' study, Kulkarni and Simon were able to simulate on a computer the details of experimentation carried out by Krebs. To do this, they relied heavily on some problem-solving heuristics that had been implemented earlier to capture human performance using simpler tasks, supplemented, of course, by specific strategies known to have been used by Krebs. The resulting simulation was quite life-like in that it was capable of generating a series of moves through the experimental problem space, stopping to query the environment (i.e. to "do experiments"), and assimilating the "answers" provided by the operators. The overall topography of the simulation's moves through the experiment space was, in the end, strikingly similar to the actual moves made by Krebs.

Klahr and his students have taken somewhat similar approaches to the analysis of scientific thinking, beginning, for the most part, with analyses of laboratory tasks and later moving to "real-world" science. Thus, Klahr and Dunbar (1988; see also Penner & Klahr, 1993 and Shrager, 1990) analysed the problem-solving strategies of student subjects attempting to discover the principles of operation of a programmable toy vehicle, the "Big Trak". They were able to sketch the strategies in terms of search through two separate problem spaces—a space of hypothesised relationships and a space of possible experiments. Again, a fair proportion of the heuristics identified in the analysis can be found in other problem-solving studies and hence are likely to be general in character. Some of the heuristics, however, are more narrow in applicability and derive from specific experiences and skills which the subjects possessed prior to their participation in the research. Dunbar has done similar research on simulated problems involving enzyme kinetics (again, with college student subjects) and is in the process of reporting on his analysis of extensive field studies of molecular biologists engaged in discovery-oriented research (Dunbar, 1993; 1995). Bradshaw (1992) has also applied dual search space models to an account of the invention of the airplane by the Wright brothers. Whereas the earliest studies of science by Simon and his colleagues and students (e.g. Langley et al., 1987) relied upon laboratory tasks and grossly simplified historical "cases", the later work by Bradshaw and Dunbar, like that of Kulkarni and Simon (1988), has focused on the rich microstructural detail of extended case studies.

A Simonian approach to the study of scientific reasoning leads to a focus upon the symbolic representation of scientific ideas; Simon has argued that these representations are capable of capturing everything that we need to account for thinking (see, for example, Larkin & Simon, 1987). In recent years, this claim has been challenged by connectionists such as Rumelhart and McClelland (1986). They have argued that models of thinking which rely upon distributed representations and distributed processing, carried out by huge interconnected nets of neural-like nodes, are closer approximations to the likely organisation of brains and provide elegant ways to achieve some cognitive results that are awkward or impossible by other means (Rumelhart & Todd, 1993). It is too soon to tell whether this effort will affect specific models of scientific reasoning, though a few attempts have been made (see in particular, Thagard, 1989 and Chitwood & Tweney, submitted, discussed below). Note however that both the Kuhnian and the Piagetian approaches discussed earlier rely heavily upon non-propositional models of scientific thought, and that connectionist models may enjoy their greatest success in capturing such thought (see, for example, Churchland & Sejnowski, 1992). In addition, connectionist work in general has placed a great emphasis upon the dynamic aspects of thinking, echoing an important theme in our review.

THE WASON TRADITION IN SCIENTIFIC REASONING

The figure for whom this book is a tribute—Peter C. Wason—stands, like Kuhn, Piaget, and Simon, at the head of an important tradition of work in the psychology of science. In the present context (studies devoted to reasoning generally, not merely studies of scientific reasoning), Wason's work takes on a special character, however, since Wason, even more than Piaget, has been concerned with the relation between formal logic and "psychologic". Indeed, the earliest empirical programmes in the modern psychology of science were all explicitly Wasonian. Since Gorman (1992 and this volume) has reviewed this work, we can be brief here, and centre on the most important issue—the role that Wason's explorations of confirmatory heuristics (as summarised in, for example, Wason & Johnson-Laird, 1972) have had on the understanding of scientific thinking.

Wason's influence is pervasive; most importantly, his elegant and profoundly simple approaches to the nature of confirmation bias convinced a number of investigators that testable questions about scientific thinking are possible. Confirmation biases speak directly to the role of reasoning in science and are, in fact, implicated in nearly all recent discussions of the rationality of science (see, for example, Cohen, 1981 and Stich, 1990). Wason's influence has thus served to focus discussion on a key issue involving heuristics in thinking, and has brought this attention to bear in a way that is markedly different to the emphasis on heuristics found in Simon's work. In particular, Wason has considered carefully the relation between formal logical processes and those that derive from non-logical processes. In this respect, his work (and that of his students—see especially Johnson-Laird, 1983 and Evans, 1989) clarifies the role of logic in reasoning and helps to justify our claim that reasoning is *more than* formal logic.[1]

For a time, it was the height of fashion to characterise confirmation bias as a potentially very dysfunctional aspect of science. Perhaps the most dramatic instance of this genre is Mitroff's (1974) book on the tenacious and emotionally anti-rational biases of a group of NASA lunar scientists—biases that were strikingly portrayed on the basis of Mitroff's extensive interviews. Mahoney (1976) used Mitroff's research and his own studies of scientists (which used some of Wason's tasks) to indict science for its pervasive confirmatory bias. For Mahoney, such biases are inherently pernicious, blocking progress at every turn. Such critiques culminated in Faust's book, *The Limits of Scientific Reasoning* (1984), the very title of which suggests its main theme, namely, "that human judgement is far more limited than we have typically believed and that all individuals, scientists included, have a surprisingly restricted capacity to manage or interpret complex information" (Faust, 1984, p. xxv). For Faust, even more than for Mahoney, the complexity of scientific problems, and the weaknesses of human cognitive capabilities, render impossible anything remotely like "objectivity" in science. For both Faust and Mahoney, confirmatory biases are the source of the limitations.

Such bleak implications seem to have faded from the recent literature, however, partly because of the emergence of a deeper insight into the nature of confirmatory tendencies like those first observed by Wason. Mynatt, Doherty, and Tweney (1978), for example, had noted that a seemingly normative disconfirmatory strategy, used by a few subjects in their artificial universe studies, was actually of very little utility; in fact, the most successful subjects in those studies used both confirmatory and disconfirmatory strategies. Tweney, Doherty, and Mynatt (1981, p. 116) noted that at least four kinds of confirmatory tendencies could be described, involving failures to:

1. Seek disconfirmatory evidence.
2. Utilise disconfirmatory evidence when it is available.
3. Test alternative hypotheses.
4. Consider whether evidence supporting a favoured hypothesis supports alternative hypotheses as well.

Note that the third and fourth type imply the presence of an alternative hypothesis, whereas the first two can occur with reference to a single hypothesis. Cognitively, this seems to be an important difference—how one acts in the presence of multiple hypotheses should, one feels, differ from one's actions in the face of only a single alternative. Farris and Revlin's (1989) account of hypothesis testing as a manifestation of a counter-factual strategy (see Gorman, this volume, Chapter 10), which implies the existence of multiple alternatives, thus is a direct attempt to invoke such differences. Furthermore, as Tweney et al. (1981) noted, much depends upon the particular viability of each hypothesis under consideration. Whether or not it is functionally useful to pursue a disconfirmatory strategy may depend on whether the hypothesis to be disconfirmed has already been associated with corroborating tests or whether it is relatively new and untested. In the latter case, Tweney et al. suggested that it may actually be better to pursue *only* confirmatory tests, postponing disconfirmatory attempts until after some corroboration had been obtained. New hypotheses may be fragile and may need to be "given a break"! On this view, the confirmatory tendencies decried by Mahoney and Faust are not so dysfunctional after all.

A similar point emerged from Tweney's studies of Faraday's diaries (see, e.g. Tweney, 1985). By categorising Faraday's experiments as either confirmatory (meeting his expectations) or disconfirmatory (failing to meet his expectations), Tweney was able to show that the majority of a set of 135 experiments (conducted in 1831 as part of his discovery of electromagnetic induction) were in fact disconfirmatory in character—and that Faraday seemingly ignored these experiments! But a closer look suggested that this was not a confirmation bias on Faraday's part. Instead, it seemed to be a sophisticated use of a mixed strategy: "Confirm first, disconfirm later." In every case, Faraday was postponing the issues raised by the disconfirmatory outcomes until he had amassed sufficient confirmatory evidence to make a potentially falsifying test worthwhile. The fragility of new hypotheses thus seemed to be taken into account in his researches.

In recent years, a number of authors have addressed the issue of what sorts of contexts imply a need for confirmatory heuristics. Thus, Klayman and Ha (1987) suggested that Wason's 2-4-6 task could only be understood as an instance in which a subject's hypotheses are likely to be less general than the experimenter's hypothesis and that the subjects were therefore less likely to generate a triple that conformed to their own hypotheses but not to the experimenter's. As a result, fortuitous disconfirmation could not be obtained; only if the subjects deliberately sought disconfirmation was it likely to be found. Klayman and Ha argued that in the real world of hypothesis testing such situations were probably rare—using positive tests when the subject's hypothesis is more general than the experimenter's ought therefore to result in disconfirmation more often. Plausible though this idea seems, however, a later attempt to confirm the notion experimentally (Klayman & Ha, 1989) produced equivocal results. Klayman and Ha manipulated the specificity of the experimenter's hypothesis from more general than the subject's likely starting point to more specific than the subject's starting point. The manipulation did result in changes in performance, but these differences were confounded with differences in problem difficulty and hence could not be attributed to the effect of the generality-specificity relationship as such. In any case, it is not clear exactly how one ought to map the generality-specificity dimension on to the more complex case of scientific hypotheses. Unlike the hypothesis spaces in the Wason task, scientific hypotheses cannot easily be related to each other along a simple generality-specificity dimension.

In fact, of course, real-world hypothesis testing occurs in a variety of diverse contexts; it would not be surprising if we eventually must conclude that the issue of the viability of a confirmatory strategy is dependent on context and that no general rule can be found. None the less, approaches like that of Klayman and Ha suggest that we ought to at least try to establish general grounds for specifying the conditions of applicability of a variety of strategies in a variety of contexts. As Cosmides (1989) has noted, reasoning strategies are potentially subject to natural selection pressures and we must therefore pay close attention to the adaptive goals of a cognitive system. For her, the general principles of evolution must be applied to the specific processes of thought in specific contexts. Cheng and Holyoak (1989) have challenged Cosmides on this point, arguing instead that the appropriate locus for explanations of thought must be sought in an understanding of pragmatic principles—i.e. at a social-cognitive level. In our view, however, both approaches seem to be relentlessly *causal* in character. Surely we must assume that an observed regularity in how people test hypotheses (and confirmation "bias" is such a regularity) has *some* adaptive value on *some* level. But the appropriate research goal ought to be a characterisation of the microstructural dynamics of thought; doing so requires close attention to the social-cognitive environment and to the adaptive significance of particular goals. We believe that this will produce more insight than attempts to argue that evolutionary or pragmatic causal explanations are correct. In some sense, both must surely be correct.

Our own research recently has used neural networks to explore the properties of the problem-solving environments of scientific thinking (Chitwood & Tweney, submitted). By starting with an extensive description of experiments conducted by Faraday in 1831 in conjunction with his most famous discovery, that of electromagnetic induction (Tweney & Hoffner, 1987), we were able to code a set of 54 of his experiments in a form that could be accepted by a neural network as input. In brief, each experiment consisted of a set of features, a vector input, such that each feature represented one distinguishing characteristic of an experiment. For example, one feature represented whether or not a battery was used as a source of current and was coded 1 or 0 to indicate the presence or absence of this piece of apparatus in the experiment. Another feature was coded 1 if the experiment included connecting a circuit as a critical manipulative feature. Outputs of each experiment were represented using a vector that coded the particular phenomenon of interest (e.g. a detected current or a spark) and a separate feature that indicated the relative size of the effect if an effect was produced. Having coded each experiment as an input vector and each outcome as an output vector, we then provided the inputs to the neural network and asked it to learn to predict the output of each experiment, as represented by the target output vector. Initially, of course, its outputs were merely guesses and bore no particular relation to the obtained output but, by using back-propagation after each attempt (a procedure which allows a network to change its weights after each mismatch between its own output and the target output; Rumelhart & McClelland, 1986), we were able to explore the "learnability" of the set of experiments conducted by Faraday.

Such learnability constituted a criterion for the nature of the epistemological environment in which Faraday's experiments participated. In brief, we can think of the neural network as a "pure empiricist": faced with the particular set of experiments conducted by Faraday and the outcomes of those experiments, the network will seek to identify patterns that hold across the entire data set. It is a *pure* empiricist in the sense that it will consider every experimental outcome to be weighted as heavily as every other experiment and is therefore entirely free of any tendencies to ignore disconfirmatory evidence.

We found that the network could learn to predict correctly the outcomes of the experiments if we limited its exposure to relatively short blocks (11 to 14 experiments, across several days of Faraday's efforts). But if we gave the network the entire block of 54 experiments, then it could not learn at all. Was this due to capacity limitations of the network? We were able to rule out this possibility. First of all, once it had successfully learned a given block, if we took the now-trained network and taught it the next block, the network lost its ability to perform well on the initially learned block (though, in some cases, further training led to a recovery of the initial level of performance). Further, when we separated the 54 experiments into 2 groups, experiments that were successful (i.e. that met Faraday's expectations) and experiments that were unsuccessful (did not meet his expectations), we found that the successful experiments were easily learned and the unsuccessful ones could not be learned at all. The limitations in the network's ability to learn was not, therefore, an inherent limitation of its architecture but must instead have been due to inherent features of the original data set.[2]

These experiments tell us something about the particular knowledge-producing characteristics of the environment in which Faraday worked. Each of Faraday's experiments is construed to be a question, the answer to which may tell him something about the current state of his belief about physical reality. He is not just in a perceptual environment, gathering "facts" to inductively arrive at knowledge; instead, he is in an *epistemological* environment specially constructed to be relevant to his hypotheses. Note that the inputs to our networks and the outputs that they produce are based on selected features of the experiments—those that we judged to be relevant to Faraday's characterisation of the experiments. Our networks, like Faraday, were responding to only selected aspects of the perceived events, those aspects that were scientifically relevant. Even so, a network, unlike Faraday, is a pure empiricist—it treats each and every input as worth equal consideration. To say then of a particular neural network that it could or could not learn to predict the outcomes of the presented experiments is to say that the epistemological environment did or did not contain a pattern inducible by a pure empiricist.

Faraday was not a pure empiricist, of course. He had a variety of theoretical expectations at the outset—expectations that were altered by the experimental outcomes but which were, for him, never absent. And, as noted earlier, Faraday was using a "confirm early, disconfirm late" heuristic. In effect, he was perfectly able to ignore some of the outcomes; unlike the purely empirical network, Faraday did not treat all outcomes with the same seriousness. This leads us to an important conclusion: in the particular epistemological environment that Faraday developed, some means of ignoring the unsuccessful experiments was *necessary*. Had Faraday not had a set of strong theoretical expectations, he would have had to have had a confirmation "bias".

We do not at present know how general our point is, but it seems as if it might be quite common to find epistemological environments that have a similar property. Nature is chaotic in its character and will frequently provide false feedback to the inquirer. In the present case, it is possible to see that many of the experiments tried by Faraday were in fact producing the expected effects but the effects were small and could not be detected with Faraday's insensitive apparatus. The task of the scientist in such an environment is to impose order on the apparent disorder. On our view, that is one of the necessary functions of a confirmation heuristic—it filters out some of the noise and may allow a signal to be detected. This is not a sure thing, which is why a disconfirmatory strategy is a necessary supplement later on. Any pattern induced by a confirmatory tendency will later need to be verified by standing up against potentially disconfirming tests.

In all, then, Wason's discovery of the pervasive human tendency to seek and to use only confirmatory evidence may need to be seen as one of the marvellous adaptive characteristics of human thought. In contrast to the usual focus on confirmation *bias* as a reflection of the limits of human cognition, the evidence suggests that a confirmation *heuristic* is one of the highly functional means by which knowledge is made possible. For the specific case of scientific thinking, rationality becomes a many-splendoured thing indeed!

CONCLUSIONS

There is an easy way to "capsulise" the message of each of the preceding brief reviews of traditions in the cognitive psychology of science. We could simply say that the Kuhnian tradition has helped to place scientific thinking within the wider social, cultural, and historical context of science;

that the Piagetian tradition has emphasised the unity of thought within a diversity of concerns and the developmental emergence of new ideas out of old; that the Simonian tradition has explored the applicability of the problem space notion to the understanding of science; and that the Wasonian tradition has produced valuable insights into the role of confirmatory and disconfirmatory tendencies in science.

Such a summary is accurate, but misses some of the more interesting generalisations that we think reside in the work as a whole. First of all, each of the traditions has contributed to an increasingly detailed examination of the *microstructure* of real-world science. Some of the research surveyed, of course, is predicated entirely upon such concern with the fine details of real-world science—for example, Gooding's diary studies, or Miller's close analysis of the role of imagery in the history of physics. But even in the cases where questions are framed in contexts that are seemingly much narrower in scope (the laboratory studies of confirmation bias, say, or Chi's work on children's use and attainment of scientific concepts), there is an inexorable tendency for the questions to move into more complex contexts before they are fully answered. This is a natural tendency, of course: scientific thinking occurs in richly dynamic contexts, and no one has felt that we could ground knowledge of science solely on narrow laboratory tasks.

Scientific studies of science thus inevitably move outward, but this also has the effect of bringing some of the research into a peculiar relationship with other studies of reasoning. Throughout the history of studies of reasoning, there has been a tendency to locate the work with respect to formal logic; to take the claim that human reasoning must be understood in relation to logically derived norms of reasoning, as a starting point. Testable questions do emerge from such starting points, as this book exemplifies, and those questions can in fact be answered. Such starting points lend themselves well to experimental approaches, of course: if a logical derivation (say a syllogism, or a *modus tollens* inference) can be specified for a particular mode of reasoning, then it is a relatively straightforward matter to frame an experimental question concerning whether human subjects do or do not conform to the logical specification in reasoning. The interesting answers derive, to be sure, from the discrepancies between the logical derivation and the actual process used by human reasoners. Thus, Johnson-Laird and Byrne (1991), for example, have argued for a general conception of mental models as the underlying processing mode by which people reason.

In applying such concepts to the real-world case of scientific reasoning, however, things do not stay so simple for very long. In the real world of science, as in everyday reasoning, the simple application of normative logical models is at best a small part of the interesting and richly varied thought that is occurring. To understand it is to engage difficult questions about the role of imagery, the role of problem-solving heuristics, and the structure of the problem spaces at hand. Perhaps most importantly, meanings can be fixed in the laboratory—taken as givens—but are constructed entities in the real world, constructions that change over time. Further, as our neural network studies imply, the enormous complexity of the world's structure may affect in profound ways the necessary strategies for imposing order upon the apparent disorder. Full understanding of science, given all this, is unlikely unless full attention is given to this complexity and diversity, both externally to the scientist and internally, cognitively, within the individual scientist.

The study of scientific thinking and reasoning thus confirms a tendency present in other areas of reasoning: full understanding depends on more than just the relation to logic. While logic can still constitute the starting point for studies of reasoning, it can no longer be the only starting point. As with scientific reasoning, so also with other domains: the full understanding of reasoning will emerge from the careful analysis of all the levels at which it is manifest. Given this, we look forward to a widening arena for such studies—one that continually reaches outward from the confines of the laboratory task to the wider environment of social, cultural, and historical contexts.

NOTES

1. Interestingly, Wason's early writings do not include a discussion of Karl Popper, whose normative analysis of disconfirmation has been much discussed and often related to Wason's findings (e.g. Gorman, 1992). Perhaps this is not so surprising, given that Popper's doctorate was taken under the direction of the psychologist Karl Buehler (Kurz, 1993).
2. We also varied the number of hidden units, the specific learning parameters, and the specific algorithms used to rule out the possibility that some such artefact was responsible for the failure to learn.

ACKNOWLEDGEMENTS

We are grateful to Elke Kurz and Michael Gorman for comments on an earlier version of this chapter.

REFERENCES

Arnheim, R. (1962). *Picasso's Guernica: The genesis of a painting*. Berkeley, CA: University of California Press.
Bechtel, W. (1988). *Philosophy of science: An overview for cognitive science*. Hillsdale, NJ: Lawrence Erlbaum Associates Inc.

Bradshaw, G. (1992). The airplane and the logic of invention. In R.N. Giere (Ed.), *Cognitive models of science* (Minnesota Studies in the Philosophy of Science, Vol. XV, pp. 239–250). Minneapolis: University of Minnesota Press.

Carey, S. (1992).The origin and evolution of everyday concepts. In R.N. Giere (Ed.), *Cognitive models of science* (Minnesota Studies in the Philosophy of Science, Vol. XV, pp. 89–128). Minneapolis: University of Minnesota Press.

Carlson, W.B., & Gorman, M.E. (1992). A cognitive framework to understand technological creativity: Bell, Edison, and the telephone. In R.J. Weber & D.N. Perkins (Eds.), *Inventive minds: Creativity in technology* (pp. 48–79). New York: Oxford University Press.

Cheng, P.W., & Holyoak, K.J. (1989). On the natural selection of reasoning theories. *Cognition, 33,* 285–313.

Chi, M.T.H. (1992). Conceptual change within and across ontological categories: Examples from learning and discovery in science. In R.N. Giere (Ed.), *Cognitive models of science* (Minnesota Studies in the Philosophy of Science, Vol. XV, pp. 129–186). Minneapolis: University of Minnesota Press.

Chitwood, S.T., & Tweney, R.D. (submitted). *Why confirmation bias? The epistemological environment of scientific experiment.* Bowling Green, OH.

Churchland, P.S., & Sejnowski, T.J. (1992). *The computational brain.* Cambridge, MA: MIT Press.

Cohen, L.J. (1981). Can human irrationality be experimentally demonstrated? *Behavioral and Brain Sciences, 4,* 317–331.

Cosmides, L. (1989). The logic of social exchange: Has natural selection shaped how humans reason? Studies with the Wason selection task. *Cognition, 31,* 187–276.

De Mey, M. (1982). *The cognitive paradigm.* Dordrecht: D. Reidel Publishing Co. (Reprinted, 1992, Chicago: University of Chicago Press.)

Dunbar, K. (1993). Concept discovery in a scientific domain. *Cognitive Science, 17,* 397–434.

Dunbar, K. (1995). How scientists really reason: Scientific reasoning in real-world laboratories. In R.J. Sternberg & J.E. Davidson (Eds.), *The nature of insight,* (pp.365–396). Cambridge, MA: MIT Press.

Evans, J.St.B.T. (1989). *Bias in human reasoning: Causes and consequences.* Hove, UK: Lawrence Erlbaum Associates Ltd.

Farris, H., & Revlin, R. (1989). The discovery process: A counter-factual strategy. *Social Studies of Science, 19,* 497–513.

Faust, D. (1984). *The limits of scientific reasoning.* Minneapolis, MN: University of Minnesota Press.

Gooding, D. (1990). *Experiment and the making of meaning: Human agency in scientific observation and experiment.* Dordrecht: Kluwer Academic Publishers.

Gooding, D. (1992). The procedural turn; or, Why do thought experiments work? In R.N. Giere (Ed.), *Cognitive models of science* (Minnesota Studies in the Philosophy of Science, Vol. XV, pp. 45–76). Minneapolis: University of Minnesota Press.

Gorman, M.E. (1992). *Simulating science: Heuristics, mental models, and technoscientific thinking.* Bloomington, IN: Indiana University Press.

Gorman, M.E., & Carlson, W.B. (1989). Interpreting invention as a cognitive process: The case of Alexander Graham Bell, Thomas Edison, and the telephone. *Science, Technology, and Human Values, 15,* 131–164.

Gruber, H.E. (1974). *Darwin on man.* New York: Dutton.

Gruber, H.E. (1989). The evolving systems approach to creative work. In D.B. Wallace & H.E. Gruber (Eds.), *Creative people at work: Twelve cognitive case studies* (pp. 3–24). New York: Oxford University Press.

Holmes, F.L. (1980). Hans Krebs and the discovery of the ornithine cycle. *Federation Proceedings, 39,* 216–225.

Holmes, F.L. (1987). Scientific writing and scientific discovery. *Isis, 78,* 220–235.

Ippolito, M.F, & Tweney, R.D. (1995). The inception of insight. In R.J. Sternberg & J.E. Davidson (Eds.), *The nature of insight* (pp.433–462). Cambridge, MA: MIT Press.

Johnson-Laird, P.N. (1983). *Mental models.* Cambridge, MA: Harvard University Press.

Johnson-Laird, P.N., & Byrne, R.M.J. (1991). *Deduction.* Hove, UK: Lawrence Erlbaum Associates Ltd.

Klahr, D., & Dunbar, K. (1988). Dual space search during scientific reasoning. *Cognitive Science, 12,* 1–48.

Klayman, J., & Ha, Y.-W. (1987). Confirmation, disconfirmation, and information in hypothesis testing. *Psychological Review, 94,* 211–228.

Klayman, J., & Ha, Y.-W. (1989). Hypothesis testing in rule discovery: Strategy, structure, and content. *Journal of Experimental Psychology: Learning, Memory, and Cognition, 15,* 596–604.

Kuhn, T.S. (1962). *The structure of scientific revolutions* (2nd edition, 1970). Chicago: University of Chicago Press.

Kulkarni, D., & Simon, H.A. (1988). The processes of scientific discovery: The strategy of experimentation. *Cognitive Science, 12,* 139–176.

Kurz, E. (1993, November). *Popper versus Quine on psychology and epistemology.* Paper presented at the 4S Annual Meeting, West Lafayette, IN.

Langley, P.W., Simon, H.A., Bradshaw, G.L., & Zytkow, J.M. (1987). *Scientific discovery: Computational explorations of the discovery process.* Cambridge, MA: MIT Press.

Larkin, J.H., & Simon, H.A. (1987). Why a diagram is (sometimes) worth ten thousand words. *Cognitive Science, 11,* 65–101.

Lovie, A.D. (1992). *Context and commitment: A psychology of science.* Hemel Hempstead: Harvester Wheatsheaf.

Mahoney, M.J. (1976). *Scientist as subject.* Cambridge, MA: Ballinger.

Miller, A.I. (1984). *Imagery in scientific thought: Creating 20th century physics.* Boston, MA: Birkhauser.

Miller, A.I. (1989). Imagery and intuition in creative scientific thinking: Albert Einstein's invention of the special theory of relativity. In D.B. Wallace & H.E. Gruber (Eds.), *Creative people at work: Twelve cognitive case studies* (pp. 171–188). New York: Oxford University Press.

Mitroff, I. (1974). *The subjective side of science.* Amsterdam: Elsevier.

Mynatt, C.R., Doherty, M.E., & Tweney, R.D. (1978). Consequences of confirmation and disconfirmation in a simulated research environment. *Quarterly Journal of Experimental Psychology, 30,* 395–406.

Nersessian, N. (1984). *Faraday to Einstein: Constructing meaning in scientific theories.* Dordrecht: Nijhoff.

Nersessian, N. (1992). How do scientists think? Capturing the dynamics of conceptual change in science. In R.N. Giere (Ed.), *Cognitive models of science* (Minnesota Studies in the Philosophy of Science, Vol. XV, pp. 3–44). Minneapolis: University of Minnesota Press.

Penner, D., & Klahr, D. (1993, November). *The effects of data error during a scientific reasoning task*. Paper presented at the Annual Meeting of the Society for Social Study of Science, West Lafayette, IN.

Piaget, J. (1970). *Genetic epistemology* (E. Duckworth, trans.). New York: Columbia University Press.

Polya, G. (1965). *How to solve it: A new aspect of mathematical method*. Princeton, NJ: Princeton University Press.

Rumelhart, D.E., & McClelland (Eds.) (1986). *Parallel distributed processing: Explorations in the microstructure of cognition*. Cambridge, MA: MIT Press.

Rumelhart, D.E., & Todd, P.M. (1993). Learning and connectionist representations. In D.E. Meyer & S. Kornblum (Eds.), *Attention and performance XIV* (pp. 3–30). Cambridge, MA: MIT Press.

Shrager, J. (1990). Common-sense perception and the psychology of theory formation. In J. Shrager & P. Langley (Eds.), *Computational models of scientific discovery and theory formation* (pp. 437–470). Palo Alto, CA: Morgan Kaufmann.

Simon, H.A. (1991). *Models of my life*. New York: Basic Books.

Stich, S. (1990). *The fragmentation of reason: Preface to a pragmatic theory of cognitive evaluation*. Cambridge, MA: MIT Press.

Thagard, P. (1989). Explanatory coherence. *Behavioral and Brain Sciences, 12,* 435–467.

Tweney, R.D. (1985). Faraday's discovery of induction: A cognitive approach. In D. Gooding & F.A.J.L. James (Eds.), *Faraday rediscovered: Essays on the life and work of Michael Faraday, 1791–1867* (pp. 189–210). New York: Stockton Press/London: Macmillan. (Reprinted, 1990, American Institute of Physics.)

Tweney, R.D. (1992). Stopping time: Faraday and the scientific creation of perceptual order. *Physis: Revista Internazionale di Storia Della Scienza, 29,* 149–164.

Tweney, R.D., Doherty, M.E., & Mynatt, C.R. (Eds.) (1981). *On scientific thinking*. New York: Columbia University Press.

Tweney, R.D., & Hoffner, C.E. (1987). Understanding the microstructure of science: An example. In *Program of the Ninth Annual Conference of the Cognitive Science Society* (pp. 677–681). Hillsdale, NJ: Lawrence Erlbaum Associates Inc.

Wason, P.C., & Johnson-Laird, P.N. (1972). *Psychology of reasoning: Structure and content*. Cambridge, MA: Harvard University Press.

CHAPTER TWELVE

The THOG Problem and its Implications for Human Reasoning

Stephen E. Newstead

University of Plymouth, UK

Vittorio Girotto

University of Trieste, Italy
CREPCO, Aix-en-Provence, France

Paolo Legrenzi

University of Milan, Italy

THE ORIGIN AND NATURE OF THE PROBLEM

The THOG problem was first reported by Peter Wason in 1977, though it was apparently devised a year earlier than this. Wason (1977) claims that one of his principal reasons for devising the problem was that the selection task was becoming too well known and that he wanted another way of looking at people's self-contradictions. It is interesting to note in this light that the selection task has since generated a vast literature and is now arguably the single most popular paradigm in the study of human reasoning, while the THOG problem remains much less well known and less widely researched. Nevertheless, we will argue here that it can provide important insights into the cognitive processes involved in reasoning.

The original version of the problem as presented by Wason (1977) is as follows:

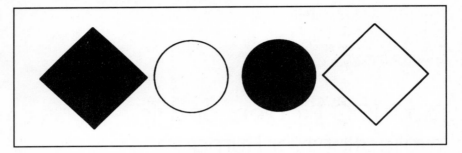

FIG. 12.1. Designs used in the THOG problem.

In front of you are four designs: a black diamond, a white diamond, a black circle, and a white circle. (The designs in Fig. 12.1 are presented at this point.)

You are given a rule which allows an arbitrary name to be applied to the designs.

Rule: In the above designs there is a particular shape and a particular colour, such that any of the designs which has one, and only one, of these features is called a THOG.

The black diamond is called a THOG. What can you say, if anything, about whether each of the three remaining designs is a THOG?

The correct response is to say that the white diamond and the black circle are definitely not THOGs, while the white circle definitely is a THOG. The reason for this is that the particular shape and colour could be either black plus circle or white plus diamond, and the same conclusion follows in each case. If black plus circle had been written down then the white diamond could not be a THOG since it contains neither of the properties; the black circle could not be a THOG because it contains both; only the white circle could be a THOG since it contains just one of the designated properties. Precisely the same conclusion follows from the other pair of properties (white plus diamond) that could have been written down: the white diamond could not be a THOG because it contains both properties, the black circle could not because it contains neither, while the white circle could be a THOG because it contains just one of the properties.

In the first published data on the problem, Wason and Brooks (1979) found that fewer than one-third of their participants produced the correct answer. The most common response was almost a mirror image of the correct one, with participants indicating that the white diamond and the black circle either were or might be THOGs, while the white circle was definitely not a THOG. Wason and Brooks (1979) termed these responses "intuitive errors". Subsequent research using the standard version of the problem has confirmed both the difficulty of the problem and the prevalence of these intuitive errors. (The interested reader may wish to look ahead to Table 12.2 where a summary of the responses obtained in three fairly typical studies is presented; the first row presents the number of correct responses.)

EARLY RESEARCH ON THE PROBLEM

In an attempt to ascertain why the THOG problem is so difficult, a number of authors have analysed the cognitive processes necessary to answer the problem correctly. The following processes at least would seem to be required: understanding the problem; generating hypotheses; testing hypotheses; and carrying out a combinatorial analysis. The possibility of each of these being the main source of the problem's difficulty is considered in turn in the context of early research on the problem.

Understanding the Problem

Solvers need to understand what the problem involves and, in particular, they need to understand the notion of exclusive disjunction contained in the rule. The problem requires people to consider the possibility of a particular colour and a particular shape, but not both, being present in a design. It seems plausible to suggest that there may be difficulties of comprehension because the problem does seem rather cumbersome and complicated. Suspecting this, Wason and Brooks (1979) rephrased the problem in their study, using what is now termed the standard version of the problem. This is their revised version:

> In front of you are four designs: black diamond, white diamond, black circle, and white circle. [The same four designs as in the original version are then presented.] You are to assume that I have written down one of the colours (black or white) and one of the shapes (diamond or circle). Now read the following rule carefully:
>
> If, and only if, any of the designs includes either the colour I have written down, or the shape I have written down, but not both, then it is called a THOG.
>
> I will tell you that the black diamond is a THOG.
>
> Each of the designs can now be classified into one of the following categories: (a) definitely is a THOG; (b) insufficient information to decide; (c) definitely is not a THOG.

We have already seen, however, that this modified version of the problem produces a substantial number of errors (it was the version used by Wason & Brooks, 1979), suggesting that the clarification has had little effect.

It could also be argued that people should have little difficulty in understanding the exclusive disjunction used in the rule, because the exclusive interpretation of disjunctives seems to be the normal one in everyday language (Newstead, Griggs, & Chrostowski, 1984; Evans, Newstead, & Byrne, 1993, Chapter 5). On the other hand, it may be one thing to understand a rule, another to use it. Research on the learning of conceptual rules has repeatedly found that disjunctive rules are more difficult to acquire than conjunctive rules, and that exclusive disjunctions are harder than inclusive ones (e.g. Neisser & Weene, 1962; see Newstead & Griggs, 1983, for a review). The THOG problem clearly requires participants to use the rule, hence the exclusive disjunction may cause difficulties. However, Wason and Brooks (1979) found that participants had no difficulty in classifying designs when they themselves had written down one of the shapes and one of the colours. What is more, even after participants had demonstrated their understanding of the exclusive disjunctive rule in this way they were still unable to solve the standard THOG problem. It would appear that, when stripped of all other factors, the exclusive disjunction used in this problem is understandable by most people; it is perfectly possible, however, that the complexity of this rule contributes to the overall difficulty of the problem, because solvers are required not just to understand the rule but to carry out other cognitive processes at the same time.

Hypothesis Formation

In addition to understanding the rule, participants must also generate hypotheses as to what the particular shape and the particular colour might be. Wason and Brooks (1979) eliminated this as the explanation for the difficulty of the THOG problem. In their Experiments 2 and 3 they showed that the majority of subjects were quite capable of indicating what combinations were permitted under the rule. Furthermore, requiring subjects to indicate these combinations did not lead to any increase in correct answers to the problem. This result has subsequently been confirmed by Smyth and Clark (1986) and Girotto and Legrenzi (1989). Once again, however, we cannot rule out the possibility that hypothesis formation may be more difficult when carried out not on its own but in conjunction with other cognitive activities.

Hypothesis Testing

Having generated the hypotheses, solvers must then test each of the designs against these hypotheses. It would appear that people do not find it difficult to check whether designs conform to a rule. As we have seen,

Wason and Brooks (1979) asked participants in their Experiment 1 to write down one of the colours and one of the shapes and then to classify each design as to whether it conformed to an exclusive disjunction rule linking these two properties. This is precisely the same analysis as is required in the standard THOG problem, but using self-generated properties involving one combination of features rather than hypothesised properties involving two completely hypothetical combinations of features. The great majority of the participants had no difficulty in carrying out this task, and we can therefore conclude that the difficulty of testing hypotheses (at least when there is only one combination of properties to take into account) does not in itself explain why the THOG problem is so difficult.

However, there is more to hypothesis testing in the THOG problem than just classifying designs; it is also necessary to keep *different* hypotheses in mind and to test them systematically. This aspect of hypothesis testing is considered more fully in the next section, and there is good reason to believe that it may be an important aspect. Using a very different type of problem—the "pseudodiagnosticity" probabilistic inference task—Mynatt, Doherty, and Dragan (1993) have presented convincing evidence that people typically consider only one hypothesis at a time. To quote their own words: "people can hold in working memory, and operate upon, but one alternative at a time" (p. 759). Roger Dominowski (personal communication) has argued that cognitive complexity *per se* cannot explain the high rate of erroneous performance in the original version. If people can solve the problem when they have only one hypothesis to consider, why can they not solve the original problem in this way—i.e. by reducing its complexity? A possible answer is that people get confused precisely because they have to consider two hypotheses (see the "Theoretical considerations" section below). It is tempting to conclude that hypothesis testing in itself is not a problem, but that the testing of more than one hypothesis at the same time might well be.

Combinatorial Analysis

In the THOG problem, solvers have to test systematically each design against each hypothesis. The type of combinatorial analysis required in solving the version of the THOG problem given above is illustrated in Table 12.1.

This analysis involves consideration of each of the designs against the two possible combinations of properties (i.e. black + circle and white + diamond), and ascertaining that two of the designs cannot be THOGs (indicated by the letter "N") and that the other designs are THOGs (indicated by the letter "Y") regardless of which combination is considered. Clearly, there is a lot to consider in this combinatorial analysis, and it would

TABLE 12.1

Combinatorial Analysis Required to Solve the THOG Problem

Design	Hypothesis	
	Black + Circle	White + Diamond
Black diamond	Y	Y
Black circle	N	N
White diamond	N	N
White circle	Y	Y

not be surprising if errors crept in. Such an analysis is, according to Inhelder and Piaget (1958), within the capabilities of any adult who has reached the stage of formal operations (which is assumed to be virtually everyone). However, Inhelder and Piaget demonstrated the ability to carry out such an analysis within rather different contexts—for example, testing combinations of liquids to see which ones produced a chemical reaction. It is possible that there is something in the THOG problem that makes the combinatorial analysis more difficult, though it is not immediately clear what this might be. Wason and Brooks (1979) assumed, almost by default, that the difficulty of carrying out the full combinatorial analysis was the principal source of the problem's complexity, but their research produced no independent evidence either for or against this suggestion.

There is another possibility that is consistent with the findings reported so far: that people are quite capable of carrying out the types of cognitive processing required to solve the problem, and that the difficulty stems from the requirement to carry out all these cognitive processes at the same time. In particular, the need to test more than one hypothesis at the same time may well overload working memory. Because of this cognitive complexity, there may be a tendency to simplify the problem by assuming that the properties of the positive example of the THOG are the properties that are written down. Wason himself thought that this might be a major factor in explaining how people tackled the problem. He says (Wason, 1978, p. 50):

> The basic conceptual difficulty with the THOG problem is that the person trying to solve it has to detach the notion of possible pairs of defining features away from the actual designs which exhibit those features.

In support of this is the finding that people often say in error that the two designs which share a property in common with the THOG design might themselves be THOGs and that the design which shares no features in common is not a THOG. This suggestion has subsequently been termed "confusion theory" and it now has considerable evidence in its support.

Before considering this subsequent research, however, we will summarise the wide-ranging research which has been conducted on a separate but related question: that of whether realistic material can facilitate performance. Wason (1977, pp. 127–128) threw down this challenge: "The logic of exclusive disjunction, pertinent to this problem, cannot readily be mapped on to everyday life situations." Many researchers took up the challenge to produce realistic versions of the problem, and much of this research has been both ingenious and theoretically productive.

THE EFFECTS OF REALISM

The search for facilitating realistic versions of the THOG problem runs very much in parallel with the similar search on the selection task (see, for reviews of the selection task literature, Evans et al., 1993, Chapter 4, and various chapters in this volume). In the 1970s it was widely assumed that almost any realistic version of the selection task would produce facilitation. In the 1980s it was realised that this was not the case and researchers concentrated their attentions on ascertaining—and explaining—which types of realism improved performance.

Wason himself (Wason, 1978), despite his scepticism as to whether this could be achieved, was actually one of the first to take up the challenge to devise a realistic version of the THOG problem. He presented the following realistic THOG devised by Wendy Stainton Rogers. There are four different ladies with different tastes:

Jane   likes progressive music
           wears "ethnic" clothes

Suzy   likes progressive music
           wears a twinset

Amy   likes classical music
           wears "ethnic" clothes

Mary   likes classical music
           wears a twinset

It is known that Suzy has "style". Having "style" means that a person has one, and only one, of two particular features: a particular kind of dress or a particular musical preference. Having both these particular features, or neither of them, makes a person "ordinary". Knowing for sure that Suzy has style, the task consisted in working out which if any of the four girls had "style" besides Suzy.

Wason did not collect data on this realistic version. He included it in a unit for a course of the Open University and let students test for differences between this and the standard version, in which "the subjects were required to deal with abstract and inherently meaningless material" (Wason, 1978, p. 54).

Four years later, Newstead, Griggs, and Warner (1982) systematically investigated the effects of realism, and in their first experiment used just the realistic version mentioned above involving four different women's fashion tastes. There were relatively few correct responses, and a preponderance of the so-called "intuitive errors". It would appear that realistic material of itself does not necessarily facilitate performance. In a second experiment, another realistic version failed again to produce facilitation. Finally, a realistic version used in a third experiment did improve performance. The experimenter told the participants that he would eat a meal if it contained just one of the two foods a friend of his had written down (a solid—either meat or ice-cream, and a sauce—either gravy or chocolate sauce). In the situation in which the experimenter claimed that he would eat meat with gravy, the correct answer was that he would also eat ice-cream with chocolate sauce, but would not eat meat with chocolate sauce or ice-cream with gravy.

In this last situation many participants correctly solved the THOG problem. However, the obtained facilitation could be interpreted as the result of the congruence between the solution of this version of the THOG problem and previous experience with food courses. It is likely that the participants did not perform a combinatorial analysis, considering each example of food course against the two possible combinations. They just "matched" their knowledge of appropriate combinations, stored in their gastronomic knowledge, with the given examples of food combinations. In this pseudo-facilitating version participants simply tended to choose the combinations of foods that would be more pleasing, irrespective of their logical status.

This interpretation of the results was corroborated by a fourth experiment, in which eight- and nine-year-old children were able to solve correctly the "gastronomic" version of the THOG problem. According to Piaget's theory, children of this age do not possess the necessary logical ability to perform combinatorial analysis. Thus, if these children too were able to give the correct answer (as was so in 75% of cases), it seems sound to conclude that their correct answer was given on the basis of their knowledge of what counts as an acceptable combination of foods rather than by following a correct reasoning strategy concerning the logical relations. The results of these last two experiments are important because they emphasise the necessity for methodological prudence: not only do the types of answer themselves matter, it is also necessary to ascertain the ways and the reasons why these answers are given by subjects.

Smyth and Clark (1986) took a different approach: they did not use familiar combinations of properties but just one familiar expression of the exclusive disjunctive relation. The concept of half-sister, based on exclusive disjunction of parents, is a real-life case in which the disjunction involved in the definition of THOG is presupposed. In fact, my half-sister is a person who has my mother or my father, but not both of my parents. If one source of difficulty is the use of an abstract exclusive disjunctive relation in defining the standard THOG, then by expressing this relation through a familiar and known concept, such as that of half-sister, it should be possible to improve performance.

Participants were presented with the names of four women and their parents (here given in brackets):

Robin   (my father and Jane)
Val   (George and Jane)
Kate   (George and my mother)
Jo   (my father and my mother)

Subjects were told: "You are to assume that I have written down one of the mothers (Jane or my mother) and one of the fathers (my father or George). Now read the following rule carefully: If, and only if, the description of a woman's parents includes either the mother I have written down, or the father I have written down, but not both, then that woman is my half-sister". Finally, they were told that Robin was a half-sister of the experimenter, and asked to decide whether each of the other three women was a half-sister of the experimenter. In this case, performance was very good (95%), but it can be argued that the task was transformed into one of classification (Girotto & Legrenzi, 1989, p. 130). In other words, particip-ants were not requested to make hypotheses about the parents of the experimenter and the parents of the women. By contrast, when the task was homogeneous to the original THOG problem—i.e. when subjects had to hypothesise who were the experimenter's mother and father—performance was again very poor.

These early realistic versions show that neither realism of the terms used (Newstead et al., 1982), nor of the relation (Smyth & Clark, 1986), make the task easy. Realism *per se* is not sufficient, neither is it necessary, as we will see shortly. These results falsify the naive and old assumption that, *ceteris paribus*, realistic problems will be easier than abstract ones. They show that realism can facilitate in a superficial and misleading way, when the pre-existing knowledge system or semantic memory leads to a representation of the problem in which knowledge "matches" the right solution. Research conducted on the selection task led to similar con-clusions at this time (e.g. Manktelow & Evans, 1979; Griggs & Cox, 1982).

Arguably, the first truly facilitating realistic version—logically isomorphous to the standard THOG—was a long story about the adventures of four Soviet spies in London devised by Girotto and Legrenzi (1989, Experiment 2). Participants were presented with the passports of four spies (each showing a type of job and a type of visa):

	Type of job	Type of visa
1) Yuri	Scientist	Tourist
2) Ivan	Scientist	Work
3) Boris	Reporter	Tourist
4) Anton	Reporter	Work

The story specified that one feature (either the job or the visa) of each passport was modified by the spies (frightened of being discovered by the British secret service) and that, after this transformation, one of the resulting passports saved a spy: Yuri. Subjects had to discover whether other modified passports also saved other spies. The correct solution is that only Anton arrived in Moscow, since his passport, once modified, will present the same combination of features as Yuri's. The performance was very good: 75% correct solutions.

Girotto and Legrenzi attributed the obtained facilitation to the temporal sequence which impeded the confusion between the properties of the positive exemplar (i.e. those presented by the successful passport before the transformation), with the properties of the passports after the transformation. A second factor in the facilitation was the fact that subjects were forced to imagine the combination(s) of job and visa which made the indicated passport successful, precisely because these combination(s) were not specified in the text of the problem.

If this interpretation of the improved performance is correct, the errors elicited in the standard version have to be interpreted as the effect of the difficulty of *separating* the hypothesised properties from those in the positive exemplar. This hypothesis was tested in a second realistic scenario: the Pub problem (Girotto & Legrenzi, 1989, Experiment 3) also studied by Newstead and Griggs (1992). The original version of the Pub problem is as follows:

Five friends meet every night in the pub. One night, Charles decides to play a game: "I have brought a deck of cards. It contains only these four types of card [subjects were at this point shown the designs in Fig. 12.1]. I deal one for myself from the deck, and I won't show it to you. Now, I'll deal each of you a card, and I will pay for a dinner for each person who has a card including either the colour of my card, or the shape of my card, but not both." The following are the cards of Charles' friends. (Subjects are then shown the cards in Fig. 12.2.) "Without showing you my card, I can tell you that I owe

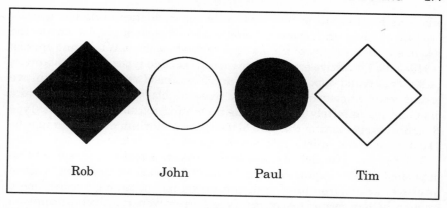

Rob   John   Paul   Tim

FIG. 12.2. Designs used in Girotto and Legrenzi's (1989) Pub problem.

Rob a dinner. Which card do you think I could have? And do you think that I have to pay for a dinner for someone else? If so, for whom?"

The correct solution is that Charles has to pay for a dinner for John as well as Rob. With this version, 89% of the subjects correctly solved the problem.

This facilitation, replicated by Newstead and Griggs (1992), is theoretically interesting for at least three reasons. First, only the context (that is the scenario of the pub) is realistic, while the material and the logical relation are abstract as in the standard THOG problem. Secondly, participants are able to perform a partial or complete combinatorial analysis (i.e. they are able to identify correctly the possible card taken by Charles). Therefore, it is difficult to consider the correct solutions as the result of pseudo-facilitation. Thirdly, it seems that the facilitation is obtained primarily through separation, suggesting that one of the main reasons why the standard THOG is so difficult is because people fail to distinguish clearly between the hypothesised combinations and the positive example of the THOG. If this is indeed the case, it may be possible to avoid errors by devising a completely abstract version of the problem different from the original one only in the clarity with which it makes this distinction. As we shall see shortly, such a problem has recently been devised by Girotto and Legrenzi (1993).

THE SOURCE OF INTUITIVE ERRORS

Our discussion so far has concentrated on the reasons why people produce so few correct responses when confronted with the THOG problem. However, there is another aspect to the findings obtained using the THOG problem to which we have alluded but which we have not yet discussed at any length. This is the fact that, although participants do not usually produce the correct response, there is nevertheless a consistency to the responses that are given: people tend to produce what Wason and Brooks (1979) called intuitive errors. There are in fact two types of intuitive error, called Type A and Type B by Griggs and Newstead (1983). Type A intuitive errors occur when participants say that the black circle and the white diamond are definitely THOGs while the white circle definitely is not; Type B errors involve saying that the black circle and white diamond might be THOGs while the white circle definitely is not.

The frequency of each of these errors (and of correct responses) in three published studies is presented in Table 12.2. It is clear that both types of intuitive error are quite common, together occurring rather more frequently than correct responses. Type A errors were relatively uncommon in the Wason and Brooks (1979) study, but actually occurred more frequently than Type B in the Newstead and Griggs (1992) study.

Wason and Brooks (1979) attribute the occurrence of intuitive errors to people assuming that the two properties of the designated THOG are the two properties contained in the rule. There is in fact an immediate problem with this suggestion, because this can explain only Type A errors. In addition, when Wason and Brooks themselves (1979, Experiment 3) asked participants to write down the properties that might be contained in the rule, not one of them wrote down the two properties contained in the positive instance. Hence this is at best only a partial explanation. Griggs and Newstead (1983) have called this explanation the "common element fallacy". The idea is derived originally from work on concept formation (Bruner, Goodnow, & Austin, 1956) in which it has been found that disjunctive concepts are difficult to acquire and that many people assume that commonly occurring attributes define the concept. This is clearly similar to what is claimed to be happening in the THOG problem where

TABLE 12.2

Responses Given to the Standard THOG Problem in Three Published Studies

	Wason & Brooks (1979) Expt. 1	Griggs & Newstead (1983) Expt. 1	Newstead & Griggs (1992) Expts. 1 & 3
Correct response	32%	2%	11%
Type A intuitive error	3%	10%	33%
Type B intuitive error	28%	25%	19%
Other	35%	61%	36%

participants assume that the positive instance defines the relevant properties for the concept of "THOGness".

An alternative explanation is in terms of matching bias, a phenomenon first investigated with respect to conditional reasoning (see Evans, this volume, Chapter 7, for an account of this research). Matching bias in the THOG problem is mentioned in Wason and Brooks (1979) but most explicitly propounded by Griggs and Newstead (1983). This explanation proposes that participants match examples to the known positive instance and respond according to how close the match is. In the standard version of the problem, they would say that the white circle is not a THOG since it shares no properties in common with the black diamond, while the other two designs are possible THOGs since they share one property in common. This explanation provides a good account of the occurrence of Type B intuitive errors; participants say that black circle and white diamond could possibly be (but are not definitely) THOGs, since they share one but only one property in common.

Griggs and Newstead (1983) carried out a number of studies using some quite complicated variants on the THOG task, including a number which introduced negatives, in an attempt to distinguish between these two explanations. The majority of the results (but not all of them) favoured the matching bias explanation. For example, one experiment used a version of the problem in which the rule was: "If, and only if, a design does not include either the colour that I have written down, or does not include the shape I have written down, or does not include both the colour and the shape that I have written down, then it is a THOG." Not surprisingly, given the number of negatives in this rule, the number of correct responses was low. What is interesting, however, is that the pattern of responses was almost identical to that found on the standard THOG problem. This is easily explained by matching bias, since this theory predicts that participants will often ignore negatives and respond as if they were not there.

Subsequent research has also largely supported the matching bias explanation. O'Brien et al. (1990) found that a number of participants did seem to assume that the properties written down were the same as those in the positive exemplar, just as the common element explanation predicts (though note that this result contrasts with the findings of Wason & Brooks, 1979). However, O'Brien et al. found that the subjects who wrote down the properties of the positive exemplar were *not* those who made intuitive errors!

Of the two theories that have been put forward to explain intuitive errors the matching bias explanation has more evidence in its favour. This may not be too surprising because in general there seems to be a preponderance of Type B intuitive errors in the literature, and these are the ones that matching bias explains best. However, it is quite possible (and indeed likely) that both theories play a role, with Type A errors resulting from the common element fallacy while Type B errors stem from matching.

CONFUSION THEORY

Both the matching bias and the common element explanations for intuitive errors have close links with the confusion theory which has been mentioned briefly in previous sections. Confusion theory claims that people fail to distinguish clearly between the hypothesised properties and those in the positive exemplar. In just the same way, matching and common element theories propose that participants focus inappropriately on the properties in the design they are told is a THOG.

Confusion theory obtains empirical support in the research of Girotto and Legrenzi (1989) who found that a number of versions of the problem which seemed to separate clearly the hypothesised properties from those in the positive exemplar all produced facilitation. Newstead and Griggs (1992) have replicated and expanded Girotto and Legrenzi's findings. And O'Brien et al. (1990) found a certain degree of facilitation (45% correct responses) in a version of the problem in which separate labels were given to the colour that the experimenter had chosen and the shape that had been chosen, a finding which they explain as being due to the fact that these labels serve to distinguish clearly between the properties written down and the properties of the positive exemplar, thus removing any possible confusion between these.

Confusion theory also seems to provide a plausible explanation of the facilitation found with various versions of the THOG problem by Griggs and Newstead (1982). One of the problems which produced consistent facilitation is the DRUG problem which, as can be seen, is rather longer than the standard THOG:

Dr. Robinson was instructing some trainee nurses on how to administer drugs. He was talking about kidney diseases and told the nurses that renal patients required carefully controlled intakes of calcium and potassium. The best way of administering these was by two injections daily, but patients became very sore with this number of injections. Thus, it was hospital policy to administer one drug intravenously and one orally. The doctor emphasised: "You must give the patients potassium either in an injection or orally every day, but of course you must not give them both the potassium injection and the potassium pill. Similarly, you must give the patients calcium but not both the calcium injection and the calcium pill."

The nurses were then told, as a class exercise, to decide what brand name of drugs they would select to administer to patients. They were told to choose some combination of the drugs Deroxin and Altanin (which are intravenous drugs, one containing calcium and the other potassium) with the drugs Prisone and Triblomate (which are orally administered drugs, one of which contains calcium, the other potassium).

At the next class, Dr. Robinson was surprised to find that the class had produced as answers all the possible combinations of the drugs:

	Injection	Drug
Answer 1	Deroxin	Prisone
Answer 2	Deroxin	Triblomate
Answer 3	Altanin	Prisone
Answer 4	Altanin	Triblomate

Dr. Robinson got as far as telling the class that the combination in Answer 1 conformed to his instructions when he was called away to do an emergency operation. Hence the students had to work out for themselves whether they were right or wrong.

Participants had to classify the remaining combinations as to whether they conformed to Dr. Robinson's instructions.

Despite its superficial dissimilarity to the original version of the THOG problem, Griggs and Newstead (1982) show, by an analysis of the underlying structures, that the problems are isomorphic and require the same logical operations in their solution. The structural tree for the problem can be seen in Fig. 12.3. The DRUG problem led to correct solutions from more than 70% of subjects. Griggs and Newstead (1982) explain this improvement in terms of problem representation, pointing out that the underlying problem structure can be envisaged as having two branches (see Fig. 12.3). This figure presents a possible problem space for the problem, and clearly indicates that it is necessary to consider two possibilities, corresponding to the two hypotheses that have to be considered. They claim that their version makes the existence of the second branch very obvious because it is clearly specified in the problem and given a verbal label, and this enables subjects to represent the problem properly. The standard THOG, on the other hand, does not make the second branch at all explicit; in effect, this corresponds to the properties not written down.

This explanation is not the same as confusion theory, but it does have certain similarities. In particular, by making the problem structure very clear, it seems certain that this also enabled participants to distinguish clearly between the positive exemplar of the THOG and the hypothesised combination. Griggs and Newstead also attach some significance to their finding that verbal labels making the structure explicit played an important role in the facilitation; once again, the main function of these labels may be to highlight the distinction between the hypotheses and the

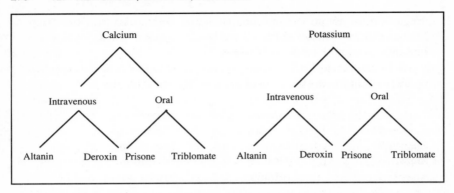

FIG. 12.3. Structural tree underlying the DRUG problem. (Adapted from Griggs & Newstead, 1982.)

positive instance. It is worth noting that this tendency to focus on positive instances is a common one in reasoning research; Evans (1989) has claimed that there is a general "positivity bias" in many areas of human thinking. According to Legrenzi, Girotto, and Johnson-Laird (1993), this bias is a consequence of the fact that the initial representation of a problem tends to be "focused". In other words, only some of the relevant pieces of information contained in the premises of a problem tend to be represented in an explicit way right from the start. (For a similar explanation, see Evans, this volume, Chapter 7.)

However, perhaps the most convincing evidence in favour of confusion theory comes from research on an abstract version of the problem. Girotto and Legrenzi (1993) have devised a version of the problem which they call the SARS problem. This involves the basic designs as used in the original THOG problem but participants are given instructions as follows:

> I have defined one of the designs as a SARS. You do not know which design this is. But you do know that a design is a THOG if it has either the colour or the shape of the SARS, but not both. Knowing for sure that the black diamond is a THOG, you have to indicate which one or which ones among the remaining designs could be the SARS. Could you also indicate whether, in addition to the black diamond, there are other THOGs?

This problem led to 70% correct responding, significantly better than the standard THOG. Girotto and Legrenzi (1993) interpret this as indicating that clear separation of the properties in the positive exemplar from the properties in the hypothesis can produce facilitation even in an abstract version of the task.

It would thus appear that a consensus is emerging that confusion theory provides an appropriate explanation of the difficulty of the THOG problem. However, the theory is not without its problems. Newstead and Griggs (1992) found that separation of the properties in the positive exemplar from those in the hypothesis was not on its own enough to produce facilitation. They found that it was also necessary to ask subjects to write down the properties in the hypothesis (something that was explicitly required in all of the versions used by Girotto and Legrenzi in their research, apart from the Spy problem in which, as indicated, the story forced the participants to imagine the combination(s) of job and visa that made the indicated passport successful). In the absence of such a requirement, no facilitation occurred. This seems to indicate that participants need to both name the possible properties and have these clearly differentiated from the positive exemplar for facilitation to occur. A further difficulty with the confusion theory, as we shall see, is that it does not provide an adequate explanation as to *why* the confusion should arise in the first place.

INDIVIDUAL DIFFERENCES

In his early reports on the THOG problem, Wason describes some preliminary but provocative research on individual differences in problem-solving abilities. He refers to some unpublished work by Mimikos comparing students from arts and science backgrounds. According to Wason (1978), science students solved the problem correctly while arts students produced predominantly intuitive errors. A similar difference in success rate was obtained in a variant on the THOG problem called the ANTI-THOG. To put more precise figures on this, Mimikos is reported as having found that 25 out of 32 science students got both problems right, while only 3 out of 32 arts students did so. In another unpublished study, Jackson (1986) found that mathematics and computer science students performed rather better than did either electrical engineering or social science students.

It is possible to suggest a number of reasons why such differences should occur. Science students (and possibly mathematics and computer science students as well) are probably accustomed to hypothesis testing and to carrying out combinatorial analysis (for example in experimental studies, cf. Lehman, Lempert, & Nisbett, 1988). Unfortunately, neither Mimikos' nor Jackson's intriguing studies were ever published and there seems to have been no published research following up these findings. Given their potential importance, it is high time this omission was rectified.

THEORETICAL CONSIDERATIONS

Although confusion theory seems to offer an adequate explanation of erroneous THOG performance in terms of confusion between data and hypotheses, Newstead and Griggs (1992) pointed out that a crucial question is still open: Why does this confusion occur? Newstead and Griggs suggested that the need to generate hypotheses, hold them in mind and, at the same time, evaluate their consequences might be a task that defeats working memory capacity. When these different steps are carried out as separate tasks, and the properties of the hypotheses are separated from those of the positive example, the problem is simplified. Otherwise, people are overloaded by the problem and confusion results.

Shafir and Tversky (1992) have proposed a similar explanation (based in part on the role of working memory capacity) of the difficulties that people exhibit in several thinking activities, and we believe that this can throw light on the difficulty of the THOG problem. According to these authors, in everyday thinking and decision making "people often fail to consider all the possible outcomes and consequences of uncertain events". An illustration of this tendency to think in a non-consequential way is the so called "disjunction effect" (Tversky & Shafir, 1992). For example, people who prefer action A over action B (e.g. going to Hawaii vs. staying at home) when event x occurs (e.g. passing an exam), and also prefer action A over action B (again, going to Hawaii vs. staying at home) when the event x does not occur (e.g. failing the exam), tend to postpone their decision about the two courses of action (e.g. await the outcome of the exam) when they do not know whether event x occurs or not (i.e. when they do not know whether they have passed or failed the exam). In other words, people sometimes violate one basic axiom of expected utility theory, the sure thing principle (Savage, 1954), by not choosing under uncertainty a given course of action that they would have chosen whatever state of the world actually occurred (cf. Fig. 12.4).

The principal source of non-consequential thinking seems to be the difficulty of considering all the hypothetical branches of an event tree, due to the limits of attention and working memory. In some cases, as in the example of the Hawaii decision problem, people fail to assess all the potential consequences of an outcome and the related likelihoods. They seem to ignore future preferences; having passed the exam, people would have chosen to go to Hawaii to celebrate their success, and, having failed the exam, they would have chosen to go to Hawaii to get over their failure; however not knowing the result of the exam, they lack a clear reason for going and, therefore, they tend to await the outcome before deciding to go. In other cases, however, people's failures do not depend on the uncertainty about their future preferences, but on the general difficulty of representing

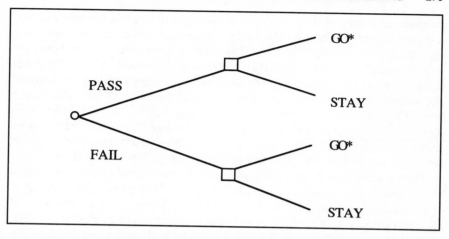

FIG. 12.4. Tree diagram for the Hawaiian vacation problem. (Adapted fromTversky & Shafir, 1992.) (Note: the circle denotes the chance node; the squares denote decision nodes; and * denotes the preferred option under each possible outcome.)

in a complete manner all the branches of the decision tree. One example of this is the failure to solve in a consequential way Newcomb's Problem, a decision task in which there is just one reason for choosing a given option (Shafir & Tversky, 1992).

Shafir and Tversky have shown patterns of non-consequential thinking in several decision-making tasks. They have also analysed the failure to solve Wason's selection task (Wason, 1966) as an example of non-consequentialism. For instance, failure to select the not-q card can be seen as a disjunction effect. In a typical version of the selection task, participants have to test the truth status of a conditional rule ("if p then q") by evaluating the hidden values of four cards representing the four logical cases (p, not-p, q and not-q). A logically correct projection of the possible consequences of turning each card would indicate that only a combination of p and not-q values would falsify the rule and, therefore, that the two cards to be selected are p and not-q. However, most participants tend to select only p, or p and q cards.

Among the very first experiments on this task, the "therapy experiments" (e.g. Wason & Johnson-Laird, 1970) showed that people are able to appreciate the falsifying value of a not-q card with a p case on its back. (In some experiments, participants were actually asked to turn over the cards and to discover the values presented on their backs.) Participants also understand that a not-p case on the back of the not-q card would not falsify the rule. Still, they tend not to select this card. In a similar way, subjects understand that neither a p, nor a not-p case on the other side of a q card would falsify the rule, and yet they tend to select this card when its other side is not known. (The verbal protocols of the "therapy experiments" are particularly interesting because they illustrate dramatically how normal adults can exhibit self-contradicting patterns of reasoning.) In short, according to Shafir and Tversky, people who do not solve the selection task behave in much the same way as subjects who choose in a non-consequential way in Tversky and Shafir's (1992) decision tasks. In both cases, they argue, deviations from the normatively correct solutions depend on the difficulty of facing a disjunction of outcomes.

This analysis can be applied to only some of the typical response patterns obvserved in the selection task. As Girotto and Legrenzi (1993) noted, in the selection task people seem to neglect the consequences of only *some* of the relevant cases. In particular, subjects tend to correctly select the p card, as well as to correctly omit the not-p card. In both cases, the hidden side remains unknown. However, despite uncertainty, reasoning about these two cards appears to be correct.

Irrespective of any difficulties, Shafir and Tversky's attempt to interpret reasoning errors as examples of non-consequentialism, and to attribute them to the sources which determine the difficulties in decision-making tasks, seems promising. Recently, Girotto and Legrenzi (1993) have interpreted the failure to solve the THOG problem as an example of non-consequential reasoning. In fact, in the THOG problem, participants fail to assess the consequences of two hypotheses by ignoring which one is the correct one. One of the early experiments by Wason and Brooks (1979, Experiment 1) showed a pattern of answers which resembles a disjunction effect. Wason and Brooks asked their participants to individuate *one* particular hypothesis, by writing down themselves a particular colour and a particular shape. As indicated earlier, participants had no difficulty in solving this task and the subsequent request to individuate the designs which derive, on the basis of the disjunctive rule, from that combination of colour and shape. However, the majority of them were not able to solve the subsequent standard THOG problem, in which they had to consider *two* combinations of colour and shape (ignoring which of them is the correct one) and to assess their consequences. Similarly, subjects who have generated the possible combinations of features written down by the experimenter (Wason & Brooks, 1979, Experiment 2; cf. also Smyth & Clark, 1986), or subjects who have individuated the designs which correspond to these hypothetical combinations (the MIB problem, Girotto & Legrenzi, 1989, Experiment 1), are not able to solve the standard THOG problem. That is, they are not able to find all the possible consequences of two hypotheses generated on the basis of a disjunctive rule. Recall, as well, that Mynatt et al. (1993), using the very different "pseudodiagnosticity" problems, also found that people had difficulty in considering more than one hypothesis at the same time.

The ensemble of these results suggests a general conclusion—one that was proposed originally by Wason himself: participants who are able to test the consequences of a *particular* hypothesis are not able to test the consequences of *real* hypotheses when "it is not known which one corresponds to reality. It may be peculiarly difficult to reason about hypothetical possibilities to reach determinate conclusions" (Wason & Brooks, 1979, p. 88).

In sum, according to Girotto and Legrenzi (1993), the erroneous inferences that subjects draw in the THOG problem are a clear example of non-consequentialism. To illustrate this, steps to solve the THOG problem are represented in Fig. 12.5 by means of a diagram tree similar to that used to represent the decision-making tasks which elicit the disjunction effect, cf. Fig. 12.4.

A further demonstration of the similarity between the erroneous performance elicited in the THOG problem and the disjunction effects in

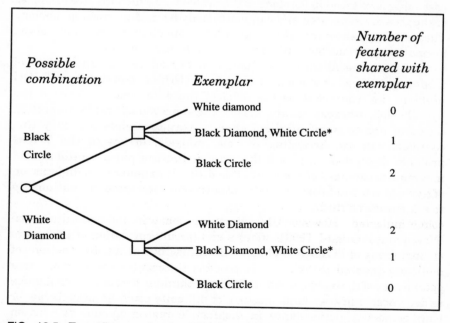

FIG. 12.5. Tree diagram for the THOG problem. (Note: the circle denotes the departure of the two branches corresponding to the two hypothetical combinations; the squares denote the three possible consequences in each branch; and * denotes the designs which have one of the two features of the hypothetical combinations—i.e. the THOG designs.)

decision-making tasks is provided by the fact that in both domains these effects disappear when the structure of the tasks is made clear. Tversky and Shafir (1992) found that a problem which elicits disjunctive patterns (the second gamble problem) can be solved correctly when subjects are asked to indicate their preferences for each possible outcome, and *immediately* afterwards to choose an option for the situation in which the outcome is unknown. In other words, when the structure of the event tree is made clear, participants are able to consider the fact that for each possible outcome their options do not change, and their answers appear to be normatively correct.

As indicated earlier, Girotto and Legrenzi (1993) have found that a version of the THOG problem in which the structure of the task was made clear and the working memory load was reduced by labelling the two hypotheses (the SARS problem), did facilitate performance. Similarly, Griggs and Newstead (1982) found that an expanded version of the problem, which made the structure of the problem very explicit, also resulted in facilitation. So, as in the previous case, non-consequential reasoning is reduced in versions of the problem in which the two branches of the tree are separated and can more easily be held in working memory. These findings show that people are able to appreciate the validity of the normative solutions both in reasoning and decision making.

In more general terms, confusion theory offers an explanation of *what* is going wrong when participants fail to solve the standard THOG problem (i.e. they confuse the level of the data and the level of the hypotheses), whereas an analysis of these erroneous performances in terms of non-consequentialism offers a way to understand *why* this confusion occurs. According to this analysis, errors in the THOG problem depend on the fact that, given the limited attentional and mnemonic resources of the mind, it is difficult to generate a disjunction of hypotheses and to assess their potential consequences in relationship to a disjunctive rule.[1]

As indicated, confusion theory too, at least in its revised version (Newstead & Griggs, 1992), offers a similar interpretation of the errors elicited in the THOG problem. However, by using the notion of non-consequential thinking, it is possible to consider these errors as a special case of the more general difficulty of thinking through consequences under uncertainty. A common source of difficulty could be responsible for both erroneous performance in disjunctive reasoning and disjunction effects in decision making.

CONCLUDING COMMENTS

In this chapter we have reviewed the literature on the THOG problem, indicated why it is so difficult to solve, and analysed how research on this problem relates to cognitive processing in general. Our main conclusions are as follows:

1. None of the basic component processes required for the solution of the problem is beyond the capabilities of the people who are typically asked to solve the problem.
2. Carrying out all of the processes together *is* beyond the capabilities of most people. We suspect that testing two hypotheses simultaneously is the major source of this difficulty because of the demands it places on working memory.
3. Because of this cognitive overload, people resort to more primitive forms of responding, including matching bias and the common element fallacy. Both of these involve a failure to distinguish adequately between the hypothesised properties and those present in the positive exemplar.
4. At a theoretical level, the results are best explained by confusion theory, which we suspect may be simply a special case of the recently proposed line of interpretation of reasoning and decision- making difficulties in terms of non-consequential thinking.
5. Realistic material does not in itself produce facilitation, but some realistic versions are effective in doing so. This is achieved either by cueing in the correct response or by overcoming confusion by clearly separating the hypothesised properties from those in the given exemplar. It is also possible to devise abstract versions which achieve this separation.

In a recent survey of the literature, Evans et al. (1993) argued that research on the THOG problem has contributed more to an understanding of general aspects of human reasoning than it has to an understanding of disjunctive reasoning processes *per se*. The attempt to link the difficulties of this specific problem with the difficulties of other reasoning and decision-making tasks seems to confirm this claim. Whether or not it is judged to be successful, this attempt is our homage to the work of Peter Wason, who invented the THOG problem and also explained its difficulty in a way which is very much in line with the most recent developments in the study of human thinking.

NOTE

1. The proposed explanation is in line with the mental model theory of deductive reasoning (see Johnson-Laird & Byrne, 1991), according to which the main source of inferential errors is the difficulty of holding in working memory several models (i.e. representations) of the content of the premises. (For an analysis of the errors that people make in decision-making tasks in terms of the model theory, cf. Legrenzi et al., 1993.)

ACKNOWLEDGEMENTS

Preparation of this chapter was partially supported by a CNR grant to Vittorio Girotto and Paolo Legrenzi.

REFERENCES

Bruner, J.S., Goodnow, J.J., & Austin, G.A. (1956). *A study of thinking.* New York: Wiley.

Evans, J.St.B.T. (1989). *Bias in human reasoning: Causes and consequences.* Hove, UK: Lawrence Erlbaum Associates Ltd.

Evans, J.St.B.T., Newstead, S.E., & Byrne, R.M.J. (1993). *Human reasoning: The psychology of deduction.* Hove, UK: Lawrence Erlbaum Associates Ltd.

Girotto, V., & Legrenzi, P. (1989). Mental representation and hypothetico-deductive reasoning: The case of the THOG problem. *Psychological Research, 51,* 129–135.

Girotto, V., & Legrenzi, P. (1993). Naming the parents of the THOG: Mental representation and reasoning. *Quarterly Journal of Experimental Psychology, 46A,* 701–713.

Griggs, R.A., & Cox, J.R. (1982). The elusive thematic materials effect in the Wason selection task. *British Journal of Psychology, 73,* 407–420.

Griggs, R.A., & Newstead, S.E. (1982). The role of problem structure in a deductive reasoning task. *Journal of Experimental Psychology: Learning, Memory, and Cognition, 8,* 297–307.

Griggs, R.A., & Newstead, S.E. (1983). The source of intuitive errors in Wason's THOG problem. *British Journal of Psychology, 74,* 451–459.

Inhelder, B., & Piaget, J. (1958). *The growth of logical thinking from childhood to adolescence.* New York: Basic Books.

Jackson, S.L. (1986). *The effects of area of expertise and level of education on performance on two reasoning tasks.* Unpublished masters thesis, University of Florida.

Johnson-Laird, P.N., & Byrne, R.M.J. (1991). *Deduction.* Hove, UK: Lawrence Erlbaum Associates Ltd.

Legrenzi, P., Girotto, V., & Johnson-Laird, P.N. (1993). Focusing in reasoning and decision making. *Cognition, 49,* 37–66.

Lehman, D.R., Lempert, R.O., & Nisbett, R.E. (1988). The effects of graduate training on reasoning: Formal reasoning and thinking about everyday life events. *American Journal of Psychology, 43,* 431–443.

Manktelow, K.I., & Evans, J.St.B.T. (1979). Facilitation of reasoning by realism: Effect or non-effect? *British Journal of Psychology, 70*, 477–488.

Mynatt, C.R., Doherty, M.E., & Dragan, W. (1993). Information relevance, working memory, and the consideration of alternatives. *Quarterly Journal of Experimental Psychology, 46A*, 759–778.

Neisser, U., & Weene, P. (1962). Hierarchies in concept attainment. *Journal of Experimental Psychology, 64*, 640–645.

Newstead, S.E., & Griggs, R.A. (1983). The language and thought of disjunction. In J.St.B.T. Evans (Ed.), *Thinking and reasoning: Psychological approaches*. London: Routledge & Kegan Paul.

Newstead, S.E., & Griggs, R.A. (1992). Thinking about THOG: Sources of error in a deductive reasoning task. *Psychological Research, 54*, 299–305.

Newstead, S.E., Griggs, R.A., & Chrostowski, J.J. (1984). Reasoning with realistic disjunctives. *Quarterly Journal of Experimental Psychology, 36A*, 611–627.

Newstead, S.E., Griggs, R.A., & Warner, S.A. (1982). The effects of realism on Wason's THOG problem. *Psychological Research, 44*, 85–96.

O'Brien, D.P., Noveck, I.A., Davidson, G.M., Fisch, S.M., Lea, R.B., & Freitag, J. (1990). Sources of difficulty in deductive reasoning. *Quarterly Journal of Experimental Psychology, 42A*, 329–352.

Savage, L.J. (1954). *The foundation of statistics*. New York: Wiley.

Shafir, E., & Tversky, A. (1992). Thinking through uncertainty: Nonconsequential reasoning and choice. *Cognitive Psychology, 24*, 449–474.

Smyth, M.M., & Clark, S.E. (1986). My half-sister is a THOG: Strategic processes in a reasoning task. *British Journal of Psychology, 77*, 275–287.

Tversky, A., & Shafir, E. (1992). The disjunction effect in choice under certainty. *Psychological Science, 3*, 305–309.

Wason, P.C. (1966). Reasoning. In B.M. Foss (Ed.), *New horizons in psychology*. Harmondsworth: Penguin.

Wason, P.C. (1977). Self-contradictions. In P.N. Johnson-Laird & P.C. Wason (Eds.), *Thinking: Readings in cognitive science*. Cambridge: Cambridge University Press.

Wason, P.C. (1978). *Hypothesis testing and reasoning*. Unit 25, Block 4, Cognitive Psychology. Milton Keynes: Open University.

Wason, P.C., & Brooks, P.G. (1979). THOG: The anatomy of a problem. *Psychological Research, 41*, 79–90.

Wason, P.C., & Johnson-Laird, P.N. (1970). A conflict between selecting and evaluating information in an inferential task. *British Journal of Psychology, 61*, 509–515.

CHAPTER THIRTEEN

Creativity in Research

Peter Wason

We that have done and thought,
That have thought and done
Must ramble, and thin out
Like milk spilt on a stone
W.B. YEATS

BACKGROUND

A propensity for doing research (above all else) might be related to scholastic achievement at a much earlier age. Psychoanalysts, for instance, would subscribe to the view that patterns of behaviour repeat themselves throughout life. Similarly, research workers are often faced with the funny question, "How did you ever think of it?" as if knowledge of the past explains the present. A brief account of my educational background may enable others, even experimental psychologists, to ponder the roots of originality.

My parents came from distinguished Liberal families, but this spirit hardly extended to the education of their children. At the age of eight, I was despatched to a prep school in the Mendip Hills. I found it impossible to learn more about even those things which interested me, let alone things which bored me. In algebra lessons the maths master used to intone: "You cannot add an apple to a banana". This obvious falsehood assumed the significance of a zen Koan which was quite beyond me.

I failed exams (Common Entrance) with monotonous regularity. My next school, Stowe, was liberal, as public schools go—perhaps too liberal. I failed the School Certificate examination twice. Nowadays I would be considered a case for the educational psychologist.

But all bad things, even 10 years of boarding schools, come to an end: there was a war. After intensive selection procedures I eventually passed out of Sandhurst, and was appointed (at the age of 20) a liaison officer to an armoured brigade in Normandy. I do not suppose I had what is quaintly called a "good war", but I never doubted that it was a just war. In 1945, I recovered in County Clare from the effects of a war which had, ironically, been therapeutic. Although severely injured I experienced a sense of spiritual freedom. In 1946 I went up to Oxford (New College) to read English, and then became an Assistant Lecturer at Aberdeen University.

Dissatisfied with the humanities, I elected to read psychology at University College London in 1950, and stayed there for over 30 years.

CREATIVITY

Perhaps I was drawn towards the topic of reasoning because most things in life seemed unreasonable. At any rate, I should like to understand the relentless drive of research which does not depend on reinforcement. But that is beyond my scope. There are several interesting theories of creativity, but the one I like best is Bruner's (1961) idea that the creative product arouses effective surprise. By searching between the lines of my papers and reliving the experience of research, I hope I may find I have met that criterion.

The significant moves in research seem as if they were done yesterday, but even the adventitious circumstances surrounding them retain a vividness of an almost hysterical intensity, and I touch on them because, in a minor way, they may reveal changing climates of opinion. Similarly, on just a few occasions I point to connections between experimental findings and everyday life.

FAKES AND FLUKES

I start with a one-off problem, the roots of which may lie fairly deep. My interest in fakes was probably stimulated by an uncle. He had a vast collection of mathematical and mechanical puzzles as well as a scrap-book on fakes world-wide. The fascination of fakes is that the owner of one may passionately resist the suggestion that it is not authentic: a phenomenon related to the 2-4-6 problem. Sam Fillenbaum, with diagnostic acumen, told me "I now see what drives you—things which are not what they seem".

In collaboration with Shuli Reich (Wason & Reich, 1979), I investigated the understanding of a seemingly innocent sentence: "No head injury is too trivial to be ignored". It seems to mean that attention should be paid to all head injuries however trivial, but the sentence is a fake—it means all head injuries should be ignored however trivial. The puzzlement is not helped by considering the following sentence with the same syntax: "No weather forecast is too plausible to be mistrusted". That sentence means exactly what it seems to mean. We found that the fake is not exposed by any appeal to grammatical analysis. Linguists tended to offer different readings. Subsequently, I devised a thought experiment which creates an absurd world to match the absurd sentence.

"In our world", said the Red Queen defiantly to Alice, "we make a point of ignoring all head injuries."

"Even the trivial ones?", murmured Alice.

"Of course, child", retorted the Red Queen, "No head injury is too trivial to be ignored."

Effective surprise—the field is reorganised to mediate the meaning directly. The example is not unique. Much education is faked because it consists of memorising inauthentic bits and pieces that tend to block insights. We are all dominated by fakes that militate against understanding.

In addition to the deceptive influence of fakes, shifting climates of opinion affect the perception of problems. For instance, my views on the study which follows were not really acceptable to the zeitgeist. At Harvard's Center for Cognitive Studies in 1963, I continued my chronometric experiments on negation. I aimed to determine whether pragmatic factors—the way in which negatives are generally used—would affect the ease with which they are grasped. George Miller and his students have been concerned with negation as a syntactical transformation, under the influence of Chomsky's early theory of grammar. My aim was to see whether contexts of plausible denial (e.g. "a spider is not an insect") would facilitate understanding more than contexts of implausible denial (e.g. "a herring is not a bird"). But in the experiment, conducted by Susan Carey, I rather perversely used abstract material to test the hypothesis. The results were promising, but there were methodological hurdles involved in their interpretation. I was told that the subtraction of reaction times was not on because it infringed the "irreducible minimum". And George Miller suggested I had "carried out two experiments and thrown away the results of one". In fact, I made the only valid *post hoc* comparison to throw further light on the confirmation of the hypothesis. Other critics said the results were a fluke, if not a fake. But some time later many seemed to agree (in my view rightly) that the results were not surprising at all—of course negatives are used to deny things which might otherwise be considered true. (I shall present a thought experiment on negation later to illustrate how the obvious can remain concealed.)

Psychologists, especially, suffer from changes in the climate of opinion. Iris Murdoch (1992, p. 43) relates something similar in philosophy. In 1940, Ayer's *Language, Truth, and Logic* was widely acclaimed, but today it may seem "brilliant and ingenious, but also unsophisticated and dotty". In our discipline we may wonder how, for instance, Clark Hull's mathematico-deductive theory of rote learning would be considered today.

RESEARCH STRATEGY

"I am looking for a problem", a friend once said to me, surrounded by a pile of learned journals. This struck me, quite unfairly, as rather funny because I would not think of working in that way. For me, problems come when they are least expected. My own experience of "creativity" is related to what others have experienced, so there may be little original (or creative) in my own account. Quite typically, the unconscious, or as Kubie (1958) would say, the preconscious (freed from distortion by the unconscious), becomes dominant. Phenomenologically, there is the impression of being guided. The distinctive criterion is one of passivity and the absence of intellectual effort. The will is not exercised; effort comes at a later stage when the problem is being formulated. All this has been described well by the analyst, Masud Khan, in a comment on a case report: "this is research into how to let oneself be used, become the servant of a process" (Milner, 1969).

I think there is an analogy here to the effective supervision of research. The balance between encouragement and criticism is often mishandled. Some supervisors are enthusiastic at the end of a research project, when they ought to be at the beginning. I frequently used to bombard my students with letters if I thought there was anything I could add to their ideas, thus giving time for digestion. An idea may be "half-baked", as Y. Bar-Hillel said of a paper by Oliver Selfridge (1959) (see also Good, 1962), but "half-baked" ideas, given careful attention, can become "baked" in the course of time, rather than burned.

This suggests a general principle. In their development of the 2-4-6 problem (Wason, 1960), Ryan Tweney and his associates (1980) supplied an interesting correction. They argued that it is inefficient to try to disconfirm an hypothesis until it has been sufficiently confirmed. In a later development, they showed that if disconfirmatory evidence for one rule was made confirmatory evidence for another rule, then the task became dramatically easier. I sent this "half-baked" idea on the back of an envelope to Tweney without considering its implication in any way at all. After it had been tested, I saw again the link to supervision: avoid disconfirmation in the early stages and withhold criticism until later. Only once was I disappointed when a student wanted me to do his cooking for him. He asked for an idea on which to do research, but later rejected it on the grounds that "it was not original enough". Life is hard.

METHODOLOGY

"Physicists talk about physics", said Poincaré, "and sociologists talk about methodology". He might as well have included psychologists, at least until recently. I like to keep my experiments as simple as possible. I have an intuitive dislike of complex statistics, especially the analysis of variance (invented by Fisher for the assessment of manure). It has been called "robust", and it seems to me just too powerful for psychological data: like taking a magnifying glass for something which should be apparent to the naked eye. But then, of course, I am prejudiced and my views reflect my lack of mathematical sophistication. I prefer rank order tests, and have been fortunate because two of their leading exponents, A.R. Jonckheere and J.W. Whitfield, have been my friends at UCL.

I dislike group testing which necessarily precludes "introspections", so-called by neo-behaviourists who consider such information gratuitous, or, at best, corroborative. They can provide a key to a problem. For instance, in the early studies of negation (Wason, 1959; 1961; Wason & Jones, 1963), if I had been concerned only with the objective data (response latencies), I would not have captured the "secret of negation": the mental deletion of the word "not" in the sentence. The "negation models" of Clark (1974) and Trabasso (1972) acknowledge this fact, but give it a rather arbitrary interpretation. At an information-processing level the rationale for the deletion is to yield an affirmative sentence which requires fewer steps to verify, but at a psycholinguistic level it looks more like a recovery of the missing presupposition. A negative without a presupposition induces bafflement. This can be illuminated by a simple thought experiment. Verify in your mind the two sentences which follow, and see which is easier:

1. Six is even and five is not even.
2. Six is even and two is not odd.

This (partly) enabled me to write an article with the paradoxical title, "In real life negatives are false" (Wason, 1972) for Leo Apostel's "Negation Project". Negatives are used to falsify presuppositions rather than to maintain truth.

The simple statement of the solution belies the time and effort taken to arrive at it. In 1958, we were all puzzled. The curves of the response times in the first experiment were differentiated clearly over a large number of trials, and there was no sign of their convergence. "You'll really learn something about the nervous system from that", said Ron Melzac, who was visiting, on entering my room. John Whitfield took the results to Canada to show them to Donald Hebb and his colleagues. "It's always good to hear from young research workers even if their work is not ripe for publication" said the Chairman of the Experimental Psychology Society when I addressed them.

On the whole, I am against talking about an experiment before it has been carried out, although I violated this principle in my graduate seminars in the 1960s. It is true that consultation may reveal a flaw, but just as often it may distort the original idea, especially if it is only "half-baked". An experimental idea is like a poem. It would be odd to ask another person about it because nobody else would know what will emerge. This may seem a highly idiosyncratic way for a scientist to work, but that overlooks the affinity of discovery between arts and science. There is a time for discussion—after the data cannot be altered and before the next experiment. I have been fortunate in having as a discussant and teacher, A.R. Jonckheere, who has inspired countless graduate students for decades at UCL with his ideas, and sometimes with their own ideas.

REPORTING RESEARCH

It is obvious that there is a dialectic between thinking and experimenting, each modifying the other. I think that if thought is not externalised by experimental tests, then it is liable to distortion. But the same thing happens in writing: the concrete expression of thought in words modifies the ideas on the topic. The process of drafting and redrafting is like experimenting on a problem. Research has not been completed until it has been written up for publication. This is critically important for the research worker. I like Freud's comment: "Write it, write it, put it down in black and white; that's the way to get it out of your system—outside you, that is; give it an existence independently of you" (Riviere, 1958).

I have presented my own practice in several articles (e.g. Wason, 1980; Green & Wason, 1982). It assumes that you do not know what you are really trying to say until you have said it. It consists in two phases. The first is an externalisation of thought without correction or criticism. There is an analogy to the confirmatory stage in the discovery of a rule in the 2-4-6 problem. I have called this kind of writing, "clearing the store" to make room for new ideas; it relieves mental congestion. The second, critical phase (analogous to disconfirmation) is an attempt to extract order and meaning from the "zero draft". But the process of concerted criticism brings with it new thought, memories, and unforeseen connections.

I have called the conventional model of writing "the tape in the head" because it implies a kind of pre-existent meaning which is run off, usually with stumbling corrections, as soon as pen is put to paper. The model for generative writing is a patchwork quilt, a crossword, or a jigsaw puzzle—a process of discovery devoid of serial order. The notion of generative writing has been independently expounded by Peter Elbow (1973) in his remarkable book *Writing Without Teachers*. I suspect, however, that it is rather difficult to make converts to this method. My hunch is that most students have an ingrained tendency to spell out the "zero draft" in too committed a manner. Ask them to improve on what they have written and (in my experience) they will make a few perfunctory alterations. Their "draft" simply does not catch alight. It is not sufficiently porous and undisciplined. In an effort to increase fluency, I have tried getting subjects to write about God in invisible ink, but the results were unclear. (The Editor of the *Quarterly Journal of Experimental Psychology* said he would be delighted to publish the excerpts so long as they remained in invisible ink.)

Some corroboration for the benefits of generative writing was obtained by David Lowenthal and myself (1977) in our survey on academics and their writing. One salient finding was that those who planned their writing in advance tended to dislike the process, but that those who used it to extend their thought generally enjoyed it. And this was so regardless of academic discipline.

Personally, I enjoy academic writing because it is a sure way to get peace of mind, due no doubt to its ordering and creative functions. Indeed I often have the fantasy that I may die before finishing a paper. This obviously inflates its importance, but suggests that unconsciously the paper is a part of myself. A rather similar irrational fantasy is rewarding, and may be more common—the paper you are now writing will be the best you have ever written.

I dislike argument unless it is written down. Most face-to-face argument is a point-scoring game which proceeds from different premises. It is not conducive to peace of mind. In any case, it hardly contributes towards progress because the protagonists seldom change their minds about the issue under discussion.

A STUDY IN PREJUDICE

Argument is a kind of debased criticism, but I take the latter fairly seriously. When people are criticised, they usually say they have been misunderstood, and usually they are right. It is my 2-4-6 studies which have given the most offence, and sometimes I wish the critics had actually done the experiment themselves. Perhaps I should have called the original paper (Wason, 1960) "a study in prejudice", as a friend suggested at the time. Recently it has met with some interesting conceptual criticism.

The most influential idea underlying the experiment was Popper's concept of falsifiability in scientific methodology. But the English translation of "Logik der Forschung" was delayed until 1959, and I had to make do with a number of scintillating articles, especially one entitled, "Philosophy of Science, A Personal Report" (Popper, 1957), which is less technical than his *magnum opus*. I attended one or two of Popper's seminars at the London School of Economics, but found them rather above my head as well as disputatious. Popper's successor, Imre Lakatos, stopped me in the street with a rather ambiguous invitation: "We've read everything you have written, and we disagree with all of it—do come and give us a seminar".

Some misgivings about my original paper were raised as soon as it was published, although the more weighty ones were not made until the 1980s, at least 20 years after publication. On two different occasions an academic rather brusquely left the room when I was lecturing, and did so at precisely the same point: when I said that the correct rule cannot be proved, but any incorrect hypothesis could be disproved. In a similar way, when I said that the subjects seemed deeply moved after the experiment, someone retorted, "That's only because it is you doing it". And there is one individual who publicly proclaims that the erroneous solutions are justified because nearly all the subjects announce them. Perhaps this should be called the modal theory of truth. I should, of course, have tried to discover more about this interesting delusion.

In 1983 Jonathan Evans argued that there is no evidence that the subjects were trying to confirm their hypotheses, but only that they tended to generate positive instances of them. It seems to me, however, that when a subject writes down on the record sheet, "to test this theory", accompanied by a positive instance of it, then that is *ipso facto* an attempt to confirm that hypothesis. Evans writes (p. 143): "It is not that the subjects do not wish to falsify, it is simply that they cannot think of the way to do it". But if a subject was not under the spell of a current hypothesis, it would surely be trivially easy to generate a negative instance of it. This could be tested by asking subjects, not to perform the task, but to comment on the protocol of another subject, or even a constructed one. Or perhaps, possible ways of proceeding could be listed, and the subject asked to put them into rank order with respect to efficiency. Simplest of all: instruct the subject to generate a negative instance and time the response.

Klayman and Ha (1987) argue that subjects are justified in using what they call "a positive test strategy" (*pace* Francis Bacon, 1621) because in so doing they are unaware of the very general scope of the rule. The highly specific initial instance, 2-4-6, may cause them to think that the rule is also highly restricted.

Fenna Poletiek (1992) in her doctoral thesis also makes the same point. I concede that there may be some truth in these criticisms, and that I may have overstated the case for confirmation, but as David Green and I have pointed out in a rejoinder (unpublished) to Klayman and Ha: "A strategy implies a voluntary decision to generate evidence in one way rather than another, but many individuals in this task seem to behave as if the hypothesis which they entertain must be correct". This is revealed by the extraordinary tendency merely to reformulate, and announce, the same rule rather than seek an alternative. It suggests a commitment to truth rather than a plausible option. It is not, of course, claimed that every subject, at every opportunity, was a prey to this kind of conceptual blindness. The technology of the original experiment, and the absence of covert timing, did not allow any other indication of this tendency (other than reformulation and the obsession with past instances) of the extent to which there is an awareness that other hypotheses could be candidates for the rule. Stuart Sutherland (1992) in his provocative book, *Irrationality*, cites a pleasing glimpse of the surprises which may still occur with this task: "I once put the problem to one of the most distinguished biologists in Britain, who proposed the rule, 'Any three numbers increasing by the same amount'. After being told he was wrong, he said, 'Well, it must be any three numbers in which, starting from the last number, each of the other two decreases by the same amount'. It is, of course, an identical rule." It is just these ritualistic moves which convey far more about the kind of thinking adopted than any numerical analysis.

Some very recent informal reports suggest that students today do better than they did in 1959. I do not know whether to be pleased or sorry—both I suppose. However, Estelle Phillips (personal communication) has tested individuals outside the academic community (e.g. a carpenter and a businessman) who yielded typical results—hypotheses that tended to become more elaborate and difficult to decipher. (It is, incidentally, extremely uncommon for announced hypotheses of the same underlying rule to become shorter rather than longer. In the original paper I made the point that this recourse to verbal exactitude is analogous to the pronouncement of a spell in magic.) It would seem that my invitation to prejudice may be as valid today as yesterday.

THE SELECTION TASK AS A PICTURE OF CREATIVE EFFORT

In their definitive book, *Human Reasoning*, Jonathan Evans and his associates (1993) state that I first described the selection task in 1966, but could hardly have suspected that in the next quarter of a century it would become the most intensively researched single problem in the history of the psychology of reasoning. Correct. But as a minor contribution to the psychology of research, it would be interesting to plot the accelerating curve of publication dates over this period. Initially, the consumers of research may have caught something of the subjects' perplexities and suspicions. But today work on the task has been called a cottage industry.

The reason for the initial disdain and the subsequent enthusiasm may have something to do with a contradiction: the task is both simple in structure and difficult to solve. Only very recently a psychologist expressed surprise that although students could not solve it they were capable of writing a computer program for it. A few individuals in the early days called it a trick, others called it "irritating". Some said it was divorced from everyday life. I felt like replying: "That is its saving grace". We don't hear so much of that kind of talk nowadays. The fact that a simple structure, without semantic support, tends to defy our wits does have a definite appeal.

Actually, the selection task was conceived a few years earlier than 1966, probably in 1960 or 1961. I had become interested in Quine's (1952) elegant notation for determining validity in the propositional calculus, but I experienced difficulty in understanding the truth functions of the conditional. So I constructed the familiar four cards, and presented the problem to two friends. Both solved it after some thought, and my assistant thought it lacked potential. I did not turn to it again until I found myself at the Center for Cognitive Studies in 1963. Here I found that sentences like, "If I go to Chicago, I catch a train", caused more hilarity than concentration. It is difficult to continue an experiment when the subjects collapse with laughter.

The first formal experiments, done partly in Scotland (Wason 1968), met with grave looks from dedicated Piagetians; the subjects' responses were clearly incompatible with "formal operations". There was even the hint that there was something wrong with the experiment—a fluke or perhaps a fake. Furthermore, there were surprises—startling discrepancies between the selection of the cards and the inferences drawn from them when they were turned over. There were extraordinary cases of divided attention which might have interested a clinician. Sometimes a single individual began to sound like two people talking. A further study (Wason, 1969) caught in my net the so-called "Mensa Protocol" in which a member of that élite organisation reasoned, with assurance and precision, from premises which, according to Piaget, are typical of young children. I called the paper, "Regression in Reasoning?"

In the 1970s, I had a fruitful collaboration with Phil Johnson-Laird which culminated in our book, *Psychology of Reasoning* (Wason & Johnson-Laird, 1972). But at about this time I became aware of murmurs of disapproval in some quarters. On one occasion, someone suddenly said, perhaps half in jest, "We're not having any more experiments on the selection task", as if the Department was in danger of being infected by some new virus. I should have met this oracular pronouncement by retorting, "We've hardly begun".

One thing that struck us was the invariable (and possibly blinding) effect of selecting the true antecedent (p). If it were to be removed from the task, the responses might be more rational. We considered the possibility of a three-card problem. I then suggested the additional removal of the false antecedent (p̄) leaving a binary choice between the true and false consequents (q and q̄). Phil greeted this as a stroke of genius, but it was really only a natural progression. In concrete terms, given the sentence, "all the rectangles are pink", with the task of proving it true as economically as possible, the solution is to inspect all non-pink objects to establish that they are not rectangles. Pink objects are vacuous. In our experiment (Johnson-Laird & Wason, 1970, Experiment 1) all the subjects eventually solved the problem. After more than 10 years David Green and I resuscitated it (Wason & Green, 1984), and investigated its potential in several ways. We called it the "reduced array selection task" (RAST).

The RAST has many advantages over the standard task. Its solution does not depend on an all-or-none decision but is seriated over a number of trials, each of which provides knowledge of results; it enables a variety of measures to be taken. The subjects usually start getting it wrong, but generally end up getting it right: an ideal situation. The RAST is so flexible that it has been used with good effect to study the thinking of children as young as seven (Girotto, Light, & Colbourn, 1988; Light, Blaye, Gilly, & Girotto, 1990).

The experiments we have done on the selection task have often been governed by chance occurrences, and the results have been surprising and non-linear. For instance, we tested the hypothesis that the phrase, "the other side of the card", could have been misinterpreted as the side which is face downwards, instead of referring to a symmetrical relation (Wason & Johnson-Laird, 1970). There was not a shred of evidence in favour of this hypothesis, but when all the information was revealed, the subjects' comments were saturated with self-contradictions which disclosed the sources of error—much to the astonishment of our assistant, Diana Shapiro. A similar serendipitous finding occurred in Wason and Golding (1974). The aim of the experiment was totally eclipsed by the subjects' inconsistent remarks (see also Wason, 1979).

Since the late 1980s, the selection task has had a liberating effect on research; it has lost its autonomy and become a catalyst which has resulted in a veritable intellectual ferment. The protagonists of social contract theory (Cosmides, 1989; Gigerenzer & Hug, 1992), pragmatic schemas (Cheng & Holyoak, 1985), mental models (Johnson-Laird & Byrne, 1993), deontic logic (Manktelow & Over, 1990), and heuristic-analytic theory (Evans, 1989) have used the task in the struggle for survival for their ideas.

The implications of social contract theory are particularly noteworthy because of their boldness which (incidentally) should delight Popper. Gigerenzer and Hug (1992) have even claimed that the results obtained so far have helped to demolish the century-old assumption of Leibnitz that human reasoning can be reduced to a calculus. It has assumed instead that the mind is a bundle of Darwinian algorithms designed for survival in a clan of hunter-gatherers rather than a reasoning machine (Cosmides, 1989; Gigerenzer & Hug, 1992). It remains to be seen whether further experimental tests will demand "a new theory of mind", as an anonymous writer in *The Economist* (1992) has suggested, but these assumptions will at least involve liaison between two disciplines—psychology and social biology. That is something for which we should be grateful.

Research on the selection task, from its earliest days, has revealed all the confusions, changes of perspective, accidental discoveries, and insights which are typical of creative work. But what progress has been made, and what achievement will endure, has been due to the work of many hands. To have been a vehicle for such research, and to have watched it grow, has taught me, beyond question, that an apple can be added to a banana with impunity, and even with satisfaction. And that, perhaps, is what creativity is all about.

ACKNOWLEDGEMENTS

My grateful thanks to:

- my graduate students, research assistants, and subjects, who have made research such a joy;
- my friends who have made this book possible;
- especially Phil Johnson-Laird and Jonathan Evans; to have either as research students in one life would have been a blessing; to have had both stretches the bounds of credibility;
- Sheila Jones, my first collaborator, whose advice I valued at every move;
- Paolo and Maria Legrenzi for convening and hosting the Selection Task Conference at Trento (1974), and for hospitality never to be forgotten;
- Jerome Bruner and George Miller for an invitation to "my-new-found-land", and a wonderful year at Harvard's Center for Cognitive Studies (1962–1963);
- A.R. Jonckheere (a man in whose company it is impossible to feel downcast) for tuition, inspiration, and criticism;

- the Medical Research Council, and especially its former Secretary, Sir Harold Himsworth, for generous financial and moral support;
- my wife, Ming (deceased), and dear daughters, Armorer and Sarah, for so much love.

REFERENCES

Bacon, F. (1621). *Novum organum*. Oxford: Oxford University Press.

Bruner, J.S. (1961). The act of discovery. *Harvard Educational Review, 31*, 21–32.

Cheng, P.W., & Holyoak, K.J. (1985). Pragmatic reasoning schemas. *Cognitive Psychology, 17*, 391–416.

Clark, H.H. (1974). Semantics and comprehension. In T.A. Sebeok (Ed.), *Current trends in linguistics, Volume 12: Linguistics and adjacent arts and sciences*. The Hague: Mouton.

Cosmides, L. (1989). The logic of social exchange. Has natural selection shaped how humans reason? Studies with the Wason selection task. *Cognition, 31*, 187–276.

Economist (1992). A critique of pure reason. 4th July.

Elbow, P. (1973). *Writing without teachers*. London: Oxford University Press.

Evans, J. St.B.T. (1983). Selective processes in reasoning. In J.St.B.T. Evans (Ed.), *Thinking and reasoning: Psychological approaches*. London: Routledge & Kegan Paul.

Evans, J.St.B.T. (1989). *Bias in human reasoning: Causes and consequences*. Hove, UK: Lawrence Erlbaum Associates Ltd.

Evans, J.St.B.T., Newstead, S.E, Byrne, R.M.J. (1993). *Human reasoning: The psychology of deduction*. Hove, UK: Lawrence Erlbaum Associates Ltd.

Gigerenzer, G., & Hug, K. (1992). Domain-specific reasoning: Social contracts, cheating, and perspective change. *Cognition, 43*, 127–171.

Girotto, V., Light, P., & Colbourn, C. (1988). Pragmatic schemas and conditional reasoning in children. *Quarterly Journal of Experimental Psychology, 40A*, 469–482.

Good, I.J. (Ed.) (1962). *The scientist speculates*. London: Heinemann.

Green, D.W., & Wason, P.C. (1982). Notes on the psychology of writing. *Human Relations, 35*, 47–56.

Green, D.W., & Wason, P.C. (1969). A rejoinder to Klayman and Ha (unpublished).

Johnson-Laird, P.N., & Byrne, R.M.J. (1993). Models and deductive rationality. In K. Manktelow & D. Over (Eds.), *Models of rationality*. London: Routledge & Kegan Paul.

Klayman, J. & Ha, Y.U. (1987). Confirmation, disconfirmation, and information in hypothesis testing. *Psychological Review, 94*, 211–228.

Kubie, L.S. (1958). *Neurotic distortion of the creative process*. Kansas: University of Kansas Press.

Light, P.H., Blaye, A., Gilly, M., & Girotto, V. (1990). Pragmatic schemas and logical reasoning in six to eight year olds. *Cognitive Development, 4*, 49–64.

Lowenthal, D., & Wason, P.C. (1977). Academics and their writing. *Times Literary Supplement*, 24th June, 781.

Manktelow, K.I., & Over, D.E. (1990). Deontic thought and the selection task. In K.J. Gilhooly, M.T.G. Keene, R.H. Logie, & G. Erdos (Eds.), *Lines of thinking, Vol.1*. New York: Wiley.

Murdoch, I. (1992). *Metaphysics as a guide to morals*. London: Chatto and Windus.

Milner, M. (1969). *The hands of the living god*. New York: International University Press, Inc.

Poletiek, F. (1992). *Toektsen*. Amsterdam en Kitgeverij LEMMA, BV.

Popper, K.R. (1957). Philosophy of science: A personal report. In C.A. Mace (Ed.), *British philosophy in the mid-century*. London: Allen and Unwin.

Popper, K.R. (1959). *The logic of scientific discovery*. London: Hutchinson.

Quine, W.V.O. (1952). *Methods of logic*. London: Routledge & Kegan Paul.

Riviere, J. (1958). A character trait of Freud's. In J.D. Sutherland (Ed.), *Psychoanalysis and contemporary thought*. London: Hogarth.

Selfridge, O.G. (1959). Pandemonium: A paradigm for learning. In D.V. Blake & A.M. Uttey (Eds.), *Proceedings of the symposium on mechanisation of thought processes*. London: National Physical Laboratory.

Sutherland, S. (1992). *Irrationality: The enemy within*. London: Constable.

Trabasso, T. (1972). Mental operation in language comprehension. In J.B. Carroll & R.O. Freedle (Eds.), *Language comprehension and the acquisition of knowledge*. Washington, DC: Winston.

Tweney, R.D., Doherty, M.E., Warner, W.J., Pliske, D.B., Mynatt, C., Gross, K.A., & Arkelin, D.L. (1980). Strategies of rule discovery in an inference task. *Quarterly Journal of Experimental Psychology, 32*, 109–123.

Wason, P.C. (1959). The processing of positive and negative information. *Quarterly Journal of Experimental Psychology, 11*, 92–107.

Wason, P.C. (1960). On the failure to eliminate hypotheses in a conceptual task. *Quarterly Journal of Experimental Psychology, 12*, 129–140.

Wason, P.C. (1961). Response to affirmative and negative binary statements. *British Journal of Psychology, 52*, 133–142.

Wason, P.C. (1965). The contexts of plausible denial. *Journal of Verbal Learning and Verbal Behavior, 4*, 7–11.

Wason, P.C. (1968). Reasoning about a rule. *Quarterly Journal of Experimental Psychology, 20*, 273–281.

Wason, P.C. (1969). Regression in reasoning? *British Journal of Psychology, 60*, 471–480.

Wason, P.C. (1972). In real life negatives are false. *Negation, Logique et Analyse, 57–58*, 17–38.

Wason, P.C. (1979). Self-contradictions. In P.N. Johnson-Laird & P.C. Wason (Eds.), *Thinking: Readings in cognitive science*. Cambridge: Cambridge University Press.

Wason, P.C. (1980). Specific thoughts on the writing process. In L.W. Gregg and E.R. Steinberg (Eds.), *Cognitive processes in writing*. Hillsdale, NJ: Lawrence Erlbaum Associates Inc.

Wason, P.C., & Golding E. (1974). The language of inconsistency. *British Journal of Psychology, 65*, 537–546.

Wason, P.C., & Green, D. (1984). Reasoning and mental representation. *Quarterly Journal of Experimental Psychology, 36A*, 597–610.

Wason, P.C., & Johnson-Laird P.N. (1970). A conflict between selecting and evaluating information in an inferential task. *British Journal of Psychology, 61*, 509–515.

Wason, P.C., & Johnson-Laird, P.N. (1972). *Psychology of reasoning: Structure and content*. London: Batsford.

Wason, P.C., & Jones, S. (1963). Negatives: Denotation and connotation. *British Journal of Psychology, 57*, 413–418.
Wason, P.C., & Reich, S.S. (1979). A verbal illusion. *Quarterly Journal of Experimental Psychology, 31*, 591–597.

Author Index

Slovic, P., 4
Smyth, M.M., 11, 264, 269, 280
Spellman, B.A., 186
Sperber, D., 139, 149, 199–200
Stafford, A., 226
Staudenmayer, H., 19
Stenning, K., 157, 159, 161, 163, 176–177
Stich, S., 250
Sutherland, E.J., 109
Sutherland, S., 295

Tabossi, P., 5
Tagart, J., 129
Taplin, J.E., 19
Thagard, P., 249
Todd, P.M., 249
Tooby, J., 97, 99, 102
Toulmin, S., 183
Trabasso, T.R., 6, 291
Tschirgi, J.E., 21–23, 26–27, 32–34, 52, 54–55
Tukey, D.D., 221
Tversky, A., 4, 107, 149, 278–280, 282
Tweney, R.D., xii, 4–5, 13, 28, 51, 72, 220, 223–226, 232, 234, 236, 241–257, 290

Valentine, E.R., 28–29
Van Duyne, P.C., 178

Vuyk, R., 17
Vygotsky, L.S., 183

Ward, S.L., 49–52
Warner, S.A., 11, 268
Wason, P.C., xii, 1–12, 14, 17, 19, 22–23, 25–26, 28–29, 44, 50–51, 54, 56, 67–68, 87, 92, 98, 115, 132–133, 135, 137, 148, 154, 164–165, 167, 174–176, 181–182, 185, 189, 191–192, 212, 217–221, 223, 226, 237, 250–252, 255, 257, 261–268, 266, 272–273, 279–281, 287–298
Weene, P., 264
Westrum, R., 185
Wetherick, N.E., 17, 221, 226, 237
Whitfield, J.W., 291–292
Whitten, A., 183
Wilkins, M.C., 2, 41
Wilson, D., 149, 199–200
Wilson, T.D., 178
Woodworth, R.S., 2

Yachanin, S.A., 28–29, 47–48, 51–52, 54, 72
Yang, Y., 206, 212
Yopp, H. and R., 3

Zwicky, A.M., 200

Subject Index